"This provocative, important, and majestically composed book about the future of cities should be essential reading for our times. An urban planner, environmentalist, and musician, Rose takes us on a rollicking, centuries-long journey through the history of cities, never forgetting to marvel at their resilience and human core. What does Bach tell us about the complexity and organization of our urban environments? What is the 'metabolism of the city'? By the time I had finished Rose's book, I began to see the city and the world around me in an entirely new light. I could not put this book down."
—Siddhartha Mukherjee, author of *The Emperor of All Maladies* and *The Gene*

"Huge in ambition, grand in scope, dazzling in accomplishment. You will never look at your city, yourself, or your neighbors the same way again."
—Andrew Zolli, author of *Resilience*

"Rose's nonstop tour of the city—an in-depth account of its history, theory, and practice—is exhilarating and complete, wherein compassion, Bach's *Well-Tempered Clavier*, and contemporary scientific thinking finally come to rest together. This is a hugely satisfying poem—rich in history and thought, and deeply felt throughout."   —Philip Glass, composer

"Gathering a lifetime of learning, discovery, and understanding, Jonathan Rose has written an astonishing book: a treasure trove of knowledge about how our urban lives have evolved, interwoven with a compellingly pragmatic case for what they can be in the future. *The Well-Tempered City* is essential and exciting reading."   —Jeremy Newsum, executive trustee of the Grosvenor Estate

"Once in every great while, a new book arrives that really addresses the things that are on my mind. Rose's *The Well-Tempered City* has given me an elegant and powerful framework in which to look at the things that interest me the most these days: contemporary culture, music, and compassion. It is essential reading for everyone who lives in cities and everyone who dreams of repairing the world."   —Laurie Anderson, artist

"*The Well-Tempered City* traverses the span of human settlements, from ancient, sacred cities that were temple complexes to modern, sensate, interconnected metropoles that mimic living systems in function and design. As the extraordinary migration to urban environments continues unabated, the question Jonathan Rose poses is whether we build squalor by default or environments that address, heal, and prevent poverty, ill health, and civic discord by intention. This is a tall order but it is not speculative. Jonathan is a preeminent developer of the most imaginative urban housing in the United States. His scholarship extends from recent discoveries in neuroscience and human behavior to the skillful and transformative practices implemented in his own work. The pragmatic and the visionary rarely integrate this harmoniously into the reimagination of what a city is and could be." —Paul Hawken, author of *Blessed Unrest*

"Jonathan Rose's powerful new book, *The Well-Tempered City*, reveals a fresh understanding of inequality, urbanization, housing, and public health. Rose weaves rigorous cognitive neuroscience research with powerful, authentic stories of people who often live at the margins of society. The book introduces a new human development paradigm—the cognitive ecology of well-being—and demonstrates how this new way of thinking offers solutions that help low-income families and communities recover and repair their lives. This book should be mandatory reading for anyone committed to the idea of successful and inclusive cities." —Darren Walker, president, the Ford Foundation

"Jonathan Rose draws on an incredible range of research to give a new, deeply insightful, and sweeping account of why and how cities develop. Many of humankind's greatest challenges and opportunities lie in cities, and *The Well–Tempered City* shows us the way to a bright urban future."
—Eric Beinhocker, executive director, the Institute for New Economic Thinking, University of Oxford, author of *The Origin of Wealth*

"In an age where nobody believes anything, this book offers a rich vein of facts. It is essential reading for all those who live in cities, but perhaps more important for those who don't and may have to."
—Sir Nicholas Grimshaw, CBE, PPRA, RIBA, AIA, founder of Grimshaw Architects

"From the very first pages of this brilliant book, I was hooked. The transformative knowledge this book conveys has enabled be to know what I didn't think was even possible to know. Weaving a captivating in-depth story about the history of city life, exploring the various and intriguing ways our human nature works with—or against—nature, and addressing the pressing needs of our fragile planet, Jonathan Rose provides us with a unique and practical guide to where we've been and where we need to go to make our global, urban-dominated home a more resilient and compassionate place. This magnificent book, based deeply on extensive science we rarely hear about, is both informative and profoundly creative in illuminating novel and achievable applications that can create positive changes in our collective lives. Bravo!"

—Daniel J. Siegel, MD, executive director of the Mindsight Institute, author of *Mind*

"Jonathan Rose shares his brilliant vision in this fascinating look at cities past and present. *The Well-Tempered City* offers a plan for urban—and ecological and social—thriving into the future. Anyone who lives in a city or cares about them will find this a rewarding read."

—Daniel Goleman, author of *Emotional Intelligence*

"*The Well-Tempered City* is a rich tapestry of the increasingly complex urbanized world. Rose's depiction of the city as a living metabolism—one requiring clean calories and water, green space and buildings, happiness and harmony achieved though connectivity, community, and compassion—resonates like the Bach fugues he alludes to."   —Arthur Segel, professor, Harvard Business School

"A comprehensive primer for how to contemplate urban spaces as they evolve for the future."   —*Kirkus Reviews*

"A thought-provoking introduction to the future of cities."

—*Publishers Weekly*

"*The Well-Tempered City* stands alongside works by Jane Jacobs, Lewis Mumford, and Christopher Alexander, deserving influence and implementation."

—*The Architect's Newspaper*

THE WELL-TEMPERED CITY

THE
WELL-TEMPERED
CITY

What Modern Science, Ancient Civilizations,
and Human Nature Teach Us About the Future
of Urban Life

JONATHAN F. P.
ROSE

HARPER WAVE
An Imprint of HarperCollins*Publishers*

For Peter Calthorpe, who inspires me to look outward
to see the form of cities,

and Diana Calthorpe Rose, who inspires me to look
inward, toward wisdom and compassion.

A hardcover edition of this book was published in 2016 by Harper Wave, an imprint of HarperCollins Publishers.

HarperCollins books may be purchased for educational, business, or sales promotional use. For information, please e-mail the Special Markets Department at SPsales@harpercollins.com.

FIRST HARPER WAVE PAPERBACK EDITION PUBLISHED 2017.

Designed by William Ruoto

The Library of Congress has catalogued the hardcover edition as follows:

Rose, Jonathan F. P.
The well-tempered city : what modern science, ancient civilizations, and human nature teach us about the future of urban life / Jonathan F. P. Rose.
Includes bibliographical references and index.
p. cm.
978-0-06-223472-8
1. City planning. 2. Cities and towns—Growth. 3. Community development—Environmental aspects.
HT165.5.R67   2016
307.1/216—dc23   2016004096

ISBN 978-0-06-223473-5 (pbk.)

23 24 25 26 27 LBC 10 9 8 7 6

CONTENTS

PART FOUR: Community

PART FIVE: Compassion

The Well-Tempered City

WHEN I WAS SIXTEEN, Philip Johnson, an influential architect and advisor to Governor Nelson Rockefeller, asked my father, Frederick P. Rose, a public-spirited apartment-house builder, for his thoughts on how to redevelop New York City's Welfare Island. Now known as Roosevelt Island, this narrow strip of land in the East River between Manhattan and Queens was long the domain of the city's outcasts, first housing a penitentiary, then a "lunatic asylum," a smallpox isolation ward, and two welfare hospitals for chronic diseases. My father took me there in 1968, and as we stood among the shells of abandoned buildings in the weedy, trash-filled landscape, he asked, "What would you do with this?"

I have been trying to answer that question ever since.

In the 1960s cities in the United States began sliding into decades of physical, social, and environmental decay. Following the murder of Martin Luther King, Jr., in 1968, African American neighborhoods across the country burned, fueled by a century of segregation and neglect. Cleveland's Cuyahoga River, thick with oil and sludge, caught on fire, an image that reverberated from the cover of *Time* magazine as a symbol of the pollution choking the nation's cities. Increased crime, hard drugs, declining schools, and decaying transportation systems pushed America's middle-class families to the suburbs, exacerbating the gap between a city's wealthy and its workers. City tax bases declined, interest rates rose, and many urban centers began to teeter on the edge of insolvency.

I grew up in the suburbs, but I was drawn to nearby New York City because it was gritty and alive with what the architect Robert Venturi called "complexity and contradiction . . . messy vitality,"[1] throbbing with street life and jazz, blues, and rock and roll.

I spent the summer before I visited Roosevelt Island in New Mexico, working on the excavation of a thousand-year-old Anasazi village. It was built of adobe bricks made from the earth, its buildings aligning with the rising sun on the spring and fall equinoxes. The ruins lay on a high mesa alive with plants, insects, small mammals, and birds. As we settled into the rhythms of nature, everything fitting together into a living, dynamic wholeness, I could feel the flow of her mysterious patterns although they were far too complex for me to understand. They were also ultimately too complex for the Anasazi. The climate changed and centuries of drought devastated their cities.

Jane Jacobs, one of the great urban thinkers of the twentieth century, said, "Intricate minglings of different uses in cities are not a form of chaos. On the contrary, they represent a complex and highly developed form of order."[2] After that summer, I set out to find that order. I sensed that its seeds were in many places—in biology and evolution, in physics and quantum mechanics, in religion and philosophy, in psychology and ecology, in the histories of cities long gone, and in cities now emerging. My goal was to integrate lessons from these varied sources in order to understand how to make cities whole. And my inspiration was a master of making wholeness: Johann Sebastian Bach.

Bach's music weaves together depth and delight in an endlessly unfolding tapestry, infused with wisdom and compassion. Listening to his music, I have a sense of the grandeur of nature, ever moving toward harmony. But it is also an urban music, written in the cities of Weimar, Köthen, and Leipzig.

The Well-Tempered Clavier, which Bach wrote in two sections, or books, in 1722 and 1742, provides a great map of counterpoint, an instruction manual for composers and performers organized into patterns of unearthly beauty, a vast integration that demonstrates both the perfection of the whole and the role of the individual within it. In each book Bach moves through all twenty-four major and minor keys in a series of preludes and fugues, weaving them together into a sublime ecology of sound.

The Well-Tempered Clavier was composed to prove that a new system of tuning notes, tempering, should replace a system that had reigned for two thousand years. Prior to the late seventeenth century each musical scale of notes used in European music was tuned slightly differently, in keeping with the theories of Pythagoras. The great Greek mathematician proposed that the ratios of the distances between the planets were the same as the ratios between musical notes, a theory he called "the harmony of the spheres." Tuning each musical key to these planetary proportions created beautiful scales within a given musical key, but generated notes that were slightly out of tune with the notes of every other key. If two different keys were played together the result was excruciating to listen to. Pythagoras's tuning system, which came to be called "just intonation," remained unchallenged for two thousand years, limiting compositions to just one key.

The solution, to tune the notes "in between" Pythagoras's perfect pitches, was first proposed by the Chinese prince Zhu Zaiyu, in his book *Fusion of Music and Calendar*, which was published in 1580. Matteo Ricci, a Jesuit monk, famed for his travels to China, recorded the concept in his journal and brought it back to Europe, where the idea gestated. In 1687, the German organist and music theorist Andreas Werckmeister published a treatise on the mathematics of music in which he described a system that became known as Werckmeister temperament. Through tempering, each key's notes were tuned in a way that sounded pleasing when more than one key was played simultlaneously. Werckmeister's system reflected another Greek philosophy, the "golden mean," which sought the desirable middle between two extremes. The founder of the theory of the golden mean was none other than Theano, wife of Pythagoras!

In 1691, Werckmeister proposed a tuning system he called "*musi- kalische temperatur,*" or well temperament. It was designed to solve the problem of musical circularity. In the just intonation system, if one started on a cyclical journey through the keys, each slightly out of tune with the prior one, when the journey came back to the beginning, the circle would not close. Werkmeister's well-tempered system, which in the twentieth century became known as equal temperament, was designed so that the distances between notes were in proper proportion, so that the end of a circle was consonant with the beginning.

The contemporary composer Philip Glass notes, "Without a well-tempered system, one could not move from the key of A to the unrelated key of E flat without going out of tune. And thus, one could only play music in one key at a time. Well temperament opened up all of the keys to a composer."

Bach believed that God had created a sacred architecture of the universe, and that his mission as a composer was to express its magnificent form through music. The well-tempered tuning system unshackled Bach, allowing his music to flow across keys in ways that no one had ever explored before. *The Well-Tempered Clavier* was composed to align our highest human aspirations with the sublime harmony of nature. It is a model of the task we have today in designing and reshaping our cities.

The world's first cities were founded on sacred sites, built around temples, and often designed in a plan that, like Bach's music, was organized to reflect the architecture of the universe. They were filled with art and sanctuaries, animated with ceremonies that gave meaning to the lives of their inhabitants.

The mission of these early communities' designers was to align people with the principles that gave birth to life, morality, order, and wisdom. As settlements grew, their priests, the most trusted members of the community, became responsible for overseeing storehouses for grain and other goods. They developed governance systems to help carry out three primary responsibilities: to provide for the protection and prosperity of their residents, to oversee the fair distribution of resources, and to maintain a balance between human and natural systems in order to increase well-being.

Today's cities are technical marvels, reflecting civilization's enormous scientific strides. Human creativity has produced unimagined power and prosperity, although that prosperity is not well distributed. Yet most of our cities have lost their original higher purpose.

The goal of this book is to knit these threads—our technical and social potential and the generative power of nature—back together, toward a higher purpose for cities. In a time of increasing volatility, complexity, and ambiguity, the well-tempered city has systems that can help it evolve toward a more even temperament, one that balances prosperity and well-being with efficiency and equality in ways that continually restore the city's social and natural capital. Many of these qualities are already at work today in cities around the world. The purpose of this book is to show how they might come together.

The Answer Is Urban

I WAS BORN IN 1952, when the world's population was 2.6 billion.[1] Since then it has almost tripled in size. In 1952 only 30 percent of the world's people lived in cities, but now more than half do,[2] and by the end of the twenty-first century that number will grow to 85 percent. The quality and character of our cities will determine the temperament of human civilization.

In 1952 conditions in many European cities were not unlike those in the developing world today. In one of Europe's southernmost cities, Palermo, the capital of Sicily, reconstruction after a devastating war was stalled by corruption; lacking affordable housing, families camped in nearby caves while the Mafia built a concrete jungle of suburban sprawl, paving over parks and farms, bribing and threatening local officials with so little regard for building and zoning codes that the result became known as the Sack of Palermo.

To the north, in Germany, 8 million of the 12 million people displaced by war remained refugees, without proper housing or work. To the west, London was shrouded by the "Great Smog," a lethal fog of sulfurous coal smoke that killed twelve thousand people in the worst air pollution event in London's history. And to the east, in Prague, the show trial of Rudolf Slánský, accompanied by Stalin's torture and execution of Jews, and their expulsion from the government, hardened the cold war lines between the Soviets and the West.

The prevailing view at the time was that economic growth was a key solution to the world's problems. Spurred by the American Marshall Plan, the postwar period in Europe gave rise to the greatest economic expansion in its history, overcoming starvation, providing work and homes for countless refugees, funding social services, and generally improving the quality of life for tens of millions of people. The United States also experienced extraordinary growth. Manufacturing wages tripled from their depression-era lows, America's middle class expanded, and the populations of many cities rose to new peaks. However, the focus on economic growth alone was not sufficient to generate true well-being.

The 1950s were not a good time for nature. The growth of the world's cities was fueled by voracious consumption of natural resources: mountains were mined, forests cut, oceans fished, rivers dammed, and groundwater was sucked from the earth—all at a rapidly accelerating pace. There was little thought given to waste. Salinated groundwater, polluted rivers, and stripped topsoil reduced nature's capacity to regenerate herself, ultimately making the task of feeding and provisioning our cities harder. Although many of the world's cities grew in the 1950s, the planning for that growth was often shortsighted, ignoring the lessons learned from thousands of years of city-making.

Look at almost any city in the world and you'll find that the part planned and built in the 1950s is probably its least attractive. Historic plazas became parking lots, rivers were covered and turned into highways, cheap "International Style" office buildings replaced beautifully crafted ones, and vast, efficient, soulless housing estates were built at the city's suburban edges, disconnected from work, shopping, culture, and community.

Certainly, by the mid-twentieth century, many nineteenth-century neighborhoods needed renewal. In Berlin's Wilhelmina Ring, thought to be the largest tenement cluster in the world, tiny, teeming apartments were heated by charcoal, and only 15 percent of apartments had both a toilet and a bath or shower. In St. Louis, Missouri, 85,000 families lived in overcrowded, rodent-filled nineteenth-century buildings, many with communal toilets. New York City's Lower East Side was the most densely populated neighborhood in the world, contributed to significant health and safety issues. These neighborhoods needed regeneration.

After World War I, the dominant approach to the design of urban renewal grew out of the ideas of the Swiss-French architect Charles-Édouard Jeanneret-Gris, known as Le Corbusier. In 1928, Le Corbusier and a group of like-minded colleagues formed the International Congresses of Modern Architecture (CIAM), to formalize and disseminate their view of city-making. In 1933 they declared the urban-planning ideal to be the "Functional City," proposing that urban social issues could be solved by a planning and building design that strictly segregated use according to function. Like Bach, Le Corbusier sought to express the architecture of the universe in his work. "Mathematics," he wrote, "is the majestic structure conceived by man to grant him comprehension of the universe. It holds the absolute and the infinite, the understandable and the ever elusive."[3] Inspired by Pythagoras's golden ratio, Le Corbusier proposed it as the ideal basis to determine the proper distances between buildings, and as the ratio between a building's height and width. The result produced isolated, evenly spaced towers, which were set in unadorned parks.

The Functional City approach was adopted all over the world. Historic, messy, vital city neighborhoods filled with dense streets lined with shops and apartment buildings were condemned, torn down, and replaced with Le Corbusier's "towers in the park," antiseptic, orderly, tall new apartment buildings with tiny kitchens and bathrooms, separated from one another by green but unusable open spaces. Shops and workshops were limited; these were only places to live. Outside Amsterdam the concept was demonstrated in Bijlmermeer, a complex constructed in the late 1960s of thirty-one ten-story

Bijlmermeer. *(Amsterdam City Archives)*

octagonal apartment buildings to house 60,000 people with not a shop to serve them, separated from the city by a wide expanse of parkland.

The Soviet Union found the Functional City concept particularly appealing, and engaged many of the CIAM architects during the Great Depression. Their ideas were applied at scale after World War II as an inexpensive way to rebuild war-torn cities, and to accelerate Soviet expansion into Eastern Europe. In January 1951, the Moscow party boss Nikita Khrushchev called together a conference on construction, proposing that the people's housing should be constructed with cheap, prefabricated concrete panels. The next year the Nineteenth Party Congress made the prefabrication of massive housing projects the law of the land, while preserving the option for luxury dachas and government buildings to be handcrafted.

Despite the Soviet Union's receptivity to their ideas, World War II drove many CIAM members to the United States, where they became deans of the nation's leading schools of architecture. The principles they taught guided the design of the nation's urban renewal program. In the 1950s new housing projects like St. Louis's Pruitt-Igoe, designed by Minoru Yamasaki, won architectural awards for their stark formality. In 1954, Dick Lee, the newly elected mayor of New Haven, Connecticut, adopted the Corbusian model of urban renewal and promised to make New Haven a model city. New Haven's efforts to replace old neighborhoods with brutally modern architecture received national attention, and won many design awards, but by the late 1960s they had largely failed because they concentrated poverty, isolated residents from services, and limited opportunity for small businesses.

In addition to housing, economic development—the creation of businesses and jobs and the improvement of living standards—is an important element of urban renewal. The prevailing urban economic model of the mid-twentieth century often focused on the development of a few large projects to revitalize a city's downtown. These deeply subsidized large shopping malls or convention centers often failed because planners didn't recognize that economic vitality functions at several scales in an overlapping, complex system. The small business—the musical instrument shop, the fabric store, or the corner grocer—is as essential as new housing and grand mixed-use centers. New Haven condemned blocks of older historic buildings to clear and build a downtown shopping mall, which struggled. As the area lost its vitality, its office buildings were only partially occupied and rents dropped. By the end of his term in 1969, Dick Lee said, "If New Haven is a model city, God help America's cities."[4]

In 1970, I arrived in New Haven to attend Yale University. It was an unsettled time. One of the first American cities to industrialize in the late 1700s, New Haven was losing middle-class jobs as manufacturers moved to the nonunion South, or offshore. The Vietnam War was dividing the nation. A persistent recession, rising interest rates, and increasing urban poverty and crime were hastening the decline of America's cities, and in New Haven the murder trial of the Black Panther Bobby Seale exacerbated racial tensions.

The goal of my undergraduate studies was to understand and integrate several big ideas: the nature and workings of the human mind, the functioning of social systems, and the way that the amazing miracle of life evolves toward ever-increasing complexity in the face of entropy and decay. My hypothesis centered on the notion that the same principles that increase the well-being of human and natural systems could also guide the development of happier, healthier cities.

Perhaps the most important ecologist of the twentieth century, the eminent biologist G. Evelyn Hutchinson, was then a Sterling professor at Yale. He graciously agreed to meet with me and discuss these early ideas that grew into this book. In 1931, when he was twenty-eight years old, Hutchinson set off for the Himalayas, to the high Tibetan land of Ladakh, where he studied the ecology of its lakes and its Buddhist culture. Hutchinson was the first to propose the idea of an ecological niche, a zone in which species and their environment intimately co-evolve, nested in ever-larger systems.

When Charles Darwin added the phrase "the survival of the fittest" to his fifth edition of *The Origin of Species* at the suggestion of the economist Herbert Spenser, by "fittest" he didn't mean "strongest"; he was referring to those species that fit together best. The magnificent tendency of nature to evolve toward the increasing fitness of its parts lies at the heart of nature's ability to adapt to changing circumstances. Hutchinson's concept of ecological niches provided a useful way to think about neighborhoods as nested in the systems of the city, its region, the nation, and the earth. Those that fit best thrive.

Hutchinson was also prescient about climate change; in 1947 he predicted that the carbon dioxide released by human activity would alter the earth's climate. If this, the planet's largest system, was threatened, then all the ecosystems nested within it would also be at risk. By the 1950s Hutchinson linked biodiversity loss to climate change. He was also the first natural scientist to explore the intersection of cybernetics (information feedback control systems) and ecology, describing how energy and information flow through ecological systems. Together with the later work of Abel Wolman, who proposed that cities have metabolisms just as natural systems do, Hutchinson provided me with elements that I would eventually integrate into an understanding of cities as complex adaptive systems.

In January 1974 I took off on my own journey to the Himalayas, starting in Istanbul and working my way across Asia as a bus mechanic. In the harsh winter I stood at the gates to the Afghan city of Herat, feeling the extraordinary tidal flow of history. Herat, which had grown to greatness as part of the Persian Empire, was captured by Alexander the Great as his armies swept through to the east, destroyed, and rebuilt as a Greek city. Herat was next conquered by the Seleucids as they expanded out of India to the west, then by Islamic invaders from the east, and so on through history. Standing there, I could feel how the tides of civilizations also contribute to the DNA of our city-making. It became clear to me that in order to understand cities, I had to learn their histories.

I also set out to understand the larger regions in which they were nested. In the fall I entered graduate school at the University of Pennsylvania to study regional planning with Ian McHarg, who had published a groundbreaking book, *Design with Nature*. McHarg proposed mapping the natural, social, and historic patterns of a region in layers and then looking at the layers together to see how they affected one another. But what I was yearning for was not yet being taught, a more integrative framework that became known as complexity.

One of the reasons that the world is so volatile and uncertain is that the world's human and natural systems are deeply complex, and complex systems can amplify volatility. To understand complexity, we should first understand its cousin, complicatedness.

Complicated systems have lots of moving parts, but they are predictable—they function in a linear fashion. And although the inputs and outputs of a complicated system may vary, the system itself is essentially static. For example, think about New York City's water supply system. Water is collected in upstate reservoirs and, powered by gravity, streams though large aqueducts toward the city. Once the water reaches the city, it flows through thousands of pipes and valves and ends up in the taps of millions of apartments and homes. This system has many elements, but they all function in a linear path from input to output. Essentially, New York City's water supply system has not changed much over the last 150 years. While the flow of water from the reservoir to a sink will vary depending on the state of the valves along the way, the structure of the system itself is fixed. Linear systems tend to have very low volatility, and are very predicable.

Complex systems have lots of elements and subsystems that are all interdependent, so that each part influences the others. It is very hard to predict the outcome of an input into complex systems. The interactions of complex systems can amplify or mute inputs. The global economy is a complex system. That's why in 2011, when Greece threatened to default on half of its $300 billion debt, the global stock markets declined by a trillion dollars, almost seven times the actual amount at risk. Nature is the earth's most complex system. And perhaps the most complex human-made systems are cities.

Wicked Problems

In 1973, facing a series of intractable planning issues, the University of California, Berkeley, planning professors W. J. Rittel and Melvin Webber published "Dilemmas in a General Theory of Planning."[5] They observed that the scientific rationalism of the 1950s, which proposed that science and engineering could solve all urban problems, hadn't worked out, and that city residents were resisting everything planners recommended. People were sitting in to halt the urban renewal that was supposed to clear blight, and to stop the construction of urban highways that were supposed to make transportation more efficient. City residents didn't like new school curriculums, and they didn't like public housing. Even Minoru Yamasaki's failed Pruitt-Igoe was demolished in a widely televised series of implosions in 1972. Everything planners tried wasn't working. What was wrong?

Rittel and Webber's conclusion was an early contribution to the emerging field of complexity, although they didn't describe it that way. They characterized problems that science and engineering could solve as *tame* ones, problems with clearly defined goals and pragmatic solutions. These are called complicated problems in this book. Rittel and Webber observed that the larger issues facing cities had no clear solutions because each intervention improved circumstances for some residents, but made things worse for others. And there was no clear framework for deciding what outcomes were the most equitable, or fair. They concluded that it was almost impossible to balance efficiency and equity. They wrote that the "kinds of problems that planners deal with, societal problems, are inherently different from the problems that scientists and perhaps some classes of engineers deal with. Planning problems are inherently wicked."

Wicked problems are ill defined and rely on "elusive political judgment." They can never be solved. Every wicked problem is a symptom of another problem. And every intervention changes the problem and its context.

The unpopularity of city and regional planning in the 1970s emasculated it. Instead of proposing transformational visions, most planners became process managers; implementing the zoning codes that fragmented cities rather than integrating them into a coherent whole. And city planners were also slow to recognize that they were subject to larger forces outside their control.

The World's Largest Blackout

New Delhi, the capital of India, is among the largest and most populous cities on earth, connected not only to other cities on the Indian subcontinent, like Mumbai and Calcutta, but also to Dubai, London, New York, and Singapore. It is home to superb medical centers, diverse global businesses, a dynamic IT sector, and thriving tourism, all of which have increased its prosperity and created a rapidly growing, well-educated middle class.

On Monday, July 31, 2012, India's northern electrical grid shuddered, staggered under its load, and then collapsed. New Delhi was paralyzed. Traffic jammed; trains, subways, and elevators froze in place; airports shut down; water could not be pumped; and factories seized up. An estimated 670 million people lost power, approximately 10 percent of the world's total population. The most obvious cause was that demand for electric power outstripped supply; New Delhi has a hot, humid climate, and as it has become more prosperous more of its people expect to live and work in air-conditioned spaces, creating huge spikes in demand during summer months. But the underlying causes are more complex and intertwined.

The world's climate is changing, generating extreme weather, including the kinds of record-breaking temperatures that drove up New Delhi's use of power-hungry air-conditioning. Climate change has also led to shorter and later monsoon rains, reducing the flow of water through hydropower plants, cutting their electrical output. India's increasingly large and prosperous population is also driving up the nation's demand for food, and for the energy needed to produce it. In the 1970s, India's farmers switched from locally adapted seeds to modern "green revolution" hybrids, which required much more water to grow. Faced with less rainfall, farmers turned to electrical pumps to lift deep groundwater to irrigate their crops. As demand for water increased, the water table dropped, requiring more and more energy to pump it from deeper and deeper wells.

India's overtaxed energy infrastructure lacks the sophisticated software and controls to balance supply and demand. To make matters worse, 27 percent of India's electricity supply is lost in transmission or stolen. Instead of reducing its energy needs with smart systems, conservation, and efficiency, India is increasing its supply, becoming the world's largest builder of coal-fired power plants. It's a pact with the devil, as burning coal only accelerates the climate change already threatening so many of India's systems. Pollution colors the air in many Indian cities a sickly yellow. On a recent visit to New Delhi I never saw the sun break through the thick, grayish yellow air that engulfed the city.

India also lacks the responsive governance needed to handle the complexity of its growth. The mismatch between supply and demand on that fateful Monday in New Delhi had been predicted. The system was sophisticated enough to track the flow of power and predict a dangerous shortfall, but it lacked the management culture to effectively act on the information. District governors were directed to reduce their districts' use of electricity for the sake of the whole system, but they did not. Instead, many governors instructed their managers to suck even more power from the grid.

That response reflects a larger general issue faced by all city leaders: the temptation to maximize benefit for an individual district, department, or company versus optimizing the whole system. From an evolutionary point of view an individual might do better in the short term by maximizing its own gains, but over the long run it will benefit more by contributing to the success of the larger system. Since the founding of the very first cities, governance and culture have been used to balance "me" and "we." Governance provides the protection, structure, regulations, roles, and responsibilities necessary to allocate resources and maintain coherence among a large and often diverse population. Culture provides society with an operating system informed by the collective memory of its most effective strategies, guided by a morality that speaks for the whole. Healthy cities must have both strong, adaptable governance and a culture of collective responsibility and compassion.

Global Megatrends

New Delhi's issues were exacerbated by climate change, one of many global megatrends that all cities must contend with. These also include globalization, increased cyberconnectivity, urbanization, population growth, income inequality, increasing consumption, natural resource depletion, loss of biodiversity, a rise in migration of displaced peoples, and an increase in terrorism. These and many other megatrends are all *known unknowns*. We know that they are coming, but we can't precisely predict their impacts.

Climate change will hit cities especially hard. By the end of the twenty-first century, significant portions of low-lying cities such as Tokyo, Miami, and Dhaka, the capital of Bangladesh, are likely to be underwater unless they invest a great deal of money to build and maintain dikes. Coastal cities such as New York, Boston, Tampa, and Shenzhen face huge infrastructure costs to protect themselves from the rising seas. Inland cities located next to rivers or in the path of upland watersheds will also suffer increased flooding, and cities located at the fertile junction of river and sea may be hit from both sides. And less physically vulnerable cities will be swamped with refugees displaced by the climate and by conflict.

Megatrends such as climate change pose threats to the security of every nation on earth. In a 2014 report, the U.S. Department of Defense concluded, "Rising global temperatures, changing precipitation patterns, climbing sea levels, and more extreme weather events will intensify the challenges of global instability, hunger, poverty, and conflict. They will likely lead to food and water shortages, pandemic disease, disputes over refugees and resources, and destruction by natural disasters in regions across the globe. In our defense strategy, we refer to climate change as a 'threat multiplier' because it has the potential to exacerbate many of the challenges we are dealing with today—from infectious disease to terrorism."6

The devastating civil war in Syria began with climate change. In 2006, a five-year drought began, the worst in over a century, which was exacerbated by a corrupt water allocation system. Crops failed and more than 1.5 million desperate farmers and herders moved into Syria's cities. Ignored by the Assad government and unable to move forward with their lives, they became frustrated by the repressive regime. Their protests sparked a civil war. In the ensuing chaos, ISIS and Al-Qaeda seized territory, further fracturing the nation.7, 8 By 2015 hundreds of thousands of Syrians had been killed, and 11 million had become refugees, flooding nearby Turkey, Lebanon, Jordan, and Iraq, as well as Europe. In the summer of 2015, the UN refugee agency proclaimed the Syrian civil war the largest refugee crisis in a generation. Germany, whose negative population growth had produced a shortage of 5 million workers, responded with expedience and moral courage by opening its doors, welcoming millions of refugees. But settling and integrating them will be a very complex task.

In the twenty-first century, many of the world's growing cities will be trapped in a vicious circle: without enough local natural and energy resources to support themselves, they will become increasingly reliant on vulnerable international supply chains for food and water. Their concentrated populations will also be more susceptible to the epidemic spread of disease, and with global prosperity increasingly dependent on a complex system of linked economies, their economies will be more vulnerable to problems that might begin in another city and cascade through the system. Next time, the kind of global financial crisis we experienced in 2009 may spin out of control. Cyberattacks are also likely to overwhelm the technical and social systems our cities depend on. And all of these conditions will affect cities' populations unequally.

Perhaps most disturbing of the known unknowns threatening cities is terrorism, because its goal is to undermine humanity's greatest collective achievement, civilization itself. Today's terrorists range from religious fanatics to narcotics gang leaders. They are motivated by racism, hatred, fundamentalism, and greed. They are often funded by the developed world's addictions to oil, diamonds, heroin, and cocaine, and rewarded with rape, pillage, fame, and promises of an exalted (and perhaps eternal) life. This fundamentalist terrorism is the antithesis of the morality with which the Axial Age thinkers infused civilization 2,500 years ago. The antidote to terrorism requires disciplined, multisectoral approaches, but it is essential that we respond by affirming the key elements of civilization—culture, connectivity, coherence, community, and compassion—inspired by a worldview of wholeness. Strong social networks that grow from free and open societies are essential to the resilience of cities under all stresses, but particularly the threat of terrorism. Fighting terrorism requires vigilance, security, and intervention, but its greatest opponent is a society that connects its parts, is committed to mutual aid, and offers opportunity for all. Connectivity, culture, coherence, community, and compassion are the protective factors of civilized cities.

Trust is also a critical element of a city's ability to respond to such stresses. Trust is built slowly; anxiety and fear propagate much more quickly. Unfortunately, trust has been undermined by growing economic inequality and injustice, as well as by tribal and religious conflicts that rack Africa, the Middle East, and India, along with growing anti-immigrant fervor in Europe and the United States.

All these challenges threaten the future of our cities, and there will be many more perils we cannot anticipate. We are tasked with planning for an uncertain future.

The U.S. military describes this condition as VUCA, an acronym for volatility, uncertainty, complexity, and ambiguity. The combination of megatrends and VUCA requires us to think differently. As the world's population increasingly moves to cities in the decades ahead, we must figure out how to make our urban systems more integrated, resilient, and adaptable, while at the same time learning how to mitigate megatrends. The best solutions are those that accomplish both adaptation and mitigation; actions with the most co-benefits will best serve the entire system. For example, simple strategies such as rigorously insulating all of a city's buildings will significantly reduce their energy use, and thus their climate impacts, while also bringing down their operating costs, making them more affordable, increasing the comfort of the occupants, and helping the buildings function better should the power go out. This in turn will create many local jobs and reduce the city's dependence on global energy supplies.

Leverage Points of Change

If we ask how human civilization will thrive in the twenty-first century the answer must be urban. Cities are the nodes of civilization. They are key leverage points for equalizing the landscape of opportunity and enhancing the harmony between humans and nature in a VUCA time.

The systems thinker Donella Meadows wrote in her classic essay on the topic, "Leverage points . . . are places within a complex system (a corporation, an economy, a living body, a city, an ecosystem) where a small shift in one thing can produce big changes in everything."[9] An example of just how effective a small lever can be—if it is applied at the right point—took place in 1995, when the National Parks Service reintroduced thirty-three pairs of wolves into the greater Yellowstone ecosystem. Prime prey for gray wolves are elks, whose population had exploded without wolves to keep it in check. Voracious eaters, elks had denuded Yellowstone's landscape.

Within six years of wolves being reintroduced, Yellowstone's valleys and hillsides were green with renewed forest, which stabilized soil that had been eroding into river bottoms. Songbirds returned. The populations of bears, eagles, and ravens grew, feasting on elk carrion from wolf kills. Wolves also reduced the coyote population, unleashing the rebound of foxes, hawks, weasels, and badgers. The beaver population grew, and as they built their dams they brought back marshlands, increasing the populations of otters, muskrats, fish, and frogs. Beaver dams slowed rivers and streams, encouraging the growth of stabilizing vegetation, and improving water quality.[10]

The reintroduction of wolves into the Yellowstone ecosystem restored a key element back into a tightly fit ecology. Their return was a leverage point that nudged countless elements back into healthy equilibrium, restoring the health of the system.

One of the key ways to increase the health of cities is to understand how their systems work, and then focus on their leverage points. In 1988, when Pablo Escobar's drug cartel was fighting an all-out war with El Cartel del Valle, *Time* named Medellín, Colombia, the most dangerous city in the world. In 2013 the Urban Land Institute proclaimed Medellín the world's most innovative city.

What turned the city around? Key leverage points included the federal government's resolve to protect its citizens from crime by augmenting the city's security forces. As a result, between 1991 and 2010 Medellín's homicide rate dropped by 80 percent. At the same time, the city invested in new public libraries, parks, and schools in its barrios, or slum neighborhoods. Previously isolated barrios were connected to downtown with an innovative transportation system of cable cars and escalators that scaled the city's steep hills where its poorest people lived. The cable cars were integrated with a modern underground metro that connected more prosperous residential, commercial, and shopping centers, making them more accessible to the poor, and thereby increasing access to jobs, education, and shopping. Safe mass transit provided an alternative to cars, reducing pollution and traffic jams.

The City was then ringed with a protective greenbelt, setting a limit against unplanned sprawl and providing land to grow food. The greenbelt transformed El Camino de la Muerte—the Path of Death, where gangs used to hang the bodies of their enemies from trees—into El Camino de la Vida, the Path of Life, a walking trail with spectacular views of the valley.[11]

By focusing its efforts on these key leverage points, in just twenty years Medellín transformed itself from a city that was barely surviving to one that was thriving. The influx of national security officers restored a natural balance in Medellín, just as introducing wolves did in Yellowstone, allowing a richer, healthier ecosystem to emerge.

New Urbanism: Toward a More Integrated Planning Paradigm

In the late 1980s several urban planners and architects who had grown up in the idealistic '60s and were familiar with older, more coherent villages, towns, and cities in Europe began to work on a new, more integrated paradigm for planning in the United States. In 1993 they formed a new organization, the Congress for the New Urbanism (CNU), which was modeled on CIAM's Functional City, but rather than tear neighborhoods apart, CNU's mission was to put them back together, with as much diversity and connectivity as possible.

Today, the principles of CNU have largely displaced the ideals of CIAM. In 1996, one of CNU's founders, Peter Calthorpe (my brother-in-law), was hired by the HUD secretary Henry Cisneros to create a new planning model for public housing. Under the HOPE 6 program, the federal government began to fund cities to demolish their failed towers-in-the-park housing projects, and replace them with new mixed-income, service-enriched, mixed-use communities. Calthorpe wrote the program's planning guidelines, which included reducing block sizes, reconnecting streets, and knitting the fabric of communities back together. Ultimately the principles of New Urbanism spread rapidly because they appealed to human nature, and because they were so adaptable to variations of place, culture, and environment.

Urban renewal also began to move toward integration, diversity, and coherence outside the United States. In Holland, the concrete towers of Bijlmermeer had grown to house 100,000 people, primarily poor immigrants from Ghana and Suriname. Shunned by the middle class, by the 1970s Bijlmermeer had become known as the most dangerous neighborhood in Europe. The ideal town had become a slum. Then, in 1992, El Al Flight 1862 crashed into one of Bijlmermeer's buildings, killing dozens. Holland's response to the disaster spurred a new wave of thinking about how to rebuild cities.

The towers in the park were demolished and replaced with denser midrise buildings enhanced by private gardens. Spaces were created for shops and small businesses, bringing services to residents as well as providing entrepreneurial immigrants a chance to rise into the middle class. The police provided better security. The metro system was extended to Bijlmermeer, connecting its residents with city opportunities. Bike riders, pedestrians, and drivers who had been carefully separated by different road systems were brought back together, creating livelier streets. And the city invested in better social services and schools. Taken together, these elements turned Bijlmermeer into a community of opportunity; today second-generation immigrants living in Bijlmermeer have the same levels of income and university education as the ethnic Dutch.

The Well-Tempered City

Eager to begin applying the ideas that I had been wrestling with, in 1976, I left planning school to become a real estate developer, focusing on the confluence of environmental and social issues in cities. My role has been to imagine and build solutions by manifesting a community's vision for its future in land and buildings. Funded by complex public and private financing, my colleagues and I coordinate the work of dozens of consultants, architects, engineers, and contractors to create projects that model the solutions needed to make cities happier, healthier, and more equitable. I have also consulted on planning issues in communities ranging from the South Bronx to São Paulo, and from Nantucket to New Orleans.

This work in cities has been extremely gratifying. I collaborate with colleagues who are smart, effective, and motivated to make the world a better place, and we see people's lives improved by our work and nature less abused. Our strategy has been to imagine and then develop projects that model a bit of solutions to the issues cities face, and then work to disseminate what we learned. It became clear that there is an eager audience for solutions that are financially viable and help solve social and environmental challenges. We discovered that creating successful models and promoting their lessons widely was a key leverage point. Our projects became early models for the green affordable housing, transit-oriented development, green building, and smart growth movements.

This work is also very difficult. The problems are wicked, the tide of megatrends is moving against our best intentions, and we are not working at a scale that is meeting the challenges of our times. I often read and write late into the night, pondering the issues of cities, how out of sync they are with nature and ourselves, and think about the shifts that could realign them—and I listen to Bach. His music is imbued with wisdom and compassion, yearning and resolution, but most important, a sense of wholeness. It came to me that the concept of temperament that helped Bach create harmony across scales could be a useful guide to composing cities that harmonize humans with each other and nature. After all, harmony lies deep in the DNA of cities; it was part of their purpose from the very first, more then five thousand years ago.

I call this aspiration the well-tempered city. It integrates five qualities of temperament to increase urban adaptability in a way that balances prosperity and well-being with efficiency and equity, ever moving toward wholeness.

The Five Qualities of a Well-Tempered City

The first quality of urban temperament is *coherence*, which can be seen at work in the temperament used to compose *The Well-Tempered Clavier*. Just as an equalizing tuning system permitted twenty-four different musical scales to integrate and to influence one another for the first time—so cities need a framework to unify their many disparate programs, departments, and aspirations. For example, we know that the best future for children is shaped by the stability of their families and housing, the quality of their schools, their access to health care, the quality of the food they eat, the absence of environmental toxins, and their connection to nature, yet each of these may fall under the mandate of a separate city agency. Most cities lack an integrated platform to support the growth of every child. Integration is the base of the first benefit of temperament. When a community has a vision, and a plan for how to carry it out, and is able to coherently integrate its disparate elements, then it begins to be well tempered. Coherence is essential for cities to thrive.

The second quality of the well-tempered city is *circularity*, which is made possible by coherence. Once notes are tempered, they can be connected. One of Bach's favorite musical patterns was the circle of fifths, a vehicle that allowed a musical composition to move from scale to scale through its fifth note, the one that fited with the first note of the next scale most naturally, finally ending up back where it began.

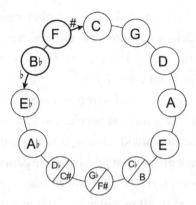

The circle of fifths. *(Jonathan Rose Companies)*

Cities have metabolisms: energy, information, and materials flow through them. One of the best responses to threatening megatrends such as limited natural resources is to develop circular urban metabolisms. Our current city systems are linear; they must become circular, following nature's way of being.

When the world's population hits 10 billion in the middle of the twenty-first century, there simply won't be enough water, food, or natural resources for all of us unless we shift from a linear system, using resources to make things and then discard them, to circular systems based on recycling. As drought-ridden California has discovered, it can purify its wastewater and turn it back into drinking water; it can take organic waste and use it to fertilize crops; it can recycle its soda bottles by turning them into Patagonia vests, creating jobs and resource independence at the same time.

The third quality of temperament, *resilience*, the ability to bounce forward when stressed, is key to cities' ability to adapt to the volatility of the twenty-first century. We can increase urban resilience with buildings that consume significantly less energy to be comfortable, and by connecting them with parks, gardens, and natural landscapes that weave nature back into cities. As our urban centers face extremes of heat and cold, deluge and drought, the well-tempered city can use natural infrastructure to moderate its temperature and provide its residents with a refuge from volatility.

The fourth quality of a well-tempered city is *community*—social networks made of well-tempered people. Humans are social animals: happiness is not just an individual state; it is also collective. This communal temperament arises from pervasive prosperity, security, health, education, social connectivity, collective efficacy, and equitable distribution of these benefits, all of which give rise to a state of well-being. When too many residents of a neighborhood suffer cognitive damage from the stresses of poverty, racism, and trauma, toxins, housing instability, and poor schools, their neighborhoods are less able to deal with the issues of a VUCA age. And it turns out that the health or illth of one neighborhood affects its neighbors in contagious ways. Our well-being is collective.

These first four qualities of temperament reveal how intertwined the world is. Just as the notes of a piano are nothing more than sounds when played separately but come alive when composed in patterns, so atoms and molecules are inert on their own but give rise to life when they are coherently related. Cities also emerge from the interdependence of related parts.

Nature naturally relates—humans must choose how they will relate. The fifth quality of the well-tempered city, *compassion*, is essential for a city to have a healthy balance between individual and collective well-being. The writer Paul Hawken notes that when an ecological community is disturbed by an avalanche or forest fire, it always heals. Human societies do not always restore their communities after stress. A key condition for restoration is compassion, which provides the connective tissue between the me and the we, and leads us to care for something larger than ourselves. Caring for others is the gateway to wholeness for ourselves and for the society of which we are part.

Donella Meadows observed, "The least obvious part of a system, its function or purpose, is often the most crucial determinant of a system's behavior."[12] For a city to truly fulfill its potential, all those within it must share a common altruistic purpose, the betterment of the whole in which they live.

At the physical level, the well-tempered city increases its resilience by integrating urban technology and nature. At the operational level it increases its resilience by developing rapidly adapting systems that co-evolve in dynamic balance with megatrends, preserving the well-being of both the human and natural systems. And at the spiritual level, temperament integrates our quest for a purpose with the aspiration for wholeness.

The Well-Tempered City in Action

The well-tempered city is not just a dream. Many of the aspects of temperament we will discuss in this book are already at work in the world today. Our current best practices in the planning, design, engineering, economics, psychology, social science, and governance of cities are moving us closer to increasing urban well-being. Even if these actions have only a modest effect when taken alone, their power emerges when they are integrated. Together they provide a pathway through resource constraints, population growth, climate change, inequality, migrations, and other threatening megatrends. Well-tempered cities will be refuges from volatility. If the United States, the world's largest economy, were to make investments in infrastructure, integrated operating systems, natural systems restoration, and the landscape of opportunity to temper all of its metropolitan regions, it would be an important stabilizing center of gravity in a volatile world.

Imagine a city with Singapore's social housing, Finland's public education, Austin's smart grid, the biking culture of Copenhagen, the urban food production of Hanoi, Florence's Tuscan regional food system, Seattle's access to nature, New York City's arts and culture, Hong Kong's subway system, Curitiba's bus rapid transit system, Paris's bike-share program, London's congestion pricing, San Francisco's recycling system, Philadelphia's green storm-water program, Seoul's Cheonggyecheon River restoration project, Windhoek's wastewater recycling system, Rotterdam's approach to living with rising seas, Tokyo's health outcomes, the happiness of Sydney, the equality of Stockholm, the peacefulness of Reykjavík, the harmonic form of the Forbidden City, the market vitality of Casablanca, the cooperative industrialization of Bologna, the innovation of Medellín, the Universities of Cambridge, the hospitals of Cleveland, and the livability of Vancouver. Each of these aspects of a well-tempered city exists today, and is continually improving. Each evolved in its own place and time, is adaptable and combinable. Put them together as interconnected systems and their metropolitan regions will evolve into happier, more prosperous, regenerative cities.

Bach's life's work was a quest to understand the harmony of the universe, to articulate the rules that allow for the expression of that harmony and then to make it manifest. Bach's music continues to move us centuries after it was written. The well-tempered city aspires to the greatness of Bach, infused with systems that bend the arc of their development toward equality, resilience, adaptability, well-being, and the ever-unfolding harmony between civilization and nature. These goals will never be fully achieved, but our cities will be richer and happier if we aspire to them, and if we infuse our every plan and constructive step with this intention.

In the pages ahead we will explore the development of cities from the beginning of civilization to the present, in order to understand the conditions that gave rise to cities, and the conditions that create the happiest communities. I hope you enjoy the journey.

PART ONE

Coherence

The transition from just temperament to equal temperament created a framework that broke down the isolation of different musical keys. For the first time they could become part of something greater than the sum of their individual parts. But although Bach's *Well-Tempered Clavier* conveys the sense of fluidity and openness, its notes are played in the same order, one measure after another.

Although inspired by Bach, the well-tempered city must be far more dynamic, ever evolving to keep pace with a rapidly changing world. To do so it must behave more like natural organisms, continuously sensing and adjusting to conditions around it. Just as humans evolve through continuous innovations that increase their evolutionary fitness, so do cities. In both the evolution of humans and cities, advances in physical form such as the opposable thumb and the street grid were essential. But the evolution of their operating systems was even more important. The human operating system is the mind.

Dan Siegel, a clinical professor of psychiatry at the UCLA School of Medicine, describes the mind as an "emergent, self-organizing process that is embodied and relational, and regulates the flow of energy and information."

There are many parallels between this understanding of the mind and the nature of cities. A city is certainly embodied in a physical place, but is much more than its streets and buildings. Dr. Siegel uses the acronym FACES to describe a healthy mind: flexible, adaptive to changes in the context, coherent (holding itself together, albeit fluidly, over time), energized, and stable. These are also the qualities necessary for cities to thrive in VUCA times.

Healthy minds continuously integrate their differentiated parts. Mental-health issues all begin with impaired integration of the brain. Chaos theory observes that when a self-organizing system is not able to link differentiated parts, it moves to chaos or rigidity. The same happens with the mind—Siegel notes that almost all mental disabilities can be categorized as chaos, rigidity, or both. Cities, too, are healthier when they link their differentiated parts.

Cities can also be overly rigid or chaotic, or find the right path in between. Rigidity often arises from centralized command and control, as in Soviet cities of the mid-twentieth century, and more recently in cities ruled by Islamic fundamentalism. In such cases, there is no place for individualism or self-expression; diversity, the source of generative capacity, is repressed. Rigid urban infrastructures are incapable of readily adapting to change.

The antithesis of rigidity is the kind of chaos we find when cities lose their ability to govern, often sprawling out of control, without clear goals and direction from a well-functioning government.

Nature's way of flowing between rigidity and chaos is to encourage the growth of differentiation, or diversity, at the same time increasing interlinkage. These qualities give rise to self-organization, which, like all aspects of nature, tends toward symmetry, balance, and coherence. Just as these characteristics enhance our personal sense of well-being, they also enhance the well-being of cities.

This section will explore how cities emerged over time, and the nine characteristics that gave rise to the very first cities. This will be seen through the lens of coherence, exploring how they were planned and where urban planning seems to be going in the near future. We will look at the growth of suburbs, underscoring how cities and suburbs can thrive only if they are integrated into a coherent regional system.

As we shall see, many of the keys to the future can be found in the past.

CHAPTER 1

The Metropolitan Tide

THERE HAVE BEEN three great waves of human history. We are now in the midst of the third. The first wave, hunter-gatherers who depended on foraging, hunting, and fishing, increased our caloric input significantly by working cooperatively and sharing their gains with their family or tribal group. This rise in calories energized the evolution of the cognitive abilities of our minds. The second wave was agricultural, a time when we advanced our social networks and applied them to growing the calories to fuel the development of civilization. In the third wave we dramatically advanced our organizational and technical capacity, making possible our largest technology, cities, which are now spreading across the earth in a vast metropolitan tide.

During the first wave humans perceived themselves to be part of nature. In the second wave, we saw ourselves as deeply embedded in nature yet also shaped by human culture. Our third wave increasingly ignores nature. If can figure out how to integrate this technical time we're living in with the natural flow of evolution, then the human species will thrive. If we cannot, we face great suffering.

The last 2 billion years of life on earth have been marked by five great extinctions, relatively short periods of time in which a significant number of species died off, followed by a new burst of life. The fossil record indicates that it takes 10 to 15 million years to rebound after a great extinction, and that afterward life always takes a new course. During the last great extinction, which occurred approximately 65 million years ago, 95 percent of all the species on earth disappeared. The dinosaur, previously the dominant form of life, never returned.

There are no fixed states in nature; populations and environments are always in flux, and sometimes these fluctuations themselves become so significant that they impact the very nature of life on earth. Life's ability to adapt to changing conditions and to regenerate after even the most dramatic disruptions is awe-inspiring. Understanding this capacity is an important key to understanding how to make our cities more resilient in these volatile times.

The flow of evolution is magnificent and mysterious. Evolution relentlessly selects for fitness without morality. But humans, who evolved a wholly new form of thinking, are imbued with intention, which, when we are at our best, is tempered with morality.

Cognition

Approximately 170,000 years ago our direct ancestors, just five thousand members of *Homo sapiens*, emerged from a long chain of evolving hominoids in southern Africa. Much of the way we think today evolved as adaptive mechanisms to that environment. Over time we have grown in number and created complex civilizations that have spread all over the planet, but our bodies, including our brains, haven't changed much over the last 100,000 years. Put a cleaned-up Holocene man or woman in contemporary clothes and you might mistake one for your neighbor.

So if we had the same brain 100,000 years ago, why did it take us so long to make the move from caves to cities? This chapter will trace that journey. From an evolutionary point of view it turns out to have been remarkably brief. And it begins with cognition, the way that we think.

Human cognition includes perception, discernment, apprehension, understanding, insight, reasoning, learning, and reflection—it is an amazing capacity. The complexity of the input that our minds digest, and the degree to which we analyze it, could make thinking a lengthy process, too slow to respond to the constant challenges of life. To counter that we have developed a series of shortcuts called cognitive biases that have been honed by evolution to help us survive. For example, when a lion suddenly emerges out of the brush, we're wired to freeze in position (and hope he doesn't see us), stand and fight, or run like the dickens. We don't have time to think. These "presets" of freeze, fight, or flight proved to be the right adaptations to the conditions in which we evolved, leading to our evolutionary success. Although they were shaped in a very different time and landscape, these ancient cognitive biases continue to affect the way we think and act today. However, most of us now live in a very different environment. When this ancient bias is repeatedly triggered by aggressive e-mails, or by living in traumatic high-crime neighborhoods, the fight-or-flight response can have a negative impact on our well-being.

In another cognitive bias, our minds evolved to value present conditions more highly than we do future ones, a tendency known as hyperbolic discounting. When we were hunter-gatherers, this bias helped us focus on immediate needs. Unfortunately, in the complex world we're living in, long-range planning is often more important than figuring out where to get our next meal. This cognitive bias is a key reason it is often so hard for our contemporary society to focus on solving the big issues that threaten us, such as climate change, whose effects emerge slowly over time.

Another cognitive bias that helped us succeed as hunters was our unusual focus on hunting large adult animals in their most reproductive years, while most other species typically hunt the young or the very old. This bias made us "superpredators," reducing the reproductive capacity of the species we ate up to fourteen times faster than the norm for other hunting species. As our population grew in size, our prey began to become extinct. As our population grows toward 10 billion, this bias is reducing our long-term ecological fitness.

Our minds are also biased toward in-group favoritism, one's warm feeling for family and friends, which is coupled with out-group aversion. In the early days of human evolution this was a positive adaptation—we survived due to the mutuality of tribe. Because tribes competed against one another for resources, we grew to view other tribes with caution. This, too, became "wired" as a very strong tendency. The work of the social neuroscientist Tania Singer shows that these two biases are deeply linked—the stronger our in-group feelings may be for our family, neighborhood, or football team, the stronger our antipathy will be for those we view as "other." This cognitive bias underlies the racism and nationalism that plague the world today.

Not all of human thinking focuses on the practical issues of day-to-day living, however. The magnificence of human cognition lies in its range. Although we don't really know what the predecessors to *Homo sapiens* thought, signs that they pondered the mysteries of life and death go back 350,000 years to the caves of Atapuerca, Spain, where archaeologists discovered what seem to be the first signs of ritual burial. The positions of the dead imply that their bodies were carefully arranged, accompanied by ocher-decorated flint weapons and tools.

Why were the oldest rituals we can find tied to death? Death inspires us to reflect on where we came from, and where we may be going, leading us to think of the larger questions about the origins of the universe, the emergence of life, and its purpose. Living in nature, exposed to the cycles of the seasons, the moon and the stars, human consciousness developed a yearning for insight into the workings of the world around us. From this we developed the capacity for symbolic thought, which gave rise to language, myth, and the search for meaning. And this was aligned with our minds' propensity to favor symmetry, balance, coherence, and harmony.

The archaeologist John Hoffecker, a fellow at Colorado University's Institute of Arctic and Alpine Research, believes that the mind emerged from the collective brain of humans in social groups. "We are smart, and intentional," he writes, "precisely because we are a 'we.' Humans obviously evolved a much wider range of communication tools to express their thoughts, the most important being language. Individual human brains within social groups became integrated into a neurologic Internet of sorts, giving birth to the mind."[1] Dan Siegel describes this as a relational process—he describes the integration of ourselves and others as not "me" nor "we" but "mwe."

Every aspect of city-making is dependent upon our cognition. It's a process that requires us to think and work cooperatively, to access our shared "neurological Internet" that has provided humans with such a dramatic evolutionary advantage.

Cooperation

Many species exhibit reciprocal behaviors. For example, two horses in a field will stand head to tail so they can swat flies off each other. Reciprocity is a key element of human behavior, too, and humans cooperate in ways that no other species does. Consider the cognitive skills required to work together on a task such as carrying a log. To make that possible, not only does one person have to consider the advantages of moving the log, but he or she also has to be able to communicate those advantages to others and convince them to join in the effort. This reciprocity is the foundation of morality.

The first humans lived in multigenerational tribes, sharing a trait that biologists call eusociality. In noneusocial species offspring are born, leave the nest, and go off to find a mate and establish their own nests. They may flock together for protection and migration, but their genetic fate is individual. Eusocial groups contain multiple generations, divide labor, and contribute a significant portion of their labor for the benefit of the group. The genetic success of eusocial species comes from their cooperative behaviors and altruism. Rather than depending on individual strength, the genetic viability of a eusocial species like *Homo sapiens* is dependent on the success of the group. As the eminent biologist E. O. Wilson noted, human collective behavior has enabled us to conquer the earth.

Human cognition provides us with intentionality, with empathy for friends, and with the capacity to discern who is an enemy. We can intuit who is telling the truth, and who is lying. We are able to make short- and long-term decisions, to make sense of the deep past, and to develop scenarios for the future. All this takes pure intelligence and a large working memory. It also requires social intelligence, the capacity to balance selfishness and selflessness, especially when the two impulses conflict. This social intelligence separated us from our evolutionary Neanderthal cousins, and vaulted humans forward. Wilson writes, "The strategies of this game were written as a complicated mix of closely calibrated altruism, cooperation, competition, domination, reciprocity, defection and deceit."[2] And these were critical skills when it came to making cities.

The first members of *Homo sapiens* initially numbered only five thousand people gathered in small bands, and evolved remarkably quickly. Some of this shift was genetic, as successful mutations contributed to the gene pool. Some was epigenetic, part of the process by which experience influences how genes are expressed, or turned on and off, and give rise to traits that become passed on. And some was cultural, changes in the human social operating system. Together, as our population modestly grew, a whole suite of behaviors evolved that have become deeply ingrained in us today.

Homo sapiens hunted more successfully in groups, protected one another, and helped raise one another's young. A child consumes 3 million calories in the span from birth to maturity, and it's difficult for one parent to gather that much food on her own while also taking care of herself. But acting collectively, it is feasible to feed an entire tribe, even its smallest, weakest members. In fact, humans are the only mammals that engage in *alloparenting*, or shared parenting.

Living so closely together, we have evolved to prefer those who are pleasant and agreeable, and contribute to the community. In fact, today if we are socially rejected the pain and embarrassment that we feel light up the anterior cingulate cortex, the same part of the brain that is activated by physical pain.[3] We are hardwired to get along. We are also wired to reject freeloaders such as the tribe member unwilling to hunt but eager to eat food provided by others. One hundred thousand years ago, rejection from the tribe was tantamount to a death sentence. This ancient evolutionary bias against freeloaders still drives us today; it's the reason phrases like "welfare cheat" and "tax dodger" are so powerful.

These human traits and thousands more like them evolved over a very short period of time, perhaps due to our limited numbers. Ian Tattersall, a paleoanthropologist at the American Museum of Natural History, observed that small groups evolve much more quickly than large ones. "Large, dense populations have too much genetic inertia to be nudged consistently in one direction. Small, isolated populations, on the other hand, routinely differentiate."[4] And we were a perilously small group! Some 73,000 years ago, when a volcano erupted in present-day Sumatra, blackening the skies with volcanic ash, it triggered a thousand-year cold spell that reduced the population of *Homo sapiens* to just a few thousand. We all have this tiny number of ancestors in common, which is why their genetic adaptations—including their hardwired biases—persist in our DNA, even now that there are more then 7 billion of us on the planet.

The Nine Cs

Cognition and cooperation are the first of nine fundamental characteristics of *Homo sapiens* necessary for the emergence of the very first cities: cognition, cooperation, culture, calories, connectivity, commerce, control, complexity, and concentration. These elements are also essential for the continued well-being of cities. In this chapter we will explore these steps along the ancient path to urbanism. Each of the nine Cs contributes to the first aspect of the well-tempered city: coherence.

Culture

Culture is our collective operating software, which continuously evolves, adapts, and regenerates, just as nature does. Culture can adapt more rapidly than genetics or neurology, helping us fit to changing circumstances. Culture also serves as our collective memory, a way to pass on adaptive behaviors like social organization, knowledge and communication systems, and worldviews[5] from one generation to the next, so that they do not have to be continually rediscovered. The adaptive capacity of culture is an essential characteristic of human resilience. Culture contains our ethics, our commonly held values that serve as the center of gravity for living together. Unless these ethical rules permeate a culture, its community will not stay together. Cultural coherence forms the basis of trust, and without trust a civilization will not prosper.

The archaeological record indicates that some 50,000 years ago, in the Upper Paleolithic era, there was a tremendous spike in human activity. At the same time *Homo sapiens* exhibited an entirely new suite of behaviors that anthropologists have labeled "behavioral modernity." Suddenly we see evidence in the archaeological record of a dramatic increase in complex symbolic thought and cultural creativity that seems to correlate with the origin of language. Before that people may have used simple words, known as protolanguages, but did not have access to complex grammar and a wide range of words. Perhaps the change came from the development of verbs, which allowed us to describe not only objects, but actions, and not only in the present, but in the past and future as well. Expressions of behavioral modernity include finely crafted and decorated tools, music and art, self-ornamentation, games, fishing, cooking, long-distance exchange, and increasingly complex burial rituals.

Shortly after the emergence of language, *Homo sapiens* began to spread around the globe in what is called the "African breakout," traveling along seacoasts east to Asia and Australia, and north to Europe. It seems that in emerging, tools, language, and symbolic thought were deeply interrelated. Interestingly, today if you scan someone's brain with an MRI machine while he or she is chipping away at flints to make tools, the core language areas of the brain light up.[6] In order to make a tool we must first imagine how to make it and how to use it, the same skills we need for language. This relationship between language and technologies persists today. When illiterate slum children are given access to computers they can teach themselves English, math, and other subjects essential to prospering in the modern world.

Equipped with language and the capacity to imagine and articulate strategies, *Homo sapiens* could plan cooperative hunting expeditions to drive large game over cliffs, or to herd their prey toward a hidden band of waiting hunters. The hunting success that followed provided more protein, skins for warmth, and bones for tools, all of which gave *Homo sapiens* a tremendous evolutionary advantage. It is also around this same time that archaeologists find the first evidence of humans making art and music. The contemporaneous emergence of religion indicates that, along with their new capacity for symbolic thought and creativity, humans began wrestling with the larger questions of their existence.

Aurochs, horses, and deer, painted in the caves of Lascaux, France, in 15,300 BCE, more than ten thousand years before the first city was built. *(Prof Saxx, via Wikimedia Commons)*

Around 40,000 years ago the first cave art emerged. Within 10,000 years, it was being created over much of the world, from Indonesia to Africa.

The oldest findings are colored disks, symbols of wholeness. These were followed by extraordinary works depicting large animals, often in motion, complexly shaded and sometimes painted on carved stone to create a three-dimensional effect. Some renderings are intended to accurately mirror life, but others are mythic, with the head of one beast imposed on the body of another. Small carved sculptures of voluptuous women, known as "Venus figures," begin to appear. Their enlarged breasts and hips celebrate fecundity, the generative capacity of life. Unlike the caves that people lived and worked in, those caves heavily decorated with art seem to be sanctuaries set apart from daily life. Cognitive science has now shown that the experience of

The Venus of Willendorf, Austria, circa 28,000 to 25,000 BCE. *(Matthias Kabel, via Wikimedia Commons)*

awe is deeply associated with increased compassion, and the practice of ritual with social affiliation. These caves are the first evidence of humans connecting spirituality with a specific place. Thousands of years later, these sacred places became the seeds of cities.

Around the same time this early art was being created, nomadic hunter-gatherers began to build temporary shelters to protect themselves from the harsher elements, and to extend the range of their territory. Drawn from their environments, shelters in the watery south were made of sticks woven together with palm fronds; those in the plains were built of dried mud; dwellings in the mountains were assembled from loose stone; and in the far north igloos were carved from snow and ice.

Twenty thousand years ago the earth's climate began to warm. During this period the human population increased in the Fertile

Crescent in the modern Middle East, starting along the Nile, moving north along the coast of the Mediterranean Sea, and then east to the Tigris and Euphrates Rivers.

Today this region includes parts of Egypt, Cyprus, Israel, Jordan, Syria, southern Turkey, Lebanon, Kuwait, Iraq, and northern Iran.

At that time, the seas were four hundred feet lower than today. (The coast of Florida was fifteen miles east of Miami!) Then, about 12,500 BCE, the earth began to warm during an event called the "meltwater pulse 1A" and the seas rose fifty feet.[7]

Around 10,800 BCE, the climate suddenly turned colder and drier, beginning a thousand-year period called the Younger Dryas. In adapting to the shift, plants developed what ecologists call "r"-type characteristics. To survive shorter growing seasons they evolved by becoming very fertile, reducing their body size, and maturing quickly. To make it through a cold winter they stored lots of calories in their seeds.

The changing climate wiped out many of the larger species that humans had been hunting. In response, the Natufian people living in the western third of the Fertile Crescent began to select high-calorie seeds to eat and watered them to encourage their growth. This required frequent visits to their crops, which in turn prompted them to reside nearby. In this way the shift in climate gave rise to the first human settlements, although their residents still obtained much of their food by hunting and gathering. Over the course of the next two thousand years, the practice of agriculture transformed the entire region, as settlers domesticated first plants and then animals. Learning to domesticate plants seems to have taken only three hundred years, the result of two processes working simultaneously: climate change and human ingenuity.

Evolution often occurs in response to stress. After all, why change when things are going well? Environmental conditions that reduce the reproductive success of part of an ecosystem create a condition

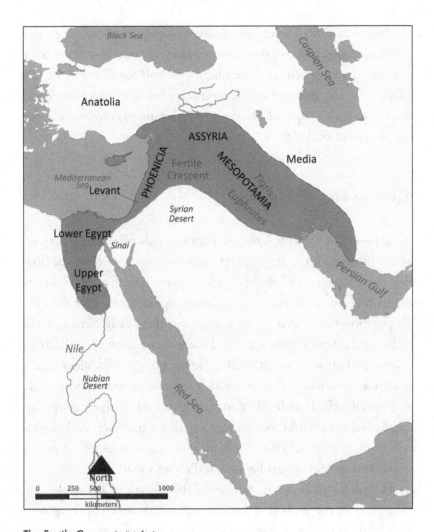

The Fertile Crescent. (Nafsa)

called evolutionary pressure. Ironically, success can create its own
pressure in the form of an ecology that has less biodiversity, and is
therefore more robust but also fragile. The system is stronger, but
less resilient. This kind of strength, lacking diversity, does not adapt
well to changing conditions; it makes the system more vulnerable to

collapse or failure. Throughout human history, climate change and population growth have created evolutionary pressures. At times these pressures have toppled civilizations, as we will see shortly with the Mayan empire. But evolutionary pressure can also foster ingenious responses, such as agriculture. As it spread, human cultivation fueled the growth of civilizations.

Calories Fuel Community

As settlers of the Fertile Crescent began to cultivate grains, they selected those with the largest seeds and thinnest seed coats, because they were easiest to cook. By 7700 BCE this selective harvesting of grains had led to plants that contained significantly more calories. Of the forty indigenous grains available to these early farmers, eight ended up becoming what are called the founder crops of civilization: emmer and einkorn wheat, hulled barley, peas, lentils, bitter vetch, chickpeas, and flax.[8] These were rich in protein, were easy to cook, and stored well. Initially they were irrigated when rivers or springs overflowed their banks, but farmers expanded the reach of these waters using modest ditches. Sophisticated, interconnected irrigation systems would not appear for several thousand years.

Humans also began to encourage the growth of fig, apple, and olive trees in the areas they settled, and cut down competing non-fruit-bearing plants. A few centuries later the migrating mountain peoples living in the Eastern Crescent, who had already domesticated dogs for hunting and protection, figured out how to domesticate goats and sheep. And then in the central part of the Crescent, near what today is the city of Damascus, pigs and cattle were domesticated. These new activities dramatically increased the number of calories available to early agriculturalists. Calories measure the energy resources of a civilization, and with a surplus of calories these early communities were able to invest in infrastructure and organizational complexity.

Villages where grains were grown became as many as six times larger than precultivation villages. Homes were larger, and these villages sometimes featured substantial public works, evidence of the beginnings of central planning and social organization. But while calories fueled the growth of communities and the rate at which they developed, Neolithic farmers themselves did not fare so well. Studies comparing hunter-gatherers with early farmers show that the farmers were as much as six inches shorter, and were much more susceptible to vitamin deficiencies, spinal deformities, and infectious diseases from living so closely together. Interestingly, the appeal of community seemed to override concerns over individual health.

First Came the Temple, Then Came the City

According to an ancient Sumerian legend, the center of the earth's surface was marked by a sacred mountain, Ekur, where heaven and earth met. Here the gods brought humans knowledge of agriculture, animal husbandry, and weaving. And the legend was remarkably accurate: DNA analysis of the genetic ancestor of the first domesticated wheat locates it in a settlement only twenty miles away.

Around 12,000 years ago a group of Neolithic settlers began to visit this sacred spot in the mountains of what is today the southeastern Anatolia region of Turkey to hold ritual ceremonies. In about 9000 BCE they began to build an extraordinary temple compound, Göbekli Tepe. Göbekli Tepe is one of the first known human constructions, and its ambitions were outsize. At its oldest levels archaeologists have identified more than two hundred carved columns set in circles like Stonehenge, weighing ten to twenty tons each on average, with some more than twice as much.

These columns were quarried nearby and carried as much as a

quarter mile to the building site, a task that likely required five hundred people per column. How they did it is still a mystery. Göbekli Tepe also has several windowless rooms with polished terrazzo floors, and stone benches were placed among the columns for sitting. The carvings on the columns are magnificent and mysterious, and include lions, bulls, boars, foxes, snakes, spiders, and birds, and images of abstract humans and phallic symbols. The site shows no signs of settlement but clear evidence of campsites from ancient visitors, and the remains of aurochs, the giant Neolithic cattle eaten at ritual feasts. Anthropologists believe these ceremonies were enhanced by the consumption of alcohol, and perhaps hallucinogenic drugs.[9]

Twelve thousand years ago, at the same time that Göbekli Tepe was attracting spiritual visitors, Ein as-Sultan near the west bank of the Jordan River was emerging as a popular camping ground for Natufian hunter-gatherers. It, too, was a sacred site, where worshippers gathered to honor the goddess of the moon, although they would not build here until 9600 BCE. Archaeologists described this settlement as a "pre-pottery Neolithic A" town, which came into being at a time when grains and fruits were still being stored in dried gourds. Pots had not yet been invented. This place, believed to be the oldest known settled community in the world, was called Jericho. Like the communities that followed it, Jericho sprang up at a site where deities were located; its name is believed to come from Yareah, the local deity of the moon.

At the core of almost every ancient settlement that followed, archaeologists find a temple dedicated to an aspect of nature. Klaus Schmidt observed, "First came the temple, then the city."[10] These sacred dwellings were occupied by priests respected by their followers for their understanding of the natural order, connecting creation theories and the earth's fecundity. The power of their leadership stemmed from their ability to understand and maintain the balance between humans and nature. Over time these temples expanded, as did the settlements that grew around them to support their spiritual activities.

Digging down through the layers of Jericho's history, archaeologists found that its earliest, deepest layer was composed of small circular dwellings built of clay and straw bricks, with the family's dead buried under their floors, evidence of some form of ancestor worship. Heads were separated from bodies and the skulls covered with plaster and painted with ocher and displayed in the rooms above, making them the earliest known portraits of the dead.

By 9400 BCE Jericho had grown to include some seventy houses and more than a thousand occupants. The village was surrounded by a stone wall made famous by its biblical encounter with Joshua almost eight thousand years later, making this the world's first gated community. The walls of Jericho were most likely used to prevent annual floods from the Jordan River from inundating the town. There is no evidence of war at that time, or for millennia to come. More than twelve feet high and six feet wide at its base, the wall enclosed the town, as well as a tower with twenty-two stone steps carved into it, which was used for lunar rituals.

Archaeologists calculate that it would have taken more than one hundred men one hundred days to construct Jericho's great wall. This level of activity was made possible only by the excess calories generated by agriculture, but it also required a new degree of governance, and a dense-enough population to raise volunteers (or command them). By 8000 BCE the residents of Jericho had organized a simple irrigation system to extend springwater to nearby fields.

The first settlements in China were also located around sacred springs or the conjunction of rivers. They grew into communities with a rigorously defined plan that reflected what the Chinese believed to be the architecture of the universe. This plan, the nine-square system, would be used across multiple scales to align farms, small regional towns, then cities, and finally the capital city itself, with the objective of creating harmony between the forces of humankind and nature.

This search for alignment between humans and nature that lies at the core of most early religions also has its pragmatic side. As we explore the collapse of cities and empires we'll see that often they lost the equilibrium between their society and the ecological system that supported it; they grew beyond their water supply, or depleted their soil and could no longer feed themselves. From the beginning the balance between civilization and nature has been essential to meeting both our spiritual and practical needs.

The Tempering Role of Religion

These early settlements also required a new degree of large-scale cooperative behavior. Although they were built by hunter-gatherers, there was something different in their culture that brought them to work together at a scale never before achieved in human history. The psychologist Ara Norenzayan of the University of British Columbia proposed that the transformation came with the emergence of a new belief system, one he called "big gods." Prior to that time, humans believed in gods who created the universe, or local spirits, who had little interest in people's behavior. In small-scale societies, cooperative behaviors were monitored by the group. Free riders were expelled from the community. But larger groups are harder to monitor, and to get to cooperate. Norenzayan believes that the belief in judgmental deities, or "big gods," provided the cooperative glue necessary to build places such as Göbekli Tepe. A watchful, punishing god or gods proved to be a very good monitor of behavior, particularly if the god had authority over your after- or future life. "Big gods" tempered human behavior.

Edward Slingerland, a historian at UBC Vancouver, observed that all-knowing big gods are "crazily effective" at enforcing social norms. "Not only can they see you everywhere you are, but they can actually look inside your mind."[11]

Societies with "big gods" need to have sufficient time and resources to be able to spend them on temples and worship. Nicolas Baumard, a French psychologist who studies the evolution of religion, observed that moralizing religions were much more likely once a community could provide its people with more than 20,000 kilocalories in total energy resources each day.

These two cultural practices, the belief in "big gods" and advances in agriculture, evolved hand in hand, and are evident in the foundation of very early cities in history.

Agriculture soon spread along riverine areas subject to seasonal floods. The practice moved eastward to the Indus (today's Pakistan), then to the Ganges (India), the Brahmaputra (Bangladesh), the Irawaddy (Burma), and finally to the Yellow and Yangtze Rivers in China. By 8000 BCE the Chinese had begun to domesticate rice, millet, mung, soy, and adzuki beans, and were settling down to grow them. Agriculture also followed a western path, moving to Anatolia, Cyprus, and Greece by 6500 BCE. From there it moved south to Egypt, and then into Africa, continuing west to Italy, France, and Germany by 5400 BCE, and Spain, Britain, and Norway by 2500 BCE.

Luc-Normand Tellier, professor emeritus in spatial economics at the University of Quebec in Montreal, named this pathway the "Great Corridor."[12] A whole series of innovations followed this route. The communities along it were most likely to trade, to grow in complexity, and eventually, to become cities. The energy of the Fertile Crescent's grain was transformational. As the practice of agriculture flowed along the Great Corridor, it transformed pastoral tribes into settled communities, planting the seeds of future cities.

Connectivity, Commerce, and Complexity

While Jericho and other towns of its era prospered, they did not grow enough to become cities, which raises a question. If agriculture was the driver of urbanization, as is popularly believed, why was there a four-thousand-year hiatus between the emergence of agriculture and the first cities? Because the last elements—connectivity, commerce, control, complexity, and concentration—had not yet emerged at a scale sufficient to drive urbanization. And once again the climate changed, stalling the growth of cities. Ice and sediment cores indicate that around 6200 BCE a three-hundred-year period of dramatic cooling occurred.[13] Mesopotamian towns like Jericho fell into decline, and their inhabitants scattered or perished.

When the climate began to warm again, the Ubaid, a new and remarkable civilization, spread along the Great Corridor. The Ubaid period, from 5500 to 4000 BCE, gave rise to hundreds of towns and at least twenty known proto-cities, large settlements that shared both rural and urban features, in an area stretching across southern Turkey to the southern tip of Iraq. When archaeologists dug through the strata of Mesopotamian settlements they found an Ubaid layer underneath every future major city. As Dr. Gil Stein, director of the University of Chicago's Oriental Institute, describes it, "This is the earliest complex society in the world. If you want to understand the roots of the urban revolution, you have to look at the Ubaid."[14]

Ubaid towns typically housed about three thousand people. The Ubaid built the first rectangular houses with multiple rooms, which could be packed closely together, giving rise to urban density. In the early Ubaid period, towns were largely egalitarian, but toward the end of their dominance, signs of social stratification appear, with a few large homes that persist over centuries, indicating that family wealth was being passed down from generation to generation.

Ubaid towns formed a loose network of communities stretching from the Mediterranean Sea to the Persian Gulf, connections that increased the flow of ideas and trade, forming what archaeologists call the *interaction sphere*.[15] Trade created arteries of connectivity through which varied cultures flowed, spreading innovation.

The first trade networks began in areas encircled by desert—in Mesopotamia, between the Tigris and Euphrates Rivers in northern Iran, and in the Levant, to the west of the Jordan. Over time these networks crossed the deserts that hemmed them in and reached south to the Nile Valley, north into Turkey, and east toward Afghanistan. Then they began to interconnect. The power of the Ubaid lay not in the advance of any one town, but in the network effect of connecting many.

One force driving commerce and connectivity was the creative surge in designing and manufacturing goods worth trading. During the Ubaid period pottery-making became ubiquitous, along with mining precious stones and smelting metals like copper in the mountainous areas. Incense, spice, and perfumes were produced in the east. Now that disparate regions of the middle east had something significant to offer one another, their proto-cities began to differentiate. The Ubaid began manufacturing on a large scale, not just for their own use, but specifically for commerce, spinning wool into cloth and using the slow pottery wheel to increase production. Pots with distinctive styles and decorations began to be widely traded. As the University of Cambridge archaeologist Joan Oates noted, "It is the first time that you see the spread of a material culture over so wide an area."[16]

The connectivity of differentiated communities, and the commerce and culture that flowed through them, enriched the network effect that not only increased the diversity of the whole system, but allowed each community to also increase its own diversity. During the Ubaid period, as communities joined the network the generative value of the whole system grew geometrically, a phenomenon described by Metcalf's law (which was developed to describe the growth of modern communication networks): the value of a network is proportional to the square of the number of connected users of the system. Communities differentiated, with localized religions, cultural traditions, dialects, or languages, and trade goods became specialized, contributing to the complexity of the network, another key "C" on the pathway to urbanism.

Calories, Cooperation, and Control

As Mesopotamian communities began to grow in size and number, they needed more food. About 4000 BCE they began to dig irrigation ditches to extend the flow of water from rivers and springs. These ditches worked well, but soon silted up and had to be continually dug out to keep the water flowing. The ditch walls also constantly needed to be repaired, and the silt, spread across fields, was needed to restore the soil it covered. As networks of irrigation systems grew, a system became necessary for fairly allocating the water and silt among the fields—and the labor required to maintain them. These activities required collective action.

Two cooperative systems arose. The first was the agreement that farmers would individually maintain the ditches that ran through their exclusive areas of cultivation, and that they would collectively maintain the system's feeder ditches. The second was the election of the wisest and fairest among them to oversee these activities, granting him the authority to manage the system. Interestingly, he used his power not to enhance his wealth, but rather to enhance his status as a leader. Electing a ditch boss, as the role came to be known, is the oldest and longest-running democratic process in the world, and continues to this day in many parts of the world.

Ubaid agriculture began to stimulate new technologies. In addition to improvements in irrigation systems, farmers developed flint sickles to more efficiently harvest grain. The need to keep surpluses gave rise to communal storehouses along with methods of management and accounting. From these grew the world's first writing and number systems, essential to the administration of control, the seventh of the nine conditions that would make the first cities possible. The management of the storehouses and the administration of the proto-city were assumed by the temple, the most sophisticated and trusted organization in the community. Along with the development of education and administrative skills, excavations of later Ubaid settlements indicate that social hierarchies were growing.

Meh

The most important proto-city in the Ubaid, Eridu, was neither the largest nor the most commercially successful, but it was the most spiritually powerful. Its great temple was considered the holder of all knowledge, *meh*—the gods' gift to humans—the key to organizing a society. The anthropologist Gwendolyn Leick describes this as "all of those institutions, forms of social behavior, emotions, signs of office, which in their totality were seen as indispensable for the smooth operation of the world."[17]

Meh was both an activating energy and the source of rules that guided the spiritual, social, and moral basis of the Ubaid culture. *Meh* provided the integrative framework and purpose that was essential for people to live together in higher densities. As a vital, sacred force and value system, *meh* was manifested in Eridu's moral, administrative, and operating systems. *Meh* was a temperament system that unleashed true urbanism.

The most important goddess of Eridu was Inanna, who was said to have stolen the sacred *meh* from her father, the god Enki, who lived in Eridu, and took it south to Uruk. Without the *meh*, Eridu rapidly declined. It lost its moxie. Its sacred power and prestige were transferred to Uruk. With Eridu's *meh*, Uruk undertook the final step in the nine Cs, concentration, a combination of sufficient population and mass with sufficient density, diversity, and connectivity. Its concentrated population created an interaction sphere that became the world's first known city.

Around 3800 BCE many Ubaid towns began to rapidly increase in size and complexity, growing into a dozen independent cities, each with clearly defined territory identified by canals and stone markers. Each also had its own patron god or goddess, temples, and priestly governors or kings, who led the city. These cities typically had populations of about 10,000 people.[18] Of all of them, Ur was in the best position for trade. But Uruk, not Ur, led the region. It had the sacred *meh*, so its culture dominated Mesopotamia.

At its height, in 3200 BCE, Uruk was the largest city in the world, with an estimated population of 50,000 to 80,000 residents living in a walled area six kilometers square. It covered an area half the size of ancient Rome. The city was led by a series of kings that the Sumerians believed descended from a line of mythic god-kings. The role of the human king was to balance heaven and earth, maintaining the prosperity and harmony of the region's people by continually cultivating the conditions for *meh* to thrive.

The kings of Uruk built monumental temples and palaces to enhance the power and fertility of their domains, the first ziggurats in the world. They were decorated with fantastic art. Their altars were lined with gold and decorated with lapis lazuli. The temple art reflected an interaction realm between humans and nature, featuring half-human, half-animal images such as human-headed bison and lion-headed men. At the center of the city were two temples, one dedicated to Inanna, the city's founding goddess, and one to An, the male god who remained in heaven. Nearby were large storehouses. Much of the region's agricultural bounty was gathered there, counted, and then redistributed. Just as the ditch boss's role was to fairly allocate water, the role of the king and his administration was to fairly allocate grain and goods. To administer its complex domain, Uruk developed more sophisticated counting and recording systems, and the world's first writing.

While Uruk was led by a king and managerial elite, the city's urban form indicates a great deal of equality. Its houses and workplaces, clustered by occupations, are mostly all of the same size, and there are no signs of private wealth in them.

By the middle part of the Uruk period it is estimated that 89 percent of the population of Mesopotamia lived in cities, a level of urbanization that we may not approach again until the end of the twenty-first century.

Uruk imported precious stones, metals, and hardwoods from far and wide, exporting a crude, bevel-rimmed clay bowl, made in molds—the world's first known mass-produced item. Bowls from Uruk are found in almost every archaeological site in Mesopotamia, indicating the city's powerful role in trade. It seems that the bowl was used to pay workers in grain, and was cheap enough for them to throw out after use. Hundreds of thousands of them have been found.

As Uruk grew to dominate its region, many of its construction and agricultural workers, and some domestic workers, were slaves. Some were debtors, while others were captured from the mountains in the north. Archaeologists believe that they were slaves for a term, not for life, and there seems to have been a fair amount of social mobility for slaves.

The nine Cs, the building blocks of cities, were exemplified in Uruk. Symbolic thought, the cognitive ability that gave birth to language, art, and religion fifty thousand years ago, took another quantum jump in Uruk with the development of writing. The complexity of the city could be achieved only by expanding cooperative behaviors beyond their evolutionary beginning, the family and tribe, to include collaboration with people who might never meet, but who shared a common purpose as residents of the same city—obedience to the gods, art, culture, ceremony, and rules of behavior. It was deeply tied to the centralized governance system, which merged two powers we now think of as separate, church and state, but in Uruk could have been conceived of only as one. Uruk's sophistication grew from its complexity, built from the diversity of talents and trades in its midst. The city grew to be larger than any previous settlement. To ease its functioning, or by natural propensity, the artisans settled in one area of the city, the butchers in another, the administrators in another, and so on. As Uruk diversified into concentrated sectors, it also increased the linkages among them, just as a healthy mind integrates diversified functions. Uruk was also externally connected to a much larger network of trade and cultural exchange. And all of this was powered by the surplus calories of a cooperative, connected, controlled agricultural system.

The invention of the city was a key moment in the evolution of civilization. It permitted people to specialize in ways that they never did before, accelerating the development of music, art, and literature. But it had a dark side, too. The city's leaders discovered that their newly found organizational capacities and ability to command their citizens could be applied to making war. Within five hundred years of the founding of Uruk, cities were raising armies for the specific purpose of conquering others.

Cities Emerge around the World

The journey of humanity, from a small band of *Homo sapiens* living in the savanna of southern Africa to the world's first city, Uruk, continued onward.

In addition to the first cities in Sumer, there are six other places around the world where ancient cities emerged: Egypt's Nile Valley, the Indus valley of India, along the Yellow River in China, the Valley of Mexico, the jungles of Guatemala and Honduras, and the coastlands and highlands of Peru. Many were initially designed to align with the sun, moon, and stars, or some form of a sacred geometry. And in all cases, their development was along the pathway of the nine Cs.

Mesopotamia's urbanism rapidly spread south to Egypt, and east to the Indus valley. The Harappan civilization developed along the banks of the Indus River and its tributaries, located in what today is eastern Afghanistan, Pakistan, and northwestern India. Its growth was driven by commerce. The Harappans built the most impressive dock systems of all early civilizations, connecting the western civilizations of Egypt, Crete, and Mesopotamia with the eastern ones along the Ganges. The city of Harappa and others that soon followed had the most advanced sanitation systems in the world at the time, with each house having its own well, distinct rooms for bathing, and clay tile–lined drains to carry away wastewater in the streets. In fact, today there are hundreds of millions of people in India (and elsewhere globally) who do not have the benefit of such good sanitation systems.

In the Indus valley, the Great Corridor met what later became a branch of the Silk Road, the trading route through the Pamir Mountains and into China.

The Evolution of the Chinese City of Harmony

Like the first cities of Mesopotamia, ancient Chinese cities first arose around a spiritual place, the Bo, a holy navel connected to the generative powers of the universe, from which life was thought to emerge. Chinese cities were designed to maximize the flow of divine energy, or *qi*, through the Bo, connecting humans with heaven and earth.

The first Chinese towns emerged about 3000 BCE, growing out of the Neolithic Yangshao culture that spread through the lower Yellow River valley near China's eastern coast. Yangshao culture was steeped in the ancient traditions of cosmology, geomancy, astrology, and numerology, all of which sought to describe the underlying order of the universe, and align human activities with it. Bànpô, China's first known large town in the area, just west of today's Xi'an, was just a typical village with its circular mud huts and overhanging thatched roofs. However, around 4000 BCE, Bànpô began to differentiate with the construction of a central great hall, just as the Uruk communities of Mesopotamia organized around a central temple. Bànpô's hall was surrounded by some two hundred houses, whose doors aligned with the sun during the winter solstice. This not only provided cosmological benefits, but also helped provide heating from passive solar gain.

The Chinese believed that the fertility of the earth was dependent upon harmony with their ancestors and their buried bones. Feng shui, the geomantic rules of order, was first described in the *Book of Burial*, which described how to align houses, cities, and graves to maintain harmony. Heaven was represented with a circle revolving around a square earth subdivided into nine squares.

This nine-square form became the fundamental geometry of all Chinese planning. For example, every farm was divided into nine squares. Eight farmers were each given the right to farm one square for themselves, along with collective responsibility for the ninth square, the emperor's. Crops harvested from this center square were transported to a great storage granary in the central square of a nearby nine-squared town, and from there to the center square of a regional hub, making their way to the center of the largest imperial city. The nine-square form ordered the flow of calories, and political and spiritual power, to and from the center.

About eight hundred years after the founding of Uruk's network of

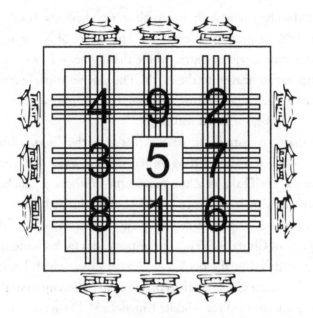

The Chinese Nine (or Magic) Square System: In the ancient Chinese city, the palace was always in the center, in square 5, and enclosed with fortifications to form an inner city. The temples of the ancestors were placed in square 7, the temples of land and grains were in square 3, and a hall for audiences with the public was in square 1. The market was in square 9. Each side of the city had three gates. This pattern was duplicated across scales, from the organization of a simple house to the nation. *(Alfred Schinz,* The Magic Square: Cities in Ancient China *[Stuttgart: Axel Menges, 1996])*

independent cities, the Great Yellow Emperor, Huang Di, developed the world's first centralized state. He also discovered magnetism, built an observatory for tracking the pathways of the stars, made refinements to the calendar, and allocated land in a more equitable way. He tempered his domain by standardizing measures, sponsored the invention of Chinese writing, and propagated a code of laws throughout his empire.

The palace of Erlitou, the oldest in China, was built around 1900 BCE at the confluence of the Lou and Yi Rivers, a sacred place known as the Waste of Xia. Triangles of land at the confluence of rivers were considered to be particularly ripe with spiritual energy, fertile for agriculture and for human procreation. The Waste of Xia marked the center of the nine-square earth, where the divine *qi* flowed from the Jade Emperor in heaven to the earth. The divine emperor resided in the center of the city, radiating *qi* throughout his city and beyond its gates, into his nine-squared realm.

The Shang dynasty fell in 1046, replaced by the Zhou, a disruptive change that was seen as upsetting the harmonious order of the universe. To restore it, the Duke of Zhou moved the aristocracy, scholars, and craftsmen from their residence in the city of Yin back to the Waste of Xia, where he designed a new holy city, Chengzhou, the first fully planned city of China (1036 BCE). The principles for building that city were later codified in the book *The Rites of Zhou*, which became the basis for all ancient Chinese urban planning to follow, up until the time the Europeans invaded the Middle Kingdom.[19] The reconstruction of Beijing as an imperial capital, completed in AD 1421, followed the same urban design rules that shaped Zhou nearly 2,500 years earlier. Twenty-first-century Chinese cities follow a rigid grid system. Unfortunately, the purpose has been to enable towers in the park buildings, and these lack the elegant integration of the earlier Chinese systems. Contemporary Chinese cities, planned to facilitate the relentless expansion of high-rise apartment towers and office blocks, share more with Le Corbusier's Functional City than they do with the Rites of Zhou.

El Mirador

The development of cities continued to unfold around the world. The Mayan culture emerged about 2000 BCE, stretching from the Yucatán Peninsula in the east, over the highlands of the Sierra Madre, across what today is southern Guatemala and El Salvador, to the lowlands of the Pacific plain. The Maya became increasingly sophisticated, growing to between 6 million and 15 million people in city-states across Central America, and then around AD 900 completely collapsed. Today the only traces of it that remain are the ruins of amazing cities, covered by the jungles and forests that have grown over them.

A key driver of Mayan success was the cultivation of corn, whose high caloric content supported the rapidly growing populace and its complex urban and social structures. Mayan farmers supplemented maize with beans, squash, and cocoa grown in terraced fields fertilized with mud from nearby marshes. The Mayans built their cities at the junction of several trade routes, which allowed their king and his favored families to control and profit from the region's trade. As Mayans grew wealthier their social system shifted from a network of local agricultural clans to a more complex arrangement that included a hierarchical class system and a religion that integrated precise astronomical observations with complex mythologies and ceremonies.

The Mayans invented a hieroglyphic writing system, and were the first people in the world to develop the concept of zero. Sophisticated mathematicians, they also developed an extremely accurate calendar, along with complex astronomic calculations of the larger patterns of the universe. They applied their knowledge of cosmic proportions to create plans for their impressive cities, organized around grand boulevards aligned with the sun's rays on the equinox. These boulevards also connected monumental stone pyramids whose mathematical proportions reflected those of the planets.

As Mayan cities grew, they expanded farther into surrounding valleys and hillsides, cutting trees and terracing slopes for fields. To enhance crop yields, their farmers developed extensive systems of reservoirs, canals, dikes, and dams that sustained the civilization for a remarkably long period of time.

El Mirador, one of the first great Mayan city-states, occupied approximately 6.2 square miles, an area a bit larger than present-day Miami, Florida. It was built according to an exacting plan aligned with the path of the sun, and every building was faced with stone, covered with a clay plaster, then decorated with dramatic paintings of sacred symbols and masks. At its peak the capital city, which housed about 200,000 people, was part of a string of politically and economically interconnected cities in a region of 1 million inhabitants.[20]

Then, suddenly, after 1,800 years of extraordinary success, the Mayan civilization collapsed.

The Fall of the Maya

There were key five contributors to the collapse of the Maya: drought, social turmoil from inequality, weakened trading partners, epidemic disease, and environmental degradation. Anthropologist Jared Diamond notes in his book *Collapse* that each of these is a megatrend we should be concerned about today, and each one is exacerbated by climate change.

The rapid expansion of Mayan cities in the century just prior to collapse taxed peasant farmers heavily. While excavating gravesites, the archaeologist David Webster observed that the bones of the Mayan ruling class got progressively taller and heavier, while the bones of the peasants became more stunted.[21] This increasing gap between rulers and subjects undermined the civilization's social contract, eroding trust. As the Mayan empire began to decline due to environmental and economic pressures, the social fabric unraveled, and in many cities, peasants and workers rose up in revolt.

Mayan economic growth had been fueled by trade with sister cities. In the early 600s a major trading partner to the north, the Aztec city Teotihuacan, then the largest city in the Mayan trade network, collapsed, most likely due to internal unrest. The loss of a major trading partner brought El Mirador several decades of severe recession; the Mayan economy eventually recovered, but the fall of Teotihuacan was a portent of things to come. Mayan cities were so deeply interconnected that they could no longer function independently.

We think of the Maya as living in a rainforest. Actually, most of their territory lay in a seasonal desert with limited rainfall. Archaeological evidence from tree rings indicates that starting in the 800s the climate began to change, causing a significant drought. Mayan reservoirs had an eighteen-month supply of water, which was adequate as long as rains came every summer, but once the climate changed, they were not large enough to buffer the droughts. An extended drought first hit the drier cities of the south, but then spread northward to affect the entire Mayan civilization. And as each node in the interconnected economy declined, the entire system weakened further.

The growing Mayan population also outpaced its agricultural technologies. Its exhausted soils produced less nutritious food, hastening the spread of disease. Precious resources needed for the common good were allocated to aggrandize the wealthy. Forests were cut to feed fires used to make lime plaster to cover buildings with layers of extravagant decorations. This exposed clay soils, which streamed down the deforested hillsides, filling in the cities' swampy reservoirs, reducing their capacity when it was most needed.

The Maya were brilliant, sophisticated city builders. They significantly advanced mathematics and science, but they failed to adapt their governance systems and cultural practices to changing circumstances. Climate change, drought, conspicuous consumption, rising income inequality, dependence on extended trade, a degraded ecology, epidemic diseases, and the inability of the food system to keep pace all played their role in the collapse of the Mayan civilization, and every one of these agents is still at work in the world today. Like the Mayans, we have the intellectual tools to understand the megatrends that give rise to the growth of cities and lead to their collapse. And like the Mayans, we are failing to act. The question our city leaders must answer is this: What does it take to transform information into understanding, and then into change? Is our contemporary culture more capable of shifting course than the Mayans who raced headlong to their demise?

Convergent Evolution

That question leads us to inquire a step further. Was the evolution of human culture down the path of the nine Cs toward cities inevitable? The writer and philosopher of technology Kevin Kelly observes that in natural evolution, structures such as the eye develop across a wide range of species, from insects to fish to mammals. As Kelly says, "Since the same structure will appear again and again seemingly from nowhere—like a vortex that instantly appears from water molecules in a draining tub—these structures have to be considered inevitable. . . . This attraction to recurring forms is called convergent evolution."[22]

The emergence of cities in the seven birthplaces of urban culture follows a similar pattern, unfolding along the pathway of the nine Cs. They were all founded in spiritually charged places, perceived to be gateways to the formative power of the universe or a particular god. Settled communities began as cooperative societies, turning to leaders who were responsible for maintaining harmony among divine powers, fertile fields, and the behavior of their people. They were fueled by agricultural technologies, and grew with commerce that fostered connections between proto-cities. As these networks became more complex, their city nodes became denser, more concentrated, but also more diverse. This combination of connectivity, concentration, and diversity gave rise to more complexity, which required more sophisticated cultures and control systems to keep them growing coherently between rigidity and chaos.

We will meet the nine Cs again and again as we explore cities together. These are the conditions of the convergent evolution of cities. And these are the elements that must be tempered by coherence.

Prioritizing Well-Tempered Well-Being

This chapter is infused with our contemporary creation myth, the story of evolution. It's a science-based worldview, and yet, like the founding myths of ancient cities, it is filled with awe and wonder, an attempt to explain the extraordinary, generative aspect of nature. And we have another myth, our belief in the selective power of markets, of economic self-determination that has made cities cauldrons of opportunity. But these threads have not been skillfully woven together. The economic model of the world's cities is out of alignment with the natural world in which they are embedded. And modern life is filled with stress, anxiety, and uncertainty. We have achieved little of the harmony that the ancients sought. Contemporary cities are only beginning to ask what is true well-being, and how we can achieve it.

Modern cities operate under an economic theory that is less than 300 years old, and our theory of evolution is less than 150, so we don't yet fully understand their implications. We have not developed an overarching *meh* to energize our cities, to permeate them with a worldview that aligns our economic, technological, and social advances with the well-being of humans and of nature. The ancients recognized that achieving such harmony was their responsibility. We have not. At least, not yet.

The first step in achieving harmony is coherence, and that can be achieved only through the integration of all of the systems of our cities' *meh*. Like the temperament that integrated the twenty-four keys of the newly developed keyboard into one musical system linked by scales, our cities need integrating systems that provide all its rules and regulations, social systems, and economic incentives with a common set of goals and one common operating language.

One of the most significant ways that cities integrate their various parts is through planning. This is the aspect of coherence that we turn to next. And once again we look to history, where we find the fragments of the DNA that will combine and evolve and lead us to the modern city.

CHAPTER 2

Planning for Growth

THE URBANISM OF Uruk and its Mesopotamian network spread along the Great Corridor, west toward Italy, east through the Harappan area of the Indus to China, and south to Egypt along the Nile.

The Egyptian city of Memphis was founded about 3100 BCE where the Nile River flows into its vast, fertile delta, 250 miles south of the future city of Alexandria. By 2250 BCE, as the Mesopotamian cities declined, Memphis became the largest city in the world. Memphis was believed to be the first city with highly differentiated neighborhoods: to the west, the extraordinary pyramids built as necropolises for the city's rulers; in the center, temples, shrines, ceremonial courts, palaces, and barracks all serving the royal court. These were surrounded by *temenos*—sacred areas bound by walls, reserved for kings and priests, which served as pathways, connecting ceremonial buildings, and provided places of contemplation and reflection. These *temenos* included sacred groves, the first known urban gardens.

Memphis was also a trading city. Its port district lined the Nile, connected to the city by roads and canals. It also had distinctive neighborhoods of workshops, where extraordinary crafts were made both for trade and to decorate the royal constructions. These were surrounded by residential areas and marketplaces, which spread into an undifferentiated sprawl for laborers and slaves.

Like those in all early cities, the streets of Memphis were laid out to follow the natural topography. It was not until 2600 BCE that street plans in the form of grids emerged in the Harappan cities of the Indus valley. From there the concept rapidly spread.

The First Codes

As we've seen, the first cities often had a clearly delineated physical form; in fact, their configuration was often more strictly regulated than it is in cities today. Centered on places of worship, these cities were planned to reflect the underlying order of nature and to impose human order on it. Cities continued to grow larger and more complex. With the rise of the great capital cities of Memphis in Egypt and Babylon in Assyria, neither sacred proportions nor mundane planning tools such as the street grid and differentiated neighborhoods were sufficient to coherently accommodate their growth. Something more was needed.

After the great Amorite king Hammurabi conquered the ancient city of Babylon in the seventeenth century BCE he rebuilt it with a grid street pattern. From this powerful city, Hammurabi expanded his reach along the Euphrates River to unite all of southern Mesopotamia under his rule. At the time Babylon was the largest city in the world, and within its walls people from many tribes and regions lived according to their own customs and mores. To integrate them into one Babylonian people, Hammurabi created a unified code for all his people to live by.

The code of Hammurabi begins by recounting the king's godly calling, and his responsibility to bring justice to his cities:

> When Marduk sent me to rule over men, to give the protection of right to the land, I did right and righteousness . . . and brought about the well-being of the oppressed.
>
> The great gods have called me, I am the salvation-bearing

shepherd, whose staff is straight, the good shadow that is spread over my city; on my breast I cherish the inhabitants of the land of Sumer and Akkad; in my shelter I have let them repose in peace; in my deep wisdom have I enclosed them. That the strong might not injure the weak, in order to protect the widows and orphans, I have in Babylon the city where Anu and Bel raise high their head, in E-Sagil, the Temple, whose foundations stand firm as heaven and earth, in order to bespeak justice in the land, to settle all disputes, and heal all injuries, set up these my precious words, written upon my memorial stone, before the image of me, as king of righteousness then Anu and Bel called by name me, Hammurabi, the exalted prince, who feared God, to bring about the rule of righteousness in the land, to destroy the wicked and the evil-doers; so that the strong should not harm the weak; so that I should rule over the black-headed people like Shamash, and enlighten the land, to further the well-being of mankind.[1]

Our current cities would do well to have such a mission "to ensure that the strong might not harm the weak . . . to settle all disputes, and heal all injuries . . . to further the well-being of mankind"!

In 1754 BCE, when the code was written, the Babylonian state was made up of peoples from many tribes and regions. Each tribe had evolved customs that made sense for their ecological and social niches, giving rise to a wide range of habits and mores. Charles Horne, an early-twentieth-century American legal scholar,[2] postulated that the code of Hammurabi was not the first of its kind, but rather marked an important transition, the shift from a wide variety of oral, locally based codes to a written universal code. By creating a written master code, and posting it on stone columns placed in the heart of the city, Hammurabi created a tempering framework for diverse cultures—a way to make many different peoples come together as Babylonians, under a unifying identity and behavioral system. Since that time powerful cities have prospered by integrating diverse cultures into a more coherent one. This has been a key to the success of a modern city like New York, which has served as a melting pot for waves of immigrants, and where new arrivals today, whether they're from Paris, Texas, or Paris, France, quickly feel that they have become New Yorkers.

Around 1500 BCE, with the development of boats capable of undertaking long journeys and carrying large loads, the centers of gravity of urbanism shifted to the seacoasts. A new corridor emerged along the Indian Ocean, connecting Southeast Asia, Sri Lanka, the Indus valley, and the Middle East. Coastal port cities rose in prominence, interior ones declined. The Phoenicians, the first great Mediterranean sailors, dominated trade along the sea's coast until they were conquered by the Greeks, who were not only excellent sailors and traders, but also city builders.

The Agora: Integrating Democracy and Commerce

The Greek philosopher Aristotle described Hippodamus, who lived from 498 to 408 BCE, as the world's first urban planner, ignoring millennia of city planning that preceded him. But even though the city grid had been used in planning for thousands of years before him, Hippodamus described and codified its use with such precision that modern grids such as that of Manhattan are still called Hippodamian plans. Hippodamus was also deeply interested in the culture, function, and economies of cities. He concluded that the ideal city should be composed of 10,000 people divided into three classes: soldiers, artisans, and farmers. Foreshadowing modern zoning codes, he proposed that a city's land be divided into three distinct parts—public, private, and sacred—and then organized in clearly defined neighborhoods.

In 479 BCE, after the Greeks defeated the Persians at the Battle of

Marathon, they captured the city of Miletus on the Mediterranean coast of what today is Turkey and engaged Hippodamus to rebuild it as a Greek city. His goal was to achieve a design that was at the same time democratic, dignified, and graceful. What a wonderful aspiration! When cities state their most ambitious goals, it seems to make them more achievable. Singapore, for example, aspires to be "a liveable and endearing home, a vibrant and sustainable city, an active and gracious community"; Medellín calls itself "a city of life, on the basis of equity, inclusion, education, culture and citizen cohabitation"; Trondheim, Norway, aspires to "Quality and Equality"; whereas Saskatoon aspires only to be the "Potash Capital of the World."

Hippodamus designed Melitus with a grid of wide streets and a large open space—the *agora*, or marketplace—in the center of the city, to be used for both civic and commercial activities. The Greek word "agora" has two roots, *agorázô*, which means "I shop," and *agoreúô*, which means "I speak in public." Hippodamus's agora integrated both. Four times a month, democratic assemblies were held in the agora to determine matters of state. Courts of law opened onto it, as did theaters and temples, and every spare inch of colonnaded space not dedicated to public functions was filled with market stalls. In ancient Greece democracy and trade were deeply intertwined. The agora was the root of democratic capitalism.

Hippodamus believed that innovation and commerce drove prosperity, so he developed a city code that granted the world's first patent on inventions and ideas. However, Hippodamus also recognized the important role that a vital city played in creating a culture of innovation, so his code split the proceeds from those patents between the inventor and the city.[3] Today cities like San Francisco are cauldrons of innovation, but their prosperity also contributes to a tremendous and unsettling income disparity between the tech and the rest. A modest Hippodamian patent tax would help bridge the affordable housing gap that innovation exacerbates.

The Founding of Alexandria

Ancient Greece was neither an empire nor a nation. Instead it was a loose association of ambitious city-states that shared religious and philosophical systems and a common language, and traded and competed with one another. What we think of as Greece arose from these interactions; there was no central governance of Greece. That began to change in 338 BCE, when Philip of Macedon formed the League of Corinth, a federation of Greek cities and states, to battle against Persia. When Philip was assassinated in 336, his twenty-year-old son Alexander took over, and marched east with a conquering army to Persia and beyond.

Along the way Alexander the Great built a series of cities to solidify his victories in battle and to glorify his name. Many were named Alexandria, but the port city in Egypt, founded in 331 BCE to connect the agricultural wealth of Egypt with the Greek cities of Macedonia, remained his greatest achievement. To build it, Alexander appointed his friend (and some say lover) Dinocrates of Rhodes as his city planner. Recognizing the need for a city's farmers to thrive, Dinocrates located Alexandria on the fertile plains of the Egyptian coast. There he laid out the city in a grid alongside a large, sheltered harbor, and engaged engineers to design its water and sewage systems.

For more than a thousand years Alexandria not only was the capital of Egypt and an important center of trade, but was known throughout the ancient world for its extraordinary library. Alexander, who had been tutored by Aristotle in his youth, deliberately set out to make the city the knowledge capital of the world. The library's mission was to obtain every single book in the world, copy it and translate it into Greek, assemble the finest scholars of the time to digest and analyze its contents, and to teach what they had learned from it.

The Alexandria library's acquisition department traveled widely to purchase books, but it also confiscated any book that a ship or traveler brought to the city's borders. After making a copy overnight in its vast scriptoriums, the library kept the original and returned the copy to the volume's owner. To accommodate all of this copying Alexandria became a leading papyrus manufacturer, a classic example of a knowledge center also developing technologies for knowledge storage and dissemination.

The system succeeded, producing such extraordinary scholars as Archimedes, Aristophanes, Eratosthenes, Herophilus, Strabo, Zenodotus, and Euclid, who in 300 BCE developed what has become known as Euclidean geometry. Euclid's system of measurement, with its methods for calculating angles and areas, formed the basis for much of the city planning that was to come. By 200 BCE Alexandria was the largest city in the world, a vibrant trading city connecting Greece with markets as far east as India. It was a superb example of a city that integrated power, trade, and knowledge.

The Ten Books of Architecture

The Greek confederation was a cranky one, with cities ever shifting their alliances, and as the united Romans to the west became stronger, they began to conquer neighboring lands to feed their growing armies and cities. The Greeks, meanwhile, had turned over their military affairs to mercenaries. Why fight if you could spend your days in the agora and your nights at the theater? At first the Romans provided armies for the various warring Greek factions, but in 197 BCE Rome started keeping the lands its legions were winning for itself, and by 146, with the fall of Corinth and Carthage, Greece had become a Roman territory.

As the Roman Empire expanded, it needed a planning framework to integrate the wide range of cities it conquered into the empire. In the first century BCE, Vitruvius, who started his career designing war

THE WELL-TEMPERED CITY

machines for the military, wrote *De architectura*, the Ten Books of Architecture, establishing the framework for much of Roman city-making for many centuries to come. Roman planning provided a centralized infrastructure for fresh water, wastewater, and storm water; gridded streets connected to intercity highways; easily divisible city blocks; central civic and commercial districts; separate zones defined by use, and often by class; building standards to protect the safety of residents; docks, warehouses, and the other elements of economy and trade; amphitheaters for entertainment; and temples to infuse the city with its religion and culture. The Roman system integrated all the elements of cities into one highly functioning whole, and eased the assimilation of cities stretching from the British Isles to Babylonia into the larger empire.

Vitruvius is remembered for describing the most important attributes of a building as *firmitas*, *utilitas*, and *venustas*, or structural strength, utility, and beauty. And only by understanding nature, Vit-

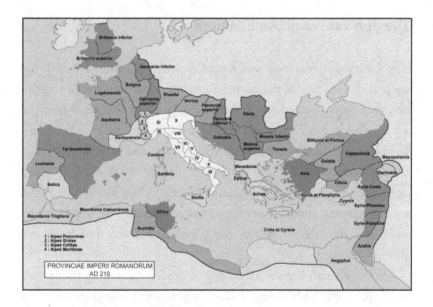

The Roman Empire and its provinces in 210 CE. *(Mandrak)*

ruvius believed, could a city builder understand beauty. Vitruvius's attributes are still taught to architects.

Eastern and Western Systems of Thought

From the early days of civilization two very different ways emerged to understand the world and the role humans play in it: Western and Eastern. These two systems gave rise to very different ways of planning cities that deeply influence how we think about cities today. The Western worldview was born in Mesopotamia; forged in Babylon; advanced by Greek philosophers; systematized, engineered, and spread widely by the Romans.

The Eastern view first emerged in the Indus valley and was advanced by the Chinese along the Yangtze River before spreading farther east to Japan and Korea, and south to Indochina and the Pacific.

The Greeks believed that the world was made up of fundamental individual units called atoms, which followed rules of combination that governed how all matter came into being. This worldview gave rise to physics, astronomy, logic, rational philosophy, and the geometry that formed the basis of Western city planning. Its political outcome was democracy, in which basic units, individuals with free will, could choose to act alone or in concert. Civic morality emerged from the collective agreements made by individuals, not from a higher realm. (In fact, their gods often were not very good models of morality.)

The Chinese, in contrast, believed in collective agency rather than free will; individuals were bound to one another by social and ancestral obligations, and the world unfolded through a harmony achieved by balancing the energies of five key elements: wood, fire, earth, metal, and water. This system did not hold the Chinese back when it came to developing advanced technologies such as stirrups and gunpowder that transformed warfare, locks that made canals possible, boatbuilding and sailing systems that opened waterways to Chinese sailors, mapmaking, immunization, deep-well drilling, and many more, but it did lay the ground for the Chinese belief in collective destiny, fate, and distrust of individualism.

The Greek view that objects and actions functioned independently gave rise to the concept that humans and nature are related but separate, and that directed by anthropomorphic gods, nature has human-like qualities, such as constancy and fickleness. The Chinese view that objects and actions are deeply integrated with their ecological context gave rise to seeing humans as part of nature, and seeing the highest goal of civilization as achieving harmony between them.

The Implications of Eastern and Western Mental Models for City Planning

The Western view of a world of independent objects following abstract rules led to a rule-based system for city planning with a clear separation of uses. It gave rise to the street grid, which provided a framework for the independent development of buildings. By creating easily sellable lots, Western cities became profitable real estate ventures. Seeing the world as comprising individual components assembled in modular fashion gave rise to the Industrial Revolution. But the shadow side of the Western view was that it failed to see the whole, labeling anything outside its domain an externality.

Western planning has long struggled with balancing individual rights and freedom with collective responsibility, because it sees these as two forces in opposition. The Eastern world's integrative worldview led to the development of city plans as maps of the forces of the universe. The result was a deeply pleasing order with little room for variation, lest the harmony it sought to maintain be disturbed. Chinese city planning placed the palace, the seat of power, in the center of the city. There the emperor served as the moral center of his realm, with absolute authority.

Hammurabi and the Duke of Zhou had the same general goal, to create a framework that integrated many local peoples into a whole, a nation. Both claimed to rule with the blessing of the heavens, and both assumed the responsibility for the well-being and harmony of their peoples. But Hammurabi accomplished his integration with a set of rules that perceived his subjects as individual actors within a larger domain. Zhou set out to integrate his domain into a collective pattern, made of nested scales of communities.

Each of these worldviews has its strengths and weaknesses. To address the issues our cities face in the twenty-first century we need both, seeing the world as quantum physics does, understanding that light can be both an individual particle and a collective wave. To thrive and adapt, cities need to enhance both our individual and our collective nature. This is the value of the first temperament, which lets each note ring individually, yet provides the framework for integrating them into a magnificent, harmonious tapestry of music.

The Axial Age

The worldviews of both the East and the West shifted dramatically during the remarkable period between 800 and 200 BCE, a time that the German philosopher Karl Jaspers named the Axial Age. During this epoch Confucianism and Taoism arose in China; Hinduism, Jainism, and Buddhism in India; Judaism and Zoroastrianism in the Middle East; and Pythagoras, Heraclitus, Parmenides, and Anaxagoras developed philosophical rationalism in Greece. This was the time that the foundational works of many of the world's religions were written—the canonical Hebrew texts that became the Hebrew Bible, the Analects of Confucius, the Tao Te Ching, the Bhagavad Gita, and the Sutras of the Buddha.

Thinkers of the Axial Age came from a wide range of cultures and geographies, but they shared a common search for meaning. As they explored the nature of wisdom and compassion and the human mind, they asked, how does the individual relate to the whole? What is ethical behavior? And how does ethics permeate society?

These questions arose in response to an increase in violence and materialism resulting from two technologies that had swept across Eurasia. The first was the chariot-riding archer, which led to the rise of large, highly mobile armies around 1700 BCE. Five hundred years later the Iron Age produced even more powerful and destructive weapons. Emperors, greedy for land and power, began a thousand years of continuous war. At the same time the invention and widespread usage of coins to represent value dramatically increased commerce, accelerating the rapid growth of wealth, materialism, and inequality.

The consequence of these two technologies was an increase in aggression and suffering. In response, the sages of the age sought to find a new balance. By turning inward they advanced methods of deep contemplation. From this inner state they developed new systems of thought that promoted discipline, compassion for others, and the search to understand the larger whole.

The religions and philosophies that emerged from the Axial Age were far better adapted to the increasingly sophisticated urbanism of their times. They gave rise to moral codes that allowed for a much more complex society to function. They enhanced systems of trust, essential for people to live closely together and to trade. They advanced compassion, a key element of a more equitable society. And they developed the idea of transcendence, the capacity of an individual to experience the ultimate nature of the universe. Transcendence eliminated the need for an emperor appointed by heaven to serve as translator of the ways of nature and arbiter of wisdom and justice. These new worldviews spread along the great trade routes, watering the soil of cities.

The Rise of the Islamic City

Significant shifts in worldviews such as the Axial Age often arise out of chaos. One thousand years later, as the Roman Empire declined, chaos certainly ensued. The great unified empire, held together with political might, infrastructure, and a voracious metabolism, began to dissolve into pieces. Too often the response to chaos is the other extreme, fascism and decadence. In 570 Emperor Justinian hastened his empire's end by mandating the Justinian codes, which imposed rigid, autocratic order on every aspect of the Roman city, from its physical form to its version of Christianity, while his wife reportedly performed public sexual acts with animals. Pope Gregory the Great wrote: "Ruins on ruins. . . . Where is the senate? Where are the people? All the pomp of secular dignities has been destroyed. . . . And we, the few that we are who remain, every day we are menaced by scourges and innumerable trials."[4]

Rome's inability to adapt to its changing circumstances led to its rapid decline and fall, marking the beginning of Europe's Dark Ages. But from Rome's ashes another civilization arose. In 570 CE, as Rome swung between rigidity and chaos, the prophet Muhammad was born in the city of Mecca. In 622, Muhammad journeyed with a small band of followers from Mecca to Medina to spread the revelations that would form the foundations of the Islamic faith. By the time he died a decade later, he had united the entire Arabian Peninsula under Islam. By 636 worshippers of Islam had conquered the eastern Byzantine Empire, and the following year Islam spread to modern-day Iran and Iraq. By 640 Islam held sway in Rome, Syria, and Palestine, and by 642 it had enveloped Egypt, Armenia, and Chinese Turkestan. By

718 Islam reigned over much of the land from Spain and northern Africa to northern India.

The spread of Islam was certainly aided by the collapse of Rome, but even so it was remarkably rapid. Islam offered the cities it captured a coherent, integrating vision, accompanied by economic and religious freedom that encouraged diversity and contributed to prosperity. Prior to Islam's arrival, Jews and Christians were heavily taxed to finance wars between Byzantines and Persians. Once the Islamic caliphate conquered a city it reduced taxes, and encouraged free trade by taxing wealth, not income. Muhammad's Constitution of Medina permitted Jews and Christians their own quarters ruled by their own laws, courts, and judges. As a consequence they supported the spread of Islamic rule. Islam replaced rigidity and chaos with a system that was flexible, adaptive, coherent, energized, and stable. Cities like Córdoba in Spain blossomed, enlivened by a mix of Christian, Jewish, and Islamic thought, infused with tolerance, appreciation, and collaboration.

Islam has long considered itself an urban religion. Rather than follow the strict form of Chinese cities, Islamic cities followed an organizational pattern that was recognizably Islamic, but flexible enough to adapt to local conditions. The main mosque always occupied the center of the city. Adjacent to it was the madrassa, a school that taught both religious and scientific subjects. The mosque area also housed social service agencies, hospitals, public baths, and hotels. Next to this was the *suq*, the marketplace. Stalls selling items such as incense, candles, perfume, and books were located closest to the mosque. Next came clothing, food, and spices. The most profane activities such as tanning hides, slaughtering animals, and manufacturing pottery were located farthest from the mosque, usually outside the city walls.

Islamic cities were designed to adapt to nature. Their streets were narrow to reduce exposure to sun and wind, and curved to follow the city's natural topography. In the Islamic moral system the individual aspired to external modesty, but spiritual resplendence within. Reflecting this, Islamic homes had plain blank walls facing the street, with only a few narrow windows. The street walls were required to stand higher than eye level for a camel rider, to protect the privacy of women, who, under sharia law and custom, spent most of their time inside.[5] A small gate opened onto a gracious internal courtyard, which was the center of family life. Depending on the owner's wealth, the inside of the home could be quite ornate.

In the 900s, at the height of Islam's golden age, Abu Nasr Muhammad al-Farabi, an important religious and scientific thinker, developed the first scientific theory of the vacuum, and significantly contributed to the engineering of urban water distribution systems. He also wrote a key Islamic text, *The Perfect City*, which described three kinds of cities.[6] The best was the virtuous city, a place in which people pursue knowledge, virtue, and happiness with humility. Next came the ignorant city, whose residents seek wealth, honor, freedom, and pleasure without aspiring to a higher state of well-being and true happiness. Last came the wicked city, whose people delude themselves, knowing that wisdom is the highest calling but justifying the pursuit of power and pleasure with arrogant, self-serving rationalizations.

Although al-Farabi derived much of his philosophy from Plato and Aristostle, he differed in one key area. The Greeks believed in pure forms, an unchanging, absolute truth such as the ideal form for a city. Al-Farabi, however, in alignment with modern social science, believed that our civic behaviors emerged collectively, and that the ideal city arose from leaders with noble intentions and a society oriented toward wisdom and compassion.

Knowledge in the Islamic City

During this period of rapid growth, Islamic thinkers made great advances in mathematics, science, medicine, and literature. Their key information technology was papermaking, most likely obtained by capturing a Chinese papermaker in the 751 battle for Samarkand and torturing him to extract his secrets. By 795, the technology had arrived in Baghdad, which became the papermaking capital of the world and the largest city in the West, second only to Chang'an in China.

The pervasiveness of knowledge—and the technology to access it—is key to the prosperity of cities. Parchment, the primary means of transmitting the written word in Europe, was expensive and difficult to make, work with, and store, and was therefore used only for the most precious documents. As a result, contemporary written knowledge in Europe had been largely limited to religious topics and available only in the libraries of remote rural monasteries. In Islamic cities, paper was cheap enough to use for shopping lists. Its prevalence fired the growth of engineering, accounting, mapmaking, poetry, literature, and mathematics. Paper-based information moved easily along trade routes and was mashed up in cities, especially in their universities.

In 859, Fatima al-Fihri, the wealthy daughter of a merchant, founded the world's oldest continuously operating university, the University of Al-Karaouine in Fez. Although its curriculum had religion at its core, it also included math, the natural sciences, and medicine. Universities rapidly spread to other Islamic cities, forming a knowledge network that became world renowned. The sons of nobility in Europe and Asia were sent to these universities to become educated, further extending Islam's sphere of influence.

In many ways the golden age of Islamic cities exemplified the key qualities of the nine Cs. They were concentrated nodes in connected networks of trade and knowledge. They developed institutions to advance scientific and medical knowledge and their practice. They welcomed a wide range of peoples and cultures, which added complexity and diversity to the city, as well as their own trade networks. They developed extensive governance systems to regulate morals without unduly impinging on freedom, creativity, or entrepreneurship. Islamic culture provided coherence by applying a flexible planning structure that balanced opportunity and pleasure with modesty, spirituality, and altruism. These are also the key qualities of thriving cities today.

The design of modern twenty-first-century Islamic cities stands in almost complete opposition to the principles of traditional Islamic cities. The central buildings of Dubai, for example, are tall, ostentatious, and commercial. Its streets are designed for automobiles rather than to provide cooling shade for pedestrians. Its edges sprawl into suburbs with gated communities. And although modern Islamic cities use low-tax strategies to attract investment, and are building universities, they lack a culture that aspires to the humility, wisdom, and compassion that al-Farabi defined as essential to the virtuous city.

While these Islamic cities were woven together in a coherent network through which culture and commerce flowed freely, Christian Europe was deeply fragmented, its cities isolated and its intellectual capital constrained. But in 1157 Prince Henry the Lion set out to change all of that.

The Hanseatic League

Prince Henry the Lion was born in 1142 in Schleswig-Holstein, a duchy of the Holy Roman Empire, located on what today is the northern border of Germany. Prince Henry, son of Henry the Black and grandson of Henry the Proud, was an ambitious prince who used military power and economic and political alliances to build his realm. Recognizing the importance of prosperous cities, he set out to grow them, connect to them, or capture them. In 1157 he founded the city of Munich, and in 1159, Lübeck, followed by Stade, Lüneburg, and

Brunswick, which became his capital. But it was in Lübeck, located on the Baltic coast, that Henry the Lion figured out how to create an economic development zone and transform the economy of the region.

Lübeck was a small town subject to frequent attacks by Slavic marauders, most recently the pirate Niclot the Obotrite. Prince Henry's army fought Niclot to the death, took control of the town, made it the seat of a diocese to impose order, and cleared its center to make way for a large marketplace. To attract merchants Prince Henry created Europe's first economic development zone, granting an unusual degree of economic and political freedom to towns and cities regulated by a clear set of fairly administered regulations. As a result, any merchant who settled in Lübeck could conduct trade throughout Henry's domain without paying customs duties to import or export goods.

Lübeck established its own mint, providing a stable and trusted currency accepted throughout Henry's territory. Twenty businessmen were elected to lead the city council, holding two-year terms, although they were often reelected for extended periods. If a father was elected, neither his sons nor his brothers could serve at the same time, to ensure that no one family would have undue influence. The council then elected four *Bürgermeisters*, an executive team that selected one of the four, typically the oldest, to be mayor. This system of governance was protected by the city's charter.

To promote his new trade zone Henry sent messengers throughout the Baltic—his promotional tools were copies of his new charter and offers of cheap land in the marketplace. Attracted by freedom and opportunity, merchants came from Russia, Denmark, Norway, and Sweden to settle in the city. By trading with their homelands they established a network of protected Baltic Sea trade routes that eventually extended from London all the way to Novgorod, Russia.

Lübeck's charter, which came to be known as Lübeck's Law, was pivotal to the success of the cities that adopted it. To accelerate the growth of trading partners Lübeck exported its law across the Baltic. Over time one hundred cities adopted it, and in 1358 they formed the Hanseatic League, a powerful multinational trade alliance that made Lübeck the most prosperous city on the Baltic.[7] In 1375, Emperor Charles IV designated it one of the five "Glories of the Empire," along with Venice, Rome, Pisa, and Florence. Lübeck's Law provided the foundation for the ascent of Amsterdam, with its democratic and mercantile culture, which the Dutch brought with them to New Amsterdam—now New York City—when it was incorporated in 1653. Many of America's principles of democratic rule that balance individual freedom and collective responsibility can be traced back to Lübeck.

The success of Lübeck demonstrates important tools for creating thriving cities that apply to this day. Even in the Digital Age, businesspeople like to get together and gossip, trade, compete, and collaborate. A city needs an economic development strategy with appropriate incentives, a responsive governance system that regulates equitably, a reliable currency, fair taxation whose proceeds are then invested in common infrastructure, and connections to a network of cooperating competitors. The Hanseatic League became an interaction sphere, the same kind of system that energized the Ubaic network. To a volatile world of competing cities, Prince Henry the Lion offers a particularly salient message. He expanded his realm by widely disseminating free copies of his rules for ordering a diverse city. The best ideas for city planning and governance won, providing the tempering system that gave rise to a powerful network.

Amsterdam: Protection, Freedom, and Growth

The city of Amsterdam, situated on the coast of Holland's North Sea, benefited mightily from trade in the Hanseatic League, and its merchants grew prosperous and powerful. In the 1500s Europe was not a stable place. Constant wars and shifting alliances threatened most of its emerging nations. The Netherlands' primary antagonist was Spain, with whom she battled on land and sea. Where Spain's Catholicism veered toward repressive fundamentalism, enforced by torture and inquisitions, the Netherlands responded with tolerance. Amsterdam, its key trading city, opened its arms to European merchants seeking opportunity, and welcomed streams of wealthy Jews from Spain and Portugal, merchants from Antwerp, and Huguenots from France.

In 1602 the Netherlands granted a group of Amsterdam business leaders a monopoly to trade with the East, forming the Dutch East India Company, one of the the world's first companies with publicly traded stock. City fathers were faced with a dual challenge: they needed a plan to both protect the city from military threats from Catholic invaders, and also to accommodate its prodigious population growth and the economic prosperity that would come from its emerging global trade. In 1610 the city carpenter, Hendrick Jacobsz Staets, was commissioned to produce a plan. He began by drawing a half-circle around the city and its seacoast that established its outer limits. Staets chose the half-circle, which generated one of the most beautiful city plans in the world, for simple economic reasons: a circle enclosed the most amount of space with the least length. Its straight edge faced the sea, where the semicircle was protected from attack by a city wall. Outside the wall a larger semicircle of land was designated open space to expose oncoming attackers. Within the protective wall Staets proposed three great semicircular canals by which goods arriving from the sea could be distributed to warehouses and shops throughout the city. Running from the city center to its edge were a series of both grand and lesser streets. This fan-shaped overall pattern provided an elegant plan for the development of the city.

Amsterdam's blueprint was built out over a half century, but its teeming immigrants were not so patient. Much like the informal occupants who surround many of today's developing world's cities, Am-

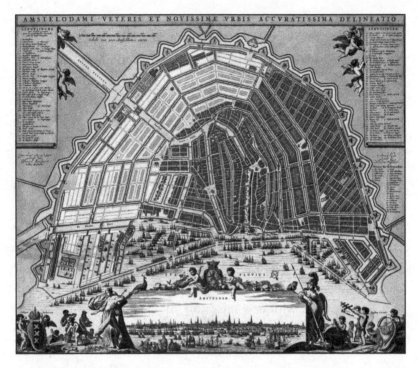

Amsterdam, 1662. *(Daniel Stalpaert, published by Nicolaus Visscher, University of Amsterdam Library, via Wikimedia Commons)*

sterdam's immigrants built slums in the open space outside the city walls, knowing that in time of war they would be displaced, but until then they had an area in which they could freely live and trade. As the city inside the walls developed, it was organized by social class with separate neighborhoods for princes, gentlemen, and the working class. Over time the immigrant suburbs were incorporated into the city and gained access to public infrastructure.

Staets's plan, while providing protection and efficiency, was also designed for grace, ease, and comfort. The city council mandated that as canals were built, their edges had to be planted with elm and lime trees, to provide "sweet air, adornment and pleasantness." Today Amsterdam remains one of the most pleasing cities in the world.

Vienna Tears Down Its Walls

Europe's cities grew rapidly in the eighteenth and nineteenth centuries, fueled by industrialization and globalization. As it became clear that connectivity was more important than defense, they began to tear down the walls that hemmed them in. One of the first cities to take this step was Vienna, capital of the great Hapsburg Empire. In 1857, Emperor Franz Joseph I razed the fortifications surrounding the city and incorporated the parade grounds that had flanked them. In the newly available space he constructed the Ringstrasse, a wide, tree-lined boulevard that circled Vienna's historic core, expanding the city with new leafy suburban neighborhoods and broad airy streets. At the same time Franz Joseph invested in the development of a modern civic and cultural infrastructure. The Ringstrasse and its intersecting boulevards were lined with new museums, an opera house, the city hall and courts of law, parks, and a university. Around these, developers built homes intended for a rising merchant class, and for the professors, musicians, and intelligentsia connected to cultural institutions and the university.

Tearing down the city's walls not only reflected a more open urban plan but also indicated a more open, liberal attitude. Like Amsterdam, the city of Vienna welcomed an influx of people from all over Europe. The more urban neighborhoods of the Ringstrasse featured large family-sized apartments, which particularly attracted secularized and educated Jews, who, since 1084, throughout most of Europe, had been permitted to live only in segregated ghettos. Traditional Jewish Talmudic education encouraged probing analysis, questioning, and a search for deeper meanings; Vienna's new university encouraged a similar intellectual exploration, encouraging the work of Jews such as Sigmund Freud and Gustav Mahler.

The Ringstrasse area soon became the Córdoba of its time, a hothouse for emerging ideas. Vienna's influx of diverse populations, the

growth of its civic and cultural institutions, its links with other leading European cities, and its increasing middle class gave rise to tremendous creative ferment. By the turn of the twentieth century this
multicultural mix was considered the most generative place on earth.

European Planning Comes to America

The native peoples of North America had their own civic cultures.
The Anasazi of the Southwest built extraordinary cities aligned with
the solar solstices. The Iroquois lived in longhouses up to 330 feet in
length. In the 1300s the Cahokia mound city, near what is today St.
Louis, was the largest urban center in North America, with a population of 40,000. No other North American city reached this size until
Philadelphia expanded in the 1780s.

As the Spanish, French, Dutch, and English invaded the continent
they brought with them their own systems of city planning. Spanish
cities like St. Augustine, the oldest continuously occupied settlement
in the United States of European origin, were organized according to
"The Laws of the Indies," a code instructing conquistadors how to
build new communities, which included street grids. Town squares
were bounded by important civic buildings, with noxious or dangerous uses clustered at the edge of town. Laws also mandated that all
of a town's buildings adopt a similar look in order to give the town a
uniform and pleasing identity.[8]

Following the birth of the United States, the Federal Ordinance
of 1785 set out plans for a grid-based survey of lands to the west
of the original thirteen American colonies, so they could be easily
subdivided into rectangular lots. Every town and city west of the
Appalachian Mountains was formed around a gridded street system,
creating a uniform American urban vocabulary, unlike the more organic European cities whose streets curve as they follow the natural

topography of the land. Daniel Elazar, a professor of political science at Temple University, called this "The largest single act of national planning in our history."[9]

The United States was founded as a rural economy, its wealth deriving from its agriculture, furs, and natural resources. In 1820 only 7 percent of the population lived in cities, but industrialization changed America's complexion. By 1870 one quarter of its people were urbanites, and by the turn of the twentieth century that share had risen to 40 percent. The nation's fast-growing cities needed plans, and five strands were emerging.

The first was the sanitary reform movement, which focused on civic water, sewer, and garbage infrastructure, founded in London in response to the waves of cholera and other diseases that swept through the city. The second element also began in London: the urban parks movement thrived in the United States under the leadership of the Olmsted brothers, who designed not only parks but interconnected systems of urban parks. The third strand was the garden city movement, also founded in England, which proposed cities with a balance of residences built around small parks, industry, and agriculture, surrounded by permanent greenbelts.

The fourth thread was New York's housing reform movement, a response to the overcrowded, unhealthy, and unsafe tenements populated by immigrants. The fifth and final element was the City Beautiful movement, which promoted cities planned to classical proportions, carefully composed with civic buildings facing grand avenues, and suffused with formal parks and gardens. Its purpose was to inspire civic virtue, spread harmony among all classes, attract the wealthy, uplift the poor, and nurture the middle class. America's rapidly growing cities eagerly embraced these five movements, creating some of our finest examples of urbanism.

Daniel Burnham's 1909 Plan of Chicago was the nation's first great City Beautiful plan. Burnham was commissioned by a group of civic businessmen who had traveled widely and admired the plans of European cities. Although the Burnham plan was advisory in nature, it significantly shaped a collective vision for how the city should develop. It proposed clustering civic buildings to create civic centers, connected by a series of wide public avenues, and, like the L'Enfant plan for Washington, diagonal streets to tie the city together, along with a series of parks and regional highways to connect the city to outlying districts. But its centerpiece was the reclamation of Chicago's frontage on Lake Michigan. "The Lakefront by right belongs to the people," wrote Burnham. "Not a foot of its shores should be appropriated to the exclusion of the people."[10]

The success of the Burnham plan illustrated the importance of establishing a collective vision for a city, one that enhanced the civic realm, provided for all its residents the best the city had to offer, and unleashed its entrepreneurs. It also demonstrated the value of an independent group of city leaders who could rise above the limitations of bureaucracy and politics to guide that vision.

As the automobile grew in popularity in the early twentieth century, American cities began to spread out from their cores. Planners began to think more regionally, led by a proposal for New York's metropolitan region by Clarence Stein, Benton McKaye, Lewis Mumford, and others. Like Burnham's Plan of Chicago, the New York regional plan was only advisory, as were the regional plans of other cites that followed it. It became clear, however, that in order to make a real difference, a plan had to be backed by the rule of law. The first comprehensive legally enforceable system for regulating land use in American cities was the zoning code, yet zoning, as old as Egypt's great capital city, Memphis, was just a tool; insufficient without the vision of a comprehensive plan, it could only regulate land use, not inspire it. As more than 22,000 cities, towns, and counties in the United States were granted their own zoning powers, integrating them into cohesive regions proved to be very difficult.

In the mid-1800s New York City became a magnet for

immigrants, first from Ireland and Italy, and then from all over the world. To house them cheaply, developers built inexpensive, unsanitary, and unsafe tenements served by outhouses. Pressured by the housing reform movement, New York State passed the First Tenement House Acts in 1867, requiring fire escapes for each apartment and a window for each room.

The Second Tenement House Act of 1879 required windows to face fresh air and light, to which developers responded by facing interior bedrooms onto narrow courtyards known as air shafts, in order to provide the required light and air. But tenants threw garbage into them, and they became breeding grounds for rats and vermin, so in 1901 the final tenement act, known as "the New Law," required that courtyards be drained and accessible for cleaning, and that residents be provided with indoor plumbing. Today New York City's Lower East Side is still home to hundreds of New Law tenements, now occupied by hipsters whose great-grandparents lived in them a century ago, a dozen crowded into a room.

In the early twentieth century rapidly improving construction technologies—including steel framing, electric elevators, and electric water pumps—allowed developers to break through previous engineering limits on building heights. However, as New York's buildings became taller, its streets became darker. So in 1916 the city passed a zoning resolution establishing height and setback controls on buildings in order to allow more light to reach the streets; the city also restricted the spread of industry into residential and commercial neighborhoods.

Purely residential districts were created, their character further delineated by height restrictions; for example, the code established a six-story maximum height limit for nonfireproof buildings. When developers were unleashed by New York City's new zoning code, large sections of the Bronx, Brooklyn, and Queens were provided with vast swaths of affordable six-story apartment buildings for working-class residents.

New York City's zoning code rapidly became a model for other cities with similar problems. Such codes typically regulated the physical aspects of land development—how a building fitted onto its lot, parking requirements, and separating usage. Although zoning codes were written for the private realm, by prescribing the distance that buildings were to be set back from the street they also framed the public realm. However, unlike the grand boulevards planned by the City Beautiful movement, America's public realm in most cases became what was left over after private development. Not until the beginning of the twenty-first century would most U.S. cities again actively design their streets as public spaces.

Zoning Zones America

New York City's first zoning laws paved the way for other cities to organize America's rapid growth. But zoning really took off in 1922, when Herbert Hoover, then head of the federal Commerce Department, led a distinguished committee to write the Standard Zoning Enabling Act (SZEA), creating a format for local governments to write zoning codes. Hoover, as it happened, was very interested in planning. "The enormous losses in human happiness and in money, which have resulted as a lack of City Plans which take into account the conditions of modern life need little proof," he wrote. "The lack of adequate open spaces, playgrounds and parks, the congestion of streets, the misery of tenement life and its repercussions upon each new generation are an untold charge against our American life. Our cities do not produce their full contributions to the sinews of American life and national character. The moral and social issues can only be resolved by a new conception of City building."[11]

Under Hoover's leadership, the Commerce Department actively promoted the idea of a standardized zoning system, and towns and cities across America responded. By 1926 forty-three of the forty-eight states had adopted SZEA in some form. Unfortunately, separating uses became the prime organizing structure of communities, rather than a larger vision of the purpose of a community and a plan for its public realm.

As planners adopted zoning codes, they increasingly became administrators rather than designers. They no longer had time for such ideals as preventing "losses in human happiness." They had roads to plan for the new automobiles to come, subdivisions to approve for America's burgeoning single-family housing industry, and then a depression and a war that stopped almost all new development. After World War II the nation experienced an extraordinary development boom and, as we will see, the appeal of the automobile and the political power of the mortgage and homebuilding industries heavily biased that growth toward the suburbs.

In the late 1960s, as America's cities became increasingly polluted and their suburbs jammed with traffic, citizens turned to the burgeoning environmental movement for a solution, but alas, this took us no closer to designing communities that enhanced the well-being of human and natural systems.

Environmental Lawyers to the Rescue?

In 1969 the United States Congress passed the first major environmental legislation, the National Environmental Policy Act (NEPA), and President Richard Nixon signed it into law. The goals of the act were noble, as captured in its opening words.

> The Congress, recognizing the profound impact of man's activity on the interrelations of all components of the natural environment, particularly the profound influences of population growth, high-density urbanization, industrial expansion,

resource exploitation, and new and expanding technological advances and recognizing further the critical importance of restoring and maintaining environmental quality to the overall welfare and development of man, declares that it is the continuing policy of the Federal Government . . . to create and maintain conditions under which man and nature can exist in productive harmony, and fulfill the social, economic, and other requirements of present and future generations of Americans.[12]

What extraordinary goals! But almost forty years after the act's passage, the "conditions under which man and nature can exist in productive harmony, and fulfill the social, economic, and other requirements of present and future generations of Americans" seem not closer, but further away.

In the ensuing years, NEPA and its state and city offspring have given rise to many individual legal victories. NEPA has been a critical tool for bringing environmental review to government actions. It was followed by the Clean Air Act of 1970 and the Clean Water Act of 1972. Since their passage, the United States' air and water have become considerably cleaner, although they are constantly being threatened by the commercial use of toxins that had not even been imagined when these laws were passed. Yet the overall health of America's environment is much worse, and the systemic threats of climate change, mass extinction, and urban sprawl are significantly larger. If the purpose of NEPA was to make it easier for environmentalists to litigate, it was a huge success, but viewed through the lens of creating the systemic conditions in which man and nature can exist in productive harmony, it was not up to the task. By almost every measure, overall human and environmental health under the purview of NEPA has declined since its passage. The incidence of place-based lifestyle illnesses like obesity, cancer, and heart disease has risen, traffic congestion has increased, biodiversity and soil health have declined, and the amount of greenhouse gas emitted has appreciably risen.

NEPA, which was drafted by environmental lawyers, viewed the "profound impact of man's activity on the interrelations of all components of the natural environment" as a legal problem, and therefore proposed a legal solution. Environmental impact statements (EIS) were to be drafted to analyze proposed significant projects, providing a basis for environmental advocates to sue to stop those projects. But the EIS process does not call for a vision or a plan. It does not look at cities or regions as whole systems. Instead, like zoning, it was designed to break systems into their component parts, but not to reintegrate them. This legacy of Greek thought, dividing whole systems into their individual elements, makes analysis easier, but it lacks the integrating vision of Chinese harmony. There is nothing in the EIS process that increases a community's flexibility, adaptability, or coherence. It simply analyzes environmental impact case by case and comes to a conclusion, for or against the specific action under review.

At the same time that NEPA was being considered, Senator Henry Jackson and Congressman Morris Udall proposed the Land Use Planning Act, to "assure that the lands in the Nation are used in ways that create and maintain conditions under which man and nature can exist in productive harmony and under which the environmental, social, economic, and other requirements of present and future generations of Americans can be met."[13] Alas, the Watergate scandal undermined the political power of the Nixon administration to pass the bill, and it was narrowly defeated by a campaign led by the right-wing John Birch Society, which equated planning with communism.

Reaching back to Egypt's Memphis we have seen that neighborhood differentiation is an important contributor to organizing growing cities. Zoning in itself is not the problem. Nor are street grids, which trace back to Hippodamus. The problem our contemporary cities face begins with the lack of a coherent vision of their well-being, along with the lack of a practical framework for bringing it into being. Throughout history the world's greatest cities emerged in civilizations with urban cultures that integrated diversity with a fabric of connectivity, guided by a sense of purpose articulated in a grand vision.

Uruk's cities were integrated by *meh*, and Babylonian cities with a code "so that the strong should not harm the weak . . . and to further the well-being of mankind." Hippodamus designed his cities to be democratic, dignified, and graceful. Alexandria was founded with a mission to support scholars who could know all known things and educate the next generation of scholars who could discover more. Vitruvius proposed that all the complex aspects of city-making could be unified through the qualities of strength, utility, and beauty. Al-Farabi saw the ideal city as a place where humans could rise in knowledge, virtue, and happiness. Henry the Lion understood that the strength of cities lay in their networks, bound by trust and common systems. Emperor Franz Joseph created a gardened platform for a diverse middle class.

Even as coherent visions for our cities have become less and less common, the twenty-first century places greater stresses on both human and natural systems. The city-planning tools of the twentieth century were not designed to deal with climate change, population growth, resource depletion, and the other megatrends. The VUCA age requires our cities to be more flexible and adaptable to rapidly changing conditions. But zoning and environmental impact statements were just two factors among many that drove city development in the twentieth century away from cities and toward the suburbs.

CHAPTER 3

Sprawl and Its Discontents

Transportation and Suburban Growth

For as long as we've had cities, we've had suburbs. The word itself comes from the Latin *suburbium*, meaning "under the city." Kenneth T. Jackson, in his seminal book on suburbs, *Crabgrass Frontier*, quotes an effusive letter written on a clay tablet in 539 BCE to the king of Persia about life in the suburbs of Ur. "Our property seems to me the most beautiful in the world. It is so close to Babylon that we enjoy all of the advantages of the city, and yet when we come home, we are away from all of the noise and dust."[1]

As the nineteenth century progressed, the United States rapidly grew and urbanized. Its population growth was bolstered by a high birthrate and an open immigration policy. Its industrial growth was founded on innovation, fueled by calories made possible first by the coal that powered steam engines, and then by oil. The growth of urban electric utilities brought light, convenience, and comfort to millions of homes; U.S. cities became more efficiently connected by rapidly spreading rail lines, the telegraph, and the telephone. The phonograph, moving pictures, and the typewriter all facilitated the integration of America's culture, while mail-order catalogs helped turn the country into one huge consumer market. The United States was the largest commercially integrated zone on earth.

In the late 1800s, rapidly growing train networks provided inter-city transportation, but the key mode of intracity transportation was still the horse. Every day, New York City's 100,000 horses produced 2.5 million pounds of manure,[2] posing a serious urban quality-of-life issue. Horse-drawn trolleys moved only 50 percent faster than one person could move on foot, so they didn't expand the urban footprint by much, limiting most American and European suburbs to modest satellites of the cities they adjoined. Although a few experimental electric tram lines were developed in Europe to connect cities with their suburbs, they didn't have the power or reliability to make a significant impact.

In 1888, however, the shape of urban development was transformed by the American inventor Frank J. Sprague. His improvements to the electric motor and his invention of the spring-loaded overhead trolley pole led to the first city-scale electric trolley system. Within two years of its success in hilly Richmond, Virginia, 110 cities on several continents had contracted to use Sprague's system. Sprague's electric streetcar changed the urban form of America's growing cities. Streetcar lines provided a framework for long, linear residential developments, in contrast to the denser walkable villages that were springing up around coal-powered commuter rail stations. The typical streetcar suburb had homes on small lots, often forty or fifty feet wide, facing the serviced street. Wherever the streetcar stopped you'd find a small cluster of local retail stores, with apartments above for the shop owners and their employees. These were entirely pedestrian and transit-served communities, with little need for private transportation. With their affordable homes and opportunities for small businesses, they were an ideal fit for the growing middle class.

Real estate developers soon began to see the opportunity to build grander projects around streetcar and commuter rail stops. In 1893 the Roland Park Corporation purchased land adjacent to Baltimore's Johns Hopkins University; led by Edward H. Boulton, the company developed three of Baltimore's most beautiful garden communities: Roland Park, Guilford, and Homeland. The firm hired Frederick Law Olmsted, Jr., as its master planner and landscape architect. The result was some of the finest examples of architecture and landscape design of the era, including graceful tree-lined streets and the first planned shopping center. But Roland Park also promoted one of the nation's most shameful housing practices, the use of restricted deed covenants to forbid the sale of homes to black or Jewish families. These restrictions even banned African American guests.

Boulton promoted his ideas aggressively through the National Conference on City Planning and the Annual Conference of the Development of High Class Residential Property. Roland Park became a model of the American garden suburb. Its development practices served as a prototype for the garden city developers of Shaker Heights outside Cleveland; Garden City, Long Island; the Country Club district of Kansas City; Palos Verdes, California; and other communities. They were gracious, green, and restricted. While Frank Sprague's streetcars spurred the growth of coherent American suburbs, the opportunity to live in them was not equally shared.

In the meantime Sprague had gone on to improve mechanical systems that made possible New York's subway system, the Chicago El, and London's Underground. His technical prowess unleashed rapid growth at the edges of those cities by eliminating the need for coal-fired engines; this allowed the development of enclosed downtown stations like New York City's Grand Central Terminal. After Sprague transformed horizontal transportation technology, he set to work on the vertical plane. With Charles Platt he invented key components of the electric elevator, setting the stage for the development of the skyscraper.

Thanks to Sprague's inventions, within a few decades the five-thousand-year-old form of the city was transformed into one that was both higher and wider. No longer did most families need to live near where their breadwinners worked. They could live in cleaner, greener suburbs a subway or train ride away from the dense clusters of tall buildings rising in the urban core.

By 1907, only nineteen years after the electric streetcar was invented, cities in the United States were served by 34,000 miles of streetcar lines.[3] Although each line was owned by a private company, together they provided a large, interconnected system. In E. L. Doctorow's novel *Ragtime*, set at the turn of the twentieth century, his characters travel from New York City to Boston on streetcar lines that run from town to town. But Henry Ford's mass-produced, affordable automobile would soon offer individual freedom of transportation on an unimagined scale. By 1924 the automobile had captured the American imagination, and streetcar use began to decline.

The rise of automobiles and the construction of paved roads to encourage their use further accelerated suburban growth. By 1929, when the stock market crashed, one in six Americans lived in the suburbs.[4] During the Great Depression and the war that followed, development in America slowed significantly. But after World War II a new American model emerged that significantly shifted the urban/suburban balance.

The Foundations of American Housing Policy

America's first national affordable housing policy was embodied in the Homestead Act of 1862, which granted 160 acres of land to anyone (including women and freed slaves) who had never taken up arms against the U.S. government, was at least twenty-one years old, and agreed to live on the land and work it for five years. This uniquely American opportunity was denied to soldiers who fought against the United States in the Civil War; how ironic that both the Southern whites who fought in the war and the blacks who were liberated by it faced discrimination when it came to home ownership. Between 1862 and 1934, through a series of congressional acts the federal government granted 1.6 million homesteads, more than 10 percent of the nation's land. But by the 1930s Americans were no longer looking to live on small farms. They were moving to cities.

During the terrible fury of World War I, much of Europe's housing stock was destroyed. In response many countries created extensive housing development programs, building not only for the poor and working classes, but also for the middle class. These building programs attracted bright, young, idealistic architects coming out of the continent's most innovative design schools, such as the Bauhaus, who experimented with new multifamily building designs, new forms of cooperatives, and communities that integrated living, working, and the arts.

But in the United States housing policy was caught up in a larger debate between capitalism and socialism. The location and organization of American development became a proxy for the divisive political discussion. The European form of mixed-income urban rental and co-op housing was branded socialist, whereas suburban single-family home ownership was labeled capitalist. In 1938 the social scientist W. W. Jennings wrote, "Ownership of homes is the best guarantee against communism and socialism, and the various bad 'isms' of life. I do not say that it is an infallible guarantee, but I do say that owners of homes usually are more interested in the safeguarding of our national history than are renters and tenants."[5]

In 1934, choosing the path of capitalism, the federal government chose to address the Depression's stalled housing markets as a financial problem by passing the National Housing Act; the goal was to make mortgages, and thus single-family homes, more affordable. The act created the Federal Housing Administration, or FHA, which used federal credit to provide lower-cost loans. It also created the Federal Deposit Insurance Corporation, or FDIC, which brought financial stability to the nation's local savings-and-loan banks, increasing their capacity to provide mortgages to home buyers. In 1938 the Housing Act was expanded, leading to the creation of the Federal National Mortgage Association, commonly known as Fannie Mae. Fannie Mae purchased FHA-insured mortgages from local banks, returning the money the banks had lent so it could be lent again. Ironically, Fannie Mae, which was designed to alleviate foreclosures and community bank failures, would end up helping to create the very same problems through its purchase of subprime mortgages seventy years later.

The Racial Bias of the Federal Housing Finance System

In 1935, one year after the federal government entered the housing finance area, the Federal Home Loan Bank Board asked the Home Owners Loan Corporation to create "residential security maps" for 239 cities. Instead of individually evaluating borrowers by income, underwriters would first rate the location of their homes. The newest or wealthiest areas—typically suburban or posh urban neighborhoods—were outlined with a blue pencil, and labeled type A; these were prime areas for lending. Type B neighborhoods were outlined in green and designated desirable. Type C neighborhoods, typically urban, were identified as declining, and outlined in yellow. Type D neighborhoods were circled in red, and designated as too risky for loans.

African American neighborhoods were always redlined, as were many Jewish, Italian, and other working-class neighborhoods. This meant that an African American doctor or Jewish lawyer couldn't get a loan to buy or renovate their home if they lived in the wrong neighborhood, despite their income. The Federal Housing Administration's underwriting manual of 1938 extended this practice, encouraging communities to enact racially restrictive zoning ordinances to protect their home values, and to back these up with restrictive covenants excluding blacks, Jews, and others whose ownership would reduce property values. The manual stated: "Recommended restrictions should include provision for the following: the prohibition of the occupancy of properties except by the race for which they are intended. . . . Schools should be appropriate to the needs of the new community and they should not be attended in large numbers by inharmonious racial groups."[6]

Within one year of its creation America's housing finance system was imbued with a deep locational and racial bias that would help to tear America apart. And this didn't happen on its own.

When the federal mortgage assistance program was created, the nation's housing and auto industries quickly realized that the more federal policy shifted toward suburban single-family homes and away from urban multifamily homes, the more profit they would make. The National Home Builders Association, the National Realtors Association, the National Mortgage Brokers Association, and the auto industry all became actively engaged in federal housing policy to promote their interests. Viewing urban renters and co-op owners as lost customers, they did everything they could to sway those who shaped the housing finance system to tilt the playing field against city residents.

The Streetcar System Is Dismantled

The auto industry also viewed riders of mass transit as lost customers. To discourage streetcar ridership, General Motors, Firestone Tire, Standard Oil of California, Phillips Petroleum, and Mack Trucks formed dummy transit companies in 1938, and began buying up cash-stretched city streetcar lines and closing them down, converting them to bus routes. Los Angeles, San Diego, St. Louis, Oakland, and dozens more cities like them suffered the fate of having their streetcar systems destroyed. The plan worked, and cities increasingly became connected to their suburbs by cars and buses.

The Federal Response to the Housing Shortage

Coming home after World War II, America's servicemen came up against a housing shortage that had been brewing ever since the Depression. Six million veterans couldn't find a place to live, and were forced to double up with families and friends. Their frustration was palpable, and in an effort to avoid a repeat of the 1932 veterans' protest march on Washington, Congress passed the GI Bill (the Servicemen's Readjustment Act of 1944), providing generous health, housing, unemployment, and educational benefits for returning vets. The housing benefits provided for zero-down-payment and low-interest loans for single-family-home buyers in green- and blue-lined neighborhoods. However, the Republican-controlled Congress refused to permit veterans' benefits to extend to urban multifamily rental and co-op apartments. Since form follows finance, most servicemen and their families moved to the suburbs, the only place that VA housing benefits could be used.

Recognizing that the nation's cities needed funding for growth and renewal, Senator Robert Taft, a Republican of Ohio and a passionate advocate for multifamily housing and urban investment, put together a bipartisan group of senators to advance a national housing bill. The lobbies for the home builders, real estate brokers, and mortgage lenders responded by funding a young, ambitious Republican senator from Wisconsin named Joseph McCarthy, whom they encouraged to stridently oppose Taft's bill. They hired McCarthy to speak out against multifamily housing, touring him around the country with a script provided by their PR firm claiming that apartment living encouraged socialism. Noting that these anti-Communist lines got the most enthusiastic response, the senator increased the vitriol of his rhetoric. Using a technique he later applied to hunt purported Communists, McCarthy established and led the U.S. Senate Joint Committee Study and Investigation of Housing, and crossed the country, holding thirty-three highly publicized hearings between 1947 and 1948. In the summer of 1947, while visiting the temporary Rego Park Veterans Housing project in Queens, New York, McCarthy claimed it "deliberately created a slum area, at Federal Expense . . . a breeding ground for Communists."[7]

Facing a huge national demand for housing, and stymied by the Republican-controlled House of Representatives, a furious President Harry Truman signed Public Law 846 into being in 1948, promoting single-family housing at the expense of multifamily dwellings, resigned to the fact it was the only housing bill Congress would pass. In his signing press conference President Truman said, "In this case, as in many others, Congress has failed miserably to meet the urgent needs of the people of the United States. . . . It fails completely to aid in meeting our greatest housing need—low-cost rental housing. . . . The failure to pass decent housing legislation is a sad disappointment to the millions of our people who are so desperately in need of homes, and to the many Members of Congress who tried so hard to break the stranglehold of the little group of men who blocked a decent housing bill."[8]

When a public housing bill finally did pass Congress in 1949, Republicans forbade the creation of mixed-income communities, mandating that public housing could be rented only to the poor. They won, and as a result the only federally subsidized options for middle-class families were mortgages for suburban single-family homes. The effect on public housing communities proved to be devastating; instead of becoming healthy, diverse, mixed-income neighborhoods, they became ghettos of concentrated poverty.

Congress's 1949 version of urban renewal primarily focused on slum clearance, providing funds for cities to condemn wide swaths of neighborhoods. In some cases new projects like the brutally functional Pruitt-Igoe were built in their place, but more often whole neighborhoods were demolished and either never rebuilt or so poorly rebuilt as to drive down property values and drive away working families. It's little wonder that urban renewal began to be derisively called "Negro removal." Today, more than half a century later, many cities still have vacant urban renewal sites from the slum clearance programs of the 1950s and '60s. Many of these demolished neighborhoods were once graced by historic buildings that just needed refurbishing.

Today the federal government provides about $120 billion in subsidies to single-family home owners, almost three times more than all of the federal subsidies for low- and moderate-income rental housing.[9] And that doesn't factor in the trillions of dollars the nation lost subsidizing undesirable, unneeded suburban sprawl during the subprime mortgage crisis.

Even these homeowner subsidies are unfairly allocated. According to the Center for Budget and Policy Priorities, an executive earning $675,000 with a $1 million mortgage will receive a subsidy of $14,000 annually, with taxpayers paying 35 percent of mortgage interest costs. A schoolteacher earning $45,000 a year with a $250,000 mortgage receives a housing subsidy of only $1,500 a year and 15 percent of interest expenses subsidized.[10]

Between 1947 and 1953, the population of the United States as a whole grew by 11 percent, but the population of its suburbs grew by 43 percent. The "little group of men" determined America's suburban development path.

The Megatrends That Shaped American Suburbs

In the United States a postwar baby boom and a full-employment economy uncorked an enormous demand for housing. For developers cities were complicated places to build in, whereas suburbs opened their arms to the prosperity that they hoped would come with growth. Zoning also gave communities the power to determine their character, and most suburban communities chose to zone for single-family homes and retail, often barring manufacturing, apartment buildings, and denser land uses they thought would lower property values. They lacked the foresight to understand that they were sowing the seeds of a jobs/housing/shopping imbalance that would force their residents to suffer from pervasive traffic.

Suburban zoning codes facilitated the development of tract housing—vast, inexpensive fields of mass-produced homes first imagined by William Levitt, the developer of Levittown, Long Island, whose success was widely copied by others. Buying inexpensive land from farmers and rezoning it for homes, developers of tract housing took advantage of new, federally funded highways as well as VA and FHA loan programs. Until the mid-1950s, many of these developments were racially restricted. Even William Levitt, who was Jewish himself, refused at first to sell to Jews, and sold to blacks only when the courts forced him to.

In 1956, President Dwight Eisenhower signed the Federal Highway Act, vastly expanding federal financing of the road systems that connected city and suburbs. By 2010 the system spanned 47,182 miles and connected most of America's cities. But the planners of the Interstate Highway System resisted all efforts to integrate highways with the nation's freight, passenger, commuter, and streetcar rail systems, refusing to even place an easement for future rail lines down the highway divider, or alongside it. And because the Interstate Highway System was almost completely financed by the federal government, privately funded rail and streetcar systems simply couldn't compete.

The Interstate Highway program slashed urban highways right through cities. Since no one wanted to live near highways, they were placed where they'd meet the fewest objections, along waterfronts where there was usually a parallel road serving the docks, and through politically weaker poor and working-class neighborhoods, effectively severing them from the rest of the city. Those residents who could afford to move left their now disconnected, noisy, polluted neighborhoods for the suburbs. And those residents who stayed behind watched their neighborhoods rapidly decline.

In the 1960s, as manufacturing moved to less expensive locations in the nonunionized South and then offshore, the good urban jobs that had attracted African Americans and immigrants to cities dried up, leaving empty and often toxic industrial sites behind. Nor were these neighborhoods safe. The war in Vietnam had sent young Americans abroad, traumatized them, introduced them to hard drugs, taught them to use weapons, and sent them home without jobs or much hope of a future. No wonder urban violence exploded, further pushing families to move to the safer suburbs.

The Decline of American Cities

The 1970s were a terrible time for American cities. Although almost every city suffered, one of the most visible was New York. When Mayor Abe Beame asked the federal government for a loan to help New York through its fiscal crisis, President Gerald Ford flew up to New York and delivered a speech in which he said, "The people of this country will not be stampeded. They will not panic when a few desperate New York officials and bankers try to scare New York's mortgage payments out of them."[11] The next day the New York *Daily News* ran the headline "FORD TO CITY: DROP DEAD." Although President Ford never actually said those words, his message had come through loud and clear. The federal government had no interest in helping the nation's cities.

Over the next twenty-five years, most American cities lost a significant portion of their population, and environmental and city planning professionals did little to stem the tide. City planners were trained to focus on regulating growth, not to respond to its decline, and environmentalists were antigrowth, failing to recognize vitality as a natural quality of healthy systems. Detroit was a very different city when its population soared past the million mark in 1921 than it was when it shrank below a million in 1990. Yet it had neither the tools nor the vision to help it manage that contraction effectively.

In his 1970 State of the Union address Richard Nixon said, "The violent and decayed central cities of our great metropolitan complexes are the most conspicuous area of failure in American life today. I propose that before these problems become insoluble, the nation develop a national growth policy. . . . If we seize our growth as a challenge, we can make the 1970s an historic period when by conscious choice we transformed our land into what we want it to become."[12] But we did not adopt the national planning act that he was proposing, nor did we have a vision for what we wanted our cities to become. The key city-planning tools created in the United States between 1916 and 1990 were inadequate to meet the challenges of the second half of the twentieth century. Zoning, for example, was created in the early twentieth century solely to solve a nineteenth-century problem: the negative environmental effects of urban industrialization. The separation of noxious from nonnoxious uses was an ancient one, but during the previous five thousand years of city-making, people had still been able to live near where they shopped and worked. By disaggregating living and working, and by encouraging separation of incomes through lot size and other characteristics, monocultural zoning became a significant contributor to the twentieth-century problems of suburban sprawl, traffic jams, few live-work-play communities, inefficient land use, and extraordinary environmental degradation.

In the 1970s busing schemes designed to integrate city schools pushed more white families to the suburbs, and as the middle class moved out of the city its tax base shrank. The recession and stagflation of the 1970s hit cities hard, and many teetered on the edge of bankruptcy. Corporations began to move their headquarters from grand downtown office buildings to suburban office parks closer to their CEO's golf course, and jobs followed. And all these factors continued to be fueled by the federally funded tilt toward single-family housing, autos, and trucks.

The 1970s also saw a significant cultural shift overtake America, driven by women entering the workforce. Baby boomers entered the housing market almost as eagerly as their parents had after the war, but there was a difference. Now, financed by two incomes, couples were able to purchase homes that were larger, and fill them with consumer goods. Between 1960 and 2010 the average American home doubled in size; in 2010 the typical American home had more TVs in it than people. This surge in consumption was accompanied by a dramatic increase in the number of suburban shopping centers. In 1960 the United States provided 4 square feet of retail per person, but by 2010 that number had grown to 46.6 square feet,[13] almost six times as much as Australia's 6.5 square feet per person and twenty times as much as France's 2.3 square feet.[14] Shopping-center zoning gave rise to much larger retail spaces than the old downtown train-station village or streetcar suburbs provided. These vast new sites with their huge parking lots set in motion a wave of upsizing and standardization in the retail industry. Between 1960 and 2009 personal consumption grew from 62 percent of the American economy to 77 percent, commanding more than three quarters of the United States' allocation of financial resources, attention, and innovation.

The Rise of Suburban Poverty

In 1940 only 13.4 percent of Americans lived in the suburbs. By 1970 that percentage it had grown to 37.1, and by 2012, although the suburban growth rate had significantly slowed, almost half of all Americans lived in suburbs. Still, there was a difference between the suburbs of 1947 and those of 2012. The Brookings Institute reported that by 2008 more than half the poverty in the United States was located in suburbs, not cities. Suburban poverty had grown at five times the rate of poverty in cities, while New York City, Providence, and Washington, DC, actually saw their rate of poverty decline over the same period. Today federal programs for the poor such as food stamps, unemployment insurance, and aid to dependent children send more money to suburbs than they do to cities.[15]

At the same time that America was suburbanizing, it was also becoming more economically segregated. A 2010 study by the Stanford University researchers Sean Reardon and Kendra Bischoff documented that in 1970, only 15 percent of Americans lived in a neighborhood that was at the extreme of either affluence or poverty, but by 2007 that number had doubled to 31.7 percent.[16] Lower-income suburban communities simply do not have the educational, social service, police, and public health infrastructure that cities have to deal with their poor. And with a declining tax base, they are falling further and further behind. This means that not only are poor suburbanites struggling, but their towns are struggling, too.

Suburban poverty and income segregation by location are global phenomena. In France poor, often first- and second-generation immigrants from Algeria and other former French colonies live in *bidonvilles*, or shantytowns, and *banlieues*. Technically, *banlieue* means "suburb," but in France it has become a euphemism for large concrete blocks of government-built subsidized low-income social housing that fills the inner suburban ring. Officially called "urban sensitive zones,"[17] 731 such neighborhoods encircle France's cities; banlieues are plagued by more than twice the unemployment rate found in cities and four times the poverty rate, and have twice as many single-parent families.[18] Banlieue youth unemployment exceeds 40 percent.

Much like ghettos in the United States, these zones are often separated from the urban core by highways that surround them but don't connect to them.

One such suburban town is Clichy-sous-Bois, part of Seine-Saint-Denis, a hundred-square-mile enclave outside Paris. After World War II, Clichy was designed to become a new upper-middle-class town, but when the proposed train line was never built, French-born residents left and Muslim immigrants moved in. Today the community provides few jobs, and facilities are just as scarce. "We don't have a cinema, a swimming pool, an unemployment office, any cafés or hangouts," says Youssef Sbai, director of a children's center in the apartment complex Bois du Temple Towers, where he was raised. "But after the riots [of 2005] they did build a big new police station."[19]

Italy's poor and working-class immigrants live in the *periferie*, the suburbs of cities such as Rome. Vienna's poor live in the city's suburban districts of Favoriten, Simmering, and Meidling, described in a rental guide as "unattractive working-class suburbs dominated by flat buildings, ranging from the 1920s tenement housing to the huge project-type blocks of the 1980s and 1990s."[20] But at least Europe's poor suburbs are served by water and sewer systems, trash pickup, electricity, and some mass transit. And although we may disagree with their Corbusian style of planning, they were planned. In Latin America, Africa, and Asia, rapidly growing slums at the edges of the cities lack the most basic services and infrastructure, such as clean water, sewers, reliable electricity, and garbage pickup.

When immigrants were given such pathways to prosperity as land tenure or decent affordable housing, the ability to create small businesses, up-to-date education, and political and economic systems with inclusive opportunity, Amsterdam, New York, and Barcelona thrived. Those twenty-first-century cities that plan in ways that provide opportunities for all of their residents, including their immigrants, are doing far better than those that isolate them or fail to serve their basic needs. The latter are sowing seeds of discontent that will inevitably yield a dark harvest of social turbulence.

The Suburbs and the Environment

The suburbanization of the world's urban areas has exacerbated not only social problems but also environmental ones. These include loss of productive soils, reduced biodiversity, and inefficient use of natural resources.

Many of the world's cities are built near rivers and estuaries, areas that have the richest agricultural soils. As cities spread onto surrounding farmlands, the economic value of urban development far exceeds the agricultural value of the land. In the United States, since 1967, more than 25 million acres were lost to urban sprawl,[21] more than two acres of farmland per minute.

And this is not just an American phenomenon. A study by China's Institute of Geographic Science and Natural Resource Research identifies almost 10 million acres of China's farmland that have been converted to urban development, displacing 50 million farmers.[22]

The suburban form as initially conceived was a wonderful extension of the city, but as currently practiced it is highly inefficient. And in an increasingly resource-constrained world whose people yearn for a more equitable distribution of prosperity, the form is no longer working well. Urban areas use resources more efficiently than suburbs because they are denser. A typical city block will contain between thirty and one hundred times more homes per acre then a typical suburban block. Because it serves so many people, a city utilizes every street, along with the water, sewer, electric, gas, telephone, and cable lines under it, much more efficiently—and therefore at a small fraction of the cost. Each resident of San Francisco consumes 45.7 gallons of water per day, whereas residents of nearby suburban Hillsborough use 290 gallons a day, more than six times as much.[23] This is partly because more than half of all residential water use in the United States goes to water lawns, which are far more common in suburbs. And automobile usage, with its consumption of fuel and its output of greenhouse gases, is twice as high for residents of those suburbs that lack mass transit as it is for city dwellers.

The Suburban Tide Turns

As cities across the United States began to empty during the 1970s, a group of hardy urban pioneers remained, anchoring their neighborhoods. With the shift from rail to truck transportation, many industries moved to the suburbs for easier highway access, emptying out entire industrial city neighborhoods. Artists moved into the large, cheap old manufacturing buildings and converted them into living and working spaces, soon followed by hip art galleries, bars, and restaurants. In poor and working-class neighborhoods, urban homesteaders bought inexpensive town houses, or squatted in abandoned buildings, and rebuilt them with their own hands. They created community development organizations that began to plan their neighborhoods, advocate for their future, and build affordable housing. They took over rubbish-filled abandoned lots and converted them into community gardens.

In the 1990s the suburban tide began to turn. Bored by suburbs, the children of baby boomers began to flock back to cities, particularly to edgier emerging neighborhoods. Cities were now much safer, and offered some of the most interesting jobs. Based on the confluence of technology, marketing, and finance, the dot-com boom of the late 1990s was urban. Since then job growth in the United States has been much stronger in globally connected, twenty-four-hour, walkable, livable cities. Coming out of the recession of 2008, GDP growth in hip cities like Portland, Oregon, was three times that of the rest of the country.[24] In the past people have always traveled to wherever the jobs were, and by 2010 the new geography of jobs was clear: companies are moving their offices to the places where the smartest, most entrepreneurial, best-educated young people want to live, work, and play: cities with universities, arts, music, culture, and parks, coherently connected by public transportation.

At the same time America's love affair with the automobile began to fade. Traffic was one of the most-cited reasons, especially the annoying unpredictability of stop-and-go traffic. As the Harvard professor Daniel Gilbert puts it, "Driving in traffic is a different kind of hell every day." Research studies indicate that the most disliked daily activity is commuting.[25] The Swiss economists Bruno Frey and Alois Stutzer describe a cognitive bias that they named the "commuter's paradox." Their research indicates that when people pick a place to live they consistently overestimate the value of a larger home, and may choose to travel a greater distance to work in order to get that extra bedroom, or that bigger yard, and underestimate the pain of a long commute. They write, "Our main result indicates, however, that people with long journeys to and from work are systematically worse off and report significantly lower subjective well-being. For economists, this result on commuting is paradoxical."[26]

The quality-of-life benefits of automobile-dependent transportation, which offered an exhilarating sense of freedom in the twentieth century, are rapidly declining in the twenty-first century due to the mismatch between single-mode land uses and the lack of diversity of adequate transportation options. In 2014, congestion increased the travel time of U.S. auto drivers by 6.9 billion hours, adding up to forty-eight minutes to trips that could have been accomplished without traffic in twenty minutes, and costing an extra $160 billion in wasted fuel.[27] Cars are typically driven only 5 percent of the day— the rest of the time they are parked. This is not a very good utilization factor for most people's second most costly investment after their home.[28, 29] As a result, automobile usage is declining. Between 2004 and 2013, the total vehicle miles traveled (VMT) in the United States dropped every single year.[30]

Surprisingly, the decline of automobile use in American cities was not the greatest in most densely populated urban centers. It was most significant in those cities with the most sprawl, such as Atlanta, where driving per capita was down 10.1 percent, and Houston, down 15.2 percent.[31] Working-class and middle-income Americans who live in the suburbs spend about 30 percent of their income on car payments, insurance, gas, and repairs. Increasingly, it's a cost they cannot afford. The decline in automobile use has been particularly evident among young people. In 1990, 75 percent of all American seventeen-year-olds had drivers' licenses; by 2010 the proportion had fallen to less than 50 percent.

So as the interesting jobs, stimulating social life, and pleasures of lively neighborhoods increased in the city, urban living became a choice for happiness and economic rationality. The handcrafted community revitalization efforts of the 1990s had succeeded in creating places where more people wanted to live and work. By 2012 the Urban Land Institute's real estate investment survey, "Emerging Trends in Real Estate," noted, "Living smaller, closer to work, and preferably near mass transit holds increasing appeal as more people look to manage expenses wisely. Interest cools on offices, especially suburban office parks: more companies concentrate in urban districts where sought-after generation-Y talent wants to locate in 24-hour environments."[31]

European cities have been even more successful in taming the urban automobile. Europe's car use increased after World War II, but its older cities simply weren't designed to accommodate auto parking. By 1960 every available public square in the city of Copenhagen had been taken over as a parking lot. Today, with the advent of an extensive bike path system, more people in Copenhagen commute by bike than by car.[32] And its public squares have become pedestrian parks.[33]

Modern Alexandria

But automobile use is on the rise in the developing world's cities. Modern Alexandria, Egypt's second-largest city, is the largest seaport on the Mediterranean, a key hub connecting Europe, Africa, and the Middle East. Alexandria, sprawling along twenty miles of Mediterranean coast, has a rapidly growing population of more than 4 million people. Eighty percent of Egypt's imports and exports pass through Alexandria, so its health is vital to the country. Alexandria is a linear city hemmed in by a long ridge, with the seacoast on one side and low-lying marshes and reclaimed lands on the other.

In the mid-twentieth century the automobile became Alexandria's prime mode of transportation. Today, the core of the city, designed long before the automobile, has far too much traffic and far too little parking. As the city sprawled beyond that historic center, it filled in its marshlands. In 2006 Alexandria went further, paving over 25 kilometers of beachfront and replacing it with an eight-lane corniche, a waterfront highway cutting off the beach from the city. "If you look at what Alexandria had to do to keep functioning, the corniche was perceived as a step forward," said Anthony Bigio, an urban specialist with the World Bank. "But the actions they've taken so far have actually worsened their vulnerability" to climate change.

The new highway cuts the city off from the sea, but not the sea from the city. It has destroyed the biologically rich transition area between low and high tide that the ancient marshlands used to provide, so the sea floor adjacent to the highway is eroding; and without the wave-blocking resistance provided by coral and sea plants, low-lying Alexandria is more vulnerable than ever to storm surges. But having recently made a major infrastructure investment in its highway, Alexandria now lacks the financial resources to invest in storm barriers.

The highway also takes up space that might otherwise be applied to the latest thinking in waterfront resilience: the restoration of natural wetlands to absorb storms and rises in sea level. Even worse, the city's main evacuation route is now in the most vulnerable location, adjacent to the very sea that threatens it. Unfortunately, Alexandria applied twentieth-century engineering to solve its problem, rather than taking an integrated twenty-first-century approach that could address multiple problems simultaneously.

While Alexandria was building a new highway along its waterfront, many U.S. cities were tearing theirs down. In San Francisco, the 1989 Loma Prieta earthquake caused significant structural damage to the Embarcadero Freeway. The Embarcadero had cut the city off from the bay, so faced with the substantial cost of rebuilding the elevated highway, the city decided instead to replace it with a European-style boulevard, which stimulated revitalization of the waterfront. In the same year New York City demolished the aging elevated West Side Highway and rebuilt it as a boulevard with a lush public park along the Hudson River's edge. An old disused elevated rail line that ran parallel to the river was transformed into the High Line, a new linear park that has become one of the city's hottest tourist attractions. And in South Korea, as we'll explore further in chapter 7, the city of Seoul removed the highway that covered its Cheonggyecheon River and restored the riverfront, creating a fantastic new park. By 2010, if you wanted to walk to work, or jog through nature, this was becoming easier to do in a city than in its suburbs.

The Return of Mass Transit

Along with highway removal, cities have been using federal, state, and local funds to rebuild their mass-transit systems, bringing back streetcars and adding commuter light-rail systems and bike sharing. In the process they're making cities more livable and more equitable, and lowering their environmental impact. This approach even makes life better for the drivers who remain, by taking cars off the road. One new light-rail line has eight times the carrying capacity of one highway lane during peak travel times, math that has led city planners to encourage new systems all over the United States, although construction tends to cluster in autocentric western cities like Los Angeles, Portland, San Diego, Dallas, Denver, Salt Lake City, Phoenix, and San Jose. In every case, mass-transit ridership exceeded expectations. These cities and their suburbs are also increasing the density of the development around their transit stations, creating new towns that draw from the successes of century-old train station communities.

New light-rail systems are being planned as parts of larger regional systems connecting to airports and city-center train stations. The most extensive ties together the entire Denver region. The city's old Union Station has been revitalized as a transit hub, connecting the national Amtrak system, the regional light-rail system, the local electric downtown mall shuttle, the bus system, and the airport. Suburban communities are densifying and diversifying their offering, appealing to young urban families. The Denver region's multiple modes of transportation offer its residents choices that make it an appealing place to live. The commuter may want to take the train into the city during the week, walk to a restaurant in the evening, and drive to the country on the weekend, all of which may now be possible.

But such systems require decades of consistent political support. Denver's regional transportation system was conceived of by Mayor Federico Peña in the 1980s, first constructed by Mayor Wellington Webb in the 1990s, vastly expanded into a larger regional system in the 2000s by Mayor John Hickenlooper and a coalition of fifty-two regional mayors and county leaders, and connected to the airport by Mayor Michael Hancock in 2016.

The extraordinary growth of the United States has been enabled by successive transportation technologies—first the steamboat, followed by the railroad, streetcar, automobile, truck, and airplane. There are two new technologies that could help make our regions even more coherent, connected, and prosperous. The autonomous vehicle (driverless cars) will provide the freedom of the current system without its burdens. Instead of owning a car, customers will be able to book or summon one, which will pick them up, drive in high-speed lanes (with the cars packed much more closely together), and drop them off—without their ever having to worry about finding a parking space. And high-speed rail can connect midsize cities and regions to larger ones. For example, if Syracuse, Buffalo, Albany, and Rochester, New York, had high-speed connections to Montreal, Toronto, New York City, Boston, New Haven, and Philadelphia, integrating them all within a two-hour ride, their intellectual assets could be much better leveraged into local economic development.

Subprime Stimulates Sprawl

Despite the lack of suburban job growth and the rise of traffic congestion, during the 2000s suburbs in the United States did continue to grow. But this growth was not fueled by natural demand; it was powered by a surplus of capital. Fannie Mae and Freddie Mac kept money flowing to the housing market by selling their loans to Wall Street banks, which rated loans for credit quality, packaged them in bundles, and sold them to investors. Loans made to high-risk borrowers with a bad credit history, or without a steady job, were characterized as subprime. In 2000, about 8 percent of the mortgages in the United States were issued to subprime borrowers. In 2002, in response to a post-9/11 housing slump, the Bush administration pushed for more liberal loan underwriting to increase home production. As a consequence, from 2004 to 2006, 20 percent of all mortgages were made to subprime borrowers.[34]

The financial system responded with a voracious appetite for subprime loan packages. To feed the demand, real estate developers ramped up the construction of easy-to-build housing, mostly at the edges of suburbs, where land was cheap, zoning was amenable, and, thanks to immigrant labor, construction costs were low. Often these homes were not located near the jobs or universities where educated young families wanted to live, or where seniors wanted to retire, so home builders simply sold to anyone who would sign a mortgage application, and lenders, chasing fees, lent to anyone whom they could entice to apply. In the United States millions of suburban homes were built for a false market, masking the real decline in demand for suburban housing. Often paying as much as 25 to 30 percent of their income for their car payments, fuel, and insurance, these families discovered that the location of their inexpensive homes carried a very expensive transportation cost. In 2007, as gasoline prices rose above four dollars a gallon, many subprime borrowers had to choose between the cost of getting to work and paying their mortgages. As they began to default, the mortgage finance system, which had overinvested in subprime debt, began to collapse, ultimately pushing Fannie Mae and Freddie Mac into financial receivership, triggering a global financial crisis. When lenders foreclosed, they were stuck with houses no one wanted or could afford to own.

Once again, America's housing and development policy was determined by the financial goals of a few, rather than hewing to a coherent, integrated public policy. The Government Accountability Office estimated that the crisis cost the U.S. economy $22 trillion. Is this any way to run a country?

Cities and Suburbs Form a Regional System

In the 1980s, when most of America's central cities were declining and jobs were moving to the suburbs, David Rusk, a former mayor of Albuquerque, studied fifty American cities whose data proved that the health of the central city deeply determined the health of the region. At a time when suburbanites were trying to "go it alone" without their central cities, he documented that their fates were deeply intertwined. One could not solve the issues of cities or suburbs alone. They functioned as metropolitan regions.

After studying weak market cities and regions in the United States, the social scientists Manuel Pastor and Chris Benner noted that those metropolitan regions with the largest disparity between city and suburban income in 1980 had the lowest level of job growth in the following decade. Weak urban centers are less capable of driving regional growth. Cities and their suburbs form a deeply interdependent system; their ecologies, economies, and social systems are all part of a co-evolving whole. And just as regions need a strong, connected center or centers, they also need healthy suburbs.[35]

In the early 1990s a new planning movement, "New Urbanism," emerged in the United States, led by young planners inspired to create great places to live. It drew its vision from Europe's walkable, bikable cities, and from America's great train-station communities of the early twentieth century. New Urbanists recognized the problematic issues of sprawling suburbs, but rather than avoid them they engaged with suburbia, working to redefine its vision and redirect its growth toward mixed-use, mixed-income, and more walkable town centers. These proved both to be better adapted to the issues regions were facing, and to have greater market appeal.

The New Urbanists also made an interesting observation. Cities, with their Hippodamian grid systems, were organized in a way that was extremely adaptable. Most postwar suburbs were served by curving, poorly connected streets ending in cul-de-sacs separated from schools, work, and shopping to such a degree that even a family living right next to a shopping center still needed to get into a car and drive a long, circuitous route to get there. Most suburbs simply weren't adaptable.

The Well-Tempered Region

The Ubaic transformation took place not because Ubaid civilization was the first with so many towns, but rather because it was the first to be connected into a network. And the power of the Hanseatic League came from its network effect. These networks and many others share the characteristic of being multicentered.

The first cities in a region are often monocentric—they have one downtown, surrounded by suburbs. As natural systems grow, they tend to form multicentered clusters. Most of the world's rapidly developing cities are now multicentric, with several "downtowns." The problem with much twentieth-century suburban zoning is that it doesn't encourage the formation of multiple mixed-use, mixed-income, walkable town centers—the result is traffic-producing, boring, environmentally destructive sprawl.

The solution is found in the nine Cs. The elements that gave rise to cities are key elements of their restitution, particularly three: concentration, or densification; connectivity, through multiple means of mass and personalized transportation systems; and complexity, or diversity achieved by mixing uses and mixing incomes.

The application of these three attributes—concentration, complexity, and connection—into existing communities guides their movement toward coherence in the same way that three rules guide the organization of flocks.

Imagine a flock of birds, flying in a perfect V formation, hundreds or maybe thousands of birds, each in its place, always on course over thousands of miles, even as the winds shift, predators emerge, and the rising currents change as they fly over field, forest, and fjord. It turns out that the birds are not assigned seats, like musicians in a symphony, with every nuance of their flight directed by a conductor.

In 1987, Craig Reynolds, an early computer animator, was challenged to realistically simulate crowd scenes for the movie *Batman Returns*. He simply didn't have time to illustrate each person in the crowd, so he came up with the idea of having the computer simulate them. After experimenting, he discovered three simple rules that produced realistic crowd movements.

Reynolds's rules were separation, alignment, and cohesion. Applied to birds in flight, separation means maintaining just enough space to fly closely with neighbors, but to avoid crowding or crashing into them. If a bird moves in another's direction, its neighbor will move away a bit. This is also called short-range repulsion. Alignment means to steer toward the average heading of one's neighbors. And cohesion, also called long-range attraction, means to steer toward the average position of one's neighboring groups. Further study has indicated that cohesion takes place in the same way that trends flow through social networks. As each individual aligns with its group, and each group aligns with neighboring groups, the overall flock maintains incredible cohesion, continuously adjusting to reach a long-range goal.

Flocking has other benefits—collective intelligence, the energy efficiency that comes with flying in each other's wake, and predator protection. Reynolds's rules have been affirmed by numerous scientific studies, not only of birds in flight, but also of shoals of fish and insect swarms, and of human group behavior.

Concentration, complexity, and connection are the flocking

rules for thriving town centers. In each community, they may be manifested differently, but the application of these general principles increases the coherence of suburban communities and the regions of which they are part. And that is a key to their well temperament.

CHAPTER 4

The Dynamically Balancing City

WHEN THE DUKE OF ZHOU set out to build Chenzhou in 1036 BCE, every philosophical, scientific, and religious aspect of the Chinese culture guided his mission: to generate harmony between humanity and nature. He didn't consult his subjects.

And when Alexander the Great and Dinocrates set out to build Alexandria, they too had a singular vision for it. Although they quickly learned that they needed to design a city that worked for farmers as well as librarians, they were solely in charge.

But the Duke of Zhou and Alexander the Great built their cities in simpler times. The twenty-first century is more complex and volatile; its cities are far larger and influenced by a much wider array of forces and trends. Great city-making requires leadership but also, today, much broader participation.

The limited city-planning tools in common use in America's twentieth century produced rapid growth and often mediocre results. But in the latter part of the century, new tools began to emerge to help communities establish a coherent vision, and to manage the systems necessary for achieving it.

Smart Growth

In the winter of 1996, Harriet Tregoning, a young staffer in the new Clinton administration's EPA, called together a group of urban thinkers and doers to discuss what policies could guide the administration as it addressed the environmental and social issues of urban sprawl. I was a member of the group. We named the policy "smart growth." No longer did metropolitan regions have to choose between rampant growth or no growth; there was a third alternative—they could apply intelligence to their growth.

In the 1990s Salt Lake City's suburbs were rapidly expanding, propelled by the area's well-educated, affordable labor force, strong work ethic, attractive natural environment (which included four ski resorts), and the intellectual capital of the University of Utah, with its particularly strong research programs in genetics and health sciences. But the city's downtown was in decline, and the growth of its suburbs was eating into the natural beauty that attracted people to the area; it was also driving them crazy with traffic. In 1997, a public-private partnership, Envision Utah, was formed to wrestle with the growth that was beginning to choke Salt Lake City and its environs. Its goal was to keep Utah "beautiful, prosperous, and neighborly for future generations."[1] As with the Burnham plan, the organizers had no legal power to plan the area, but by building a consensus vision for the rapidly sprawling area adjacent to the Wasatch Mountain range, Envision Utah gained moral authority.

Envision Utah brought together elected officials, developers, conservationists, business leaders, and residents young and old, urban, suburban, and rural, to develop a coherent vision of the qualities they wanted to preserve in their communities, and the kind of communities that they wanted to become. Over a two-year period, Envision Utah conducted public values research, held more than two hundred workshops, and listened to more than 20,000 residents.

Working with the regional planner Peter Calthorpe, Envision Utah generated several future scenarios. At one extreme they developed a scenario of the future sprawl generated by continuing on the same course as the region's current pattern of sprawling development. As an alternative they explored concentrating future growth in higher-density transit-connected centers, and a third option provided something in between the first two. A model was generated for each scenario, showing what the region would physically look like if it were enacted, along with its economic and environmental consequences. The benefits and liabilities of each plan were quantified, with metrics of the minutes of additional traffic, acres of lost or preserved open space, and so on.

During the process residents expressed their love of the mountains and nature, and their concerns that these precious qualities were being undermined by traffic and sprawl. After being presented with the various alternatives accompanied by realistic projections, they came to understand the economic and environmental benefits of smart growth and mass transit. They branded their vision with terms like "the 3 percent strategy," which would concentrate 33 percent of all future development on 3 percent of the land, connected by a world-class mass-transit system.[2]

Envision Utah never filed an environmental impact statement. It has no zoning authority, no taxing power, and no ability to regulate growth: those responsibilities remain with the more than one hundred communities in the Wasatch Mountains. However, the power of the group's vision proved to be extraordinarily compelling. Within fifteen years, development patterns in the region dramatically shifted. A light-rail system was built, and new, higher-density development clustered around it. Between 1995 and 2005 the number of downtown residential units increased by 80 percent, and it now continues to grow rapidly. At the same time more of the natural environment has been preserved, the economy has grown, and the region has prospered, just as envisioned in the first scenario. Salt Lake City and its environs are frequently listed as one of the top ten best places to live in America.[3] In 2014, the Milken Institute ranked the Provo-Orem metropolitan area the third-best economically performing area in the country. And it is one of the most income-equal communities in the United States.

The Cornell University law professor Gerald Torres notes that politicians follow the wind; if you change the wind, they will follow.[4] Envision Utah changed the wind.

Community Participation

Founding the United States of America in the last quarter of the eighteenth century was an extraordinary experiment, one that challenged the prevailing autocratic, centralized governance model of the time. The American democracy proposed that power be vested in citizens, who would come together to form a government that would regulate itself for the common good, in order to, as the Declaration of Independence says, "effect their Safety and Happiness."

Democracy works best when the broadest range of citizens both provide input and take responsibility for its success. In the nineteenth century the United States began to promote universal public education in the belief that an educated public would make for better citizens, and thus provide wiser governance. Being open to immigrants from so many nations and teaching them to read and write in a common language also provided a coherent tempering system to democracy. As the twentieth century progressed and planning became more technical, the number of residents who really understood the choices at hand and participated in the planning process shrank, leaving a few loud voices, NIMBY neighbors, and those who stood to gain financially to have the most influence. If you have not attended a public meeting of your community's planning board, give it a try. The planning board, often made up of volunteers, would appreciate hearing unbiased views advocating for what is best for the community.

The Envision Utah plan modeled a new form of civic engagement, based on much broader public outreach accompanied by graphic ways to visualize the choices faced by the community. Calthorpe visited dozens of communities, equipped with a map of the region and boxes full of blocks representing the different types of development in the region—large lot subdivisions, smaller lots, town houses, apartment projects, shopping centers, main-street retail, and so on. Each block represented a square mile. A square-mile block zoned for one house per acre would accommodate about five hundred homes, whereas a mix of town houses and apartments might accommodate fifteen thousand. Residents were challenged to shape the region's projected growth into any land-use pattern they wished. The only requirement: they had to put all of the projected growth on the map.

At first residents spread all the houses, hotels, offices, and stores out across the landscape using the lower-density development patterns with which they were most familiar. However, this placed sprawling housing developments in the mountains where they enjoyed hiking, and produced even more traffic, which many residents had left other parts of the country to escape. As they experimented by moving around the wooden blocks representing various types of development, they began to create denser mixed-use downtowns, not unlike older western towns. They also created models for the new, vibrant, denser, walkable communities that thrive around universities and attract smart young employees.

Envision Utah captured the choices these public planning sessions were grappling with and published them in a Sunday edition of the *Salt Lake Tribune*, to inform those who hadn't attended the community workshops. The visual models and renderings made the choices easy to grasp. Projections of key indicators quantified the economic, environmental, and quality-of-life outcomes for each scenario. The process created an informed and empowered public, which came not only to understand the zoning choices the communities needed to make, but also to appreciate the benefits of higher-density affordable housing and mass transit. By envisioning alternative regional scenarios, residents were able to understand the likely futures they were facing, and to make informed choices to shape those futures. As it turned out, they didn't need an emperor to strike the best balance between development and nature: the wisdom of the crowd worked well.

Indicators of Community Health

Scenario plans typically define a set of key indicators of community and environmental health. By tracking past and current conditions, and by projecting trends, planners can use data to illuminate various outcomes. The Envision Utah plan not only was based on a consensus derived from extensive community participation, but also was deeply informed by facts on the ground. Peter Calthorpe noted, "Envision Utah defined a broad range of metrics—land consumption, air quality, economic development, infrastructure costs, energy use, water consumption, housing costs, and health, to name a few. This multidimensional analysis allowed many differing interest groups to become engaged. Environmentalists, fiscal conservatives, religious groups, developers, and city officials all had data that spoke to their issues."[5]

To help cities plan more dynamically, Calthorpe went on to develop Urban Footprint, a data-based scenario planning tool that calculates the outcomes of zoning code, planning, and development alternatives.* It contains a library of thirty-five different place types (such as main streets, grocery-anchored shopping centers, and quarter-acre subdivisions) and fifty building types, each based on real-world examples. The program also contains the economic, transportation, climate, and other impacts associated with each place type. Communities can then model different

---

*I am an investor in the company that owns Urban Footprint.

physical plans, and a range of incentives and regulations. Add in variables for fuel and water costs, etc., and the model can project the outcome for the inputted scenarios. Urban Footprint helps residents more accurately understand the consequences of their planning decisions.

In 2001 the economist Mark Anielski and a group of colleagues established a broad set of indicators for the city of Edmonton, in Alberta, Canada. The project tracked twenty-eight measures of the health of community and natural systems, in five categories of well-being: human capital (people); social capital (relationships); natural capital (the natural environment); built capital (infrastructure); and financial capital (money). The human and social indicators ranged from personal consumption to crime, from rates of cancer to the advancement of intellectual and knowledge capital. Environmental

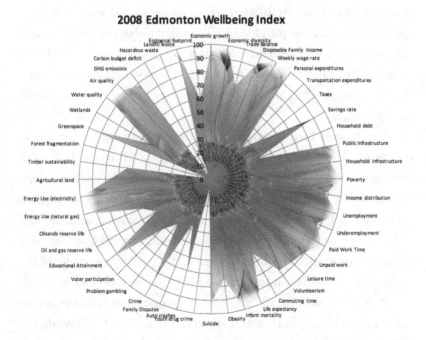

2008 Edmonton Wellbeing Index

Edmonton Well-Being Index, 2008. *(Mark Anielski, Anielski Management Inc., 2009)*

indicators ranged from measures of the health and diversity of wet-lands to the amount of greenhouse gases the city emitted.[6]

Now, for the first time, Edmonton had clear measures of its well-being and a way to track its progress toward its goals.

The combination of Envision Utah's visualization techniques and Edmonton's community health indicators provides a powerful tool for communities not only to plan their futures, but to track their progress and make adjustments as the plans unfold.

PlaNYC

In 2007, Mayor Michael Bloomberg was overseeing a thriving New York City. After decades of shrinking, in the early 2000s New York City began to grow. By 2030, it was projected to add another million people, but it had no plan for accommodating that population surge. In fact, Bloomberg realized, although the city had a capital plan, a transit plan, a housing plan, and many others, it didn't have an inte-grated strategic plan. So he asked his deputy mayor, Dan Doctoroff, to create one.

The process brought together twenty-five city agencies to figure out how to integrate their separate domains. Through their work emerged a vision of an environmentally sustainable city. Although it seems that Bloomberg had asked for a strategic plan, not a green plan, he was remarkably supportive of his innovative commissioners. The plan's green framework immediately won approval from the city's many environmental NGOs (who probably would have opposed the same plan if it had been framed as a blueprint for economic growth).

PlaNYC described 127 initiatives, grouped into ten categories: Housing and Neighborhoods; Parks and Public Spaces; Brownfields; Waterways; Water Supply; Transportation; Energy; Air Quality; Solid Waste; and Climate Change. For the first time a city clearly articulated the connections among each of these areas of operations and established measurable ways to track progress in making them more environmentally responsible. For example, PlaNYC set a goal of planting one million new trees. Each new tree was geocoded so that residents could see where it was on a map of the city, and track how many trees had been planted that day, month, or year, as part of the Parks and Public Spaces initiative. Every additional planted tree also helped the city achieve its storm-water-absorption goal, clean the air of particulates, reduce ambient summer air temperatures, and increase residents' sense of well-being. The growing amount of available data helped make the plan's objectives measurable and its agencies accountable. It also helped everyone be more effective.

Big Data

Once cities have a clear vision of what kind of place they want to become and a set of indicators to measure their progress, the next step is to measure results on the ground in order to guide progress toward better and better outcomes. Urban regulators now have the benefit of the "Internet of Things," a term coined by Kevin Ashton, a British scientist and co-founder of the Auto-ID Center at MIT. There Ashton developed global communications standards for radio frequency identification (RFID) and other sensors. These tiny electronic tags, when embedded in objects, or "things," can transmit a huge amount of information, including location, surrounding conditions like weather, and the performance of any device to which they may be attached.

The Internet of Things takes in data from a vast array of remote-sensing devices, including those in water and energy systems, mobile phones, vehicles, and weather and air-quality monitors, and integrates it into a vast, ubiquitous information network. It then adds human-generated information from hospitals, Social Security offices, employment centers, and schools, along with the personal data that people generate with every phone call, noncash purchase, and social network log-in. Taken together, the Internet of people and things is providing cities with enormous sets of information, which have become known as "big data."

Big data, a term coined by Doug Laney, vice president of research at Gartner Research, is a data set too large to be housed by any one computer. Its size is measured in petabytes, or one quadrillion bytes (1,000 terabytes). Currently the only way to deal with Big Data is with massive parallel-processing computing systems. These systems can mash it up, analyze it, extract trends, and feed it back to urban operating systems in real time, providing nearly instantaneous feedback loops on city strategies. Well-digested Big Data gives cities the ability to compare its actual conditions with community health indicators in real time, and adjust their regulations, investments, and operations to support behaviors that increase human and natural well-being, and to discourage those that don't. Energy systems can be made more efficient by tuning to real and anticipated demand. Water systems can detect leaks and wasteful usage patterns and intervene to correct them. Transportation systems can adjust to changing demand from sporting events, the weather, and changing usage patterns of bike riding and car sharing. Social service systems can individualize services to achieve better outcomes. Health-care systems can stimulate the social determinants of health to reduce reliance on more costly medical interventions.

The Levers of Governance

There are seven primary levers of governance than can guide urban development and operations: an aspirational *vision* of the city; a *master plan* for how to implement the vision, with specific indicators of its components; *data collection* so that the city has intelligence about its circumstances and can create feedback mechanisms to adjust the steps being taken toward achieving its vision; *regulations*, such as zoning and building codes; *incentives*, including tax credits and loan guarantees; and *investments* in infrastructure such as transportation, water, and sewer systems. Also, the vision must be *communicated* to the city's citizens. Ultimately, these tools will lead to success only if collectively they become part of the city's social and cultural DNA.

Regulations restrict behaviors detrimental to the overall objectives of the community. For example, building codes keep builders from constructing unsafe homes. Environmental regulations prevent toxic substances such as lead from finding their way into homes. Incentives do the opposite; they encourage the growth of things that the community desires. In high-cost cities, for example, developers may be given additional development rights in exchange for creating affordable housing, and in struggling communities incentives bring in businesses and the jobs that come with them. Investment in infrastructure provides the framework on which the vision unfolds.

Twentieth-century zoning and environmental review systems just can't keep up with the challenges of a volatile and complex world because they are static and unintegrated. Cities now have the capacity to replace them with a more dynamic, integrated system utilizing all seven levers of governance. Truly smart growth aims us toward a community vision of well-being carried out by the seven aspects of governance working together in real time, using indicators of human and natural system health to create feedback loops.

Smart Operating Systems

Mayor Bloomberg understood the power of data. After all, he had made his fortune by aggregating as much financial data as possible and communicating it in ways that were useful to his customers.

When he became mayor in 2002 the city's ability to provide agencies with usable data was primitive at best, so Bloomberg created a department of data analytics and appointed Mike Flowers to serve as its first director.

Flowers's goal was to develop actionable insights from the city's data. When he started working, one of the first problems he was asked to tackle was illegal apartment conversions. Landlords were turning basements into apartments, or subdividing existing apartments into tiny rooms, installing bunk beds, and renting them out to poor people and recent immigrants. These illegal conversions were likely to lack proper windows and sanitation, and had a higher number of fires. Because they did not follow fire safety codes by installing proper sprinkler systems and safe exit paths, their residents were fifteen times more likely to be killed or harmed in a fire. Illegal conversions also were hotbeds of drug dealing.[7] Unfortunately, the city wasn't very good at tracking them down. When it sent inspectors to respond to complaints about illegal conversions, they succeeded in finding them only 13 percent of the time. This was a huge waste of manpower. Flowers was challenged to use the city's data to help bring up their success rate. For example, overcrowded apartments should have abnormally high water usage. Cross-correlating information on permitted occupancies with water bills could indicate overcrowding. And if instead it revealed a water leak, solving that wouldn't be a bad secondary outcome of the project.

His team started by accessing the database for the city's 900,000 buildings, as well as data sets from nineteen different agencies containing such information as foreclosure records, rodent complaints, ambulance visits, crime rates, and fires. But before he could pool all this information, Flowers had to develop a common language for it. To complicate matters, each agency had been keeping information such as building addresses in different formats: the Buildings Department assigned every structure a unique building number; the Tax

Department identified buildings by borough, block, and lot numbers; the Police Department used Cartesian coordinates; and the Fire Department used an old, proximity-to-call-box system, even though the call boxes themselves were no longer in use.

Flowers created one building identification system for all of the city's agencies. Then his team went into the field and listened to housing inspectors as they made their rounds, in an effort to quantify hunches based on years of experience. From these, Flowers developed algorithms that identified patterns most likely to indicate overcrowded, unsafe, illegal conditions. Within a few months the inspectors' rate of discovering illegal conversions climbed to over 70 percent. Flowers's actionable analytics were saving lives.

As cities become increasingly effective at defining their vision, and identify the indicators of success, we are only beginning to see the ways in which dynamically tuning the cities' seven levers of governance and their operating systems will increase the well-being of both their human and their natural systems.

Sharing Big Data

Just as community participation has improved planning, it is also improving the usage of big data to make cities function better. Governments are often not the most entrepreneurial organizations, but they can be excellent aggregators of data. When they share the data, social entrepreneurs can use it to make the city better. In 2011, Washington, DC, released data from GPS transponders on the roofs of its buses. Almost immediately young companies like NextBus created smartphone apps that could tell riders when the next bus on their route was coming, and how long it would take to get to their destination. Today the system also directs passengers to alternative routes in case of traffic or an accident. With the app customers can sit in their homes or a nearby coffee shop on a rainy day and relax until their bus arrives. NextBus has increased bus ridership in every city where it has been used, taking cars off the road, improving air quality, and reducing traffic. And the bus riders themselves are happier.

The information needed to fine-tune cities doesn't even have to come from city government. Waze is a real-time route-mapping program that draws on crowd-sourced data from its millions of users, whose smartphones send in their travel speed, accident reports, roadwork, and other traffic issues they encounter. It then calculates the best route for the driver to take. Because the data is provided by a community, users feel socially connected to other users, and grateful for their input, which encourages users to contribute data for the benefit of the whole. Streetbump.com is an app that records whenever a driver goes over a pothole and sends the information to a city's department of transportation to schedule a repair, while warning its community of tire-wrecking potholes in the streets ahead.

The Smart City

A smart city uses digital technologies or information and communication technologies to enhance the quality and performance of urban services, to reduce costs and resource consumption, and to engage more effectively and actively with its citizens.

Although the core ideas for smart cities may have come initially from the United Kingdom and the United States, their most advanced applications are taking place in the rapidly growing cities of the developing world. South Korea is planning to build fifteen "ubiquitous cities," its name for the ubiquitous computing that underlies its version of a smart city. Its first U-City, Hwaseong-Dongtan, opened in 2007 and features what it calls U-Traffic, U-Parking, and U-Crime Prevention systems. Korea's New Songdo City (a 1,500-acre district outside Seoul) is using RFID tags and a wireless network to link all its building, business, medical, and governmental information systems. Its trash is tracked as it is collected by an underground vacuum system. The environmental performance of its buildings, all LEED certified, is managed by smart building systems.[8]

The city of Rio de Janeiro has developed an extensive city operations center in partnership with IBM, which has invested heavily in Rio in anticipation of global visibility in 2016 when the city hosts the Summer Olympics. The center was first used to improve Rio's security cameras, police communication systems, and traffic control. Now it also takes in information from cell phones, radio, e-mail, and text messages, while also storing and analyzing historical data. In case of a traffic accident, flood, or crime, the system not only assists with interdepartmental coordination, but also provides helpful suggestions based on various scenarios.

By squeezing out inefficiencies, smart cities could use resources far more efficiently, reducing their environmental impact while increasing the availability and quality of services. Data analysis makes it easier to find patterns such as the relationship between air quality and health, and to track the economic benefits of stronger environmental regulations. Identifying these various relationships allows costs to be charged more accurately to the source; for example, the health impacts of automobile pollution could be identified and a health-care surcharge levied according to the pollution the car generates and the number of miles driven.

The smart-city movement is a global one, promoted by the corporations that see a burgeoning market for equipment and services. Cities are eagerly sharing their experiences with one another. But along with the opportunities that this smartness brings, there also needs to be caution. Every algorithm used to analyze data will incorporate the biases of its creators, and these are not likely to be explicit. As urban operating systems become more computerized, they are more vulnerable to crashes, such as the 2006 malfunction of the software that controls San Francisco's BART system, an event that caused it to shut down three times in seventy-two hours. Smart cities are vulnerable to cyberattacks, hacking, and the inherent bugs in code that cause our personal computers to freeze at the most inopportune times. Smart cities are also vulnerable to systemic issues, such as the Internet going down. And imagine the chaos that would ensue if the global satellite positioning system failed. The solution is that every smart system has to have a human, mechanical, or analog fail-safe mode. For example, emergency services need to be equipped with walkie-talkies as well as cell phones, and compasses and maps as well as GPS. Cities need to be able to function on manual.

Agent-Based Modeling

Cities and their regions are complex, multilayered systems in which every part affects the whole. Advances in computing are now allowing planners to begin to model not just large-scale trends like population growth, but the behavior of individual groups, or "agents," like home buyers, commuters, shop owners, small companies, and so on. Each agent is assigned a specific range of behaviors that can be varied according to the circumstances. With such systems, planners can more realistically forecast the outcomes of their use of the seven levers of government to better achieve their goals.

In 2012 the economist John Geanakoplos and his colleagues created an agent-based model to test different housing finance policies to see if they could find one that could have averted the world financial crisis in 2008. They created a model of all the mortgage borrowers in the Washington, DC, area. Their computerized agents represented individual households with a wide range of circumstances; some could afford their mortgages, some couldn't. Some had fixed-rate mortgages, some adjustable. Some refinanced their homes when interest rates dropped, while others didn't want to be bothered. Geanakoplos and his team then ran a range of scenarios to analyze the collective behavior of their agents. First they raised interest rates, but this slowed the growth of the economy and caused a crash. When they lowered interest rates too many people borrowed, destabilizing the system. But when they modeled modestly tightened mortgage qualification standards, it produced the best behavioral outcomes in all sectors of the system. By modeling the collective behavior of a large group of agents, they identified an approach that could have averted the financial crisis.

Using agent-based models, planners can test the efficacy of differing regulations, incentives, and investment plans to help move their city toward their vision. Alternative scenarios can be run to determine their effect on various indicators of the well-being of human and natural systems. For example, a city facing a drought can test a combination of strategies such as raising water rates, investing in wastewater recycling plants, offering incentives for residents to plant xeriscapes (low-water-using landscapes), banning car washing, and so on to find the ones that will produce the best results. The Mayan empire collapsed because the people didn't understand the effect of their behaviors in time to change them. Smart cities can rapidly adapt to the VUCA world.

Self-Organization

When the various individual agents in a system interact, they begin to self-organize into something larger, a community whose collective behavior allows it to function cohesively. This phenomenon, in which complex capabilities emerge from combining simple elements, is the basis for creating social clusters. These may be simple at first, but as they link they take on an entirely new character and become a system. This happens when individuals become a family, families become neighbors, neighbors become a community, communities become a city, and cities become metropolitan regions. At each level qualities emerge from the relational context that did not exist in the individual context.

The word "system" comes from the ancient Greek word *sunìstemi*, which means "uniting or putting together." Systems, like communities, have boundaries, something that defines what is inside and what is part of the larger environment. However, since everything is deeply interdependent, the boundaries of both systems and communities exist largely for the convenience of identity. Although theoretical systems might be isolated, real systems are always exchanging energy, information, and matter with their surroundings.

Biocomplexity

While humans are just beginning to develop information feedback loops to guide the development of our complex creations like cities, nature has been doing it for a long time. And nature's feedback process is far more elegant, integrated, and complex than ours. This integration of the components of living systems into larger systems is called biocomplexity.

Biocomplexity is the key to nature's coherence, its ability to heal itself after a disruption such as a wildfire or an earthquake, and its adaptability under stress. It's a model that could inform how we bring these qualities to the development of cities.

The Biocomplexity Institute at Indiana University defines biocomplexity as "the study of the emergence of self-organized, complex behaviors from the interaction of many simple agents. Such emergent complexity is a hallmark of life, from the organization of molecules into cellular machinery, through the organization of cells into tissues, to the organization of individuals into communities. The other key element of biocomplexity is the unavoidable presence of multiple scales. Often, agents organize into much larger structures; those structures organize into much larger structures, etc."9

Biocomplexity is the basis for the integration of the cycles of life. It is the process by which genes shape the forms and locations of proteins, which build organisms whose metabolisms are deeply tied to the rest of the web of life, all done in such a way that both individual organisms and the larger system of life "learn" what works and what doesn't, and evolve to adapt.

Biocomplexity emerges from the collective behavior of a biological system. This wholeness is accomplished in part by the sharing of genetic material, which is shaped by the system's environmental conditions.

Life on earth is a magnificent biocomplex system, integrated by our shared DNA. This body of shared genetic information is the key to the extraordinary cycles of life. It's the reason the outputs of one species serve as the inputs for another, so that there is no waste in nature. And it is regenerative, designed to keep energizing and organizing an inherently entropic system.

In Botswana's Okavango Delta, a wildebeest is eaten by a hyena, who chews every bit of the wildebeest, including its bones. They are broken down in the hyena's digestive system, and pass out as white, calcium-rich excrement. Land turtles eat the excrement as a source of calcium for making their shells. Their excrement in turn is eaten by dung beetles, whose own excrement is broken down by bacteria in the soil to become essential elements for the growth of plants. And those plants will be eaten by wildebeest. As the nutrients pass through this system from the wildebeest to the soil, they become simpler, and have lower levels of energy and information, following time's arrow of entropy. But when they are drawn into a plant through its roots and up to its leaves, the plant's chlorophyll captures the sun's energy that reorganizes elements into higher levels of complexity, information, and energy.

Our cities mimic the general aspects of biocomplex systems. Each citizen, company, building, and car is a component of the city; collectively, like the elements of nature, they form a far more complex system than does any individual component. But they do not yet incorporate nature's regenerative qualities. The best cities of the future will.

The complete collection of an individual organism's DNA is called its genome. A *metagenome* is the genomic information of all the organisms in a community or system that shapes how it grows and functions. It is not kept in one central place, but distributed throughout the community. A single sample from a river of its environmental DNA, known as eDNA, can tell the story of all of the fish, plants, algae, and other microorganisms that make up their integrated ecology.

Our cities have a metagenome, the Alexandrian library of all their knowledge, processes, and social systems. It's why each city has a different signature of sounds, smells, and sensibilities. As we begin to collect and analyze big data, we can begin to see its outlines.

Metagenomes are composed of genes, which are made up of strands of DNA. Think of DNA as the blueprints for buildings, streets, and all the other elements of the city. Its genes, which are made of compilations of DNA, are similar to its building code. The metagenome of the city is its master plan, its zoning code, and all the organizational social, economic, and environmental systems of the city. Perhaps this is what was meant by the ancient concept of *meh*.

In nature, the genes of an organism contain many blueprints, but not every one is expressed. In fact, only 1.5 percent of all the DNA in a human is expressed in the protein building blocks of our body—we do not yet know what much of the remaining DNA does. In the same way, although a city may have a zoning code permitting thirty-story buildings in a neighborhood, this doesn't mean that every building will be that tall. But they all have the same potential to become that tall.

In the biocomplexity of a healthy system, the metagenomics of the whole system are constantly being influenced by the evolution of the individual components within it, and are influencing them at the same time. This process occurs through epigenetics, the switching system for genes. Environmental conditions such as stress or plenty are monitored and fed back into the genome, and change how DNA is expressed by turning some components off and others on. These changes are then passed down to future generations. This continuous feedback loop between the current adaptive needs of the system and its individual and collective DNA keeps it evolving.

Life unfolds through three macromolecules: DNA, which contains all the information in a system; RNA, which translates it; and proteins, the physical building blocks of the system. The *proteome* is the total set of proteins in the system designed by its DNA. The physical expressions of a city—its buildings, streets, and infrastructure—are its proteome. But proteins need more than information to grow; they need energy, materials, and water. These are supplied by an organism's metabolism. The total metabolism of a system is its *metabolomics*. (Think of it as metabolism's version of economics.) In the next chapter, we will explore the metabolism of the city, and how essential it is to a city's resilience. The genes of individual organisms, the proteins that build life, the metabolism that powers it and regenerates its decaying energy, information, and complexity, and the feedback loops that monitor the results of the process form the cycle of life. The biocomplexity of life on earth is built from this common set of operating instructions that tie us together. Every organism contributes its genes to the gene pool of life on earth. This ever-unfolding gene pool helps ecosystems adapt to changes in the environment.

Biocomplexity provides the best model for city planning and development systems to be able to adapt to the volatility ahead. It requires that city planning and governance be much more dynamic, starting with data-sensing and feedback systems so that they can continuously learn, and then the dynamic application of the tools of governance to adjust the city's growth and metabolism in real time. Cities also must encourage a wider range of innovation—the richer the gene pool of solutions, the greater the adaptive capacity of the city. And to achieve these, the city must be capable of changing and willing to change.

Nature does not have to think about these things; it does not have to decide which course of action to take. Humans do. Our cities are reflections of our perceptions and intentions, our aspirations, our cognitive biases, and our fears. These shape how we choose what our cities shall be from the vast metagenome of possibility.

Coherence

The first of the five qualities of temperament is coherence, which grows from integration of information, feedback systems, and an intention, or direction, toward which coherence flows. Most urban operating systems are as disconnected as Pythagoras's separate musical scales. Just as the well-tempered music system integrated all scales into one much larger universe of compositional opportunity, capturing and integrating all of a city's information in a single system enhances its ability to adapt. When the information of each component of a city can contribute to the metagenome of the whole, then the city can learn, and more effectively evolve. A lesson that biocomplexity brings to city planning is that when all elements of the system share a common metagenome, they fit together. The magnificent fitness of nature comes from our common evolutionary heritage. And such fitness is a key to efficient, resilient cities. It is a key to the regenerative, adaptive capacity needed in a VUCA world.

But integration and coherence are not enough. Our cities must be planned to move toward a vision. That vision must embrace the well-being of life, and include the health of its human and natural systems. In reality they are not separate—humans and nature are mutually dependent. But often we humans do not act as if this is so.

The Dynamically Balancing City

When the function of awareness is merely observing, it cannot be truly adaptive. However, when a system has the capacity to be aware of its awareness, to recognize itself, it can naturally, intelligently adapt to its environment. This awareness of awareness may have been the transformational evolution of human cognition that led to the first cities.

The formal urban plans that structured Uruk, Memphis, and China's nine-square cities were brilliant concepts for building early cities, but they are no longer up to the task of growing modern ones. Although each plan aspired to maintain the balance between humans and nature with Pythagorean pureness, its rigidity was not in harmony with how nature works. In a world that moved more slowly, those organization plans worked for a long while. However, in a VUCA world, traditional planning fails because it does not adapt quickly enough.

In a rapidly changing, interconnected world, each diverse, niche-adapted solution to urban issues contributes to the metagenomics of the whole. Alexandria's thirst for and use of diverse knowledge allowed it to thrive for centuries, and Islam's acceptance of diverse religions and cultures gave rise to the vitality of its cities. The Hanseatic League went even further. Its common set of rules provided the genomic code needed to encourage connectivity among its differentiated parts. Its expansion was supported but not directed, so the system unfolded organically and flexibly, without the rigidity that comes from one nexus of control. And Amsterdam thrived by encouraging

diversity, discouraging religious fundamentalism, embracing entre-
preneurialism, and creating public stock corporations to more broadly
share with both the city and its residents the economic benefits that
arose from these conditions.

By the early 2020s, the major cities of the world will likely be
suffused with 5G wireless systems, vastly increasing their capacity to
connect everything and everyone. The dynamically balancing city
will continuously sense its economic, environmental, social, and ecological conditions and use those to tune its levers of governance to
optimize the well-being of its residents; its businesses; its cultural,
educational, and health systems; and its environment. For example,
guided by the goals of its community health index, it may tune its
zoning code, infrastructure investments, and incentives in real time
to encourage the development of affordable housing, the mix of uses
that reduces traffic, or the need for more open space.

The role of city leadership in a VUCA world is twofold. The first
aspect is to create the conditions whereby a vision for what the city
can be continuously emerges. No longer must we depend on an emperor to provide a city's vision. It may come from many sources—
from a strong mayor, a wise group of leaders, its longtime residents,
and recent immigrants. Second, city leaders must nurture the capacity of a city to adapt to rapidly changing circumstances. With vision
and adaptive capacity, cities can thrive. Nations are often too large
and polarized to fully integrate their parts; states, too removed from
the daily lives of their citizens. Cities, when sufficiently empowered
by their federal and state governments, are the size of polity capable
of adapting to rapidly changing circumstances. To do so, they need
resources. In Denmark, 60 percent of the nation's public expenditures
are spent in cities. That, writes Bruce Katz of the Brookings Institute,
is why Copenhagen "has become one of the world's happiest, healthiest, and most livable places to be."[10]

The nine Cs that gave rise to cities—cognition, cooperation, culture, calories, connectivity, commerce, complexity, concentration, and control—matter just as much today as they did when cities were emerging. Thanks in part to information technologies, cities can be connected, not only to enhance commerce, but so that they can learn from one another. Fortunately, this is what we're seeing. The rise of global urban knowledge networks is rapidly spreading the DNA of solutions across urban ecologies.

As metropolitan regions discover that the twentieth-century pattern of sprawl is sapping their efficiency, they are returning to having more concentrated urban and suburban centers, integrated into a multicentered region. The best are enhanced by culture, the human genius that enriches our lives.

In later chapters we will discuss how important rich social networks are to the vitality and resilience of cities. But the next step is to examine the second feature of the well-tempered city, circularity, which depends on the movement of energy, water, and food as they are processed by the metabolism of the city.

PART TWO

Circularity

The second aspect of well-tempered cities comes from the circle of fifths, a harmonic pathway from scale to scale used in the composition of *The Well-Tempered Clavier*. The circle of fifths uses the fifth note above its starting point as a connection to the next scale, continuing until it returns to where it began, a journey possible only with tempered tuning. It is a model of circular metabolism, biocomplexity, and the grounds of resilience. Circularity transforms linear systems into regenerative ones. It's a key strategy for cities to thrive in this century, a pathway through the challenges of climate change and resource constraints. As the world's population grows and consumes more, a well-tempered city must excel in the second temperament, providing efficient, resilient, integrated metabolic systems that function in a circular manner that mirrors nature's own process, through which one system's waste is another system's nourishment.

We can better understand how a completely self-sustaining community metabolism functions by looking at a very simple system. The village of Shey sits high on the Tibetan plateau at an elevation of approximately 15,000 feet. Best known for the cave where the famous Tibetan meditator Milarepa stayed, Shey has survived in dynamic

Shey, Tibet, near Milarepa's cave. *(Jonathan F. P. Rose)*

balance with its spectacular yet harsh environment for almost a thousand years.

Shey is largely self-sufficient; it meets almost all of the needs of its residents. The form of the village is quite compact, with clear boundaries between the closely set buildings and the surrounding agricultural fields. If we look at the structure of successful biological organisms, we see a similar efficiency of form.

The high Tibetan plateau is one of the driest regions of the world, receiving on average only three inches of rain a year, so what does fall must be carefully gathered and husbanded to sustain the village's residents. The Tibetans have learned to take tiny streams of water and collect them in irrigation ditches for distribution to their fields.

Shey's population is just the right size to maintain a healthy dynamic balance between a village and the amount of food it can produce. There is just enough irrigated land to grow barley and vegetables to feed all the people in the village. The soil is enriched by waste from humans and animals, which both fertilizes the crops and eliminates stinking piles of waste that might otherwise contribute to disease. Buildings in Shey are made of stone, as they are in most mountain communities, their roofs fashioned from willow boughs and branches, covered with clay. Willow trees are planted alongside irrigation ditches, shading the water and reducing evaporation as it flows to the fields. Long ago villagers figured out how many willow trees were needed to provide enough branches to reroof all their buildings every ten years or so. When branches are cut, new shoots are grafted on. The willow stumps live for roughly four hundred years, so at long intervals new trees are planted to sustain continuous bough production. In common with ancient irrigation system practices, Shey's irrigation and willow tree system is collectively managed, with decisions on the allocation of water and labor made by a trusted elected ditch boss.

This arid, high-altitude landscape can support only a limited number of people, so the Tibetans practice polyandry, a system in which one woman will marry all of the brothers of a family, as a natural form of population control. One son in each family is usually sent to the monastery to become educated, which also helps keep the population down and infuses the village's Buddhism with the latest teachings. Shey, with its trees and rich, irrigated fields, poses a stark contrast to the harsh land beyond, revealing just how much the Tibetans have increased biodiversity in this valley. The villagers' warmer months are filled with planting, cultivating, and harvesting their fields, sharing dzos (a cross between a yak and a bull used to plow fields), plows, and other expensive field items, and collectively helping one another harvest the crops in the fall. Once the harvest is in, they spend much of the wintertime relaxing, their days filled with meditation, conversation, and Buddhist festivals.

Self-sufficient though it is, Shey is connected to a larger world by travelers—nomads, pilgrims, and traders. Nomads trade yak butter, meat, and skins with the villagers for barley. Traders exchange their sea salt for butter and barley, and pilgrims carry the prayers and teachings of Buddhist masters. So even this remote village is connected to the flow of goods, ideas, and culture from a larger region. Travelers occasionally bring new seeds to diversify the genetic stock of local plants and animals, but as important, they bring new ideas that cross-fertilize the culture.

The farming community of Shey provides an example of how to achieve a healthy dynamic balance between human beings and nature. Yet these Tibetan villagers have a far simpler task than we do, with our vastly more complex and interconnected world, buffeted by macro trends. Most modern people do not wish to live in a remote place, without electricity or the Internet, but there are lessons from Shey that we can apply on a much larger scale: how to use inputs like water carefully and efficiently, how to eliminate the concept of waste through complete recycling, how to match the size of the community and its needs to the resources available, and how to invest in the long-term health of the system. These are all qualities of organisms with balanced metabolisms.

CHAPTER 5

The Metabolism of Cities

IN 1965, BALTIMORE, MARYLAND, was a city in transition. Like Alexandria, it was an important port, the second-largest on the United
States' Atlantic coast, the most convenient port for America's mid-
western manufacturers to export their goods. Baltimore also made
things itself. Bethlehem Steel's Sparrows Point steel mill was the
largest in the world, over four miles long. The mill made steel that
built America's infrastructure, including the girders in San Francisco's Golden Gate Bridge and the cables for the George Washington
Bridge. The plant's steel was also used in the adjoining Sparrows
Point shipyard, one of the nation's most active producers of ships,
which by the 1970s was building the world's largest supertankers.[1]
Making steel and building ships were grueling, hard work, but they
provided union jobs with good wages, although job classifications
were severely divided by race, with African Americans excluded
from managerial jobs. The composer Philip Glass earned money for
his Juilliard School tuition by working at the steel mill.

The industrial vitality of the city masked its problems—its population was beginning to move to the suburbs, along with retail activity and better jobs. Poverty, drug use, crime, and unemployment
were beginning to rise. These conditions drove not only Baltimore's
middle-class whites to the suburbs, but also its middle-class African
Americans. The urban scholar Marc Levine described Baltimore as a
third world city in the first world.[2] Like many third world cities, it
was very polluted.

And so, when the American steel industry crashed in the 1970s following the oil shock and recession of 1973, it exposed a declining city without the resilience to respond to the issues it was facing.

During the 1920s, when the population of Baltimore was growing, the city voraciously consumed water. Abel Wolman, the city's chief engineer from 1922 to 1939, developed the first reliable system for chlorinating public water supplies which became a global standard. He was a long-term thinker who designed a water supply and treatment system so robust that it would serve the city well into the twenty-first century. But Wolman's greatest contribution was not what he built, it was the way he thought. After observing a wide range of urban responses to drought and water pollution over many years, Wolman published "The Metabolism of Cities" in a 1965 issue of *Scientific American* devoted to the future of cities. His goal was to get urban planners to think about their water and other urban systems over the long term, across the line of centuries. To do so he encouraged city and regional planners to model the inflows of water, energy, and food to their cities, and also to model their outflows, including waste, which he noted often ended up as water pollution, a threat to the city's water supply. To make his point, Wolman introduced the idea that cities have metabolisms.

Wolman wrote, "The metabolic requirements of a city can be defined as all of the materials and commodities needed to sustain the city's inhabitants at home, at work and at play. Over a period of time these requirements include even the construction materials to build and rebuild the city itself. The metabolic cycle is not completed until the wastes and residues of daily life have been removed and disposed of with a minimum of nuisance and hazard. As man has come to appreciate that the earth is a closed ecological system, casual methods that once appeared satisfactory for the disposal of wastes no longer seem acceptable. He has the daily evidence of his eyes and nose to tell him that his planet cannot assimilate without limit the untreated wastes of his civilization."[3]

Using the computational tools of his day Wolman was able to create only simple linear models of the urban inputs of water, food, and fuel, and the outputs of sewage, solid refuse, and air pollution. However, he planted the seeds of several important ideas: that cities, much like biological organisms, had metabolisms, and that ultimately the earth was one closed system that had to accommodate the metabolisms of all cities. Wolman's work gave rise to the field of industrial ecology, which today examines not only the urban flows of a much broader range of materials and energy, but also the interactions among those flows.

Two primary activities drive biological metabolism. The catabolic process breaks materials down, releasing energy to power the organism. The anabolic process uses that energy, combined with the patterns provided by the system's DNA, to construct complex proteins and shape them into the building blocks of the organism. During both processes waste is produced, which needs to be carried out of the organism. Interestingly, the earth's ecology has evolved in such a way that the waste created by one process becomes the input, or food, of another. So complex natural systems do not pollute; instead, due to the integrating temperament of the metagenome, organisms exquisitely fit together, each nested in a larger whole that both supplies it with nutrients and absorbs its wastes. If our cities are going to thrive, they will need to evolve toward this model of biocomplexity.

Calculating the flow of nutrients, energy, and other materials into a city is enormously complex. In fact, even establishing the amount of energy and materials needed to create a single building is exceedingly complicated. The Canadian scholar Thomas Homer-Dixon set out to calculate the number of calories needed to build one of the world's most iconic structures, Rome's Colosseum. And his work ended up providing insight into the collapse of an entire empire.

How Many Calories Does It Take to Build a Colosseum?

Construction of the Roman Empire's grandest public arena began in 72 CE, and took eight years to complete. In order to determine the number of calories needed to complete the building, Homer-Dixon had to calculate not only the number of people it took to build the Colosseum, but also the number of workers required to quarry, mill, and otherwise produce the materials that went into it, as well as the energy needed to transport them. In his book *The Upside of Down: Catastrophe, Creativity, and the Renewal of Civilization*, Homer-Dixon wrote, "Erecting the Colosseum required more than 44 billion kilocalories of energy. Over 34 billion of these kilocalories went to feed the 1,806 oxen engaged mainly in transporting materials. More than 10 billion kilocalories powered the skilled and unskilled human laborers, which translates into 2,135 laborers working 220 days a year for five years."

These numbers don't include the labor needed to harvest the wood timbers used for scaffolding, or to fire bricks, or to make the building's decorations, which included more than 150 fountains, as well as countless statues, frescoes, and mosaics that took another three years to finish. Homer-Dixon's calculations do take into account the number of calories that went into the construction of the building itself. At the time of the Colosseum's construction, the typical Roman ate a mixture of grains, fruit, especially olives and figs, legumes, vegetables, wine, and a small amount of meat. Oxen used to transport the Colosseum's building materials were fed hay, millet, clover, wheat chaff, bean husks, and other vegetation. Homer-Dixon concluded that it took 55 square kilometers of land—an area about the size of Manhattan—to produce the energy needed for each year of the Colosseum's construction. The metabolic boundary of just one building extended far beyond its physical boundary.

In the early days of the Roman Empire, its cities were fed by small, independent regional farms, but as the empire grew it needed more food. During the second century CE, at its peak, the Roman Empire encompassed a population of 60 million. Its capital, the city of Rome, had a population of more than a million people. To increase food production, the city sponsored *latifundia*, or huge plantation-like estates, operated with slave labor. These were typically set up on conquered lands and owned by Roman senators. Earnings from latifundia were the only approved income for senators, so not surprisingly the senate made latifundia income-tax exempt. (Many things have changed over time, but not the self-interest of the politically powerful!)

As the network of latifundia grew to the edges of the empire, the system became more vulnerable. Absentee landlords were often incompetent and abusive, their slaves reluctant to work, and an active pirate network sprang up to plunder food as it made its way from the far reaches of the Mediterranean to Rome. Because the system was designed to maximize profit, the latifundia's owners and managers made little investment in the long-term fertility of their fields.

As the soil became exhausted, Rome had to conquer more and more land to feed its people. In order to subdue and maintain control of these lands, and to protect the supply chains back to its urban centers, Rome had to raise, pay, house, and feed ever-larger armies. And to appease its mass of urban workers, Rome's leaders had to provide "bread and circuses," free food and entertainment that masked huge disparities in wealth that threatened the empire from within. At the city's peak as a world capital, more than half of its residents were receiving free food.

Managing Rome's extended territory required more extensive and complex communications and control systems as well. As the empire's control over its edges eroded, its lack of coherent leadership brought chaos and conflict to its core. In the end, Homer-Dixon concluded, when the empire ran out of rich kingdoms to plunder, the administrative, logistical, and military requirements of the Roman agricultural system outstripped its ability to provide the calories needed to fuel its level of civilization. When Rome's food system failed, the empire became unsustainable.

Once the Roman Empire began to decline, the city of Rome did not recover for a thousand years. By the end of the fifth century, Rome's population had declined to 50,000, and its extraordinary infrastructure—including its system of roads and aqueducts—fell into disrepair. Without its extensive food system, Rome lacked the energy source to maintain the complexity of its civilization. By the year 1000, Rome's population had dwindled to 10,000, with its remaining residents gathered in huts around the Tiber River, living in primitive conditions. Rome did not reach a population of one million again until 1980.

The Empire of the Pig

The global reach of a nation's food systems is even greater today.

Pork has always been a valued part of the Chinese diet, but a small one. In 1949, before the Maoist revolution, only 3 percent of the Chinese diet came from meat. Pigs were raised on small family farms where they were deeply fitted into the ecology of the local food system—they ate garbage and cast-off tops of root vegetables, and their manure was recycled as fertilizer. Today, pigs are raised for the insatiable Chinese market on huge industrial farms.[4] Their billion tons of manure pollute China's precious water supply. To feed them, China imports more than half of the global supply of soybeans. To meet this demand for soybeans, more than 62 million acres of Brazilian land has been converted from rainforest and natural fields to soybean production. In 2013, China purchased the venerable American Smithfield Ham company, the world's largest pork producer, for its large landholdings in Missouri and Texas. By 2014, Argentina was exporting almost all of its soybeans to China—growing two or three crop cycles a year by using herbicides linked to cancer and birth defects. China is buying land in Africa on which to grow soybeans. To supplement soybeans, the Chinese also feed their pigs corn. At current growth rates, by 2022, China's pigs will be eating up to one third of the world's supply of corn.[5]

Pork is only one of the many global commodities that China is consuming at unsustainable rates. The metabolism of its cities mirrors Rome's.

By 2050, the world's population will reach 9–10 billion or more. As we become more prosperous and numerous, we will consume more calories. At the same time, the world's supply of arable land is shrinking due to urbanization, changing weather patterns, erosion, and the depletion of groundwater reserves. There is only one way to feed the world's cities: we must increase the efficiency of food production and reduce waste by connecting the inputs and outputs of the system in a more natural cycle. Otherwise, as anthropologist Jared Diamond has shown us in the case of the Romans, the Maya, and other great civilizations, overextension, a vulnerable food chain, poor stewardship of soil, and significant economic inequality will pave the way to collapse.

Energy Return on Investment

Measuring efficiency is one of the most important tools for managing the metabolism of cities—and empires. One measure of energy efficiency is the EROI, or energy return on investment, calculated by dividing the amount of usable energy generated in a system by the amount of energy used to create it. The higher the EROI, the more efficient the system. For example, in 1859 the first modern oil well in western Pennsylvania used one barrel of oil to fuel the extraction, production, and distribution of every hundred barrels produced, for an

EROI of 100. Today the EROI of much oil production has dropped to 4, and where extraction is very difficult, as it is in the Canadian tar sands, the EROI is often negative.

The EROI formula can be applied to the return on investment of all a city's inputs, not just energy, but food, water, construction materials, and so on. In fact, the very process of urbanization is tied to leaps in EROI. Irrigation produced the caloric energy needed to grow the world's first cities in the Middle East. The Chinese began to burn coal for heat during the Warring States period from 480 to 221 BCE, when a large number of minor cities consolidated into major city-states. James Watt's 1789 steam engine powered both the industrial revolution and the dramatic growth of manufacturing cities that followed. Inexpensive electricity powering lights, elevators, subways, streetcars, and trains fueled the growth in global urbanization that began in 1900, when only 13 percent of the earth's one billion people lived in cities. And after World War II, electric-powered air-conditioning furthered the growth of cities in hot and humid parts of the world.

Civilizations can become more complex only when their EROI increases, and cities often decline when it does not. Joseph Tainter, an anthropologist at Utah State University, defines collapse as occurring when a society involuntarily sheds a significant portion of its complexity. Studying the rise and fall of the Mayan, Anasazi, and Roman civilizations, Tainter observed a pattern: societies become more complex as a way to solve more and more complex problems. These require social and economic specialization, and institutions to manage and coordinate the information and actions that they generate. Management provides societal benefits, but doesn't generate energy itself, so it has to be subsidized by the surplus energy of the system.

Typically, when a civilization confronts a drop in EROI, as Rome did when its soils wore out, it responds by adding more complexity, because that's what managers tend to do. Rome tried to solve its problem by conquering new lands, which required more complex communications and governance systems to manage. China is currently dealing with its falling EROI by buying energy from the rest of the world. But the management required to extend a civilization's reach only adds to its EROI burden. The alternative is to localize, and like natural systems, to more efficiently weave the city's inputs and outputs into a thriving ecology. The drivers of efficiency? Good governance, smart infrastructure, and innovation.

Toward a More Resilient City Metabolism

There are five steps a city can take to improve its metabolic resilience. The first is to recognize how important a city's metabolism is for its survival, and to track its metabolic inputs and outputs from source to destination. Natural systems continually sense metabolic conditions in order to adjust to them, and cities, as biocomplex systems, need to do the same. The world of big data can provide an enormous amount of information on a city's metabolism. The key is to develop analytic tools that mine for meaningful data such as EROI trends, and identify areas of metabolic opportunity and vulnerability, so that the city can anticipate and adapt to them.

The second step is to use imported resources more efficiently, so that fewer are needed.

Third, a city needs to diversify sources of food, water, energy, and materials so that it's not overly dependent on any one. In a globally connected world, a small increase or reduction in demand from the United States and China for a commodity can have a huge impact on its availability and price.

The fourth step is to generate more resources within the city, which also has the benefit of creating more jobs. Last, and most important, the well-tempered city recycles and reuses as much of its waste as possible. This reduces disposal cost while providing inexpensive local resources. Taken together, these strategies help make a city's metabolism more efficient and resilient. And they all can be shaped using the seven tools of city management: a guiding vision, data collection and analysis, planning, regulations, incentives, investment, and communications.

Tracking a City's Metabolism

The role of information is to help the city become more conscious of itself; the role of planning is to intentionally set strategies for the future. Together these serve as the DNA of the system. Regulations, incentives, investments, and communications guiding implementation of the plan are the RNA, translating the DNA into action, building the city.

Before a city can make its metabolism more efficient, it needs to measure it and identify leverage points to increase its resilience. For example, a key element of New York City's PlaNYC was to inventory inputs like energy and water consumption, and outputs like carbon dioxide and solid waste. The data revealed that 80 percent of the fossil fuels burned in New York City were being used in buildings, which made its buildings' energy efficiency a key leverage point in decreasing the city's fossil fuel use. This also increased the city's resilience to fossil fuel price volatility, and reduced the output of carbon dioxide. To achieve its goals the city enacted regulations that required large building owners to measure their energy use and climate impact, and offered these owners incentives to shift their heating systems from oil to natural gas, reducing their carbon footprint.

New York City also calculated that 80 percent of its food flowed into the city through its Hunts Point Food Market. If Superstorm Sandy had reached the market just three hours later than it did, at high tide, it would have flooded nearby fuel and chemical depots, and washed their toxic wastes into the low-lying market. The whole region would have lost its food supply, with no alternative sufficient to meet its needs. Major wholesale food centers like Hunts Point are very efficient, but also much more vulnerable than a more distributed food system. John Doyle, professor of control and dynamic systems at the California Institute of Technology, describes systems like a central food market as robust but fragile. As systems become more robust, they draw resources toward what they do best, and withdraw resources from alternatives. This increasing lack of diversity sows the seeds of a system's vulnerability. When a robust system is challenged, the city has few alternatives, rendering the system very fragile.

While New York City carefully tracks its population and its number of housing units to determine its current and future metabolic needs, Lagos, the megacity and financial capital of Nigeria, doesn't know how many people live in it. "It keeps swallowing smaller cities so we can't define the boundaries," says Ayo Adediran, director of the city's regional and master plan department. Samuel O. Dekolo, associate lecturer in the University of Lagos department of Urban and Regional Planning, describes the city's data-gathering capacity as "pathetic . . . creating an information gap void between urban development and intelligent management."[6]

Detroit is somewhere in between Lagos and New York. According to Susan Crawford, co-author of *The Responsive City*, "The urban blight that has been plaguing Detroit was, until very recently, made worse by a dearth of information about the problem. No one could tell how many buildings needed fixing or demolition, or how effectively city services were being delivered to them (or not). Today, thanks to the combined efforts of a scrappy small business, tech-savvy city leadership and substantial philanthropic support, the extent of the problem is clear."[7] Revenues are a key element of a city's metabolism, and Lagos and Detroit shared a common problem. Not understanding what properties lay within their city's boundaries, they couldn't tax them, and as a result lost revenues. And both cities desperately needed revenues to provide essential services.[8]

When Detroit was wrestling with bankruptcy, a young San Francisco tech transplant, Jerry Paffendorf, and his company Loveland Technologies proposed to map and photograph every property in the city and record all of its attributes. To accomplish the task, Loveland invented a geographic data system tied into a smartphone app. With fifty crews of two, a driver and a surveyor, the company cataloged the condition of all 385,000 of the city's lots in nine weeks for a total cost of $1.5 million. Paffendorf describes his map as "the genome of the city."

For the first time in decades Detroit had the data to understand its tax base, and to help it overcome the revenue gap of $450 million a year that drove it into bankruptcy. Paffendorf's data also showed, among other things, the size and location of the city's burgeoning community gardens, which were contributing to the diversity of its food supply.

In 1999, Lagos was collecting only 600 million naira, or $3.7 million, a month in taxes. It simply did not have sufficient data about its residents to collect all the taxes that were due. After deciding to outsource its tax collection, Lagos in 2013 had increased collection by 3,400 percent to more than $125 million a month—without raising its tax rate. That provided the city with the funds to invest in bus transit, a new light-rail system, and other urban infrastructure that is making Lagos more resilient, helping to diversify an economy that had been overly concentrated in oil exports.

Baltimore, Abel Wolman's home, provides one of the most integrated examples of a city collecting, using, and sharing its metabolic data. Once Martin O'Malley was elected Baltimore's mayor in 2000, he launched CityStat, a publicly accessible city data system designed to make government responsible, accountable, and cost-effective. O'Malley modeled CitiStat on a similar program used by

New York City's police department to engage statistics in the fight against crime, but Baltimore extended the concept to all municipal functions.

In regular meetings with the Office of the Mayor, each agency had to review subpar performances and come up with solutions. O'Malley's first goal was to reduce the culture of absenteeism among city workers. Every week, CitiStat publicly posted who hadn't shown up to work, and why. Within three years absenteeism fell by 50 percent, and overtime dropped 40 percent. Using CitiStat data and GIS mapping, the city redesigned its trash-collection routes and increased recycling by 53 percent. It saved $1.5 million a year in the costs of mowing the lawns in its central median strips.[9] By 2007 CitiStat was saving Baltimore $350 million a year, and had led to significantly improved city services for its residents. Several years later CitiStat was being used to crowd-source community needs and set city budgets based on community objectives rather than departmental inertia—one of the leading causes of inflexible government systems.

In 2004, CitiStat won the Harvard Kennedy School's Innovation in Government award, and began to spread to dozens of other cities. Today, CitiStat is used not only to track Baltimore's citizen goals and tie them to the city's budget, but also to track how efficiently the city's resources are being used to accomplish those targets. And it is helping Baltimore's Food Policy Initiative increase access to fresh, healthy, and affordable foods. Information helps cities become more conscious of all their activities, and integrate them into a more coherent, responsive, and efficient whole.

Using Resources More Efficiently

On average, Americans consume 3,770 calories of food per day, more per person than any nation on earth. Our national food production and distribution system has become enormously complex, adding in-efficiencies and energy costs along the many steps from the source to the consumer. When people eat foods grown far away, significant costs are added in their transport. It takes 127 calories of energy to fly a single calorie of iceberg lettuce from the United States to the United Kingdom, 97 calories of energy to import 1 calorie of asparagus from Chile, and 66 calories of energy to import 1 calorie of carrots from South Africa.[10]

Food processing and refrigerated storage also consume a great deal of energy. The Swedish Institute for Food and Biotechnology has been analyzing the life cycle of food production since the 1990s. One of its classic studies examines the energy required to make a tube of Swedish tomato ketchup.[11] Researchers tallied all of the energy, wa-ter, and material needed to grow the tomatoes and convert them into tomato paste in Italy, add ingredients such as vinegar and spices from Spain, process and package the ketchup in Sweden, and then store, ship, and sell the final product. The entire effort required fifty-two transport and process steps, involving products from all over Europe. This study was followed by a similar investigation of all the elements that go into a McDonald's Big Mac—the meat, cheese, pickles, on-ions, lettuce, and bread that accompany the ketchup. The conclusion? Big Macs require about seven times more energy to produce than they provide.

The EROI of our food system is even less efficient than this would indicate, because so much of the food we produce is wasted. In a 2011 report, the United Nations Food and Agricultural Organization cal-culated that of the nearly 4 billion tons of food grown or raised across the planet, close to one third, or 1.3 billion tons, is thrown out.[12] In the United States that percentage is even higher: about 40 percent of the food we grow or import is never eaten. In fact, food is the largest component of our municipal solid waste stream. Only 3 percent of U.S. food waste is composted.[13] At the time of the construction of the

Colosseum, every calorie of human and animal input produced 12 calories of food. Today, the industrialized American food production system requires 10–20 calories for every calorie that it produces; this means that on an EROI basis it is more than 120 times less efficient than the ancient Roman system (which eventually collapsed)!

But there are more intelligent solutions on the horizon. The private food sector in the United States has developed some remarkable examples of efficiency. The Cheesecake Factory, a national restaurant chain, serves 80 million people a year; to maximize its food use, the company developed a computer program, Net Chef, to track every aspect of its consumers' preferences and adjust its food orders accordingly. Net Chef takes into account the weather, the economy, the time of year, gasoline prices, and even TV broadcasts of sports events, adjusting its orders to maximize efficiency.[14] As a result the Cheesecake Factory uses 97.5 percent of the food that it buys, throwing out only 2.5 percent.

Cities provide food for schools, jails, hospitals, recreational centers, and other facilities. Using systems like that of the Cheesecake Factory, they could use food much more efficiently, control the quality to better deliver healthy foods, and create a substantial market for local farmers. And they can use data and tools of governance to encourage more local food production.

Generating Resources in Cities: Urban Agriculture

Throughout history, if a city could not provide sufficient food for its residents it would not survive. Today no city in the world generates enough food to feed itself. The most food-productive cities in the world, Hanoi and Havana, use small gardens woven throughout their tropical urban landscapes, yet even they generate only half the food their residents need. Most cities generate barely any at all, but feed themselves from a much larger food shed. Eighty percent of Hanoi's fresh vegetables; 50 percent of its pork, poultry, and freshwater fish; and 40 percent of its eggs come from the transition region between rural and urban areas, the rurban zone. In Lagos, urban and rurban agriculture is increasing,[15] with farmers growing African spinach, waterleaf, fluted pumpkin, lettuce, cabbage, and other vegetables. Unable to find jobs in the city, they grow food both for their own nutrition and for the cash that it brings. They typically squat on government land and sell their produce to women who then take it to the markets.

Although in the United States some food comes from the region in which it is eaten, the average food item typically travels 1,500 miles from its farm of origin.[16] Our food comes from a wide range of places: tomatoes from California, mushrooms from Pennsylvania, oranges from Florida or Brazil, cherries from Chile, rice from Thailand, and more. Eighty percent of our seafood is imported from other countries,[17] as is 85 percent of our apple juice, mostly from China.[18] Consumers are connected to growers by a vast, complex web of production and distribution. The greater the distance between producers and consumers, the more vulnerable the chain is to the cost of transportation and other disruptions.

The city of Detroit was built on rich alluvial soils, perfect for farming. In fact, since many of the world's cities lie astride rivers or in natural harbors, they are often built on the region's best agricultural soil. In 1841 Detroit built its first farmers' market. In 1891 that market, now one of three in the city, moved to its current location and was renamed the Eastern Market. When the depression of 1893 hit Detroit's residents hard, the city responded by initiating America's first municipally sponsored urban garden program. Mayor Hazen S. Pingree asked landowners to let destitute residents use vacant lots to grow vegetables, not only to help keep them off the relief rolls, but also to provide them with self-respect. The gardens were nicknamed Pingree's Potato Patches.

Detroit rebounded from the recession, and by the turn of the nineteenth century the city was a thriving and diversified manufacturing hub. With the success of Henry Ford's Model T in 1908, the auto industry increasingly dominated the city's bustling economy. But just as the energy crisis, globalization, rigid union contracts, and inflation of the 1970s struck Baltimore's steel industry hard, Detroit's auto industry was also not able to adapt to these challenges. Instead of developing the higher-quality and more fuel-efficient cars that its consumers wanted, and adopting more flexible labor practices and supply chains, the auto industry clung to its old systems and practices. Its institutional inertia was not up to the growing challenge posed by more innovative Japanese and European auto companies, which manufactured vehicles more efficiently and built cars that traveled farther on a gallon of gas.

In the face of the macro trends threatening America's industrial economy, it was doubly unfortunate that Detroit's business and political leaders, dominated by the auto industry, failed to take steps to diversify the city's economic base beyond that industry, to invest in education, or to develop mass transit. As a result, the city began a long decline, hemorrhaging both jobs and residents.

The decline of Detroit over the past half century has been brutal—today, Detroit looks like a city that had its guts kicked out. Vast areas of the city are burned out and abandoned, weedy lots where blue-collar homes and brick industrial buildings once stood. At its peak in 1950 Detroit was home to 1,849,000 people. By 2013, its population declined by more than half, to 688,000. In sixty years Detroit had gone from being roughly the same size as Los Angeles to less than a fifth the size. Until 2013, when a small Whole Foods opened, there was not a single large supermarket within the city limits, not even a Walmart or Costco, although there are a scattering of locally owned smaller independent supermarkets.

Urban geographers describe this absence of fresh, nutritious food as a "food desert"—a region in which fast or packaged food is at least twice as prevalent as fresh food. In food deserts the few fruits and vegetables available are typically less fresh and more expensive. There are food deserts all over the United States—in its rural areas, and in many of its older suburbs. If one lives in a food desert, typically, the only antidote is an automobile so that one can drive to a market with cheaper and healthier food. Lower-income residents of cities like Detroit are far less likely to have a car than their suburban counterparts.

There is a critical link between fresh vegetables, fruits, and nuts and health. People who have lower levels of vitamins B, C, D, and E perform worse on cognitive tests than those with higher levels. Omega-3 fatty acids have been demonstrated to be particularly critical for the cognitive development of children. People who lack these critical vitamins and omega-3 fatty acids are also more likely to be depressed. Older people who lack folic acid are more likely to suffer from Alzheimer's disease. And people with higher levels of trans fats in their blood have lower cognitive capacity, and even brain shrinkage.[19, 20] Fresh vegetables, fruits, and nuts are rich sources of the cognitive stimulating vitamins and omega-3 fatty acids. Junk, fast, and fried foods contain lots of trans fats. Alas, for much of Detroit and other urban food deserts, junk, fast, and fried food is the norm. Poor food systems are stunting the cognitive and competitive capacity of our nation.

To meet the nutritional needs of its inner-city residents, in 1989 Detroit's community development organizations began raising urban farmers. Originally begun as an environmental campaign that focused on planting trees, Detroit's garden movement evolved into an urban livability movement. In 1997 a Capuchin monastery founded what is today Detroit's oldest organic farm, in order to grow food for its soup kitchen. The monks now operate seven gardens within two blocks of their headquarters. In 2006, the urban gardens were providing enough food to develop a brand, "Grown in Detroit," featured in the city's farmers' markets. By the summer of 2012 Detroit had some twelve hundred community gardens, nine per square mile, more per capita than any other city in America.[21] What began as an environmental movement has helped Detroit reimagine itself as a green, regenerative city.

Today Detroit has vast amounts of open space: more than forty square miles of the city are empty. It has a cheap and willing labor force, including many immigrants from agrarian backgrounds. Its community gardens already provide 15 percent of Detroit's food during the summer growing season. A study by the American Institute of Architects concluded that if the city were to consolidate its people and buildings into fifty square miles and add greenhouses for winter crops, Detroit could feed itself on its remaining ninety square miles of land.[22] That's not the vision Detroit had for itself in its glory days as an automobile manufacturing powerhouse, but it may turn out to be an important element of its future.

Detroit is not alone. Urban agriculture is sweeping America. The movement to replace abandoned manufacturing plants with edible plants is giving urban residents a powerful sense of purpose. Urban gardeners are using the regenerative power of nature to revitalize their cities by developing human and natural systems at the same time. The contemporary urban food movement that began in the abandoned lots of North Philadelphia, the South Bronx, East L.A., and West Oakland now permeates every neighborhood in America. Farm-to-table food is now grown on the roofs of industrial buildings in New York by farms like the Brooklyn Grange, and fine vinegars are fermenting in Woodberry Kitchen's old oak barrels in the heart of Baltimore's Clipper Mill. Will Allen transformed Milwaukee with Growing Power, a nationally recognized nonprofit that promotes urban farming, hands-on education, and job creation. And although the urban agriculture movement is not likely to lead to food-independent cities, it is encouraging cities to think about this aspect of their metabolisms in new ways, including establishing farms close to the city's periphery.

In many of the developing world's cities the food-generating capacity of the rurban zone is being challenged by relentless, unregulated sprawl. In the United States, real estate development of the rurban zone accelerated thanks to the subprime mortgage market of the early 2000s, with its recklessly easy loans. But with the advent of the Great Recession in 2007, rurban development came to a standstill, and it is not likely to return for some time. This has freed up land for farming. Also, as urban farmers' markets become more and more popular, farms on the outskirts of cities are beginning to make more economic sense. GrowNYC, the largest association of farmers, fishermen, and farmers' markets in the nation, has 54 markets providing livelihoods for 230 family farms and conserving 30,000 acres of land, much of it in New York City's watershed, where development is discouraged.[23]

The growth of urban farms selling to New York City's farmers' markets has been matched by the growth of urban rooftop farms. New York has more than any other city in the country. In 2012 the City Council passed a set of green zoning revisions that make it even easier to add rooftop greenhouses and gardens. Commercial farms such as Brooklyn Grange, Gotham Greens, and Brightfarms now sell not only to farmers' markets but also to large grocery chains. And they are diversifying: Brooklyn Grange not only grows vegetables but also raises chickens and keeps bees, whose role as pollinators is so essential to the city's ecology.

Many local restaurants in cities all around America are now growing vegetables and herbs on their roofs, or in adjacent lots. Hydroponic systems, which raise plants in water or mineral mediums without soil, increase the productivity of smaller rooftops. On the roof of its building, the Bell, Book and Candle restaurant in New York City's Greenwich Village hydroponically grows seventy kinds of herbs, vegetables, and fruits, and two thirds of the vegetables it needs to feed its customers. And many are connecting urban and rural food centers. Daniel, David, and Laureen Barber's Blue Hill grows food and raises pigs, sheep, and chickens in the extraordinary Stone Barns Center about thirty miles outside the city. The caterer Great Performances grows food on its Katchkie Farm.

Urban agriculture comes with overlapping benefits. It increases the EROI of food production in the United States, where one gallon of diesel is used to ship every hundred pounds of food the 1,500 average miles it takes to get from farm to market,[24] and diversifies the city's economic base, providing jobs for less tech-inclined workers. It absorbs storm water, reducing flooding in heavy storms. It reduces urban heat by utilizing the sun that strikes urban roofs, and increases the availability of fresh local food. And community gardens grow not just food, but community.

Urban agriculture has the potential to become a significant contributor to the healthy metabolism of cities, but that metabolism includes not only inputs, but outputs as well. And one of the biggest of these is garbage, known in the urban management business as municipal solid waste.

Recycling and Reuse

A key lesson from ecological economics is to keep an eye on waste: less waste means greater efficiency. In biocomplex systems every output of one part of the system is an input to another. Small communities such as Shey are similarly integrated, but humans have not yet figured out how to develop the same dynamic, closed-loop systems at the scale of our current civilization. In 2014, we generated an estimated 4 billion tons of waste. Manufacturing and mining industries produce about 1.6 billion tons of nonhazardous waste each year, and almost 500 million tons that are hazardous.[25] Seventy percent of the 1.9 billion tons of solid waste cities and towns produce ends up in landfills, 19 percent is recycled, and 11 percent is burned to generate energy. Globally, 3.5 billion people have no access to municipal disposal, so they often burn garbage, the toxic emissions from plastics, batteries, and other items polluting their air and leaching into their water. By 2025, the amount of municipal solid waste is projected to double.[26] These wastes can be either a terrible burden on the environment or, if we properly recycle them, a wonderful resource to help reduce the coming resource gap.

In 2012 the United States generated 251 million tons of municipal solid waste in its cities and towns, about 34 percent of which was recycled. Until 2010, Detroit had the lowest recycling rate in the country, zero. Faced with dramatically rising energy costs after the 1973 energy crisis, the city built the largest municipal solid waste incinerator in the nation, and then, unable to afford it, sold it to an independent operator along with a contract requiring Detroit to burn its waste through 2009 at a cost of $150 a ton. As a result, Detroit was the only major city in the United States without a recycling program. The incinerator produces 1,800 tons of hazardous air pollution per year, spewing lead, mercury, nitrous oxide, and sulfur dioxide, impacting the health of the nearby low-income community as well as the rest of the city.[27] It wasn't until 2014 that citizen activists lobbying to close the plant down managed to convince the city to begin curbside pickup of recyclables. Today even Lagos recycles more than Detroit.

Many American cities are seriously focusing on recycling waste. San Francisco recycles 80 percent of its garbage, giving it the highest recycling rate of any city in the world, with cities like Seattle not far behind. San Francisco's stellar performance began with a vision: recycling 100 percent of its waste. In 1999 the city's waste carter, Recology, began the march toward zero waste by requiring residents to separate their garbage into bins earmarked as recyclables, organic material, and so on. The easiest parts of the waste stream to recycle are glass and plastic bottles, and cans; most cities and states have laws requiring refundable deposits to be built into their prices, which give recycling market value. Next comes paper, for which there is a global market, and the more carefully it is separated, the higher its value.

The most difficult part of the waste stream to recycle has been organic material such as food. Unfortunately this is the largest part of the municipal garbage stream, and the messiest, the part people least want to deal with. It also pollutes the rest of the waste stream. Cities can sell clean separated wastepaper for about $100 a ton, but if it's contaminated with food waste, the city has to pay to haul it away. Wrapping fish bones in newspaper makes the newspaper worthless to a recycler and the fish uncompostable. Dr. Allen Hershkowitz, an entrepreneurial scientist who has spent his career studying recycling, says, "Each category of waste has its ecologically optimal disposal route. Public policies and private investment should encourage the routing of each category of waste to its best use. Metals are amongst the easiest and most economical materials to recycle. Recycled aluminum uses 96% less energy than making aluminum from bauxite. PET plastic can be remade into bottles or clothing, and HDPE can be recycled into structural plastics such as railroad ties, or made into more rigid plastic containers. Rubber and textiles can be recycled into rubber and textiles, waste paper can be mashed into pulp and reused in paper manufacturing."[28]

In San Francisco everything recyclable goes into blue containers that are picked up by Recology's biodiesel and natural-gas-fueled trucks, and then carted to Recycle Central, a 185,000-square-foot former warehouse owned and operated by residents of the nearby Bayview/Hunters Point community. Every day 750 tons of recyclable wastes are separated and shipped to various manufacturers for reuse. Organic material like food waste, yard trimmings, and food-soiled paper goes into green containers, from which Recology picks up 600 tons of material each day and takes it to Jepson Prairie Organics, where it is composted, turned into fertilizer, and sold to local farms whose food is sold back to the stores and restaurants of San Francisco.[29] This is a large, urban version of the Tibetan village of Shey's waste-recycling system, modeled after nature's own process. San Francisco's remaining waste goes to a landfill, but the city is analyzing this waste to determine how to recycle it. That will require not only new technology, but also a further shift in the behavior of San Francisco's residents.

Shifting Human Behavior

Our behaviors are shaped by a mix of cognitive biases, habits, and social cues, as well as by our culture, with its incentives and penalties. Interestingly, factual information, which is so crucial to city administrators, turns out to be the least influential component in shifting people's behaviors. For example, the state of Arizona was having difficulty getting Hispanic mothers to use baby seats while driving their small children, even though these car seats significantly reduced childhood mortality in an accident. It turned out that many of these mothers were devout Catholics who felt that the safety of their children was in God's hands. The state asked the Catholic Church to hold blessing ceremonies for baby car seats in local parishes, and as a result their use dramatically increased.

Dr. Ruth Greenspan Bell, a public policy scholar at the Woodrow Wilson Center in Washington, DC, notes, "Whether we like it or not, up to 45 percent of our daily actions are not decisions, they're habits. This necessarily affects our daily choices, like whether or not to recycle the many pieces of waste we create each day. Of course, socioeconomics, education, and policy all play a role, but the idea that humans are on auto-pilot much of the day is a topic ripe for exploration."[30]

Many of the cognitive biases that helped humans make the right survival decisions 50,000 years ago can be used to help encourage right-minded urban behaviors today. For example, we humans evolved with a strong herd instinct, a bias to act in concert with larger groups. Recycling programs that communicate "Everyone does it," and focus on ties to other neighbors who recycle, are especially effective. People also have an in-group bias, so they feel most closely aligned with people of similar backgrounds. When Hispanics view recycling as something that only white middle-class liberals do, they are less likely to recycle. When they view it as something that people in their own ethnic group do, then they join in. Understanding how to promote beneficial behaviors is now a key element of any large-scale environmental program.

To encourage the recycling of food waste, in 2014 the Seattle City Council passed an ordinance prohibiting food in Seattle's residential and commercial garbage. In 2015 the city asked garbage collection workers to check regular garbage bins for organic food scraps. If residents had placed organics in the regular garbage bin, their bin was marked with a bright red, hard-to-remove sticker for all the neighbors to see. It was also accompanied by a fine: $1 for private homes, $50 for multiunit buildings. The city is testing the premise that the shame of not being a good recycler, and the inconvenience of paying a one-dollar fine, would be a more powerful motivator of behavioral change then a large fine.[31] The red-badge-of-shame program also provides another important behavioral change strategy—feedback. When people receive relatively real-time feedback about their behavior, they are much more likely to change.

Like San Francisco and Seattle, many European and modern Asian cities are also focusing on moving toward zero waste, but they are following Detroit's strategy: combustion. They burn much of their garbage in plants that use the garbage as fuel to provide electricity or heat. The island nation of Singapore simply doesn't have land to set aside for a waste dump, so it recycles or composts 57 percent of its waste and burns 41 percent. The resulting ash and the small percentage of garbage that is nonrecyclable or compostable becomes landfill on an offshore island. Vienna burns 63 percent of its waste, Malmö 69 percent, Copenhagen 25 percent, and Berlin 40 percent.[32] Burning waste is not a viable strategy, however; it not only creates pollution and adds climate-changing greenhouse gases, but also requires us to mine or grow more materials than if we recycled them.

As the world's population grows larger and more prosperous, it consumes more and generates more waste. An astounding 98 percent of everything that flows into the metabolism of our cities leaves it as waste within six months. And much of what remains in our cities is also wasted. A century ago we repaired goods like shoes so they served us for years. Now we're much more likely to throw them out and buy another pair. In 2014, 89 million mobile phones were being used in the UK; more remarkably, there were also another 80 million functioning mobile phones in the UK lost somewhere in drawers, in closets, or under car seats! Valuable resources are trapped in those phones. There is more pure gold in a ton of mobile phones than in a ton of gold ore.[33]

While San Francisco and some Asian and European cities focus on zero waste, cities in many low- and middle-income countries are still working to get infrastructure and citizen participation to the point where they can collect all of their garbage. The United Nations Human Settlements Program estimates that low-income countries collect 30–60 percent of their garbage, whereas middle-income countries collect 50–80 percent of theirs.[34] Uncollected garbage is second only to human waste in its negative impact on public health. Garbage pollutes rivers and pond water used for cleaning or cooking. It harbors rats, vermin, and parasites; it often contains toxic materials; and burning it without the proper equipment causes respiratory disease. Children, who often play in or near garbage, are particularly vulnerable to these harmful effects.

In much of the developing world, garbage pickers swarm over the dumps in search of recyclable plastic, metals, cardboard, and clothes to sell in secondary markets. Often, the most hazardous items in the industrial world, such as electronics filled with mercury, lead, and other toxic chemicals, are shipped to developing countries to be disassembled by workers in an unregulated environment. It's a hard, unhealthy life.

Lagos has long struggled with its municipal waste. By 2014, only 40 percent of its waste was being collected. It just didn't have the infrastructure to reach the rapidly growing, informal slums at its expanding edge. And recycling was not part of the slum dwellers' culture. In response, the city implemented an innovative recycling program, Wecycling, giving small independent entrepreneurs recycling franchises and financing inexpensive, bicycle-powered mobile recycling centers, a program that combines inexpensive technology, entrepreneurship, and behavior-shifting strategies. Each bike driver rides around a designated neighborhood, going door-to-door collecting recyclables. Residents are paid by weight for bags of separated garbage, and brightly colored recycling containers promote the concept. Wecyclers then sell their goods to recycled material consolidators. Among the many co-benefits of the program is that less garbage on neighborhood streets means fewer clogged drains, which means less standing water in which malaria-carrying mosquitoes can breed.[35]

In the coming VUCA world, as global supply chains are likely to become less reliable, cities that locally produce more of their food, energy, and raw goods will be more resilient. One of the most efficient sources of those metabolic inputs is material that was formerly wasted, but can now be recycled and reused.

Ecological Economics

Our current economic system ignores the cost of waste generated in the production or disposal of goods. It seeks to maximize the profitability of the product, and shift the burden of societal and ecological costs to others, which often means the government, with its responsibility for the common good. A wiser economic system closely follows the flow of energy and materials and encourages the health of the whole, rather than the profits of a few. Building on this idea, Germany initiated a move to shift the cost of waste back to producers.

Prior to 1991 about one third of the material in German landfills came from packaging. As Germany's cities faced rising landfill costs, they pushed for a federal ordinance to shift the responsibility for collecting, sorting, and recycling packaging wastes from cities to industries that made and sold consumer goods. The result was the Ordinance on the Avoidance of Packaging Waste. Now the cost of recycling a product's packaging is included in the product's price, or it comes out of the producer's profits. Not surprisingly, once producers are responsible for the full cost of recycling their products they become highly motivated to redesign them to use less packaging, and to design packaging materials to be more easily recycled.

Based on the success of this initiative, in 2000 the European Union passed the Directive on End-of-Life Vehicle,[36] requiring automobile manufacturers to take back, recycle, and reuse 85 percent of the parts (by weight) of an automobile by 2006, and 95 percent by 2015. Faced with the cost of recycling entire cars, auto designers have had to rethink how they design their products. European automobiles are now built for easy disassembly, and for the recycling, remanufacturing, or reuse of as many parts as possible. It's no wonder that the world's most profitable car companies, Porsche, Volkswagen, and Toyota, are all based in countries with very high auto-recycling requirements. They serve as strong incentives to control resource costs and design with more rigor.

Such regulations would have helped Baltimore's Sparrows Point steel plant survive. It struggled through several owners after Bethlehem Steel went bankrupt. In 2013, its cold mill was disassembled and sold to Nucor, the largest and most profitable steel company in the United States. Nucor's business model is the antithesis of Bethlehem's. It makes steel from recycled material, often crushed cars. Rather than operate large centralized plants, Nucor builds mini and micro mills spread across the nation in forty-three locations, and has its own steel scrap broker and processor to provide its plants with recycled material for steelmaking. And its labor force is typically nonunion, but deeply empowered, engaged in the policies and operations of each plant.

Circular Economies

In 2012, Paul Polman, the chairman of Unilever, a global consumer goods company, wrote, "It is evident that an economy that extracts resources at increasing rates without consideration for the environment in which it operates, without consideration for our natural planetary boundaries cannot continue indefinitely. In a world of soon to be 9 billion consumers who are actively buying manufactured goods, this approach will hamper companies and undermine economies. We need a new way of doing business. The concept of a circular economy promises a way out."[37]

The most powerful way to enhance the adaptability of systems is to connect their inputs, outputs, and information, and create conditions in which they can respond to changing stresses. Cities and their metropolitan regions are at just the right scale to make the shift to the economics of prosperity and well-being that result in a more integrated system. They are large enough to enjoy the benefits of diversification, and small enough to be well managed, and to feed information back into more productive loops.

Entropy, the thermodynamic decline of a system from order toward disorder, affects systems in two ways—it causes them to move from higher to lower states of energetic organization, and higher to lower states of information. And as systems become less energized and organized, they become less adaptable. For example, as the Roman civilization declined, it lost its ability to provide itself with the calories and information needed to energize itself, and along with that, its ability to govern itself at a level that matched its complexity. The Roman Empire slid into simpler and less-organized states. It finally stabilized at a population that was less than 0.5 percent of its size in its heyday.

No economic system can overcome entropy; like gravity, it's a non-negotiable quality of the universe we live in. But circular economics takes entropy into account in ways that classical economics does not. This allows a city with circular economies to reward strategies that increase its EROI, and reduce its voracious appetite for external sources of energy, food, and raw materials. It can also encourage continuous feedback, information that can help raise its level of organization. A circular economy shifts a city from linear industrial systems to cyclical, regenerative systems. As cities adopt programs such as food waste composting in San Francisco and Seattle, and encourage remanufacturing as at the Nucor plants scattered across America, their systems become less vulnerable to national and global disruptions, and the income generated stays in the community.

There are four pathways in a regional circular economy. The first maintains systems and products, rather than throwing them out. This requires a return to a pre–World War II design and manufacturing ethos, when goods were made to be both maintainable and repairable, and a twenty-first-century system of hardware designed to be improved by software updates. The second reduces use through behaviors like collaborative consumption, which can expand access to goods while reducing their cost and environmental impact. For example, car-sharing programs like Zipcar have a ratio of one car for every seven members, offering increased convenience while significantly reducing the need to manufacture cars, with all the attendant waste.

The circular economy of urban systems. *(Jonathan Rose Companies)*

In the coming decade, each new autonomous vehicle is projected to replace ten cars, reducing the resources mined to make the cars by 90 percent, and if they are electric vehicles, oil use and attendant greenhouse gases by 71 percent. The third pathway encourages refurbishing and remanufacture. Patagonia, for example, will repair, free, any garment that it has sold. The fourth is to create the regulations, incentives, and infrastructure to develop markets and industries that recycle unused or waste materials. When polyester is recycled into new polyester, for example, 99.9 percent of the material is reused.

Now imagine connecting Germany's auto-recycling laws with Nucor's steel-recycling systems. Then think of the power that would come if they shared information—Ford designing car parts that would be easier to reforge, and Nucor designing steel that was lighter and stronger and easier to make cars from, and cities designing the infrastructure that connected them.

The most efficient recycler is nature. Some of the most interesting emerging recycling systems are using nature's own ubiquitous, low-maintenance recycling plants: microbes. At Wageningen University in the Netherlands, Louise Vet is working with Waste2Chemical to develop bacteria that can turn mixed waste into raw materials for the chemical industry. For example, they are extracting fats from food waste and turning them into polymers that can be used in plastics, paint additives, and lubricants at prices that compete with fossil fuels.[38]

First Steps

Circular economies are most efficient when they can readily connect inputs to outputs, and the two elements that help that happen, density and infrastructure, are prominent characteristics of cities. China, which invests more in urban infrastructure than any other nation in the world, recognizes the value of creating a circular economy. In 2011, China's Eighteenth Party Congress introduced the concept of creating an ecological civilization with Chinese characteristics. *Qiushi,* a publication of the Central Committee of the Communist Party of China, noted that the term "ecological" "pertains to the state in which nature exists, whereas the term civilization refers to a state of human progress. Thus ecological civilization describes the level of harmony that exists between human progress and natural existence in human civilization."[39]

The congress's report states that China "should depend more on saving resources and a circular economy . . . to substantially reduce consumption intensity of energy, water and land and improve efficiency and benefits." It concludes that China needs to advance reduction, reuse, and recycling in the process of production, circulation, and consumption. Its goal is to do so by "promoting the circular distribution, combination and circulation between industries, production, and living systems, domestic and foreign, speeding up building a circular society promoting circulating development in all."[40]

These concepts are now being put into action. China's lead planning agency, the National Development and Reform Commission (NDRC), has approved circular-economy pilot plans in twenty-seven cities and provinces with the goal of "ten/one hundred/one thousand": focusing on ten major areas of activity, executing them in one hundred cities, and building a thousand industries or eco-industrial parks.

In 2012, the European Union committed itself to moving toward a circular economy. "In a world with growing pressures on resources and the environment, the EU has no choice but to go for the transition to a resource-efficient and ultimately regenerative circular economy."[41] In 2014, Amsterdam released an ambitious plan to become a circular city. The alderperson for sustainability, Abdeluheb Choho, noted: "In a circular city everything that we want to achieve will come together: less pollution, less waste, and buildings that produce their own energy."[42] By utilizing a governance strategy that includes businesses, governmental agencies, citizens, and NGOs, Amsterdam's approach is much more cooperative and resilient than China's top-down strategy.

Nature's biocomplexity lies at the core of its growth and its ability to thrive and to adapt to changing circumstances. As climate change increasingly impacts our cities and the regions that supply them, applying circular thinking to their metabolic processes will be essential to the future. And, as we'll see in the next chapter, this will be particularly important in our treatment of water.

Water Is a Terrible Thing to Waste

BRAZIL HAS BECOME known as the "Saudi Arabia of Water": one eighth of the world's freshwater flows through it. Yet São Paulo, its largest and most powerful city, may soon go dry. In the fall of 2014, for as many as six days at a time the city provided its residents with no water at all; nothing to drink, to flush toilets with, to take showers with. Nothing.[1] The city's Cantareira water system was down to 5.3 percent of capacity. Just as the city was about to cut back to providing water only two days a week, in February a series of long, hard rains raised the reservoir levels to 9.5 percent. But cities cannot thrive when they live this close to the edge of their metabolic support.

Like India's power outage, São Paulo's water crisis has many causes. Over the last decade southeast Brazil has been contending with the worst drought in almost a decade. São Paulo and its suburbs have grown prodigiously, and it now must provide water for 20 million people. However, the city has not tended well to its infrastructure: between leaky pipes and theft an estimated 30 percent of its water is lost. Nor has São Paulo planned well for its future. Only now, in the midst of a crisis, is it proposing to build new reservoirs, and to raise water rates to encourage conservation.

The Tietê and Pinheiros Rivers run through São Paulo, but they are so terribly polluted by industrial wastes that their waters cannot be cleaned to drinking level standards. And Brazil's larger natural hydrological system has been threatened by massive clear-cutting of the rainforest. Just as the Mayans destroyed their natural landscape to feed themselves, the Brazilians have cut vast swaths of rainforest to raise cattle and soybeans for themselves and the world market. The northwestern rainforests release humidity into the air, producing rain in the southeast. With reduced forests, the rains are less frequent.

São Paulo, Rio de Janeiro, and other major cities in southeast Brazil now need to understand the interconnections among their water, food, wastewater, and energy in a new way, and very quickly. They are not alone. As the metropolitan tide sweeps across the world, and climate change progresses, every city is facing metabolic challenges. And to resolve them, cities are going to have to think, plan, build, and operate their infrastructure differently.

Human instincts evolved to promote survival, and one of our strongest cognitive biases is to avoid drinking dirty water or eating human wastes or putrefying foods. Early religious texts contain numerous strictures about drinking water, sanitation, and diet. As civilizations developed densely settled communities, they advanced communal solutions to these issues, including a separate but nearby garbage dump, which has become a fascinating cache of everyday articles for modern archaeologists to explore. The Harappan cities of the Indus valley featured individual wells for almost every house, and lined drains alongside each street carried off waste. Roman architects and engineers developed sophisticated aqueducts to provide water for drinking, cooking, and bathing; to carry away human waste; and to flush streets clean of manure from horses and oxen.

In the late third century CE, Rome's emperor Diocletian began to construct a great palace at the location of what is today the city of Split on the Croatian coast. Diocletian's Palace was an extraordinary example not only of Roman architecture but also of long-range planning. Knowing that Roman emperors were very susceptible to assassination, Diocletian announced that as soon as his palace was completed, he would move to it and give up his post as emperor. This proved to be a successful strategy, and Diocletian lived to have a long and happy retirement. His palace was designed for a population of 10,000, mostly soldiers to protect him, but its water supply system was planned to accommodate a population of 175,000. This oversize system was designed to weather droughts, sieges, and other likely threats. Its aqueducts served the city of Split until the middle of the twentieth century, when the population finally began to reach the water system's capacity. Spare infrastructure capacity is essential for urban resilience.

Throughout history a prime reason for the decline of cities and civilizations was that during years of plenty they expanded to the limits of their food and water capacity. When the climate changed, or other circumstances took a turn for the worse, those systems could not produce enough to sustain the society, leading to its collapse. In America's Southwest, advances in corn growing and irrigation allowed the Anasazi people to prosper in the 700s–800s, and to build populous communities such as Mesa Verde and Chaco Canyon. Pueblo Bonito, the sophisticated multifamily dwelling in Chaco Canyon, stood four to five stories tall and housed as many as 1,200 people. Anasazi communities featured kivas, or spiritual buildings, along with plazas in which they held seasonal ceremonial dances. Plotted with mathematical precision, Pueblo Bonito's Grand Kiva was designed so that at sunrise on the day of each equinox, a shaft of light would pass through slots in its circumference and shine on a designated spot on the opposite wall. Lines drawn through the axes of the Grand Kiva align with the centers of smaller kivas dozens of miles away, indicating that all of the villages in the region were aligned with one another as well, all aligned to the astronomical cycles of the universe.

Unfortunately, the Anasazi were less attuned to the climate here on earth. By examining the rings of ancient trees scientists have pinpointed two extended periods of drought in the American Southwest, from 1128 to 1180, and again from 1270 to 1288. By then the Anasazi had expanded their population to the limit of the land's capacity to feed them. Just like the Mayans, when the droughts came the Anasazi were no longer able to sustain themselves. After reaching a peak of prosperity in the early 1100s, over the next several hundred years the Anasazi were forced to abandon their major settlements. History could repeat itself in today's drought-ridden Southwest, where the population has increased dramatically, but the water supply has not.

An ample water supply is essential for cities to grow. New Yorkers built their first public well in 1677 in the public square that fronted the Bowling Green fort; until then every building in the city had its own private well. A century later, in 1776, New Yorkers not only signed the Declaration of Independence, but also constructed their first public reservoir, on the east side of Broadway near today's City Hall; its water was distributed under the streets through hollowed-out logs. In 1800 the Manhattan Company, a forerunner of the Chase Manhattan Bank, financed a deep well, reservoir, and pipe system to serve much of lower Manhattan with water. By 1830 that system had switched over from wood to more durable cast-iron pipes, and New York developed its first urban water-delivery system for fire protection.

However, the supply of water must be pure as well as ample. In 1832, New York City suffered its first cholera epidemic. As the *Evening Post* reported, "The roads, in all directions, were lined with well-filled stagecoaches, livery coaches, private vehicles and equestrians, all panic-struck, fleeing the city, as we may suppose the inhabitants of Pompeii fled when the red lava showered down upon their houses."[2]

Water, Waste, and the Spread of Disease

Until the advent of modern sanitation systems in the mid-1880s, Europe's cities were dangerous places, where cholera, measles, and smallpox regularly decimated their populations, along with episodic waves of bubonic plague. From the advent of the Italian Renaissance to the industrial era, Europe's urban population did not grow, as deaths outnumbered births; so that the population in 1345 was much the same as in 1780, when industrialization began to draw vast numbers of workers from the countryside to the cities.[3] Almost a century later, in 1842, the British social reformer Sir Edwin Chadwick published *The Sanitary Condition of the Labouring Population*, a report on the health of lower-income Londoners. The news was not good.

Throughout much of the history of cities, poor neighborhoods have typically been more crowded than others, with lower-quality buildings and insufficient water, as well as inadequate wastewater and garbage removal. As a result these lower-income communities suffer from higher rates of disease. Chadwick was a strong believer in the now-debunked miasma theory of disease, which held that diseases such as cholera were caused by something harmful in the atmosphere, known as "night air." However, that didn't keep him from initiating changes in London that would have a major impact on public health. To reduce the spread of miasma-borne diseases, Chadwick proposed the development of clean water–delivery systems, sewers to remove waste, and drainage systems to remove standing water in which mosquitoes bred.

Today we think of malaria as a rural disease of impoverished countries, but through much of the nineteenth century it was very much an urban disease. In the United States it repeatedly struck warmer cities with bodies of stagnant water such as Washington, DC, and New Orleans. Soon after Chadwick's report was published, New York City's Common Council, with the foresight of Diocletian, funded the impounding of the Croton River in Westchester County to the north and the building of an aqueduct and reservoir system to bring freshwater into the city. But it took the death of a baby girl in London from cholera to transform our understanding of urban water and sewer systems.

Dr. John Snow and the Broad Street Pump Handle

On September 2, 1854, Sarah Lewis and Police Constable Thomas Lewis lost their five-month-old daughter, Frances, to the wave of cholera sweeping through their London neighborhood. Cholera had long been prevalent in India's Ganges delta, but in 1817 it spread to Russia and then west to Europe, arriving in London in 1854. During the long days and nights of tending to her daughter, Sarah soaked the baby's diarrhea-covered diapers in a bucket to clean them and poured the dirty water into the communal cesspool in front of their home. As London had grown into a large city these deep, brick-lined pits were built as temporary containers for human waste, which was periodically carted away and sold to rural farmers as fertilizer. Proceeds from the sale of the sludge were then used to pay for the maintenance of the cesspools. Originally this was part of a healthy, interdependent balance between city dwellers and rural farmers, but as London grew ever larger the distance between the cesspools and the farmers also grew. By 1854 London had about 200,000 cesspools, and those toward the city's center were burdened with higher waste-transportation costs, which left few funds for their maintenance.

There was a further problem: globalization had struck the British and American manure markets. In the 1830s Peru had begun to mine its huge guano deposits. By using the essentially slave labor provided by indentured Chinese and Filipinos, and by filling the holds of trading ships that were otherwise returning empty to London and other major cities, Peru became a dominant supplier of cheap fertilizer. The trade was so profitable that Peru became the only country in the world with no internal taxes, and was still able to pay its president twice the salary of the U.S. president. In 1847 Peru issued an export license for guano to the London firm Antony Gibbs & Sons, which then proceeded to undercut the cesspool sludge market for fertilizer. With lower sludge prices, poorer communities could not meet the cost to cart their sludge away or to maintain their cesspools. Instead, they gave up on maintaining their cesspools and dumped waste into nearby rivers.[4] So it was that the cheap supply of guano from the faraway country of Peru accelerated to the spread of cholera in London.

In the 1800s English localities were divided into parishes responsible for providing basic government services, including the oversight of public health. Broad Street, where the Lewis family lived, was part of Saint James Parish, governed by a Board of Guardians made up of local tradesmen elected by local property owners. On the evening of September 7, 1854, five days after the death of Frances Lewis, a stranger, Dr. John Snow, appeared at the Saint James Parish Board of Guardians meeting at Vestry Hall, and quietly asked if he could speak about the recent cholera outbreak. Snow had made a map of the Broad Street area, carefully marking the location of homes in which residents had died of the disease. The map showed that those families who drew their water from the Broad Street well were much more likely to become sick. Snow proposed that the well was being polluted by seepage from the nearby sewage cistern and asked the Board of Guardians to order that the handle to the pump of the Broad Street well be removed in order to save the area's residents from a horrible death.[5]

When Dr. Snow proposed that cholera might be caused by something in the water and not the air, he was challenging deeply held assumptions. The miasma theory of the spread of disease was the official theory of the London health profession, and was so deeply entrenched that when in the very same year, 1854, the Florentine scientist Filippo Pacini discovered the cholera bacillus, *Vibrio cholerae*, and published the germ theory of disease, his discovery was roundly ignored. The same skepticism greeted Dr. Snow, but after a nightlong debate the pump handle was removed.

Deaths from the neighborhood outbreak quickly declined, and with this simple act of mapping the locations of disease and removing a pump handle, the modern era of epidemiology and public health was born. Nearly 150 years later, in 2003, John Snow was voted the greatest doctor of all time by the British medical profession.[6]

The Nature of Water Purification

The very first urban wastewater systems simply carried sewage away, usually to a nearby river. In small quantities, human and animal wastes are purified by five natural processes. Contaminants in water are *filtered* as they flow through sand, or sandy soil. Bacteria *digest* the pollutants, a process that is speeded up by *aeration*, or the oxygenation of water as it flows over waterfalls or through shallow, rocky rivers. When water moves slowly, or sits in still ponds, contaminating particles drop to the bottom through *sedimentation*. Last, the heat of the sun can speed up bacteriological processes and its ultraviolet light *disinfects* contaminants. Every modern wastewater-treatment system mimics these natural processes.

Twentieth-century waste-treatment systems largely follow nature's process, but use pumps and mechanical systems to treat large volumes of sewage in a small space. Wastewater first goes into a sedimentation tank, where the solids and suspended particles settle, and then into an aeration tank. The water may also be heated to increase microbial activity before it's run through a sand filter to remove any remaining waste particles. In more advanced systems the water may also pass through a membrane with holes so small that all chemicals are removed except pharmaceuticals, which are notoriously difficult to remove; fish living near wastewater treatment plants have been known to be sterilized by the presence of birth control compounds in the water.[7] If the water flows under ultraviolet lights, it will be completely disinfected and drinkable, although many systems also chlorinate the output. Solids removed from the wastewater are collected as sludge that is usually carted away, and if sterile enough, used as a fertilizer.

It's a good system; it took most of the nineteenth century to figure it out.

Water and Sewer Systems Make Cities Livable

The first contemporary citywide sewer system that used water to flush waste away was built in 1844 in Hamburg, Germany.[8] Until then, cisterns like the one Dr. John Snow confronted were the most common urban waste-collection system. The first American sewer systems were designed and built in Brooklyn and Chicago in the late 1850s, following the German model. Only after indoor plumbing systems featuring flush toilets and baths became prevalent later in the century did cities start to consistently build sewers to transport water. At the same time cities began to develop storm-water systems to cope with stagnant, garbage-filled rain that ponded and provided breeding grounds for yellow fever and typhoid.

As urban public health infrastructure developed, the design of water, wastewater, and storm-water treatment systems co-evolved, the advances of one informing the others. In the 1880s it was believed that the most cost-effective urban systems collected storm water and sewage water and combined them into one pipe, saving the cost of multiple pipes. But by the 1920s it became clear that while the combined system might lower construction costs, it made it difficult to operate sewage treatment plants efficiently. Low levels of storm water made wastewater more concentrated and harder to treat, whereas powerful storms flooded the system, overflowing treatment plants, dumping raw sewage into nearby rivers and bays. It seems strange that of all the uses we could find for precious, life-giving clean water, we would mix it with our excrement, and then have to clean it up again before we piped it to rivers or the ocean. Today many coastal cities in the United States are still wrestling with old combined water and sewer systems.

On the positive side, these water and sewer systems dramatically reduced the health risk of urban living. In 1840, 80 percent of all deaths in New York City came from infectious diseases. By 1940, just prior to when penicillin first became available as a drug, infectious diseases caused only 11 percent of New York's deaths. This vast improvement in public health came from civil engineering. Investments in the city's water and sewage infrastructure, along with the introduction of building-code regulations and public health campaigns to change behaviors like public spitting, significantly improved the health of urban residents.

In the late 1800s urban water delivery and treatment systems became increasingly centralized, collecting clean water upstream and uphill of the city, moving it through the city mostly by gravity, and flushing it as wastewater downstream—which often was upstream of the next city!

Today, municipal wastewater treatment is beginning to adopt the zero-waste goals of the solid-waste world, developing circular rather than linear systems, using advanced biological processes to treat water and wastewater and reuse the system's outputs. Where land is available there is also a trend toward smaller distributed systems rather than larger megasystems.

Reducing Consumption

Some uses of water consume it, others do not. Consumption converts water into a form from which it cannot be captured and reused. Most agriculture consumes water: growing a pound of cotton, for example, takes 101 gallons of water that cannot be recovered. In California, the process of extracting one gallon of ethanol fuel from corn consumes 2,138 gallons of water.[9] By contrast, municipal water is mostly put to non-consumptive uses such as drinking and bathing. When the state's cities are competing with agriculture for water that is in short supply, subsidizing the production of ethanol is not a wise allocation decision.

Most of the world's sewer and wastewater treatment begins with a flushing toilet, so that's the first place to focus on water reduction. In 1994 the United States began to require that all new toilets meet an efficiency standard of 1.6 gallons per flush, reducing water use by at least 30 percent, but the standard didn't require any upgrades to existing toilets. In 1995, facing a severe water shortage, Santa Fe, New Mexico, decided that in order to avoid the fate of its Anasazi predecessors, it needed to initiate a serious water conservation program. One of its key elements was the requirement that for every new toilet a builder added to the city, ten old toilets had to be replaced with newer, more efficient ones.[10] Over the next decade almost every old toilet in the city was replaced, with a huge net reduction in water use.

Low-flow toilets reduce water use; waterless urinals eliminate it. Since the early 2000s, waterless urinals have been part of the green building tool kit. Each waterless urinal in a high-traffic location like an office building or airport can save up to 45,000 gallons of freshwater each year. Other ways to reduce urban water use include low-flow showerheads and faucets, water-conserving dishwashers and washing machines, and water-efficient central cooling towers on large office and institutional buildings. These technologies can reduce water use by 10–30 percent.

In the United States, the biggest water-using behavior to focus on is lawn care, since 50 percent of all the water used in America's suburban communities goes to watering lawns. In the Southwest, water-challenged cities are paying residents to rip up their lawns and replace them with xeriscapes, gardens made of native desert plants and grasses that don't need watering. Mesa, Arizona, pays its residents $500 for the first 500 square feet of xeriscape garden. The water utility in Las Vegas, Nevada, is even more serious about the strategy. Its program pays home owners and commercial building owners up to $1.50 a square foot for the first 5,000 square feet of xeriscape garden, and then another dollar a square foot, up to $300,000![11]

New York City has done a particularly good job of improving the resilience of its water system. In 1979 the city's water consumption peaked at 1.5 billion gallons a day, an average of 189 gallons per person. By aggressively monitoring and repairing leaks, increasing the accuracy of the way water was billed, and passing regulations aimed at changing behavior, New York City reduced its water consumption to 1 billion gallons a day by 2009, with an average consumption of 125 gallons per person.[12] New York City is currently building a new water tunnel at a cost of $6 billion to increase the resilience of its system by permitting the closure of older tunnels for inspection and repairs.

According to the United States Geological Survey (USGS), in 2010 public water systems in the United States used 355 billion gallons of water a day, 13 percent less than was used in 2005.[13] If we can save 35 percent more with improved technologies and behavioral strategies, that's a lot of water saved. The benefits of minimizing water use have even bigger impacts in the world's newly emerging cities.

The McKinsey Global Institute estimates that by 2025 global demand for fresh urban municipal water will have risen by 40 percent over usage in 2012, and about half of this water will be needed to serve the 440 most rapidly growing emerging cities.[14] New freshwater sources will be hard to find, since humans are already consuming 87 percent of the world's freshwater supply, so reducing demand will be essential. Singapore requires all water-using devices to be labeled with their efficiency, to encourage wiser purchases, and raised its water rates to encourage water-use reduction. Singapore's goal is to reduce consumption to 37 gallons per person per day by 2030, which would be one-third of New York City's current use.

But most of the world's cities have not set such clear targets, nor do they have a plan to achieve them.

Despite the progress being made in water conservation and re-use, there is still much to be done. Flush toilets currently serve only about 60 percent of the world's population. As Bill Gates put it, "The flush toilets we use in the wealthy world are irrelevant, impractical and impossible for 40 percent of the global population, because they often don't have access to water, and sewers, electricity, and sewage treatment systems."[15] The Gates Foundation has been funding exper-iments in water-saving toilets and small local treatment systems that can function independently of central sewer systems—and therefore can be rapidly deployed in underserved communities.

Generating Value with Wastewater

Fortunately, every city already controls one of the very best sources of freshwater—its own treated wastewater. There are now more than 400,000 central wastewater treatment plants serving cities around the world, producing more than 730 million cubic meters of treated water every day. The emerging future of wastewater treatment is not only to reuse the system's water and increase the efficiency of the treatment process, but also to put treatment by-products to good use. Waste-water treatment plants are becoming net energy producers, burn-ing methane created by the biological digestion of waste to generate enough energy not only for these plants' own use, but also for their neighbors. And since 30 percent of the operating cost of a typical plant goes to cover its energy bill, free energy helps make wastewater treatment viable in a world of volatile energy prices.

Chris Peot is part of the team that is turning Washington, DC's, Blue Plains Advanced Waste Water Treatment Plant into a resource factory. Like many other older cities in the United States, Washington has an aging infrastructure. The Blue Plains plant, built seventy-five years ago, currently processes 370 million gallons of water a day coming from the region's more than 2 million residents and its huge commuting office-worker population, making it one of the ten largest wastewater treatment plants in the world.[16] In 2015 it completed a $1 billion upgrade, reducing the 1,200 tons of sludge, nitrogen, and phosphorus that the plant produced every day by 50 percent, energy use by 30 percent, and emissions by 41 percent. The project will save Washington and the neighboring areas about $10 million in power costs plus $10 million in reduced sludge-disposal costs each year.

Typically, sludge from wastewater treatment plants needs to be carted away and dumped into landfills, or mixed with lime and spread on farmland. The Blue Plains upgrade processes sludge in a new bio-solids reactor and pasteurize it with a thermal hydrolysis process.[17] About half of the sterile sludge that comes out is then converted into methane in a biological digester, and burned to power the plant's operations. The other half is turned into compost for the region's farms.

Turning sludge into energy can reduce greenhouse gases significantly. If just 10 percent of China's wastewater plant sludge was converted to energy, its carbon emissions would decline by 380 million tons per year.[18]

Wastewater treatment plants leave a lot of nitrogen and phosphorus in their effluent. Excess nitrogen and phosphorus from wastewater cause algae to bloom in freshwater systems, choking off other aquatic life. Yet both are primary components of fertilizer, and the world is facing a serious phosphorus shortage that threatens food security across the planet. If wastewater treatment plants could capture the phosphorus and nitrogen in wastewater and sell them as fertilizer, they could turn waste into food. The Hampton Roads Sanitation District in Suffolk, Virginia, is doing just that, using a chemical process to capture about 85 percent of the plant's phosphorus to produce

500 tons of fertilizer a year. The system is generating income from the sale of nitrogen and phosphorus, saving almost $200,000 a year in chemical and energy costs, and taking carbon dioxide out of the atmosphere![19]

The next frontier for wastewater treatment is using microbes to produce electricity and useful chemicals directly from the waste. The key lies in advances in microbial electrochemical technologies driven by exoelectrogens, a breed of bacteria that consume organic material and while doing so transfer electrons through their membranes to insoluble electron acceptors, making electricity. This electricity can be used to drive a power plant, but it can also do much more. When electricity is applied to a biochemical system it can yield many useful products, such as biofuels. It can even split water to produce the oxygen needed for a treatment plant's aeration process, and hydrogen to create hydrogen peroxide for the disinfecting process. Another emerging technology combines wastewater with waste CO_2 gas from power plants to grow algae, a biological fuel source that the U.S. Department of Defense has been processing to use in its planes and ships. Algae can also be used as animal feed, so that tropical forests need not be cut down to grow soybeans.

Reusing treated wastewater as drinking water may be the salvation of cities like São Paulo. In fact, reusing treated wastewater makes increasingly good sense everywhere. In a world shaped by climate change–induced droughts, rapid population growth, and a burgeoning middle class, water usage is likely to dramatically increase. One piece of the solution is to clean wastewater to potable standards and reuse it.

Judging Water by Its Quality, Not Its History

Namibia, in southwestern Africa, is the most arid country in sub-Saharan Africa, and the most sparsely settled. Almost all of its economic, political, and civic institutions are based in the nation's capital city, Windhoek, which is growing at a rate of 5 percent a year. In 1969, recognizing the insufficiency of its water supply, Windhoek converted its Goreangab water treatment plant to treat not only the surface water from the Goreangab Dam, but also effluent from the Gammams Wastewater Treatment Plant, giving rise to the Goreangab reclamation plant. The plant blends river water from the dam and reclaimed water from the plant to yield potable water. To make this work, several key practices were put into place. The first was the rigorous separation of industrial and domestic water treatment systems. Only domestic water is reclaimed. And the output of the plant is continuously tested and monitored for quality.

While the quality of the recycled water remained excellent, in the 1990s the condition of the river water feeding the Goreangab dam began to decline. Windhoek, like many cities in the developing world, was growing rapidly, with unregulated informal settlements at its edges. Lacking proper sanitation, these sprawling slums were polluting the city's groundwater and nearby rivers. Challenged by both increased demand and lower water quality, Windhoek responded by upgrading and increasing the capacity of its water-recycling program. In 2002 a new wastewater reclamation plant was built with funding from the European Union, using reverse osmosis technology to deliver 35 percent of the city's water directly from its waste.[20]

Wastewater recycling works: it's local, it's reliable, and it significantly increases a city's resilience. So why are there so few direct wastewater recycling plants in the world? Dr. Lucas van Vuuren, a South African pioneer of water reclamation, says, "Water should be judged not by its history, but by its quality,"[21] but this rational approach is challenged by our cognitive biases. Valerie Curtis, an evolutionary psychologist at the London School of Hygiene and Tropical Medicine, notes that humans developed a deeply rooted aversion to excrement as we evolved. "Pathogens were probably a greater overall threat than predators. That's why we have a strong, intuitive sense of disgust," she says. "Pretty much all of the things that we find disgusting have some kind of connection to infectious disease."[22]

In the 1980, Paul Roznin, a psychologist at the University of Pennsylvania, set out to test the strength of this disgust bias. He found that when he presented college students with a piece of chocolate fudge shaped to look like a dog turd, almost all of them were unable to eat the fudge, even though the students knew that it was made of chocolate. Their bias against contact with excrement was simply too strong.[23] However, when it comes to wastewater, people are more receptive to the concept of *indirect* reuse. Instead of plumbing treated wastewater right back into the water-intake system, as happens in Namibia, more and more cities are injecting treated wastewater into the ground, where it filters through the soil before going back into the aquifers from which the cities draw their water. Calling this "groundwater replenishment," rather then "wastewater reuse," makes it more palatable. Another approach is to return the treated water to rivers many miles upstream of the water-intake system, so that by the time it arrives at the intake, it is well diluted.

Fountain Valley, California, boasts the world's largest groundwater replenishment system. It began production in 2008, and generates 70 million gallons of recycled water per day. This provides about 20 percent of the water used by the more than 2 million residents of Orange County. The system also has a secondary benefit. Ordinarily, when aquifers near oceans are overtapped and the groundwater level drops, seawater often flows in to take its place, raising the salinity of the groundwater; however, injecting water into the ground helps prevent seawater intrusion. Also, since more than 20 percent of California's energy goes to pumping water, much of it over long distances, recycling water locally provides significant energy savings. It also may be the only solution to the growing tension between agricultural and municipal users of water in limited supply.

The desert city of Mesa, Arizona, is the thirty-eighth-largest city in the United States. A suburb of Phoenix, its population is larger than that of Atlanta, Cleveland, Miami, Minneapolis, or St. Louis. Those older American cities have denser cores, surrounded by suburbs, but Mesa is almost all suburb. In fact, it claims to be the largest municipal suburb in the United States. The area was first settled by the Hohokam people, who settled in small clusters along the Gila River. Between the seventh and fourteenth centuries they built complex irrigation systems for cultivating cotton, tobacco, maize, beans, and squash. In its day the Hohokam canal system was the most extensive in the New World. At its multiple intersections with the Gila River, the canal's head gates were as large as 90 feet wide and 10 feet deep. By 1100, the canal system was irrigating 110,000 acres of the Sonoran Desert and supporting an increasingly sophisticated population.

First living in small, *rancheria*-style settlements, by the 1100s the Hohokam people were moving into denser, more complex proto-cities. Because these communities were more vulnerable to the changing climate, droughts and floods often decimated the Hohokam population. The final blow came in a series of floods in the fourteenth century that scoured the bottom of the Gila River and lowered it below the depth of the canal heads, rendering hundreds of miles of canals useless. By 1450 most of the Hohokam's settlements were abandoned, and their inhabitants dispersed.

Mesa was resettled as part of America's nineteenth-century westward expansion in 1877 by the First Mesa Company, which reopened the old Hohokam canals, and within a year settlers were living off irrigated farmland. Mesa's early growth was slow. In 1900 its population was only 722 (by comparison, St. Louis's population at the time was 575,000). But after World War II, as air-conditioning became more prevalent, Mesa's population began to expand. By 1950 it had reached 16,790, and by 2015 it had grown to 462,000; to keep up with this growth Mesa had to dramatically expand its water supply.

The city began by establishing a goal: having a hundred-year supply of water. To help it meet its objective, the city now treats all its wastewater, and uses it either to replenish groundwater sources, or for irrigation. Its recycled water program is designed to deliver 42 million gallons of recycled water a day. Instead of one large central plant, Mesa built three plants in different parts of the city. The system also provides water to irrigate local golf courses and municipal landscaping, but much of it is swapped with the Gila River Indians, who use it for agriculture. In exchange, they give the city rights to their freshwater use of the Gila River. In order to meet their hundred-year goal, the people of Mesa also must behave differently. In 1999 the cities of Mesa, Scottsdale, and Phoenix jointly launched a "Use It Wisely" campaign, which has become one of the most extensive water-conservation educational outreach programs in the nation.

The Four Taps

To meet the needs of its growing population the island city of Singapore has developed what it calls the "four taps" water-supply system.[24] The first tap comes from its extensive reservoir system, surrounded by protected natural land to help keep the reservoirs pure. The second tap is desalinated water from the bays that surround the city. The third tap is recycled sewer water (labeled NEWater to overcome biases about it), and the fourth is imported water piped in from Malaysia. Singapore's goal is to be able to grow its population by 2.5 million people and still be water-independent from Malaysia by 2060. To achieve it Singapore has become a global research hub for new water technologies. Its future strategies include densifying its town centers, better connecting them via mass transit, and taking land formerly occupied by roads and converting it to reservoirs and open spaces.

Another island city, Hong Kong, has focused on the second tap, seawater, by implementing a dual water system that provides fresh-water for everyday use and seawater to flush toilets. This system has been in operation for more than fifty years, reducing municipal water use by 20 percent. It's so successful that the city is now experiment-ing with a three-part water system for supplying its new airport with freshwater, seawater, and gray water (from sinks).

There is also a fifth tap that can provide a low-cost, low-energy-use, distributed system of water supply: capturing rainwater on build-ing roofs and storing it in cisterns. Almost every ancient Roman home collected rainwater in an *impluvium*, a shallow cistern that occupied the center of the home's entry court. This was used to water gardens and for other household uses, and when it was hot, evaporation from the *impluvium* provided natural cooling. Today rainwater capture is a key component of the green building tool kit.

It All Adds Up

The wide range of water-conserving technologies and behaviors we've discussed can reduce the current water use of most cities by as much as 35 percent. Recycled water can also provide 30–40 percent of a city's water needs. Together these approaches can reduce freshwater usage in most cities by 70 percent. When you add more widely distributed systems of rainwater capture and storage along with desalination, one of the key causes of the collapse of ancient cities—drought—starts to look preventable. But there is a larger challenge: cities use only about 25 percent of the world's water supply. Most of the balance is used by industry and agriculture. As the world's population grows, industrial and agricultural water demands will also increase, unless they, too, shift from linear to circular metabolisms.

Traditional agricultural societies developed exquisite systems for allocating water. In the Balinese *subak* system, farmers recognize that they are all in it together, integrating the flow of water across their rice fields via a shared irrigation system called *subaks*. These are collectively maintained, guided by priests who oversee temples placed at each spring or river source. The priests advise on planting and harvesting schedules based upon the cycles of the moon. Ditch bosses propose work schedules and mediate disputes over the fair allocation of water. Each segment of the system is led locally; no one person is in charge of it all; and yet the *subaks* have thrived for a thousand years, providing irrigation, restoring soils, and limiting pests while continually adapting to climate changes.

The farmers in Bali continually monitor one another's performance. When one farm shifts its planting schedule or changes its rice species and becomes more productive, its neighbors quickly follow, leading to waves of improvement throughout the system. The interconnected *subaks* give Bali a vast, dynamically balanced system with distributed governance resulting in one of the world's most productive agricultural systems.

Unfortunately, most of the world lacks the culture of collective, adaptive governance systems needed to fairly allocate water among these uses.

As cities map their urban metabolisms, and are getting real-time data on inputs and outputs, they are increasingly understanding the power of metabolic management. And as their infrastructure systems move from linear to complex integration, they are expanding their capacity to thrive in a VUCA age. By interconnecting these systems, by distributing and increasing the information flows among them, they are increasing their resilience. But, as with the Balinese *subak* system, at the core of any high-functioning infrastructure system lies the understanding that we are all in it together, and a commitment to optimizing the allocation of resources so they benefit the system as a whole.

Infrastructure: From Maximizing to Optimizing

Infrastructure is the armature upon which civilization is built. It provides the integrated systems that enable prosperity, nurture well-being, and, if properly designed, can begin to restore the natural systems that cities so often degrade. The wisest cities, like Singapore and Mesa, are thinking like Diocletian and planning their water systems to meet the needs of the next century.

Infrastructure by its very nature is a collaborative system. From the irrigation systems of Mesopotamia to the Internet, infrastructure systems create higher levels of material flow, energy, and information by combining shared resources and processes. They are the core of a civilization's resistance to entropy.

Infrastructure systems are time-shifters, providing benefits not just for the present, but for the future, too. Reservoirs collect rain for today, and also store it for tomorrow. Health-care systems heal people as they become sick, but also provide prevention to reduce illness in the years ahead. This means that investing in infrastructure is an ideal leverage point, borrowing today to enhance well-being in the future.

Infrastructure is the fabric from which circular economies are woven. The more their parts are distributed, connected, smart, and efficient, the more they will enhance the emergence of new, adaptive patterns of organization. This requires city leaders to shift from thinking of infrastructure as *complicated* systems to understanding it as *complex* systems. Connecting various systems into one metasystem that co-evolves with the city's metabolism requires leaders to improve not only a system's efficiency, but also its coherence. It's the urban model of biocomplexity.

In a resource-constrained world, the most successful cities will learn to optimize their metabolic consumption. To do so, they will shift from linear systems to circular ones that are more adaptive to the uncertainties of a VUCA world.

Most cities cannot fund the infrastructure of the twenty-first century on their own. They need the support of their national governments. India, China, Japan, South Korea, Russia, Brazil, and many other nations are funding vast urban infrastructure investment programs. The United States Congress's reluctance to invest in the nation's infrastructure is befuddling. The American Society of Civil Engineers rates the condition of the nation's roads, bridges, drinking and wastewater systems, airports, transit systems, dams, and so forth a D+.[25] A significant infrastructure program would create millions of local jobs for steel and concrete manufacturing plants, construction workers, design engineers, and maintenance crews. It would improve the nation's economic resilience to volatility, and its competitiveness, health, safety, and quality of life. Additionally, wise infrastructure investment has excellent economic returns. A response to globalization is not isolation, it is infrastructure.

PART THREE

Resilience

Tempering Cities in a Time of Climate Change

THE THIRD ASPECT of well-temperedness, resilience, is the adaptive capacity of a system to deal with stress and volatility. The ecologist C. S. Holling was the first to describe the resilience of ecosystems in his seminal 1973 work "Resilience and Stability of Ecological Systems." Holling defined resilience as "the capacity of an ecosystem to tolerate disturbance without collapsing into a qualitatively different state that is controlled by a different set of processes. A resilient ecosystem can withstand shocks and rebuild itself when necessary. Resilience in social systems has the added capacity in humans to anticipate and plan for the future."[1]

Holling's initial work viewed stability as a system's preferred objective, with the goal of returning to a previous state after a disturbance. Very often, when communities suffer from a calamity, whether caused by weather or structural shifts in the economy, their first instinct is to want to return to their previous state. But that often is not the best objective for the system's long-term health. Today, urban resilience is viewed as the capacity of a city to bounce forward, to a new and more adaptive state.

Mitch Landrieu, the mayor who oversaw much of the rebuilding of New Orleans after Hurricanes Katrina and Rita, described the floods as a "near-death experience." When the recovery began, there was tremendous local pressure to rebuild New Orleans as it had been. But many outside consultants recommended rebuilding a much more resilient, future-facing city. Landrieu reflected upon the state of the city the night before the hurricane, and realized that almost every aspect of the city was in decline. He chose the harder, more courageous path, to keep the best of the past, but to reimagine many aspects of the city going forward. The new New Orleans has the feel of the old, but in almost every way, it is functioning differently.

Cities live at the intersection of dynamic environmental, economic, metabolic, social, and cultural systems. Responding to changing circumstances can be difficult because it is in our nature to want to return to the status quo rather than to risk moving on to an uncertain future, even if it might be a better one. This bias keeps human culture stable and reliable. In our evolutionary past, when change unfolded much more slowly, this was an important adaptive strategy. But in volatile times, when the context is so rapidly changing, we need to shift from old habits to find new, adaptive strategies more quickly.

One of the key drivers of volatility is temperature, whose etymology comes from the latin word *temperare*, which means "to restrain" or "to mix," and has the same root as "temperament." This section of the book looks at ways to make cities more resilient, particularly to climate change. A key to resilience is to temper their extremes.

Earth's climate has always been variable, and its changes have had a profound effect on the planet's ecosystems and civilizations. But its more recent swings have been exacerbated by our modern civilization's use of fossil fuels as our primary source of energy, and by industrial forestry and agriculture practices.

The wells that harvest oil and natural gas emit prodigious amounts of methane gas. When we burn fossil fuels, we release carbon dioxide. When we burn or clear-cut forests, we not only release carbon dioxide, but also reduce nature's capacity to absorb it. The carbon dioxide and methane gases that we are emitting into the atmosphere are forming a blanket, trapping heat and raising the temperature. This is melting the polar caps and glaciers, causing sea levels to rise. It is also shifting weather patterns, increasing storms in some places and drought in others.

The urban distress caused by increasingly volatile weather can be dramatic, as evidenced by Hurricane Katrina and Superstorm Sandy, which caused loss of life and damage that cost tens of billions of dollars. Other storms undermine a city's ability to function, such as the almost ten feet of snow that crippled Boston in the winter of 2014, disabling the mass-transit system, making it impossible for tens of thousands of people living one paycheck from eviction to get to work. And some new weather patterns create effects that accumulate over years, like the droughts that threaten the water supplies of cities in California and the Southwest. Rising sea levels put more than 177 million people worldwide at serious risk of flooding. Cities near sea level may be underwater a century from now.

Volatile weather also threatens the metabolism of our cities. By endangering our supplies of food, water, and essential natural resources, global warming is making many rural parts of the world more difficult to live in, causing mass migrations of people to cities.

But not all climate change is caused by humans. There is much to learn from the urban impacts of naturally occurring climate change.

Naturally Occurring Climate Change

In the late 1500s, Boris Godunov, a lowly archer in the Russian secret police, worked his way up through the hierarchy of power through murder, marriage, and manipulation. In 1598, he was proclaimed the tsar of Russia. It was a time of great income disparity. Russia's wealthy families owned huge estates worked by poor serfs, and instead of investing in the country's infrastructure, Russia's elite used their income to build luxurious palaces and buy exotic silks.

Halfway around the world, a volcano in Peru, Huaynaputina, began to stir. On February 19, 1600, it erupted, the largest recorded volcanic explosion in South America's history. Millions of tons of volcanic ash spewed into the atmosphere, blotting out the sun and triggering abnormally cold weather and drought. Across northern Europe and Russia, crops failed for three straight years.

In the famine that followed, more than one third of the Russian people died from starvation and cold, most of them rural serfs. But the cities suffered, too. In Moscow, mass graves were dug to bury 127,000 victims. Recognizing that their government was incapable of protecting them, the people revolted. Chaos and civil war ensued as rival factions struggled for power. In 1609, Poland invaded Russia and occupied the Kremlin to restore order. The combination of climate change, income inequality, and selfish governance is toxic to the health of cities, and often leads to collapse.

In the twenty-first century human-caused climate change will last longer, and cause more suffering, than the eruption of Huaynaputina. The civil war that is destroying Syria began when the changing climate caused a drought that forced 1.5 million rural farmers and herders to the cities, because President Assad allocated precious water to the elite and their agribusinesses. Without work and a political voice, Syria's displaced became the seeds of the war that is flooding Europe with tens of thousands of people seeking a better life.

And climate change is not the only megatrend of the twenty-first century. Our cities will also be impacted by a population that will grow to 10 billion people, cyber-vulnerability, natural resource depletion, biodiversity loss, increased income inequality, and an increase in terrorism, all accompanied by the increased migration of displaced peoples.

The impact of these and other megatrends on the earth's ecosystems and human populations is going to hit cities hard. By the end of the century, low-lying cities such as New Orleans and Dhaka are likely to be underwater unless they make dramatic investments in dikes. Dikes won't work for Miami, which was built on porous limestone. The seawater is already rising through the rock, a threat with no current technical solution.[2] Others cities such as New York, Boston, Tampa, Osaka, Nagoya, and Shenzhen are all facing huge infrastructure costs to protect themselves from rising seas, rising heat, and growing income inequality.

To thrive under such volatile conditions our cities will need to be able to rapidly adapt, to evolve with the enormous changes of the coming century. To do so, they need a resilient temperament. The most effective strategies are to dramatically increase the beneficial buffering role of nature within and around our cities, and to make our buildings themselves greener and more resilient. In the following two chapters we'll be exploring these strategies.

CHAPTER 7

Natural Infrastructure

Biophilia and Human Resilience

Nature has a marvelous way of adapting to climate change, and at the same time, mediating its effects. But nature also brings humans other benefits. Our desire to be in nature seems to be ingrained in our very being. The word "biophilia" was coined by the psychologist Erich Fromm, who used it to describe the instinctive bond between human beings and other living systems. The biologist E. O. Wilson also observed that we humans have "an urge to affiliate with other forms of life."[1] Even in the most urban environment people have a deeply ingrained need to connect with nature. And why not? Our very existence depends on nature's bounty—air, water, and the plants and animals we consume as food. There is also increasing scientific evidence that urban environments that provide us with more contact with nature enhance our cognitive health and well-being and increase our resilience.

In the mid-1980s Roger Ulrich, a Swedish professor of architecture, conducted a groundbreaking study in which he compared two sets of hospital patients recovering from surgery.[2] The first group had rooms with windows looking out onto a brick wall. The second had windows with views of trees. The study, which has now been replicated in many settings, showed that patients with a view of trees spent fewer days in the hospital and required less pain medication compared with those whose windows faced a wall. This work gave rise to a new field of architecture known as therapeutic design,[3] which uses natural environments to facilitate health and improve medical outcomes. It turns out that therapeutic designs aren't just good for patients; they also reduce stress for visitors, as well as the burnout and turnover of health-care workers themselves.

The benefits of nature for human well-being are pervasive. In his groundbreaking book *Last Child in the Woods: Saving Our Children from Nature-Deficit Disorder*,[4] Richard Louv presented research correlating the rapid increase of attention deficit hyperactivity disorder (ADHD) among children who experienced increased disconnection with nature. He proposed that contact with nature enhances children's ability to pay attention, and improves their capacity for social and emotional learning. Biophilia, which began as an intriguing hypothesis, is now being supported by a growing body of science.

In 2012 the *Journal of Affective Disorders* published a study indicating that people with major depressive disorder show more significant cognitive gains after nature walks than they do after walking in urban settings devoid of nature.[5] The American Horticultural Therapy Association reports that sensory gardens are increasingly becoming standard aspects of therapy for dementia.[6] A United Kingdom–based horticultural charity called Thrive is cultivating a network of therapeutic gardens to enhance the lives of people who are disabled, ill, isolated, disadvantaged, or generally vulnerable. The Sensory Trust is taking this work to Cornwall, building biophilic centers to support people whose lives are affected by social exclusion, including older people and those with physical, sensory, and intellectual impairments. And Maggie's Cancer Care Centers, a network of community-based facilities, are being built as biophilic, therapeutic drop-in centers for people affected with cancer throughout the United Kingdom. But should biophilic environments benefit only special-needs populations? Or can they help heal neighborhoods and cities, too?

The Garden in the City

Throughout history city planners have integrated parks and gardens into their visions. Perhaps the most famous ancient city gardens were the fabled hanging gardens of Babylon. These were built by King Nebuchadnezzar II for his wife: she had been raised in the mountains, and her life in the flat, arid Babylonian capital left her longing for the lush peaks and valleys of her childhood.[7] The homes of the ancient Greeks and Romans featured private gardens located in an interior courtyard nearest to the entry.

In ancient China, gardens were the province of the rich and mighty. Designed primarily for pleasure, these were lavishly constructed and decorated for feasting and carousing with concubines. Around 500 BCE, influenced by the Axial Age teachings of Confucius and Lao-tzu, the purpose of Chinese gardens shifted toward the sublime. Their design began to encourage contemplation, to promote a sense of harmony between humans and nature, and to open the visitor to *jen*, or altruistic feelings. Through the careful use of rocks, water, trees, and flowers representing the forces of nature, along with architecture, painting, and poetry representing human forces, Taoist gardens sought to model a balance between the two.

Gardens also appear throughout the life of another great Axial Age thinker, Sakyamuni Buddha, who was born in a garden, became enlightened under a tree, gave his first sermon in a deer park, or sanctuary, and died in a garden. The Buddhist Nalanda University, one of the world's first great universities and one of its longest-lasting, surrounded each of its teaching halls, monasteries, and stupas (burial structures) with a garden.

The Persian garden form advanced throughout the great Islamic flourishing of the eighth to twelfth centuries. Islamic cities featured three kinds of gardens: the *bustan*, a formal contemplative garden organized around rectangular pools and water channels in the inner courtyard of a home, representing paradise on earth; the *jannah*, an irrigated orchard of palms, oranges, and grapevines located outside the home; and the *rawdah*, or kitchen garden. The Islamic garden provided an oasis from the business of the markets and the distractions of the household, a place of refuge and contemplation in the heart of a busy city.

The Islamic conquest of Spain brought the Persian garden to Europe, where its highly geometric form, framed by walls and centered on a system of canals and fountains, can still be seen in gardens ranging from the Alhambra to the Palace of Versailles. These gardens were all private, providing pleasure for the aristocracy and wealthy merchants. It took the British to bring gardens to the public—but not without a fight.

The Emergence of the Public Urban Park

In 1536, King Henry VIII purchased common land on the outskirts of London to serve as his private hunting grounds. To privatize it, he enclosed it, or fenced it off from common usage as grazing and hunting grounds. At the time the enclosure of common lands was quite controversial. This practice had begun several centuries earlier, when plagues and famines decimated England's population and the great manor houses could not muster enough tenant farmers to work their land. To generate income, landowners fenced off what had been commonly occupied farmland and converted it to sheep grazing, which required fewer laborers. As Europe grew more prosperous and the demand for fine English wool increased, the enclosure of the long-held commons by the nobility increased, depriving local famers and herders of their livelihoods. King Henry VIII's enclosures were particularly resented because the income they produced was used to support his extravagant lifestyle.

This privatization, known as the enclosure movement, gave rise to a virulent debate about the balance between public and private benefits, between the *we* and the *me*, which has dominated discussions of land use ever since. Privatization of public property is often accompanied by a growing disparity between the wealthy and the rest. In England, in response to a decade of seething social unrest, in 1637, King Charles I opened Hyde Park to all, and London's great public parks movement was born. Today there are eight parks in London owned by the Crown but enjoyed by the public: Bushy Park, Green Park, Greenwich Park, Hyde Park, Kensington Gardens, Regent's Park, Richmond Park, and St. James's Park.

The year 1857 was a good one for the greening of the city. At the same time that Emperor Franz Joseph was tearing down Vienna's city walls and replacing them with the Ringstrasse—a vibrant new neighborhood full of trees and parks—a group of wealthy merchants in New York City lobbied for the formation of the Central Park Commission to design a park in the grazing lands north of the city's most populated neighborhoods. Their objective was to create a place where they and their families could take constitutional strolls or carriage rides, and where working-class families could socialize outside of the local saloon. The Central Park Commission held the first national landscape design competition for the new park, which was won by Frederick Law Olmsted and Calvert Vaux. Their enormously successful plan for Central Park led to a wide range of urban commissions, including Brooklyn's Prospect Park.

Central Park is an extraordinary place, an idealized natural landscape in the heart of the densest city in the United States. But Olmsted and Vaux's main contribution to the urban form of cities came later, with their development of the concept of an emerald necklace, a network of parks and parkways that often followed natural systems such as rivers. Among these are the Emerald Necklace in Boston; the Emerald Necklace of parks in Rochester, New York; Detroit's Belle

Isle Park; the Grand Necklace of Parks in Milwaukee, Wisconsin; and Cherokee Park in Louisville, Kentucky. These park systems were all built in the late nineteenth and early twentieth centuries, and were expanded by the Great Depression era's WPA and CCC projects. But in the 1970s, as cities began to struggle with increasing deficits and declining populations, their parks budgets were the first to get cut.

The Rise of Community Gardens

New York's South Bronx became a national symbol of the urban decline that took place during the second half of the twentieth century. In 1948, Robert Moses began construction of the Cross-Bronx Expressway, the world's most expensive road at the time. When it was completed in 1963, the South Bronx, a bastion of working- and middle-class communities, had been effectively severed from the rest of the city, triggering the neighborhood's rapid degeneration. By the 1970s it was decimated by drugs, crime, and abandonment. The borough's social networks had been torn apart, and there were few jobs to be found. And then the South Bronx began to burn, as junkies set buildings on fire to expose the copper pipes and wires they could strip and sell to buy heroin or crack. Landlords torched money-losing buildings to collect on insurance, and squatters burned them by accident while making fires for heat. The best the City of New York could do was to tear down the unsafe shells, creating vast, rubble-strewn lots lit in winter by the fires of homeless people gathering around trash-filled oil drums to keep warm.

The devastated South Bronx was often compared to Dresden, the German city razed by a firestorm sparked by Allied bombers in 1945, only the South Bronx was firebombed in slow motion. Despite these dispiriting conditions, the residents who remained took over a handful of empty lots and began to build community gardens. Some planted to provide themselves with an inexpensive source of nutritious food, others as an act of community building. These neighborhood gardens became safe havens where residents could connect with one another and with the healing power of nature. Recent immigrants from the Caribbean or Latin America, or African Americans just a generation or two away from the rural South, gathered in their local garden and built *casitas*, makeshift community centers, where they gathered to play music, cards, and dominoes.[8] There is now a great deal of research showing that gardens like these provide tremendous health benefits. Often the only source of fresh food in low-income urban neighborhoods, they also provide exercise, social networks, and a way to decompress from the crushing stresses of living in poverty.

The community garden movement rose in parallel with the growth of not-for-profit community development companies, which first focused on renovating abandoned buildings to create affordable housing, and then went on to build new apartment houses on vacant land while providing social services to their residents. Both movements were self-organized, widely distributed, and largely independent of city authority.

Little rankled New York City's command-and-control mayor Rudolph Giuliani more. In 1999 he proposed to auction off informal gardens on city-owned land to private real estate developers. Thanks to the efforts of the not-for-profit Trust for Public Land and the New York Restoration Project, the gardens were purchased just before the auction, given protected status, and connected by combining individual gardens into borough-wide land trusts.

The community garden movement now touches almost every city in North America. By 2012, the American Community Garden Association estimated that there were 18,000 community gardens throughout the United States and Canada.[9] This movement reflects the deep, biophilic desire of urban residents to connect with nature in the city, and its scale has grown enough to make it a meaningful element of city metabolism.

Parks, Gardens, and the Health of Cities

Of all America's national land conservation groups, the Trust for Public Land (TPL) has been working in cities the longest, having launched its urban program in 1976. As research documenting the health and economic benefits of urban parks and gardens grew in the 1990s and early 2000s, TPL began to focus on their equitable distribution throughout cities, recommending that urban residents live no more than a ten-minute walk from a park, waterfront, or garden. Parks, greenways, and gardens, it turns out, are among the most cost-effective ways to simultaneously improve public health, create climate resilience, and increase economic value.

The trust's 2009 study, "Measuring the Economic Value of a City Park System,"[10] reported seven major direct benefits of urban parks and open space: property value, tourism, direct use, health, community cohesion, clean water, and clean air. The first two factors provide cities with direct income. Studies in a wide range of cities substantiate that real estate near parks and other natural open spaces is more valuable, generating higher property tax revenues for the city; great parks also attract tourists who spend money in or near them, which increases income from the sales tax. The next three factors—direct use, health, and community cohesion—provide residents with direct savings or avoided costs. Parks provide people of all incomes a place to exercise and recreate without having to pay for health clubs or other private services. Numerous studies point to exercise as a prime way of reducing the most pervasive and costly expensive contemporary ailments, such as obesity, diabetes, heart disease, and cancer.

The average American walks only 400 yards a day. More than 60 percent of Americans are obese or overweight. By the 2000s, this lack of physical activity became second only to tobacco use as a leading cause of death among Americans.[11] Obesity adds $190 billion to the nation's annual medical costs.[12] And this is a global phenomenon.

As China moves more of its people into high-rise residential blocks, they too are walking less. The World Health Organization notes that in 2011 more than 350 million Chinese were overweight and almost 100 million were obese, five times more than just half a dozen years earlier, in 2005.[13]

One inexpensive solution to this crisis can be found in the proven correlation between the walkability of a city and exercise: people who live within a ten-minute walk or bike ride of a park (and with a safe sidewalk to get to it) exercise more. Paradoxically, many people choose to live in the suburbs in order to be closer to nature, yet city dwellers often spend more time walking outdoors than suburban residents, and as a result weigh less.

The link between urban nature and mental health has also been firmly established. Mark Taylor, a public health researcher at the University of Trnava in Slovakia, examined two of London's public data sets: the first tracked the number of antidepressant prescriptions in each of the thirty-three boroughs, and the other documented the number of street trees per block. After adjusting for factors such as unemployment and affluence, Taylor and his colleagues found a clear correlation between street trees and well-being: those areas with the fewest street trees had the highest number of residents taking anti-depressant prescription drugs.[14] Parks and park activities also help create social cohesion, which not only has significant health benefits, but also leads to reduced costs for police and fire protection, prisons, counseling, and rehabilitation. We'll explore the essential role of social cohesion for well-being in chapter 10.

Parks and open spaces also generate tremendous environmental benefits for cities. These natural landscapes absorb pollutants in the air, which is especially critical for residents of lower-income neighborhoods, who tend to be closer to the toxic output of industry, highways, and bus depots. Trees also cool surrounding air by providing shade, and by drawing up groundwater and transpiring it through their leaves. Trees temper cities by moderating the effects of climate change; when temperatures rise over 90 degrees, neighborhoods with trees can be up to twelve degrees cooler than those without. The U.S. Department of Agriculture reports, "The net cooling effect of a young, healthy tree is equivalent to ten room-size air conditioners operating 20 hours a day."[15]

Parks and open spaces also improve a city's ability to retain and clean rainwater. As the climate changes, rain in many cities has shifted from a more even distribution to cycles of drought and deluge, so that when it rains the city's storm-water system is frequently overwhelmed. Almost eight hundred communities in the United States are currently out of compliance with the Federal Clean Water Act, and need to make investments to reduce raw sewage overflowing from their storm-water systems. In Seattle, the combination of oil, heavy metals, and grime that rain washes off streets and through the storm-water system into nearby rivers is so toxic that it can poison migrating coho salmon, killing them within two and a half hours of contact. But if the same storm water first flows through soil, tests indicate that it is harmless to fish.[16] It's much cheaper for a city to build new parks to absorb and clean the water than it is to rip up streets and install larger concrete pipes and detention tanks, while at the same time providing health and social benefits.

The tempering effects of nature are an essential element of a city's infrastructure, enhancing its metabolism while providing economic benefits, climate resilience, well-being, and livability, all at a much lower cost than traditional civil engineering.

The Return of Natural Infrastructure

The city of Philadelphia's combined sewer system spews billions of gallons of toxic waste into the Schuylkill River whenever it rains, violating the Federal Clean Water Act. In the mid-2000s the EPA mandated that Philadelphia spend $8 billion to build a huge underground storm-water retention system and increase the size of storm-water pipes throughout the city, requiring almost every major street to be ripped up. Such interventions are very expensive to build and maintain, and they haven't necessarily been effective in other cities. Milwaukee, for example, spent $2.3 billion on a system in the 1980s that didn't solve the city's storm-water issues. So Philadelphia proposed an alternative plan to the EPA: instead of building a hard system of concrete and pipes, it would spend $1 billion on a soft, or natural system, building new parks, removing asphalt in schoolyards and replacing it with turf, and encouraging private owners to add green roofs to their buildings and trees and permeable paving to their parking lots. The city itself would also invest in the natural restoration of stream habitats and riverfronts.

The EPA agreed to the proposal. To pay for it, Philadelphia raised its storm-water fees. The result was a $7 billion savings over the cost of the EPA's original plan, and an increase in the quality of life and health of the city. The project is also reducing carbon dioxide emissions, improving air and water quality while restoring wetlands and other natural habitats. It's also increasing property values in newly green areas.[17] Increased waste and storm-water treatment fees are shifting behavior, giving residents feedback on the true cost of runoff; in response they are planting green roofs and sidewalk trees to reduce their fees.

Perhaps the most dramatic reintroduction of natural infrastructure to a city took place nearly seven thousand miles from Philadelphia, in Seoul, South Korea. Seoul was founded in 17 BCE along the Han River. The Cheonggyecheon River, a 5.2-mile tributary of the Han, runs through the heart of today's metropolis. When Seoul became the capital city of the Joseon dynasty in 1394, King Yeonjo funded the construction of a proper urban infrastructure system. To increase the ability of the river to drain adjacent land and carry away storm water, the river was dredged and its banks were lined with stone. Bridges were built to encourage development. Over time the river became the city's economic dividing line, with the wealthy living to its north and the poor to its south. After the Korean War, hundreds of thousands of refugees swarmed into Seoul, packing the banks of the Cheonggyecheon with makeshift shacks, and filling its waters with trash and human waste.

As South Korea became more prosperous, its residents began to buy cars and move to the suburbs. To accommodate the resulting traffic the Cheonggyecheon River was piped and covered by a road in the 1960s, and in 1976 an elevated freeway was built above that. By 1990 the freeway, carrying 160,000 cars a day, was perpetually jammed, and beginning to crumble from the stress.

When Kee Yeon Hwang, a professor in the department of urban planning and design at Hongik University, was brought in to rethink

Houses along the Cheonggyecheon River, 1946. *(From Seoul under Japanese Rule [1910–1945], Seoul Metropolitan Committee)*

the city's transportation plan, he came up with a radical idea: tearing down the road and highway that covered the Cheonggyecheon River. "The idea was sown in 1999," Hwang says. "We had experienced a strange thing. We had three tunnels in the city and one had to be shut down. Bizarrely, we found that car volumes dropped. We discovered it was a case of the Braess Paradox, which says that by taking away space in an urban area you can actually increase the flow of traffic, and, by implication, by adding extra capacity to a road network you can reduce overall performance."[18]

Braess's paradox, developed by the German mathematician Dietrich Braess, observes that adding capacity and connectivity to a user-optimized system such as a road network does not increase its efficiency if each user makes selfish choices. This is because of the Nash equilibrium theory, according to which systems are optimized only when the benefits of all are taken into account with each decision.

Americans generally believe that enhancing individual choice is a good thing, and we believe that adding capacity and connectivity to road networks solves traffic problems. But it turns out that combining them together leads to *reductions* in efficiency, and more traffic jams. A system's efficiency is enhanced by increased connectivity and capacity only when the individuals choose to optimize the whole.

From the beginning the Cheonggyecheon River restoration process was designed to maximize the benefit to the community. Hwang enlisted local participation by asking thousands of city residents what mattered most to them, and the answers were consistent: water and the environment. As the idea of tearing down the elevated highway gained momentum, Hwang developed a simulation model that predicted a slight improvement in traffic. The teardown was put to a vote of the electorate, and approved. In 2005, the $380 million project, designed to simultaneously reduce traffic, increase livability and biodiversity, and culturally transform the areas along the river's banks, was completed. It was an extraordinary success.

As part of the Cheonggyecheon River revitalization project, the city also integrated its data and transportation networks. Areas along the riverbanks were enriched with high-speed Internet access, and zoned for arts and innovation. Hundreds of new businesses and cultural organizations sprang up or relocated to the area. The increased density of residents and workers spawned hip restaurants and cafés along the river's edge. As the balance between jobs and housing improved, fewer people who worked in the area needed to drive to it. The city increased parking fees in the area, but also increased its bus services and created walkways along the restored river. As predicted, overall traffic in the city dropped and speeds increased, so even motorists benefited. Hwang said, "The tearing down of the motorway has had both intended and unexpected effects. As soon as we destroyed the road, the cars just disappeared. A lot of people just gave up their cars."[19]

The benefits of the Cheonggyecheon River restoration far exceed its impact on transportation, which first sparked the project. As Lee In-keun, Seoul's assistant mayor for infrastructure, put it, "We've basically gone from a car-oriented city to a human-oriented city."[20] The surface temperatures in summer along the restored river are now an average 6.5 degrees Fahrenheit cooler than urban areas 1,200 feet away. Wind speeds along the river have increased by 50 percent because of thermal shifts, and small particulate matter in the area has dropped to almost half of its previous levels. The restored river has enriched local biodiversity, as the number of fish and species in the Cheonggyecheon more than quadrupled, and local insect species rose in number from 5 to 192.[21] "Our life has been changed," says Inchon Yu, an actor and cultural advisor to the former mayor of Seoul, Lee Myung Bak. "People feel the water and the wind. Life becomes slower . . . it reminds people of their own hearts. It gives a new heart to the city."[22]

Sadly, Braess's paradox, which served Korean city planners so well, was not taken into account when Boston decided to significantly expand its road network, bury it, and cover it with a park, a project known as the Big Dig. The park did generate an increase in real estate values and urban livability, but the expansion of high-speed traffic lanes actually doubled commuting times along some sections of the roadway, and reduced its performance overall.

The beauty of the Cheonggyecheon River project was that it applied the principles of nature to restore both the human and natural systems of the city, and to enhance their resilience to future volatility.

Biodiversity and Coherence

Restoring nature in and around urban centers is critical to our well-being, lends vigor to city metabolism, and generates multiple environmental, economic, social, and health co-benefits, outcomes that are welcomed by the world's rapidly growing cities. As São Paulo becomes denser, it plans to develop a hundred new parks. The city of Shanghai is building twenty-one new parks around its suburban edge. New Delhi is planning a new 1,200-acre park, 50 percent larger than New York's Central Park. However, planting trees and grass alone does not necessarily re-create nature. Natural systems require complexity and diversity to thrive. But first, a brief lesson on the way that natural systems are organized.

G. Evelyn Hutchinson, the father of modern ecology, observed that the nutrients in a natural ecosystem flow through the food chain in a "trophic structure," a cycle of nutrients. At the first trophic level are the primary producers, such as plants and algae, which combine sunlight, carbon dioxide, and the elements in the soil to create living matter. This provides the nutrient and energy base for the entire ecosystem. The second trophic level consists of consumers, including all animals: since they cannot manufacture their own food, they have to eat other living things. The third and final level is made up of the decomposers, such as fungi and bacteria, which break food down, primarily returning it to the soil, so that it can be recycled back into the system. These three trophic levels organize the metabolisms of all living systems. It is an interesting framework for reflecting on the metabolisms of cities.

Eugene Odum, who together with his brother Howard wrote ecology's first textbook in 1953, described an ecosystem as a community in which organic and inorganic elements interact to create a dynamic, interdependent system based on these three trophic levels. Howard Odum later observed that not only do nutrients flow through the system, but energy does, too. Entropy dictates that the energy flowing through a system dissipates over time, but Howard proposed that in healthy, generative systems, when energy and information combine, they become what he called "emergy," or new, stored information. While entropy is always wearing down a system, emergy helps build it back up. For example, it takes very little energy to store information in DNA, but it is a hugely valuable investment, as it contains the design instructions for each organism, and collectively, the ecosystem. This library of genes that shapes an ecological community keeps changing, filtered by selection pressures and switched on and off by epigenetics so that the adaptive capacity of the system is enhanced by the diversity of its evolutionary options.

For an ecosystem to thrive, it must be sufficiently diverse, providing opportunities for multiple connections between species' inputs and outputs. If the elements of a system are too similar, something ecologists call "limiting similarity," the variety of its interconnections is reduced, and it becomes more vulnerable to stress and volatility. Just as a healthy ecosystem integrates diversity into coherence, so too must a healthy urban metabolism.

Bringing nature back into cities enriches the diversity and adaptability of its metabolism and is one of the most cost-effective, pleasing ways to increase a city's health. These principles apply not only to a city's ecology, but also to its economy. As the collapse of the automobile-based economic ecology of Detroit demonstrated, the dependence of a city on a single industry is a limiting similarity. A diverse yet coherent economy like that of New York City, with its tech, marketing, design, publishing, and financial sectors working together to generate innovation, is far more likely to thrive. Its burgeoning economy has a balance of producers, consumers, and digesters, but they are producing, consuming, and digesting information, not nutrients. Cities also need healthy natural ecosystems—and biodiversity is a key to their health.

Biodiversity and Urban Parks

Alas, many of the world's urban parks are not particularly biodiverse. For example, new parks being developed around Shanghai are planted with just a few species of trees, grasses, and ornamental bushes that may look good, but are ecologically sterile. These parks don't host the primary producer species that provide food for birds and flowers for pollinators. When the first trophic level of the ecology is limited, the rest follow. Recognizing that the lack of biodiversity reduces nature's regenerative capacity, mayors of several rapidly growing cities have come together to shine a light on this issue and share solutions.

In 2007, Carlos Alberto Richa, the mayor of Curitiba, Brazil, held the first global meeting on "Biodiversity and Cities," which produced the Curitiba Convention. It called for a global movement to increase the biodiversity of cities, and expressed the mayors' deep concern over "the unprecedented rate of loss of biodiversity of our planet and its far-reaching environmental, social, economic, and cultural impacts, exacerbated by the effects of climate change."[23] The thirty-four mayors who signed it on behalf of their cities resolved "to integrate biodiversity concerns into urban planning and development, with a view to improving the lives of urban residents, in particular those affected by poverty, securing the livelihood base of cities and developing appropriate regulatory, implementation and decision-making mechanisms to ensure effective implementation of biodiversity plans."

It is telling that this declaration came from a group of mayors. Throughout the world, national governing bodies such as the U.S. Congress often can't come to a consensus to take far-reaching actions within their borders, much less make agreements with other countries. But mayors function at a level of governance at which the environmental, social, and economic issues palpably impact everyday life. Mayors are held accountable by their constituents to take action, and when they do their leadership can make a real difference. And thus, for example, Tulsa and Oklahoma City have become leading urban parks innovators, while the senators representing them in Washington resist all ecological funding and goal setting.

In 2009, Singapore, one of the signatories to the Curitiba Convention, recognizing how essential biodiversity was to its island ecology, developed an urban biodiversity index to track its progress.[24] Since the 1970s Singapore has consciously been shifting from a manufacturing-based economy to a sophisticated knowledge-based economy. Its leaders recognize that Singapore must compete for talent with every other city in the world, and that two keys to making it more competitive are the quality of Singapore's education systems and the city's livability—where biodiversity plays a vital role. Over the decades Singapore has built a superb public education system, ranked fifth in the world.[25] In order to advance its understanding of urban biodiversity Singapore's National University developed a superb biodiversity research center and a joint environmental leadership training program with Yale and the Smithsonian.

Like Curitiba, Singapore had spent decades making itself greener. From 1985 to 2010 the population of Singapore, a land-constrained city-state on the southern tip of Malaysia, doubled in size, from 2.5 million people to 5 million, and is expected to grow beyond 7.5 million by 2030. Yet by 2010, the city's green cover of parks, open space, and rooftop gardens grew from one third of Singapore's land area to one half. This simultaneous increase in population and green and open space was accomplished by increasing the density of the city's current footprint, rather than spreading outward. Singapore recognized that to be healthy, it needed to increase not only its green space, but also its biodiversity.

In 2008 Singapore set out to generate a long-range plan similar to New York City's PlaNYC 2030. Its goal was to shift from being a garden city to being a city in a garden by 2030. "The difference might sound very small," said Poon Hong Yuen, chief executive of the country's National Parks Board, "but it's a bit like saying my house has a garden and my house is in the middle of a garden. It means having pervasive greenery, as well as biodiversity, including wildlife, all around you."[26]

Since Singapore began to replace the monoculture of palm trees that lined its roads with a diverse range of trees more than five hundred new species of birds have been identified. Its biodiversity index has become a model for other cities, including Nagoya, London, Montreal, Brussels, and Curitiba. In 2010 the Summit on Cities and Biodiversity in Nagoya, Japan, attracted 240 mayors who committed to the Curitiba principles by signing the Aichi-Nagoya Declaration on local authorities and biodiversity. The declaration was framed by the following four ideas: biodiverse ecosystems provide important services to cities, such as purifying their water supplies, reducing flooding, and mitigating rising temperatures due to climate change; the well-being of ecosystems and urban populations is deeply interlinked; the ability of cities to shift the methods of production, distribution, and consumption of natural resources can contribute substantially to the recovery of the health of the planet's ecosystems; and by increasing partnerships with citizens, businesses, NGOs, and other governments, cities will achieve biodiversity that local governments cannot achieve alone.[27]

Natural Infrastructure and Climate Change

Natural infrastructure has helped save cities a great deal of money by absorbing storm water before it flows into sewer systems, but it can also help cities deal with one of climate change's most vexing issues: rising sea levels and increased storm surges. One of nature's most adaptive systems for dealing with these issues is found in wetlands. These are areas of shallow water typically found where a coastline, river, or marsh meets dry land. They benefit from what ecologists call the "edge effect": when two ecological systems meet, their DNA mixes and nutrients flow across the edges. This enhances the conditions of life, making wetlands important breeding grounds. Wetlands' edges are among the most biologically rich and diverse habitats on earth, as they lie at the heart of nature's water, nutrient, and carbon cycles.

Wetland plants transpire water into the atmosphere, seeding inland rains. Wetlands replenish groundwater, clean human toxins, remove nitrogen, absorb carbon, mitigate carbon dioxide, and transfer nutrients to plants and animals. While coastal wetlands occupy only 2 percent of the world's oceans, they're responsible for 50 percent of carbon transfer from oceans to sediments, an important and free method of taking carbon out of the atmosphere.[28] Wetlands also generate much of the world's fiber and timber. They provide fertile areas for growing rice, shrimp, and other foods that feed much of the world's population, especially in Asia. They were also the birthplace of the world's first cities.

Ironically, the urbanization to which wetlands gave birth is increasingly posing them an existential threat. Since 1900 more than half of the world's wetlands have disappeared. And as the world rapidly urbanizes, the speed of wetland destruction is increasing. Wetlands near our cities have been drained to make inexpensive land for development; filled to make way for new roads, as happened in Alexandria; or, in the case of Baltimore, turned into docks and shipyards. Urban and suburban wetlands are often inundated with fertilizer runoff and human wastes, overproducing algae and destroying their ability to serve as breeding grounds for fish and other species. They are vulnerable to invasive species transferred by boats. Wetlands are also drying up as their sources of water are consumed by growing populations. And if human activity won't directly finish them off, then the rising levels of heat, storms, and drought from climate change likely will. Unless we do something about it.

Although urban growth is among the biggest drivers of wetland destruction, city leaders are beginning to realize that biologically rich wetlands and natural coastal systems provide some of the least expensive and most effective ways for coastal cities to deal with climate change. Around the globe cities are restoring their natural buffers and combining them with human-made infrastructure to increase their resilience. Rotterdam, the largest port in Europe, is restoring its natural wetlands, in addition to using green roofs and a network of parks and street trees, as integrated elements of its climate change adaptation strategy. Seattle is rebuilding part of its central waterfront by burying the highway that ran through it and creating a long, biodiverse park at the water's edge.

Integrating Natural and Human Infrastructure

New York City has always been proud of its extraordinary water system, but in the 1980s, as development increased in the 1,600 square miles surrounding the city's upstate watershed, its water quality was threatened by sewage leaking from sprawling new homes. In 1991 the federal EPA required New York City to build a water filtration system at an estimated cost of $10 billion. Like Philadelphia, the city proposed an alternative: to purchase huge swaths of land surrounding its reservoirs and preserve them as natural filters for water flowing into the system. The cost of the preservation strategy was $1.5 billion, which offered significant savings from the capital outlay requested by the EPA, and the cost of labor, chemicals, and power for a series of large filtration plants, expenses that would only have escalated over the years.[29] The plan worked. Today New York City's water remains among the purest in the world, and its water system's operating expenses have been contained.

After this success New York City began to focus on enhancing benefits from other natural elements of its infrastructure. In 1996 two city departments—Parks and Transportation—began to work together on a Green Streets program to transform unused roadside areas into green spaces that could beautify neighborhoods, improve air quality, reduce air temperatures, absorb storm water, and calm traffic. Since the program's inception, more than 2,500 Green Streets projects have been created citywide. In 2010 the city expanded the program into a green infrastructure strategy by adding the Department of Environmental Protection to the collaboration. By restoring school playgrounds to grass from asphalt, planting swales of natural plants along sidewalks, and adding a million new trees, the city aims to reduce its combined sewer outflow by more than 3.8 billion gallons a year. By integrating differing agencies to achieve common objectives, the city is developing more coherent communities with quantifiable co-benefits such as cooler summers, reduced energy use, increased property values, and cleaner air.

New York City's JFK International Airport is a significant piece of infrastructure. Thirty-five thousand people work there, and planes carrying more than 48 million people take off or land there every year, consuming fuel, food, and replacement parts, and emitting air pollution, noise, solid waste, and runoff. But airplanes aren't the only frequent fliers into and out of the JFK area. Directly adjacent to the airport is Jamaica Bay, where more than 325 species of migrating birds rest and feed—more than twice the number of bird species in the Galápagos! The bay is an important part of the Hudson River Flyway, a corridor for annually migrating birds from Canada and New England flying south for the winter and returning north for the summer. Jamaica Bay lies in the heart of Gateway National Park, America's first urban national park and the only one in the country that can be reached by subway.

Surrounded by an airport, intense urban development, and four sewage treatment plants, Jamaica Bay suffers from intense nitrogen pollution that causes algae to bloom, suffocating its biodiversity. However, in 2011 the City and State of New York signed an agreement with the Natural Resources Defense Council (NRDC) and other environmental groups to cut by more than 50 percent the amount of nitrogen flowing into the bay from sewage treatment. The settlement commits $100 million to upgrades to the treatment plants, and $15 million to natural solutions, such as restoring the oyster beds that originally flourished in Jamaica Bay, using their cleansing power to reduce pollution and increase the biodiversity of its wetlands. It turns out that a single oyster can filter 35 gallons of water a day—with no operating expenses.[30]

When the Dutch arrived in New York's natural harbor early in the seventeenth century, it had 220,000 acres of oyster reefs, part of an extraordinary, pristine, productive ecology that thrived along the edge between the saltwater ecology of the Atlantic and the freshwater flowing in the Hudson River. During the 1800s, oystermen harvested more than half a billion oysters each year from the reefs, but by 1923, the last New York City bay oysters had been rendered inedible by pollution, or had been dredged or buried along with the nearby wetlands. New York City lost not only an important food source but also the protection that oyster reefs provide by acting as barriers to rough seas, dampening the force of large waves in heavy storms, and protecting shorelines from damage and erosion. In 2010, the Urban Assembly's Harbor School made a pledge to plant and grow a billion oysters in New York Harbor by 2030. In the process the school is training middle and high school students in marine biology, engineering, and food production.

Rebuild by Design

In 2012, Superstorm Sandy struck the New York metropolitan region hard. Sandy was the second "once-in-five-hundred-years" storm to hit New York City in two years, and in its wake the city, state, and federal governments began to take much more seriously projections for the coming century of climate change. The direct cost of Sandy has been estimated at roughly $50 billion, with the federal government picking up almost half the cost of repair. Knowing that such storms are likely to increase, Shaun Donovan, then secretary of HUD and the leader of the Presidential Hurricane Sandy Rebuilding Task Force, asked what we could be doing differently. How could we repair the damage wrought by Sandy to make the region more resilient to future extreme weather events? What would be the least expensive, most effective way to reduce storm risks in the future? To answer these questions he proposed a research and design competition, Rebuild by Design. The winning solutions all combined natural and human infrastructure.[31]

Rebuild by Design proposed a process very different from the normal disaster-recovery program's approach to rebuilding. It began by calling for teams of scientists, designers, economists, and sociologists to spend time in selected areas affected by Sandy, meeting with residents, government officials, businesses, and local not-for-profits to study the issues. Based on what they found, selected teams proposed new ways of redeveloping targeted areas in ways that simultaneously increased their environmental and economic resilience. Six teams were selected to carry out ten proposals, integrating human and natural systems. Each used extensive community outreach in its planning, big data, and Geographic Information Systems, GIS, which help communities visualize, question, analyze, and interpret data to understand relationships and patterns, and project future scenarios, all in service of environmental, economic, and educational goals.

One of these proposals, the Living Breakwaters project, was inspired by the Billion Oyster program. Its goal was to reduce stormwater surges along Staten Island by combining risk reduction, ecological regeneration, and social resilience. Rather than propose a single engineered breakwater, the landscape architect Kate Orff designed a necklace of underwater reefs, natural breakwaters, restored upland beaches, and wetlands. These integrate technical and natural coastal-protection systems and provide a coherent, multistrategy defense against storm surges. Using computer models and GIS data, Orff and her team were able to predict likely wind and water patterns, and design ways to mitigate them. At the same time, they planned their reefs to contain minipockets of habitat, increasing biodiversity, including shellfish, fin fish, and lobsters. Working with the Billion Oyster program and local schools, the project is also serving to educate students and the community. By integrating natural elements into a technical framework, the Living Breakwaters project will evolve with change rather than resist it.

The Hunts Point Lifelines Team, led by Penn Design and the landscape architecture firm Olin, looked at the vulnerability of one of the most important food hubs in the region's metabolism, the Hunts Point Market, sitting on a 690-acre peninsula jutting into the East River. If Hurricane Sandy had hit just a few hours later, coinciding with high tide, Hunts Point would have been flooded with toxic chemicals from adjacent wastewater treatment and chemical plants. The market is located in the South Bronx, home to the poorest congressional district in the United States. It is the region's largest source of fresh produce, fish, and meat, and yet because it is fenced for security, it is surrounded by a food desert. The team asked, "How can the market mitigate the dangers of climate change while also doing a better job of connecting with its neighbors?"

In response, the team designed a levee lined with natural wetlands to protect the market from flooding. The levee will be tied into the South Bronx Greenway, making it publicly accessible, with ecology study labs along its length to serve as a recreational and educational resource for the entire South Bronx community. To ensure a reliable source of energy to meet the market's huge demand for refrigeration, the team proposed a co-generation plant, which would provide power to waiting trucks, which currently must idle their engines to power their refrigeration systems. This will reduce costs and asthma-causing pollution. And to better serve the neighborhood, they proposed that the wholesale market create a community-serving fresh food market.

The Bjarke Ingels Group/Starr Whitehouse team proposed to protect lower Manhattan from storm surges and rising sea levels with the creation of a huge arcing berm, functioning like a Dutch dike, protecting ten miles of vulnerable waterfront and the neighborhoods adjacent to them. The area includes New York's most densely settled area, the largest central business district in the nation, with a GDP of $500 billion, and Wall Street, which is a key hub in the global financial system and is increasingly becoming a tech/publishing hub. It also includes the homes of 95,000 low-income, elderly, and disabled residents, who in times of climate distress have nowhere else to go. The berm is designed to be permeable, easily crossed when there is no storm, and covered with native-species gardens, community gardens, tai chi platforms, skate parks, and movable panels that double as storm protection and walls for public art. The adjacent streets will be planted with cooling trees and bioswales, water-catching depressions lined with indigenous plants, to capture and clean rainwater. Weaving it all together is a system of bike paths and walkways that connects residents to other parts of the city.

These Rebuild by Design plans combined extensive community-based participation with science- and engineering-based solutions to increase the resilience of their targeted neighborhoods. Each proposal concluded that natural infrastructure was an essential part of the solution, a key element in enhancing the well-being of the community and the natural environment that envelops it all.

As climate change accelerates, cities are increasingly turning to innovative combinations of technical and natural infrastructure to solve urban environmental issues in affordable ways. Building on Olmsted's concept of an emerald necklace, cities are once again beginning to connect natural networks, tying together local gardens, small and large parks, natural corridors along rivers, and restored wetlands to create a thriving natural environment, rich in biodiversity. These systems temper cities, increasing their resilience to climate change, cooling their temperatures, and improve the temperament of their citizens.

CHAPTER 8

Green Buildings, Green Urbanism

BUFFETED BY THE megatrends of climate change and resource depletion, our cities will need multiple strategies to resiliently adapt. In previous chapters we discussed the investments cities can make in transportation, food, water, wastewater, solid waste, and natural infrastructure to make their metabolism more resilient. These provide much of the flexible armature upon which cities thrive.

Another important element of any city's metabolism is energy. In the suburbs, automobiles often are the largest energy consumer, with the energy expended to get to and from homes often as high as the energy used in the home itself. But the story is different in cities. For example, 80 percent of all energy used in New York City is consumed in its buildings. If one wants to make a city more resilient, greening its buildings is a high-leverage place to intervene. A city can reduce the energy and water use of its buildings with an integrated package of regulations, incentives, investments, measurements, and feedback to shift occupant behaviors. Such programs also make economic sense. Energy and water reductions of up to 30 percent typically cost very little to achieve, and generate a return on investment on the order of 20 percent a year for their owners. With appropriate financing, even deeper reductions are achievable.

Green Buildings

The green building movement began in the late 1960s as part of the cultural flowering of alternative ideas. Local builders and architects began experimenting with new technologies, designing and building homes made of logs, adobe, and other local, natural materials; using solar systems for electricity, heating, and hot water; and using composting toilets for waste. E. F. Schumacher, a British economist who wrote the influential book *Small Is Beautiful: Economics As If People Mattered*, described the systems needed for the world to regain its natural balance as "appropriate technologies." These, he proposed, are technical systems that are small-scale, decentralized, labor-intensive, energy-efficient, environmentally sound, and locally controlled.[1]

In 1973 instability in the Middle East caused oil prices to shoot up from $20 a barrel, where they had been for nearly a century, to $100 in less than three years. The United States was completely unprepared for this dramatic spike in energy costs, which affected almost every aspect of the economy, and hit the building and transportation industries especially hard. Real estate values dropped. Higher oil and electricity costs pushed many struggling building owners in inner-city neighborhoods like the South Bronx over the edge, leading to an increase in abandonment. American automakers lost market share to much more efficient Japanese and European car manufacturers, forcing the closure of plants throughout the Midwest. The ensuing economic crisis provided a sobering glimpse into how dependent our civilization had become on fossil fuel.

President Jimmy Carter, who was deeply interested in science and the environment, responded by significantly expanding government investment in renewable-energy research. As a symbol of his commitment to create alternatives to foreign oil, President Carter put solar panels on the roof of the White House. Unfortunately, Carter also created incentives to shift most of the nation's electricity-generating plants from burning foreign oil to burning domestic coal, accelerating climate change and spewing mercury and other toxic waste into the air.

The oil shortages of the mid-1970s that awakened the United States to its energy vulnerability hit low-income families hardest, often forcing them to choose between paying for heating oil and gasoline, or other necessities like food and medication. To provide relief, in 1976 Congress created the Weatherization Assistance program, which helped low-income and senior owners of existing homes make them more energy efficient, freeing up funds for food, health care, education, transportation, and housing.

The Other 99

In 2016 there were roughly 140 million buildings in the United States, of which a majority were single-family homes. All together these buildings consume 40 quadrillion BTUs of energy annually.[2] In boom economic years the United States increases its stock of buildings by about 1 percent, whereas in slow times the nation's building stock increases by only about a third of a percent. Although it's important for all new buildings to be as energy efficient as possible, they consume only 1 percent of the nation's energy. Increasing the efficiency of the other 99 percent, the nation's *existing* building stock, has a much larger impact. Weatherizing and upgrading existing homes—sealing up cracks and gaps in the exterior walls, adding insulation, replacing old single-pane windows with double-pane low "e" windows, substituting new, efficient water heaters and boilers for old ones, and installing Energy Star–rated appliances—is an easy first step toward creating greener and more economically viable communities, and reducing the emission of climate-changing greenhouse gases. And weatherization makes economic sense. Federal studies show that every dollar invested in home energy conservation pays back $2.51.[3]

These simple fixes not only can reduce energy use in our buildings by 30–40 percent but also can increase employment. A study by the Center for American Progress projected that the United States could create 650,000 permanent jobs by weatherizing 40 percent of its homes. Ninety-one percent of those jobs would be with small businesses, companies that employ fewer than twenty people. And 89 percent of the materials used in weatherization are made in the United States.[4]

If a nation wants to be more resilient in the face of climate change, economic volatility, or potential energy shortages, the easiest place to begin is with energy-efficiency retrofits of its existing buildings. We also need to make new buildings greener, and it's not hard to do.

Designing and Constructing New Green Buildings

The energy shortages of the 1970s were followed by an energy glut in the 1980s. Americans quickly forgot the oil crisis and the energy conservation measures it inspired. The Reagan administration, with its pro-oil energy policy, took the symbolic step of removing President Carter's solar panels from the roof of the White House and, more detrimentally, cut the budget of the National Renewable Energy Lab by 90 percent. But the most damaging legacy of the Reagan administration was its promotion of the false notion that investing in environmental strategies, and regulating environmental impacts, must inevitably undermine economic vitality. We now know that environmental protection and economic development can be very mutually reinforcing, but it's been hard to correct the misunderstanding that we must make a choice between the economy and the environment. In fact, China is now spending 12 percent of its GDP on health and other costs related to its horrendous urban air pollution. So failure to protect the environment is very expensive.

But until the 2000s, the American environmental community also didn't recognize the conjoined environmental and economic potential of green cities. It, too, believed that the economy and nature were deeply separate.

Even today, despite the fact that twice as many Americans work for solar industries as work in the coal industry,[5] many Americans still believe that environmental regulations, incentives, and investments stifle growth. In fact, nothing could be further from the truth. Wind, solar, and biomass generate 2.5–9.5 times as many jobs as coal, oil, and gas for every $1 million contribution to GDP.[6] The World Economic Forum's 2013 Green Investment Report notes, "Economic growth and sustainability are interdependent, you cannot have one without the other. . . . Greening global economic growth is the only way to satisfy the needs of today's population, and up to nine billion people by 2050, driving development and well-being while reducing greenhouse gas emissions and increasing natural resource productivity. . . . The investment required for water, agriculture, telecoms, power, transport, buildings, industrial and forestry sectors, according to current growth projections stands at about US $5 trillion a year to 2020. . . . The challenge will be to enable an unprecedented shift in long term investment from conventional to green alternatives to avoid locking in less efficient, emissions intensive technologies for decades to come."[7]

As the 1980s gave way to the 1990s, a small group of committed architects, engineers, builders, and academics began to consider how to develop more environmentally responsible and energy-efficient new buildings. In 1993 the U.S. Green Building Council (USGBC) was formed as a nonprofit trade organization with a mandate to promote the design, construction, and operation of green buildings. The USGBC had no regulatory power, but its founders, Mike Italiano, David Gottfried, and Rick Federizzi, surmised that if they could create a market for green buildings and green building services, this leverage point could change the design and construction industries' culture. To do so, they proposed to independently certify green attributes of buildings so that their greenness could be evaluated and compared, and "bragging rights" could be conferred on buildings that achieved the highest ratings.

In 1998, the USGBC issued its first green building rating system, LEED, an acronym for Leadership in Energy and Environmental Design. The LEED system assigns points for a variety of environmental attributes, including energy efficiency, use of recycled materials, water efficiency, and use of low-toxicity materials: the higher the point score, the greener the building. Buildings that meet minimum standards can be certified as LEED buildings, and those that perform better than baseline achieve rankings of silver, gold, or platinum. By 2015 the LEED system had spread from the United States to much of the rest of the world. More than 3.3 billion square feet had been certified under the program, a number that was growing at a rate of almost 2 million square feet a day. LEED particularly appeals to the higher end of the market: almost half of all new buildings valued over $50 million are being LEED certified. The founders of LEED were right—voluntary certification and transparent information could transform markets. LEED gold certification is now part of the definition of the world's best office buildings, and top companies and law firms will not consider moving into a new building without it.

The growth of green buildings improves the resilience of cities, helping them use less energy and water. Green building also supports the development of local cyclical economies—construction and demolition wastes are easily recycled into new construction materials. LEED-certified buildings on average are now diverting more than 40 percent of their demolition and construction wastes from landfills to recycling, with the best reaching 100 percent. This involves recycling about 80 million tons of waste a year, and the amount is expected to grow to 540 million tons by 2030.[8]

One of the strengths of LEED is that its point system is continuously being improved by feedback from the owners, architects, and contractors who use it. It is also increasingly focusing on outcomes, requiring that certified buildings measure and verify their green achievements. The program has also diversified, rating hospitals, industrial buildings, and university labs.

In its early years LEED was not well suited to multifamily housing, and this was especially true when it came to affordable housing. The solution to this problem came in the form of the Enterprise Green Community Guidelines.

The Greening of Affordable Housing

Enterprise Community Partners is a national not-for-profit that brings more than a billion dollars a year of financing, technical assistance, and other community-enhancing solutions to low-income neighborhoods throughout the United States. In 2004 Enterprise launched the Green Communities program to encourage the design and construction of green affordable housing.

Over the last decade a great deal of research has been focused on the nexus between transportation, health, and affordability for low-income families. After the cost of housing, transportation is the second-largest expense for low-income and working-class families who depend on the automobile to get to and from work, school, shopping, and so on. When affordable housing is well served by public transportation and residents can easily walk to nearby workplaces, schools, retail stores, and medical providers, it not only saves them the cost of auto ownership, but is healthier for both people and the environment. The Enterprise Green Community Guidelines encourage the development of affordable housing in transit-rich locations with other services within walking distance.

The Green Community Guidelines also encourage developers to address other issues typically faced by low-income residents. For example, they often live in poorly insulated homes, with huge winter heating and summer air-conditioning costs. Reducing their energy and water usage helps lower the high utility bills low-income families must pay for heat, air-conditioning, lighting, and washing. The air quality of low-income neighborhoods is often quite toxic because they tend to be located on cheap land, close to industrial areas, power plants, bus depots, highways, and incinerators. These direct exposures not only make residents of low-income communities more prone to illnesses, but also reduce their resilience, making them more susceptible to environmental triggers in the home such as glues, caulks, binders, and other volatile compounds found in typical paints, kitchen cabinets, and flooring. The Enterprise Guidelines require not only the use of nontoxic materials in the home, but also sufficient air circulation to clear out toxins.

To increase the scale and impact of its green guidelines, Enterprise focused on another key leverage point in the metabolism of urban development: financing. All affordable housing is funded by a complex package of public and private financing, so Enterprise began to educate the banks, investors, cities, and states that fund affordable housing on the benefits of its guidelines. The green program added only 1 or 2 percent to a building's construction budget, an amount that was easily repaid from lower operating costs. Enterprise Green Community criteria are now required for construction of affordable housing by most major cities in the United States, by more than half of its states, and by all of the major banks. By 2020 is it very likely that all new affordable housing built in the United States will be built green, the first building sector ever to meet this goal.

Via Verde—Gardens in the Sky

At the groundbreaking ceremony in May 2010 for Via Verde, a new model of green affordable urban housing located in the heart of the South Bronx, Borough President Ruben Diaz, Jr., proclaimed, "Let it be known throughout the world, that where the South Bronx once burned, we are building gardens in the sky."

Via Verde is full of green design features, but none is more visible than its garden-covered roofs. The project sits on a long, narrow site running north to south, bordered by a rail line. It has public housing and a high school on one side, and a long, low retail and office building on the other. Via Verde's design strategy turned the site's odd shape into an advantage. The tallest part of the complex was placed on the north side, and then stepped down so that it is lowest on the south side, allowing its roofs maximum exposure to the summer sun. These roofs provide the community with an orchard, fruit and vegetable gardens, and outdoor places for children to play, for seniors to read and relax, and for all to exercise.

The project was an outgrowth of the "New Housing New York Legacy Competition," a brainchild of the New York branch of the American Institute of Architects, Enterprise Community Partners, and then–New York City Housing Commissioner Shaun Donovan. The contest challenged developers to come up with a new model for green affordable housing development. The winning co-developers were Phipps Houses and my own company, Jonathan Rose Companies, with the design by the architecture firms Dattner Architects and Grimshaw.[9] With Via Verde, we set out to see if we could not only provide energy-efficient affordable housing in a transit-rich location, but also improve health outcomes for its residents. Our premise was that green affordable housing constructed from healthier materials— with lower energy costs; lots of public transit, shopping, and other services nearby; and an on-site health clinic—would increase a family's resilience, its ability to absorb adversity. In addition, if the project was architecturally stunning, it would contribute a sense of pride to its neighborhood. The premise proved to be true.

Via Verde, completed in 2012, was designed to serve families with a mix of incomes, as income diversity tends to create healthier communities and better opportunities for the children of lower-income families. When it opened, its 151 affordable apartments rented for $460 to $1,090 a month to families earning between $17,000 and $57,000 a year. The project's 71 co-op apartments sold for $79,000 and $192,000, depending on size, and were affordable to households earning between $37,000 and $160,000 a year. Unit layouts include flats, innovative duplexes, and live-work units with a first-floor workspace. The building also has a ground-floor health-care center operated by Montefiore Hospital, a pharmacy, and community facilities that include a terrific gym, a community room, a kitchen, a wonderful outdoor children's play area, an amphitheater, orchards, and gardens.

Via Verde's apartments were designed to be at least 30 percent more energy efficient than a standard new building. Motion sensors in stairways and corridors conserve electricity, turning lights on only when needed. Its apartments feature Energy Star–rated appliances, nontoxic materials, and high-efficiency mechanical systems. Its large windows provide panoramic views, daylight, and fresh air. Its elevators, corridors, heating system, and pumps are powered during the day by a 64-kilowatt solar system.

More than 80 percent of the project's construction and demolition waste was recycled, and more than 20 percent of the materials in the building came from recycled sources. Another 20 percent of the materials were locally manufactured, minimizing transportation energy and supporting the local economy. For example, the concrete blocks in Via Verde were made a hundred miles away in a working-class Hudson River town by the Kingston Block Company, using regionally recycled materials in its concrete products. Via Verde was also designed to consume less water by using water-conserving toilets, showers, and sinks. And the community gardens and orchards are watered with rainwater, which is captured and saved in rooftop storage tanks. This also reduces runoff into the city's sewer systems.

In keeping with the Enterprise Green Community Guidelines, Via Verde's residents can easily walk to shopping, they live literally adjacent to schools and sports fields, and are just a few blocks away from subway lines that reach the job-rich East and West Sides of Manhattan.

Green Roofs

Via Verde is not alone in celebrating green roofs. Their rapid spread to all kinds of buildings is based on their many benefits. The first is aesthetic: they look great, and enhance real estate values. Many market-rate apartment and office buildings now use green roofs as a leasing feature. Green roofs also provide direct economic benefits. They protect the underlying waterproofing layer so that it lasts longer. By retaining and then evaporating water, they cool the roof and the area under it, easing air-conditioning demands; this also reduces flow into the storm-water system, and the water that does flow out of the building is naturally filtered. Plants on a green roof also capture particulate matter and filter noxious gases, cleaning the air. They absorb sound, reducing street noise by 40 decibels. Properly planned, they can improve a city's biodiversity. And like weatherization programs, green roofs create construction and maintenance jobs, they increase occupant well-being, and finally, they grow healthy food, available to residents with minimal transportation costs.

When green building strategies are able to generate multiple benefits like these, they are rapidly adopted into the mainstream of development practice.

Passive Resilience

In 2005, Alex Wilson, editor of *Environmental Building News*, was ruminating on the length of time it took New Orleans to achieve even the most basic levels of recovery after Hurricane Katrina. Electric power was out for months. In the damp, hot climate, buildings quickly grew moldy, making them uninhabitable. Wilson proposed that in addition to being green, buildings needed a quality he called passive survivability, "the ability of a building to maintain critical life-support conditions for its occupants if services such as power, heating fuel, or water are lost for an extended period."[10] For example, if a building collected rainwater in a cistern and the city water supply system was disabled in a storm, the cistern could provide residents with some fresh water. And if its first-floor walls were made of mold-resistant materials like concrete block rather than drywall, the building could continue to be occupied after it was cleaned up, instead of having to be evacuated until the drywall could be replaced.

In the aftermath of both Katrina and Sandy, oil refineries were shut down and fuel storage and pumping facilities lost power; as a result, gas stations ran out of diesel fuel and gasoline, and a few days after that, diesel generators died. Hospital surgeries were finished by candlelight. Patients had to be moved, often carried down flights of stairs in the absence of working elevators. People, buildings, communities, and cities thrive when they are connected to larger networks and systems, but they need to be designed to function when they're disconnected. They need to be able to survive when urban systems go down.

Via Verde was designed with passive survivability in mind. If the power goes out in a stifling hot summer, residents can open windows and benefit from natural cooling, since every apartment is designed to face in at least two directions. This, along with ceiling fans and concrete ceilings and floors, reduces each apartment's use of energy during a hot summer, and stores that heat in winter. The walls are well insulated, and windows have exterior sunshades that protect them from the hot summer sun, but allow in the sun's warmth in winter. The project's colorful stairwells are adjacent to the outside of the building and provided with windows so that if the power goes out they will be naturally illuminated by day, saving the battery-powered emergency lighting for nighttime.

Passive Houses

The most advanced examples of passive resilience are "passive houses," a term developed in 1998 by Professors Bo Adamson of Lund University, Sweden, and Wolfgang Feist, at the University of Innsbruck, in Austria. Passive houses are so well insulated they can be kept warm by the body heat of their residents, lights, and a few small appliances. When the power goes out they may become colder, but they won't freeze. They typically use less than 20 percent of the energy of normal buildings.

Currently passive houses cost 10 percent more to build, although that cost is rapidly declining. The economic and environmental benefits of the energy they save year after year are enormous.

Brooklyn Passive Townhouse. The lighter buildings of this infrared photograph represent heat passing through the facades of typical brownstones. The well-insulated passive house in the center shows very little heat loss. *(Sam McAfee, sgBuild)*

Healthy Buildings

The first round of green buildings focused on reducing their impact on the natural environment. The next generation added an emphasis on the health of their residents. In 1997 my firm co-developed Maitri Issan House with the Greyston Foundation, a Yonkers, New York–based not-for-profit that provides housing, jobs, preschool, and health-care facilities for homeless and low-income families. Maitri Issan House was designed for people with HIV/AIDS who, at the time it was built, were dying from the disease. It was one of the nation's first green buildings to specifically focus on the health of its residents. Along with seniors, young children, and people with chronic respiratory disease, HIV/AIDS patients, with their compromised immune systems, are very sensitive to volatile organic chemicals (VOCs). In developing Maitri Issan House we sought to eliminate every source of VOCs, even building our own furniture to avoid the chemical-laden furniture that was then the only choice in the market. The project also included an on-site medical center that provided both traditional and integrative therapies.

By the early 2000s it had become clear that VOCs were connected to a global epidemic of childhood asthma. We now know that VOCs in the home can cause damage to the liver, kidneys, and central nervous system, as well as cancer, in addition to allergic skin reactions, nausea, vomiting, headaches, fatigue, dizziness, and loss of coordination. Modern buildings are full of these toxic compounds. Kitchen cabinets are made with glues that emit formaldehyde, and carpets, vinyl flooring, and the adhesives that hold them to the floor, as well as paints and caulks, are often laden with VOCs. The Healthy Building Network notes that vinyl sheet flooring, used increasingly in both affordable and market-rate housing, is laden with carcinogens, mutagens, and developmental and reproductive toxicants. A sixty-unit apartment building with vinyl flooring is likely to contain eleven tons of hazardous chemicals. Eventually, it is likely that cities will ban the use of these toxic compounds, as the evidence of their negative health effects becomes more widely known.

The health impacts of VOC emissions, chemical toxins, mold, and insect infestation are significant drivers of health-care costs. Columbia-Presbyterian Hospital in northwestern Harlem struggled to deal with the epidemic of asthma that was overloading its emergency room. In an effort to reduce the number of visits, it identified its top hundred asthma patients and increased their drug prescriptions, but that didn't work. The hospital eventually figured out that the most effective way to cure these patients was not to give them more drugs but to go to their apartments and clean up the mold and other toxins that were triggering their asthma. The lives of the hospital's patients rapidly improved, their health-care costs dropped significantly, and the emergency room was freed up to address other kinds of urgent care. Recognizing this connection between health and the home environment, doctors in Boston are now authorized to write a prescription for a building inspection if they believe that a health problem is caused by an issue in a patient's home. But there are other aspects of a building that can also improve its residents' health.

On Via Verde's seventh floor, a gym full of up-to-date exercise equipment opens out into a roof garden designed to encourage fitness. The garden also provides quiet, reflective space, as meditation and yoga have proved to be very effective in reducing stress and increasing human resilience. The ground-floor community medical center, run by the Bronx-based Montefiore Hospital, serves both Via Verde's residents and people in the neighborhood, encouraging a shift from expensive emergency room health care to more effective and less expensive preventive health care. A local pharmacy sits beside it, and nearby bicycle storage areas encourage biking, while state-of-the-art playgrounds encourage youngsters to run and play outside, in the complex's secure, sunlit courtyard.

New York City's health department is carrying out a five-year study to determine if living in Via Verde makes a difference to the health of its residents. Every resident who moved into the building when it was first leased was given a health survey. An equal number of residents who applied to the building but did not move in were also surveyed. After five years of data collection, they will be able to compare and see if the building made a difference.

Via Verde's emphasis on health and exercise is intentional. People living in low-income communities are particularly susceptible to chronic health issues, including depression. As the Gallup-Healthways Well-Being Survey notes, "Americans in poverty are more likely than those who are not to struggle with a wide array of chronic health problems, and depression disproportionately affects those in poverty the most. About 31 percent of Americans in poverty say they have at some point been diagnosed with depression, compared with 15.8 percent of those not in poverty. Impoverished Americans are also more likely to report asthma, diabetes, high blood pressure, and heart attacks— which are likely related to the higher level of obesity found for this group—31.8% vs. 26% for adults not in poverty."[11] Given the special vulnerability of impoverished families to suffer from depression and chronic diseases, the benefits of exercise and a healthy diet have an even more positive effect on low-income families than they do for those who are better off.

As the health-care payment system moves toward paying hospitals, HMOs, and other providers a fixed price per person per year, they are motivated to keep their patients healthier at lower costs. One of the least expensive ways to do this is by encouraging healthier buildings. And the Robert Wood Johnson Foundation's work demonstrates that neighborhood attributes such as walkability and ten-minute access to parks and open space have positive health benefits. So the built environment affects the quality not only of nature's health, but also of our own. Perhaps soon our health insurance rates will vary depending on the greenness of our homes and our neighborhoods.

The Impact of Human Behavior

As buildings become more and more energy efficient, the behavior of their occupants becomes an increasingly significant determinant of energy use. The United States Army discovered this when it tried to figure out how green it should make the new family housing that it was planning to build. It created a test community with four model homes—one designed to normal army standards, one to modest green standards, one that was very green, and one that was designed to be net zero, with enough solar power on its roof, and energy-efficient appliances inside, that it should not need any additional energy at all. But after the army collected a year's worth of data on how the homes performed, the results were confounding. The normal house used the least amount of energy, the net-zero house used the most. What happened? The answer lay in the behavior of the residents. The family that lived in the normal house was very careful—they turned off their lights and TV when they left a room, dried their wash on a clothesline, and used their ceiling fan for cooling except when it was very hot. The net-zero family was the opposite, with lights, TVs, electronic games, and air-conditioning running all the time. The way we build is not enough, the way that we live also matters.

And behavior also matters in office buildings. In 1985, plug loads, the power drawn by plugged-in devices, consumed 15 percent of the energy used in a typical office building. By 2010, office plug loads had grown to 45 percent. Every year we seem to accumulate more and more devices that require electricity—computers, smartphones, iPads, smart whiteboards, coffeepots, microwaves, and popcorn makers. Some of our behavior in buildings is affected by the building's design; if a room is poorly lit, for example, we're more likely to add a desk lamp; if the heating system is not well balanced, we might open a window in the middle of the winter when a room is too hot, or plug in an electric heater if it's too cold. Many behaviors are the result of designs that could be easily improved.

One such strategy is called choice architecture. The way our technology is designed creates a natural bias toward certain behaviors. The toilets in another green demonstration building, the National Renewal Energy Laboratory (NREL) in Boulder, Colorado, were designed to save water with a handle that single-flushes when it's lifted up, and double-flushes when it's pushed down. Despite the water-saving technology, very little water was actually saved. Most people are used to pushing down to flush. And it turns out that a surprising number of people flush public toilets with their foot. If the toilet had been designed to single-flush with a downward push, far more people would use that feature—and save water. Another example can be found in American hotel rooms, where it's all too easy to leave the room for the day with all the lights on; in European hotels occupants must turn on the lights by placing their keys in a switch that turns them off when the key is removed and the occupant leaves.

People also set their behavior according to what they perceive as social norms; as we've seen, composting is a social norm in San Francisco, but not in São Paulo. When most people in an office turn off their lights when leaving a room, others follow, even those who may not do so at home. Shifting behaviors has two advantages: it's quick and it's essentially free. So in designing an environmental strategy it always makes sense to think through the behavioral issues that could impede or improve its efficacy.

The Garrison Institute's Climate Mind and Behavior program, an early voice in the role that behavior could play to reduce the human impact on the climate, identified feedback as a key leverage point to shift behavior: the same signal that tunes natural ecologies can also tune our behavior. People who live or work in places where they pay their own energy or water bill will use much less energy or water than those who don't pay for it. They are more likely to turn off the lights when they leave a room, or to wait for a full load before washing their clothes. When utilities are included in the rent we are more likely to waste them, because we think of them as free. The problem is that we often don't get our utility bills until a month later, so it's harder to connect our actions with their costs. Smart meters can give people real-time feedback. For example, a TV on standby gives the illusion that it's off, but uses more electricity than an efficient refrigerator. With a smart meter display in the home, a resident is more likely to unplug the TV when the meter then reports how much that would save a month.

Behavior-change strategies are increasingly being used by cities to increase their health and resilience. By creating separated bike lanes, they are making biking easier and safer. As a result, it is the fastest-growing method of commuting for trips under ten miles in the United States. In cities that require smart meters to give real-time feedback to residents, energy usage is down. When cities raise water rates, water usage declines. When cities fine residents for not separating their garbage, recycling increases. When a city makes its environmental goals explicit and thinks through how to encourage behavior shifts, it gets the best results.

The Living Building Challenge

In 2006 the International Living Building Institute and the Cascadia Green Building Council issued the greenest and most holistic building guidelines to date, the Living Building Challenge. They posed the questions, "What if every single act of design and construction made the world a better place? What if every intervention resulted in greater biodiversity; increased soil health; additional outlets for beauty and personal expression; a deeper understanding of climate, culture and place; a realignment of our food and transportation systems; and a more profound sense of what it means to be a citizen of a planet where resources and opportunities are provided fairly and equitably?"[12]

These are extraordinary questions that call for a shift from designing and constructing green buildings with the goal of reducing their environmental impacts, to designing and constructing buildings that contribute to restoring a healthy, integrated natural and social ecology. Imagine a city as a forest where every plant, animal, and soil organism contributes to the health of the entire ecosystem. The Living Building Challenge calls on us to think of each new building in the same way.

The first urban multistory building to meet the Living Building Challenge was the Bullitt Foundation's office building in Seattle, the Bullitt Center, opened in 2014. The building's flat rooftop solar system generates 60 percent more electricity than the building requires and sends the balance back to the grid. This remarkable net positive energy outcome was achieved by optimizing several building systems to reduce energy use, and integrating them. For example, the building's windows use highly insulating glass, and computer-controlled sensors and timers open and close exterior blinds to maximize comfort while minimizing energy use. Windows automatically open and close to circulate air throughout the building. Blinds can even be tilted at different angles to let in more or less of the sunlight to warm and light the building, while a solar-powered geothermal system uses the constant 55-degree temperature of the earth to supplement the sun's heat and to cool the building.

The solar photovoltaic panels on the roof also collect rainwater that is used to water the building's gardens, to flush its toilets, and to flow through its showers. The building's wastewater is recycled, collected, and filtered in the basement before being pumped to a natural wetland on the roof where it is cleaned by natural organisms, then piped under the building to recharge the natural groundwater system, now every bit as clean as it was when it started the cycle as rain. And the building's managers have promoted a green culture to shift its occupants' behaviors to support the building's green goals.

Microgrids

Our urban systems tend to be connected, but not interconnected. Buildings are directly linked to street, water, sewer, electrical, and data systems, but these are usually fixed one-way relationships. Once we begin to construct buildings like the Bullitt Center, which generate excess solar power and clean water, we can begin to interconnect them into ecological neighborhoods, or ecodistricts. One of the easiest places to begin is with electrical power. In most cities electricity is generated at a few large plants, often powered by fossil fuels, and then fed into the electricity grid. These grids are often managed by outdated analog systems, which do not respond well to volatility. When the grid is overstressed, the whole system crashes, as it did in northern India in 2012. In the United States, grid disruptions cost the economy between $25 billion and $70 billion each year in lost output and wages, spoiled inventory, delayed production, and damage to the grid.[13]

One of the advantages of extended power networks is that they can connect cities to remote solar, wind, and hydro energy resources. But the energy system becomes much more resilient when it integrates the large-scale centralized power system known as the bulk power supply with smaller, local, smart, digitally controlled systems like the solar system on the roof of the Bullitt Center. This combination of a range of energy suppliers and scales of supply, along with local battery storage, controlled by intelligent feedback, is called a microgrid. According to Robert Galvin, former chair and CEO of Motorola, "This emerging web of smart micro grids is like a medieval knight's chain mail, a flexible array that is stronger than the sum of its parts."[14]

Without such integration, the current bulk power system is hugely inefficient. A steam-turbine coal-fired power plant is able to convert only 39–47 percent of the coal's heat to electricity. Another 6.5 percent of the energy is lost due to line losses, or "friction" in the grid.[15] The bulk power system is also inflexible. Coal-fired power plants, designed to run twenty-four hours a day, are not easy to turn on and off. And they are terribly polluting.

Microgrids can integrate several sources of power: solar, wind, biogas from waste treatment plants, co-generation, which combines power generation and heating, and bulk power. Local sources of power suffer much smaller line losses. Buildings like the Bullitt Center connected to a smart grid can be both consumers and producers, sometimes buying power, sometimes selling it. Their occupants can also provide power from battery-powered cars parked in their garages during the day, when energy prices are high, and recharge them at night when energy prices are lower. As battery technology improves, more buildings will use them to provide power during the day when it is most expensive, and buy energy at night when its cost is lower, smoothing out demand and increasing the resilience of the system.

Microgrids come in a range of sizes; they can be small enough to power a single building using rooftop solar panels, or gas-fired co-generation plants. Neighborhood-scaled microgrids are becoming increasingly viable. As we have seen, water-treatment plants can generate excess electricity from their biogas digesters to power thousands of nearby homes. Solar power on the roofs of large industrial buildings can also produce excess power to share with neighbors.

Smart grids form mesh networks, where each node has the capacity to generate and disseminate its own energy and information, but is also able to relay the energy and information of other nodes. If one or more links in the networks go down, others can pick up the slack. This allows microgrids to be self-healing. Because multiple, dynamically balanced energy and information pathways are woven together, if one link breaks, the others continue to provide power. Smart grids can detect power imbalances or outages, analyze the causes, and respond. They observe the behavior of the humans and equipment that use power, learn to predict their patterns, and can provide feedback to help reduce use in times of stress. This integration of energy and information begins to function as emergy, Howard Odum's pathway to increase the complexity of a system in spite of entropy.

Smart microgrids are informed not only by big data about the larger electrical system that they are part of, but also by small data, localized data that may be of little interest to the larger system but is meaningful on a smaller scale. For example, one of the most energy-consuming aspects of a refrigerator is its defrosting system. During a power shortage a smart local grid could identify all the refrigerators it is serving and signal them to disable their defrosters until the emergency is over. A meshed energy/information network can provide consumers with direct feedback on their energy use, helping to shift energy behaviors, and through social media to encourage a culture of energy conservation. Microgrids also support equality in ecological economics. In contrast to an electrical system operated by a few giant investor-owned utilities, most elements of a meshed energy system are owned by users. Their prosperity arises from the diversity, coherence, and sustainability of the whole.

As the world urbanizes it is electrifying, and this is good. Perhaps no modern system transforms people's lives as much as electricity. It is responsible for tremendous increases in productivity. Its light makes it easier for children to study at night; it supports cell phone and Internet access, enhancing people's connections to one another and to a world of information.

The conventional grid system simply isn't up to the task of bringing electricity's benefits to every home on earth. The International Energy Agency projects that globally $250 billion per year needs to be spent on energy infrastructure investments for the next fifty years. But there is another model for how this could be spent. As the world's telecommunications systems expanded into the developing world, they skipped over the expensive, centralized fixed landline model and went directly to the distributed wireless cell phone model. As a result, by 2014, 6 billion of the world's 7 billion people had access to a mobile phone, 1.5 billion more than had access to flush toilets. In the same way, micro-grids can spread the benefits of electrification more quickly and cheaply to the world's rapidly growing new cities and urban slums, and more easily incorporate green energy sources such as solar and wind power.

Ecodistricts

Ecodistricts, neighborhoods that work together to plan and imple-ment integrated systems, apply the intelligence, range of scale, and diversity of microgrids to as many urban infrastructure systems as possible. Minneapolis's University Avenue District Energy System proposed to integrate a diverse cluster of users including BlueCross BlueShield of Minnesota, CenterPoint Energy, Minneapolis Pub-lic Housing Authority, the University of Minnesota, private build-ing owners, and Xcel Energy. Its goal is to integrate its power, heat, cooling, open space, storm water, parking, and other elements of its metabolism so as to make them more ecological, cost-effective, and resilient. For example, the heat in one building's wastewater can be recovered, added to a circulating water loop, and used to heat other buildings. Solar thermal energy from building rooftop systems, and ground-source geothermal systems, can be added along the way, as well as the excess heat from servers and refrigerators. Every building connected to the system becomes both a producer and a consumer of heat. Little heat is wasted. And each building is spared the cost of a boiler. Studies show that such systems are cheaper to build and oper-ate, are more resilient to failure since they have a diversity of contrib-uting parts, and have much lower environmental impacts.

Ecodistricts require us to think differently. Rather than designing our buildings to function independently of our neighbors, we need to first think of them as co-dependent, and see how that co-dependence enhances their resilience in a VUCA world. As more and more systems become integrated into ecodistricts, they begin to take on the adaptive characteristics of biocomplex systems. Ecodistricts create active resilience.

Passive and Active Resilience

The twenty-first century will be racked by climate change. Our cities will be subjected to heat and cold waves, flooding, and drought. The third quality of temperament, resilience through green urbanism, can help mediate this volatility. In doing so it helps reduce the impact of climate change and adapt to it.

The world's energy systems are riddled with waste. Globally we produce 15 trillion watts of power every day, emitting 32,000 million metric tons of CO_2 into the air per year, along with many other pollutants.[16] While this waste is changing our climate and poisoning our water and air, we are largely unconscious of it. Perhaps the time has come to ask, how much are we willing to waste? The answer should be nothing, and no one.

This requires a reset in our approach to the environment. No longer can we only hope to do less harm. We must set the goal beyond harm, to act in ways that are restorative of both people and places, of the individual and the city and its environment.

The concept of temperament calls on us to see the environment not only from our point of view but from that of nature, where nothing is wasted. Because there is no waste in nature, everything is pure, naturally pure. Only when we aspire for the metabolism of our cities to be just as naturally pure will we be able to bring it into balance with nature.

PART FOUR

Community

THE WELL-TEMPERED CITY should not only mediate the stresses of the changing environment, it should also heal the cognitive and social stresses of our VUCA age. Its goal should be to nurture well-tempered people and social systems that equalize opportunity for all. Just as cities do not stand alone, but thrive in a deeply interconnected metabolic web of water, food, and energy, people thrive in a deeply interconnected web of families, communities, and cognition. These, too, have a metacultural and behavioral influence that permeates the lives of their residents as deeply as the biological metagenome influences ecologies.

Recall that the evolutionary success of *Homo sapiens* comes from our sociability, our altruism, our group intelligence. Recent cognitive science research indicates that connectivity and culture are core conditions of happiness. Well-being, it turns out, is a collective activity, carried out through the fourth quality of temperament, community. The quality of our communities deeply influences not only the character and quality of our lives, but also the fate of our children.

The healthiest communities are built upon the nine Cs (cognition, cooperation, culture, calories, concentration, commerce, complexity, connectedness, and control). It turns out that these foundational conditions of the world's first communities are also key to its best communities. Healthy communities enhance their residents' lives, and nurture the collective efficacy that is key to healthy cities.

CHAPTER 9

Creating Communities of Opportunity

WHAT ARE COMMUNITIES OF OPPORTUNITY? The root of the word "community" goes back to the Latin word *communitus*; *cum* means "with" or "together," and *munus* means gift. The word "opportunity" comes from the Latin word *opportunus*; the Latin root *ob* means "in the direction of," and *portus* means port or harbor; *opportunus* describes the winds that took travelers to their destination, a safe harbor. Today we use the word "opportunity" to describe a venturing forth, but in its root lies the return to safety, perhaps to home. So, taken together, the Latin roots of the phrase "community of opportunity" refer to the gift of being together, and returning home from our ventures to a safe harbor.

PolicyLink, a national research and action institute advancing economic and social equity in the United States, defines communities of opportunity as "places with quality schools, access to good jobs with livable wages, quality housing choices, public transportation, safe and walkable streets, services, parks, access to healthy food, and strong social networks."[1] Enterprise Community Partners describes its vision for the housing element of a community of opportunity this way: "One day, every person will have an affordable home in a vibrant community, filled with promise and the opportunity for a good life."[2] This should be the goal of community development for every human being on earth.

These definitions are suffused with connectivity, presuming that the community is connected enough to meet its metabolic needs, such as a safe supply of energy and water, access to wastewater and storm-water treatment, and regular solid waste pickup and disposal. Often taken for granted in the United States, these basic services are still not widely available in many developing cities.

And a community of opportunity should be safe from physical and social threats, including violence or trauma of any kind. It should be free of toxic compounds in the water, land, and air. Its residents should have access to affordable health care, and to social and mental health services. It should have an excellent public education system, equal to any in its region. It should include diverse people, housing types, and opportunities. Its governance should be transparent and free from corruption, and its citizens should be able to play a significant role in both its long-range planning and its short-term decision making.

All of these elements are essential for the well-being of a community and its residents. The key lies in the Latin root *cum*, "together." All these elements must be integrated, to weave the fabric of community. And the community must have a culture of we-ness, of collaboration, recognizing our mutual dependence.

Social Networks

Since the Enlightenment, the great cognitive and cultural shift toward rationalism in the mid-eighteenth century, Western or classical economics has increasingly viewed people as individual actors, each focused on fulfilling his own needs. It assumes that the sums of their individual choices are expressed though markets. This perspective powerfully influenced the twentieth-century Chicago School of Economics, known as neoclassical economics, which proposes that the source of societal well-being is free markets made up of individuals making informed and efficient choices to enhance their own circumstances. This view posits that the sum of these individual choices achieves the best societal outcome, and any government intervention that distorts the sum of individual choices leads to worse outcomes.

This economic worldview has had a strong influence on public policy in the United States since the Reaganism of the 1980s. But it has turned out to be incomplete. While individual choice is one element of a well-functioning society, collective needs also are essential. And, as we learned from the Nash equilibrium and Braess paradox, a system's design influences the outcomes that emerge from it. Furthermore, we know that individuals are deeply influenced by social networks; individual choice is not pure. Neither are markets, which never have complete information and can never value all consequences of an action. For example, if a company increases its profits by cutting costs and, as a consequence, pollutes its neighborhood, exposing residents to cancer-causing toxins, it will be more highly valued, even though the system will be worse off. In neoclassical economics, the toxic assault on neighbors and the cost of the neighbors' health care, loss of livelihood, and suffering are externalities, irrelevant to the market value of the company. Instead, unsuspecting individuals and the society at large involuntarily pick up these costs. Neoclassical economics' partial understanding of the true nature of systems has led to tremendous environmental damage, to the treacherous global financial crisis of 2008, and to the destabilizing rise of income inequality thereafter.

On the other hand, if an economic system can be constructed that begins to connect companies to their systemic impacts, then companies could not only be penalized for costs they impose on others, but also benefit from savings. There is an emerging movement to connect housing and health, and to reward healthy, stable, affordable housing for the reductions in local health-care costs that it produces. For example, the YWCA of White Plains introduced a telemedicine program in its housing for low-income senior women, and reduced hospital emergency room visits by its residents from eleven a month to two, producing net savings of over $150,000 a year. If the hospital and Medicare systems that were burdened with the emergency room costs shared some of the savings with the Y, they could help pay for even more housing-based health and social services.

In the early 2000s, the school of behavioral economics began to counterbalance some of neoclassical economics' limitations by studying the way people actually behave, rather than how economic theory assumes that they are supposed to behave. It turns out that we don't each make choices as independent entities; instead, our behavior is deeply influenced by our social and cultural setting, as well as by the cognitive biases we discussed earlier. Our behavior is even influenced by events that happened generations ago, which varied how our genes are expressed. (For example, studies show that people whose grandmothers experienced famine when pregnant are more likely to be obese.) As a result, human beings act irrationally; we don't always make decisions in our own best interest. And social science concludes that human existence is relational, not independent. We follow the crowd.

If we wish to produce behavior that enhances the resilience of our cities, we will need to shift the behavior of interrelated groups rather than simply regulating or incentivizing individuals. To do so we will need to know how social networks function.

One of the most noted urban thinkers of the twentieth century, Jane Jacobs, observed that it is impossible to make a community without creating networks. Social networks are complex adaptive systems that emerge from the relationships among individuals, groups, and organizations. Although these networks are composed of individual people, their qualities emerge from the relationships between people. This doesn't mean that individuals don't have their own agency: of course they do. But we humans are highly social beings, and the agency we exercise is shaped by the influence that cascades through social networks. And the collective agency that arises is as important to the resilience of a community to volatility and stress as is the resilience of its energy and other systems.

Hurricanes, tornadoes, and floods cause tremendous destruction to physical assets of cities, but heat waves are more deadly, causing more deaths than all other weather events combined.[3] In July 1995 temperatures soared across the American Midwest, devastating crops and roasting its cities. A number of people were killed, but the toll was highest in Chicago, where 739 people died as a result of the heat wave. (For perspective, seven times more people succumbed in Chicago than would die when Superstorm Sandy hit New York and New Jersey.)[4] Most of the victims were poor and elderly. Many didn't have air-conditioning, or if they did, they couldn't afford to turn it on; they were afraid to open their doors or windows at night because they lived in dangerous neighborhoods; alone and unable to cool off, they died.

Of the ten communities with the highest death rates, eight were predominantly African American and also suffered from high rates of crime and levels of unemployment. But, curiously, three of the ten communities with the lowest death rates were also primarily African American, with similarly elevated levels of unemployment and crime. What was different about these neighborhoods?

Englewood, on Chicago's South Side, had been hit hard by the decline of urban manufacturing; between 1960 and 1990 more than half the neighborhood's residents moved out, leaving behind vacant lots, abandoned houses, struggling strips of retail stores, and a few churches and community centers. By contrast, the adjacent neighborhood of Auburn Gresham, despite a similar loss of jobs, retained its population. Its shops stayed open, its churches maintained their membership levels, and block associations prospered. While Engle-wood had one of the highest death rates from the 1995 heat wave, Auburn Gresham had one of the lowest—in fact, it fared better than many prosperous white neighborhoods on Chicago's North Side.[5] Eric Klinenberg, sociologist and author of *Heat Wave: A Social Autopsy of Disaster in Chicago*, concluded that the variation was due to the quality of the social networks in each community.

Betty Swanson, who had lived in Auburn Gresham for more than fifty years, said, "During the heat wave we were doing wellness checks, asking neighbors to knock on each other's doors. . . . The presidents of our block clubs usually know who is alone, who is aging, who is sick. It's what we always do when it's very hot or very cold here."[6]

The same power of social networks influenced survival rates eight years later, in July and August 2003, when Europe experienced the longest, hottest heat wave recorded in centuries. All together 70,000 deaths were attributed to the heat, 14,802 of them in France. As in Chicago, the most likely to succumb were the elderly. Europe's heat wave was completely unexpected, and France was unprepared to deal with it. Typically, summer nights in France are cool, and even when they're not, the stone, brick, and concrete homes that most French live in lower temperatures enough in the evening so there's little need for air-conditioning. The deadly heat wave of 2003 was made worse by the fact that August is the month when almost all French people take a vacation, so few were around to check on their elderly parents.

Surprisingly, the highest death rates were experienced by relatively healthy seniors, not the most mentally or physically infirm. Those seniors whose infirmities required extensive family support, or who were living in nursing homes, fared much better than healthier, more independent seniors. Those who lived alone bore the heat stoically, failing to turn on fans or drink enough to keep hydrated.[7] Much as in Chicago, the survival rate of seniors in France during the heat wave was directly related to the depth of their social networks.

Social networks can be mapped by interviewing people and charting who is connected to whom. On a social network map each person is represented by a dot, and connections between people are indicated by lines between dots. Highly connected people have lots of lines running to and from them, whereas isolated people do not. As a map of social networks grows, it develops a shape. For example, networks formed around one dynamic leader will feature a central point with many lines radiating outward, but few connections between them. On the other hand, networks of friends with roughly equal numbers of friendships might look like interconnected snowflakes. The shape of a community's social network map tells us a lot about that community, revealing the highways along which ideas and behaviors are most likely to spread. Surprisingly, the most influential people are not always the most powerful; they are often the most collaborative.

As you may recall, Metcalfe's law states that the value of a telecommunications network is proportional to the square of the number of connected users of the system. This explains why the connectedness of cities during the Ubaic period gave rise to a civilization that was far greater than the sum of its parts.

Metcalfe's law noted that as a network of fax machines or cell phones grows, the more people on it, the more useful the network. But his theory doesn't distinguish between individual nodes; each one is considered equal. Human beings don't quite work that way. One of the key variables in a social network is a person's position in it. Imagine two secretaries. One is secretary to the president of the United States, and the other is secretary to the mayor of a small city. They both have access to information and influence, and in both cases they are close to the center of a dense cluster of connections, but the secretary to the president has far more power because of the president's position in the larger network.

Social Contagion

The social sciences of the first decade of the twenty-first century have provided us with research to support something that we have felt intuitively: the size and shape of our individual and community networks, and our positions in them, have a great deal to do with our health, our economic prospects, and our overall well-being. The more central we are in a network, the more its content flows through us and the more we are affected by it. That content might be useful information such as instructions, a rumor, or even a disease. But whether it's positive or negative, the closer we are to the center of the network the more we're affected by what's flowing through it.

Nicholas Christakis and James Fowler, authors of *Connected: The Surprising Power of Our Social Networks and How They Shape Our Lives*, define connections between people as either dyadic, between one person and his friends, or hyperdyadic, between a person and her friend's friends. Behavior spreads hyperdyadically from one cluster to the next, dispersing along the lines of the social network. If your spouse or close friends smoke, you're more likely to smoke, and if they quit, you're more likely to quit. You may think that you are making your own choices, but they are highly influenced by the choices being made by others in your social network. The spread of behaviors across a community of people is called contagion, and contagions can be nudged, or intentionally stimulated.

To better understand this phenomenon, in 1968 the Yale psychologist Stanley Milgram and his colleagues positioned research assistants on a crowded sidewalk in New York City. The assistants had been instructed to stop walking and look up at a randomly selected window on the sixth floor of a nearby building for one minute. Meanwhile a hidden camera filmed the crowd on the sidewalk, documenting its behavior. Milgram found that when one assistant stopped and looked at a window, approximately 4 percent of the people in the crowd would also stop and look. But if fifteen assistants stopped and looked up, remarkably 86 percent of the people on the sidewalk would look up too, and 40 percent of them would stop walking.[8] Their behavior was affected by the contagion of crowds, nudged by the researchers' prompts.

Contagion spreads behavior very rapidly. We often see this in financial fads, first described in Charles Mackay's book *Extraordinary Popular Delusions and the Madness of Crowds*, which described the Dutch tulip craze. In the early 1600s, as Amsterdam's merchants became wealthy, they displayed their prosperity by planting beautiful tulip gardens. Since it takes seven to twelve years for a flowering tulip to grow from seed, tulip bulbs bred to flower became the rage. As demand for bulbs outstripped supply, their prices rose. Demand was particularly strong for tulips with a rare, impressionistic-looking flower. By 1634 speculators entered the market, buying these rarer bulbs and reselling them for up to four times the original price.

As profits rose more people entered the market; tulip speculation spread like wildfire, peaking in 1637, when Mackay claims that a single tulip bulb was traded for two lasts of wheat, four lasts of rye, four fat oxen, eight fat swine, twelve fat sheep, two hogsheads of wine, four tuns of beer, two tuns of butter, one thousand pounds of cheese, a bed, a suit of clothes, and a silver drinking cup. And then in February buyers failed to show up at a tulip bulb auction in Haarlem, which was experiencing an outbreak of the bubonic plague. Perhaps buyers stayed away because of the sickness, but word of the failed auction spread, and fearing that the markets were collapsing, tulip owners rushed to sell their bulbs, and prices crashed. Tulip bulbs had little functional value, but they had perceived social value. In their rise and fall, we can see the contagion of imputed value through social systems.

Understanding the way that values flow through social systems is key to shaping healthier communities. Positive health behaviors such as exercise, and environmental activities such as recycling and conservation, can be encouraged, nudged.

Six Degrees of Separation, and Three Degrees of Influence

In 1967, when Stanley Milgram was an assistant professor of sociology at Harvard, he organized another famous study of what became known as "degrees of separation," although they're really degrees of connection. He asked randomly chosen individuals in Wichita, Kansas, and Omaha, Nebraska, to figure out how to get a letter from their home to one of two people, in either Sharon or Boston, Massachusetts. Each person was asked to mail a letter to someone who might know someone else who might be able to get the letter to its destination, or at least help get the letter closer. It turned out that on average every letter was able to get to its destination within 5.5 steps, which Milgram rounded up, leading to the theory that everyone is connected to everyone else by just six links; if we want to reach someone, we just have to find out who those connectors are. In 1967 these links were cumbersome to map, but given today's Web-based social networks it's much easier.

Stanley Milgram's research subjects did not randomly send letters in hopes that the recipients might know someone in Boston. They considered all the people they knew and sent the letter to someone they thought was most likely to know the end recipient. For example, they might have recalled that their doctor went to school back east and might know people in Boston, or they remembered that a friend had moved to Massachusetts. Their actions were intentional, not random, and that intentionality was essential to harvesting the intelligence of the system.

To explore this idea of connectedness further, in 2002 the sociologist Duncan Watts and his colleagues recruited 60,000 Americans on the Internet and tracked how many links it took for them to reach thirteen preselected targets, including an Ivy League professor, an archival inspector in Estonia, a policeman in Australia, and a veterinarian in the Norwegian army. Again, it took approximately six links between the person who started the search and the target. With the world's population at over 7 billion, we think that most of us are far apart from one another, but the work of Milgram and Watts underscores how tapping into a few intentional pathways can quickly bring us closer. As a result, our mental model of global humankind can shift from one that is inconceivably large to one in which we are much more intimately connected.

Although we may be connected to much of the human race by six degrees of separation, it turns out that our influence does not spread that far. To study the way behaviors move through large groups of people, Nicholas Christakis and James Fowler examined the records of the Framingham Heart Study, one of the largest continuous population studies in the world. The study began in 1948, when two thirds of all the adults in Framingham, a suburb of Boston, agreed to share their health data from regular checkups with doctors running the study, who were looking for long-term patterns of heart health and disease. Over time, many of the children of the original patients—and even their grandchildren—also agreed to be studied, even though many of them have moved away from Framingham.

Christakis and Fowler first used the Framingham database to track obesity, whose spread has been traced to behavioral choices such as lack of exercise and poor diet. Obesity is a predictor of heart disease and many kinds of cancer. Those who live with it often suffer from pain, diabetes, heart disease, hip and joint issues, depression, and other disabilites. Obesity reduces life expectancy by seven to eight years,[9] and over the last half-century the incidence of obesity in the United States has grown from 13 percent of the population to 34 percent. And obesity has an economic cost to society. In the United States in 2012, more than $190 billion was spent on obesity-related health issues.[10] Understanding the causes of its spread matters. In Framingham obesity settled into clusters, but these clusters of obesity were not linked to specific neighborhoods. Their common element turned out to be friendship.

When Christakis and Fowler looked at the effect of social networks on behavior they found that the impact of how we behave doesn't stop with our friends (the first degree of influence), but extends to their friends, and to their friends' friends—out to three degrees of influence. After that it dissipates, but within those first three degrees the effect can be very powerful. When it comes to obesity, for example, Christakis and Fowler found that when a person you consider a friend becomes obese, your own chance of becoming obese goes up by a remarkable 57 percent.

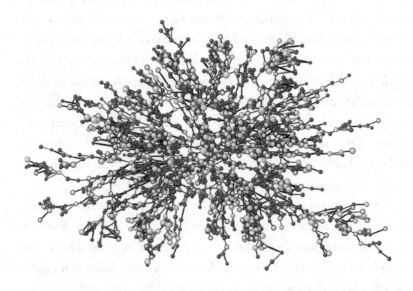

A social network map of obesity. *(Nicholas A. Christakis, James H. Fowler)*

Among mutual friends—cases where both people name each other as friends—the effect is even stronger, with the chances of obesity increasing by a stunning 171 percent![11]

When researchers tracked smoking and drinking patterns, they found that, like obesity, these also spread contagiously through the three degrees of influence. However, not every connection had the same power of influence. For example, if a woman began to drink heavily, both her male and female friends were also likely to start overdoing their alcohol intake. But if a man increased his drinking, it had less of an effect on both his male and female friends. It seems that women have more social network influence.

Understanding the power of social networks has enormous implications for generating positive health outcomes in cities. People are more likely to get a flu shot if their friends get a flu shot. People lose more weight—and keep it off—if they are part of a group like Weight Watchers, and often the spouses of members lose weight too, being only one degree of influence away. People are more likely to take a regular walk in the park when family and close friends have established that healthy habit.

Each of us occupies a position in many networks. If we are on its edge, we are less likely to influence it or be influenced by it. There are many aspects of community health that are dependent on everybody participating. For example, if too many people leave puddles in their yards, mosquitoes will breed, spreading malaria and West Nile disease. Diseases like smallpox and measles can be suppressed only when everyone is vaccinated, and parents who choose not to vaccinate their children for childhood diseases, whether in Seattle or the Sudan, put not only their own children but others at risk.

If a city wants to promote positive behaviors such as immunization, the most effective strategy is to target people who are at the center of social clusters and have them reach out to those who are less connected. According to Christakis and Fowler, "If we want to get people to quit smoking, we would not arrange them in a line and get the first one to quit and tell him to pass it on. Rather, we would surround the smoker with nonsmokers."[12]

Using this strategy to improve the health of residents in Harlem, Manmeet Kaur and her husband, Dr. Prabhjot Singh, created City Health Works, an organization that selects highly empathetic, well-networked residents from a neighborhood to serve as community health coaches.

They reach out to those less connected, who often suffer from chronic physical and mental health issues. The coaches become points of contact for a holistic system of care that spans the boundaries of health care, social needs, and opportunities to help residents achieve their own goals. This approach, which blends motivational interviewing skills with technology, is leading to better patient health and lower overall cost than the traditional emergency-room care that many lower-income residents turn to.

The Strength of Weak Ties

Mark Granovetter, a Harvard-trained sociologist, divided social connections into two categories, strong ties and weak ties: we have strong ties to our closest family members and friends, and weak ties to acquaintances we barely know. Granovetter proposed that our weak ties are more useful than our strong ties.[13] Why? Because strong ties don't extend our reach into the larger world and diversify our knowledge and contacts. Our best friends and family members tend to already know one another and spend lots of time together, reinforcing their worldviews. Our weak ties, by contrast, not only give us access to a wider range of ideas and contacts but connect us to other network clusters, with their extended ideas. As Milgram's original letters passed through their six degrees of separation, they typically flowed through a mix of strong and weak ties.

Weak ties are particularly useful for finding work. For example, when employment drops in one part of a city, as it has dropped in South Chicago, strong ties within the neighborhood are not likely to help with finding a new job; everyone in one's close network will more or less know of the same opportunities, or not know of any at all. A weak tie with an acquaintance who lives in another area where jobs are growing is much more likely to be helpful.

After studying a group of people in the Boston area who had recently found employment, Granovetter discovered that 17 percent found their job through a close friend, 55 percent through someone with whom they had only occasional contact, and 28 percent through someone with whom they rarely had contact. "It is remarkable that people receive crucial information from individuals whose very existence they have forgotten," Granovetter wrote.[14] In a 1983 update to his original work, Granovetter cites a variety of studies indicating that the higher one's social class, the more likely one will be to use weak ties to obtain a job.[15]

Weak ties are also the key to transmission of knowledge and attitudes across socially separate groups. A classic example can be seen in the Pullman porters, who worked for the Pullman Railroad Company and clustered together in Chicago's South Side. Founded in 1862 by George Pullman, the Pullman Railroad Company became the largest manufacturer and operator of sleeper train cars in the United States. Pullman sleepers were leased to railroad lines staffed with porters to carry bags for passengers, make their beds, shine their shoes, and serve their meals. Pullman chose recently freed house slaves as his porters, since they were willing to work for low wages and were well trained to provide the services that Pullman cars offered.

At its peak in the early to mid-1900s, the Pullman company employed more than 20,000 porters, all of them African American. They developed a great deal of pride in their work, and a strong esprit de corps. These ties between Pullman porters led to the formation of the first African American union in the 1920s. With the tips that supplemented their salaries, Pullman porters earned middle-class incomes, most were able to purchase homes, and many sent their children to college. A. Philip Randolph, leader of the Pullman porters' union, the Brotherhood of Sleeping Car Porters, became an early force in the American civil rights movement.

Why were Pullman porters more likely to make the difficult move from slavery to the middle class than other African Americans living in Chicago? In part this was due to their weak ties to the passengers they served, among them doctors, lawyers, businessmen, entertainers, and politicians. These contacts provided them with a far broader knowledge of the ways of middle- and upper-class Americans than most African Americans had access to. By drawing on these weak links the Pullman porters were able to infuse their own strongly tied communities with a middle-class culture.[16]

Trust Matters

Typically, strong ties bind a community together, but they can also make communities insular and less adaptive to change. The historian Francis Fukuyama notes that societies with very strong family values tend to have weaker radii of trust outside the family. These cultures tend to develop smaller, less dynamic business networks. Cultures, such as Amsterdam's in the 1600s, that encourage a broader diversity of social relations have more vital economies because they connect people and social networks to new ideas and relationships with which they may not normally come in contact.[17]

These weak ties are most valuable to societies that are capable of building trust. There's a strong relationship between the degree of broader trust in a society and its economic performance. Eric Beinhocker, author of *The Origin of Wealth*, writes, "High trust leads to economic cooperation, which leads to prosperity, which further enhances trust in a virtuous circle. But the circle can be vicious as well, with low trust leading to low cooperation, leading to poverty, and further eroding trust."18

In their book *Culture Matters*, Lawrence Harrison and Samuel Huntington ranked the world's nations according to trust. They observed that societies with the highest levels of internal trust, such as Sweden, Norway, and Germany, had the most prosperous economies. The societies with the lowest levels of trust, such as Nigeria, the Philippines, and Peru, had the lowest overall GNPs of those studied.

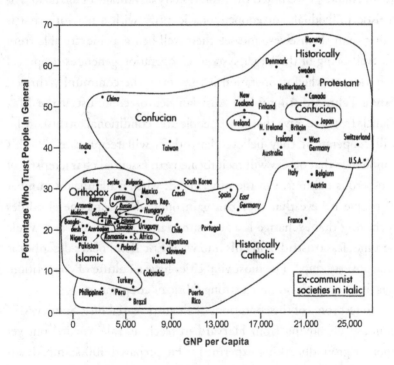

The Relationship between Trust and Economic Performance.

The greater the degree of trust in a society, the higher the GNP per capita.

Note that in general historically Protestant countries have the highest levels of trust, the historically Catholic nations tend to have lower levels of trust and moderate GNPs, and Muslim nations tend to have lower levels of trust and GNPs.

This applies within nations, too. Studies of regional trust differences in the United States show that there is a high correlation between percentage of people who trust others in a region and its indicators of economic growth, longevity, health, crime, voter participation, community involvement, philanthropy, and child school-achievement scores. The most trustful regions perform higher on all of the above indicators. As one moves from north to south, the level of trust drops, and along with it, health, voter participation, school scores, and all of the other indicators.[19]

In chapter 1 we noted the evolutionary advantage of altruism. Altruistic individuals, or cooperators, identify with a network that is larger than themselves, and see their well-being as inextricable from the well-being of the larger system. Cooperation generates reciprocal behavior, so when cooperation is the norm, the community thrives. Ernest Fehr, a distinguished Austrian neuro-economist at the Max Planck Institute, says that most people are "conditional altruists, who will cooperate if they believe that others will reciprocate."[20] This confidence that others will reciprocate is an essential characteristic of prosperous cultures. On the other hand, when a significant number of people believe that they can gain only when someone else loses (believing that exchange is a zero-sum game), the society as a whole becomes less trustful, and falls into what Eric Beinhocker describes as "the poverty trap." The most vital cities have a culture of coopetition, weaving competition into a strong fabric of cooperation.

To test some of the conditions of altruistic variability, Stanley Milgram, after moving from Harvard to teach at Yale, carried out yet another groundbreaking experiment. He prepared 300 stamped, addressed letters and dropped them on New Haven's sidewalks. Some of the letters were addressed to a fictitious person named Walter Carnap, others to medical research institutes, and still others to Friends of the Nazi Party and the Communist Party. Milgram's thesis was that those people who chose to pick up and mail a letter they found did it purely to be helpful, as they obtained no recognition or benefit from doing so. But they did not return all of the letters in equal numbers. Milgram's experiment indicated that altruism is mediated by social judgment. The letters addressed to the medical research associates had a 72 percent rate of return, followed closely by the personal letter to Walter Carnap, with a 71 percent return rate. However, only 25 percent of the letters addressed to Friends of the Nazi Party and the Communist Party were posted.[21] The dropped-letter test has been used since then to assess the cooperativeness and tolerance of communities.

Free riders try to utilize the benefits of social networks, but don't contribute to them. Their selfish behavior, which is often masked by charm and a talent for manipulation, undermines the viability of altruistic systems. If everyone were a free-riding egoist, the social system would collapse. The sociologist Peter Hedström calculates that if just 5 percent of a society were made up of egoists, by undermining the contagion of reciprocity, they would reduce the altruistic actions of the conditional altruists by 40 percent.[22] That is why the Chicago School of Economics view that society is best served when people seek only to maximize their own returns is so wrong. If people do not altruistically invest in their communities, then the soil upon which individual and family success can grow is destroyed. As Darwin observed, groups that are internally altruistic will always outcompete non-altruistic groups. To enforce the altruism of groups, we have evolved so that free riding really annoys "punishers," people who take it on themselves to mete out consequences to those who take no responsibility for others.

At the far end of the spectrum from charming free riders we find loners, or outliers who are largely disconnected from social networks, living on the fringe, barely giving or taking. One of the key roles of a community leader is to balance these different kinds of people so that the community remains trusting, sharing, and coherent. In good times the best community leaders maintain positive social norms, creating a stable social base that builds trust.

However, in volatile times, social norms may not be best adapted to changing conditions. In these cases, societies need input from "positive deviants," people whose behavior deviates from social norms in ways that are more adaptive to the circumstances. The phrase "positive deviants" comes from the work of the Tufts University nutrition researcher Marian Zeitlin, who noted that in very malnourished communities sometimes families developed new behaviors that produced better outcomes for their children. In 1991, Jerry Sternins, who studied with Zeitlin, became the new director of Save the Children in Vietnam at a time when 65 percent of the nation's children suffered from malnutrition. Sternins was tasked with reducing the number of starving children within six months or his visa would not be extended.

He and his wife, Monique, immediately began visiting villages, using existing social networks to create health committees selected from trusted community members. These committee members interviewed every family in the village and identified the families with the healthiest children. They discovered that the parents of healthy children were mixing tiny shrimp found in their rice fields and greens from sweet potato plants into their children's food. They also fed their children four times a day, rather than twice. Both of these practices produced very positive results, but deviated from the community's social norms.

To figure out how to scale up these practices, the Sterninses approached the village health committees in four small communities, with a total population of two thousand children. Once the committees understood the efficacy of the new way of feeding children, and tried to spread it, they discovered a principle now well known to cognitive scientists: changes in attitude follow changes in behavior, not the other way around. Behavior is an embodied experience—once people shift their behavior, then their attitudes change. Giving lectures on the feeding practices was not going to work. Instead, the village health committee went from house to house, showing families how to gather shrimp and potato greens, and mix them into their children's food. Proud of their success, the committee members then went on to describe their results at a national meeting of health committee leaders. Within six months, malnutrition in Vietnam's children fell by 80 percent. The Sterninses' visas were renewed.

The reason positive eating behaviors in Vietnamese villages had not spread before their arrival was that they were practiced by outliers, families on the edge of a village's social networks. But that is also what freed those families to experiment with new feeding methods. The health committees then connected these positive deviants and their ideas to the heart of the network. It took an outsider with weak ties to the community to see what the community could not see itself, because its health practices were so bound by strong social conventions. And it took insiders to help create wide acceptance of those new behaviors.

Neighborhood Effects

Cities are made of neighborhoods, each with its own characteristics.

It turns out that just as people affect their neighborhoods, neighborhoods affect people, too.

The social scientist Robert Sampson taught at the University of Chicago for twelve years, and while he was there he organized the Project on Human Development in Chicago Neighborhoods (PHDCN).[23] The PHDCN collected data that would allow him to compare the social performance of the city's neighborhoods, and to determine key drivers of neighborhood social health as well as what impact social health had on children and adolescents. Sampson compared neighborhoods with a wide range of incomes, racial mixes, and measures of violence. The study also tracked 6,000 randomly selected children, adolescents, and young adults over seven years. Neighborhood cultures, it turns out, significantly affect their residents' behavior.

Sampson's research showed that neighborhoods with the best school performance also had the best health outcomes, the lowest crime levels, and the lowest percentages of teen pregnancy. These outcomes were all interrelated. Fascinatingly, they were persistent over time and place: neighborhoods with the best outcomes remained the best, *even as residents moved into and out of them.* In his groundbreaking book, *Great American City: Chicago and the Enduring Neighborhood Effect*, Sampson concluded that neighborhoods themselves have enduring characteristics that both attract residents and shape their behaviors. Sampson determined that the two most important factors affecting the quality of neighborhoods are the perception of disorder in a neighborhood, and collective efficacy, which he defines as "social cohesion combined with shared expectations for social control."[24] These two conditions are deeply interrelated.

Neighborhood Disorder

The perception of neighborhood disorder has two forms, social and physical. Physical disorder is manifested by graffiti, abandoned or poorly kept buildings, uncollected garbage, and broken windows. Social disorder is reflected in open prostitution and drug dealing, public intoxication, verbal harassment, loud music, and rowdy groups of young people. In their article "On the Factors of Neighborhood Well-Being, Neighborhood Disorder, Psychological Distress and Health," Catherine Ross, Terrance Hill, and Ronald Angel note that exposure to neighborhood disorder leads to cognitive distress in residents, which brings with it increased levels of depression, a sense of powerlessness, and a decline in well-being.[25] A study by the Atlanta VA Medical Center and Emory University indicates that consistent exposure to a disorderly neighborhood has the same cognitive effects as PTSD.[26] Conversely, neighborhoods that have neat, tree-lined, garbage-free streets; residents who greet one another; and classical music floating out of sidewalk cafés give rise to a higher sense of well-being.

In 1982 the social scientists James Q. Wilson and George L. Kelling published "Broken Windows" in the *Atlantic Monthly*, introducing the now famous "broken windows" theory. Trying to understand the growing signs of urban disorder in many neighborhoods, they observed that if a building had a few broken windows and those windows were not promptly repaired, vandals would be more likely to continue breaking windows. On noticing that the building was uncared for, others would be more likely to drop trash in front of it. The apparent acceptance of these minor crimes communicated a social norm that supported criminal activity, leading to an increase in car thefts and break-ins.

The "broken windows" theory proposes that disorderly behavior is contagious, and that if a city aggressively signals that minor crimes are not acceptable, it will put a stop to behavior that would otherwise spread and lead to more major crimes.

This theory has had both positive and negative consequences for cities. Inspired by these ideas, in the late 1980s, New York City assiduously began to clean up the graffiti that plagued its subways and encouraged owners to do the same for the graffiti on their buildings. In the 1990s Mayor Rudy Giuliani's police department began to aggressively arrest panhandlers and small-time street drug dealers, signaling an expectation of a more orderly social norm of behavior. This policy was particularly focused on areas tourists would visit, such as the Times Square area, where the perceived (and real) sense of safety in the city generated a positive impression on visitors. However, this aggressive policing also had a deeply negative effect, sending many more young black men to jail for minor crimes, significantly decreasing their chances at a successful life and introducing more "prison culture" into their communities.

Collective Efficacy

Collective efficacy is the shared belief that a social network or group can get things done for the benefit of the community. Dense personal ties and the social contagion of behavior help facilitate collective efficacy, but they do not cause it. Collective efficacy requires pro-social leadership, a shared culture of altruism, the presence of trust, and few freeloaders. The church groups and block associations in South Chicago's Auburn Gresham neighborhood, which survived the 1995 heat wave so well, had a high level of collective efficacy. Sampson observed that when neighbors share expectations of social control in their neighborhood, trust one another, and feel social cohesion, their neighborhoods generate much better outcomes. Neighborhoods with high levels of collective efficacy have lower levels of crime, and are more likely to have lower future levels of crime. Neighborhoods with high levels of effective social regulation have people who watch out for one another's kids, scold teenagers for loud behavior on the streets, check in on their senior citizens, and generally take care of each other. They also have lower rates of teen pregnancy, lower infant mortality, and higher measures of health and well-being. This holds true whether the neighborhood is black or white, rich or poor.

Collective efficacy also seems to be strongly correlated with altruism, and with low levels of moral cynicism. By mapping the location of all of the city's not-for-profit groups—neighborhood associations, community gardens, Parent Teacher Associations, neighborhood watches, tenant associations, and other hubs of collective action— Sampson discovered that their density was one of the strongest predictors of collective efficacy. And as we have seen, a key determinant of their density is trust.

Three Degrees of Neighborhood Influence

When Robert Sampson placed his study's neighborhood data on a map of Chicago, an interesting phenomenon emerged. Just as people have three degrees of influence upon each other, it turns out that the same is true of neighborhoods. When crime is high in one, it's more likely to be high in neighborhoods immediately adjacent to it, and in the ones next to them. If the homicide rate in one neighborhood goes up by 40 percent, its direct neighbors experience a 9 percent increase in homicide, and their neighbors a 3 percent increase. On the other hand, if indicators of collective efficacy increase in a neighborhood, the homicide rates for adjoining neighborhoods, and for their neighbors, decline.

The three degrees of neighborhood effect explain some of the racial disparities in Chicago, and elsewhere around the country. Middle-class white neighborhoods are usually adjacent to other middle-class white neighborhoods, or even more prosperous ones. Due to the historical patterns of discrimination, middle-class black and Latino neighborhoods are typically adjacent to lower-class neighborhoods. Therefore a middle-class black neighborhood may have a higher level of collective efficacy and visible order than a white one, but will be disadvantaged by its adjacent poorer neighbors. The good news is that when a city focuses on improving the health, safety, and well-being of a given neighborhood, the effect of that improvement will spread by three degrees.

Social Capital and Positive Social Behavior

Social networks and trust are two key components of social capital, which the Harvard sociologist Robert Putnam, author of *Bowling Alone: The Collapse and Revival of American Community*, defines as connections among individuals—social networks and the norms of reciprocity and trustworthiness that arise from them. In that sense social capital is closely related to what some have called "civic virtue."[28] David Halpern, author of *The Hidden Wealth of Nations* and head of the UK government's Behavioral Insight team, calls social capital "our hidden wealth, namely, the non-financial resources comprised of local skills, trust and know how, useful contacts and care based exchanges."[29] Robert Putnam describes two kinds of social capital: bonding and bridging. Bonding capital is generated by the connections among very similar groups, such as families, immigrants, or neighbors. Very often, residents of low-income communities have a great deal of bonding capital, based on strong social ties.

People in bonded networks stand up for one another. Sports teams, local bars and pubs, and even gangs provide a great deal of bonding capital. Bonding capital is deeply connected to "taking care of one's own," and is tied to altruistic care for one's children and elderly parents. The high survival rates during Chicago's heat wave came from the power of bonding capital. In South Korea, this bonding is called "woori," meaning we-ness. But because these clusters are so tightly bonded, they tend to be very internally focused. Sociologists call the gaps between tight network clusters structural holes.

Bridging capital comes from the connection between groups or networks; it's based on the weak social ties we explored earlier in this chapter. Bridging capital is essential for discovering new ways of doing things, gaining employment, and finding investors. When clusters are connected across structural holes, members' information, options, and worldviews are significantly expanded. As we've seen, people who are well off often make an active practice of "networking," so they tend to have much broader networks than lower-income people. Putnam's work focused on two strong bronding networks—bowling leagues and community choirs. He noted that as they declined, the social efficacy of neighborhoods declined. Professional associations like the American Institute of Architects or the American Medical Association provide their members with a tremendous number of connections to other people, and new ideas that can help advance their work and expand their opportunities. Bonding and bridging capital are both needed for communities and their members to thrive. In 2001, Michael Woolcock, who teaches public policy at Harvard's Kennedy School, proposed that a third kind of social capital, linking capital that connects people across different social classes, is also essential for a community to prosper. He describes bridging capital as making horizontal connections, whereas linking capital makes vertical connections between people and institutions.[30]

During stable times the reliability of bonding capital may be sufficient. But in VUCA times, bonding capital is too isolating; bridging capital is needed to expand the community's gene pool of ideas and relationships. And linking capital is needed to expand its ability to bring in adaptive resources, which is increasingly important in combating the physical and social disconnection of the poor in places such as remote U.S. suburbs, France's banlieues, and the developing world's rapidly growing city edges.

The Social Capital of Leadership

Robert Sampson's Chicago studies tracked both the connections of residents to their neighborhood leaders, and their leaders' connections to one another. The more poorly the neighborhood performed on measurements of well-being, the less likely it was that residents felt connected to a leader who could change things for the better. Neighborhoods benefit from both perceived efficacy and real efficacy. It seems that neighborhoods first need residents to believe that their efforts to improve the neighborhood will make a difference. Then, if these efforts do produce positive outcomes, their confidence in collective efficacy rises.

The Chicago study also mapped the social capital of leaders in business, ministers, school principals and college presidents, police captains, members of the city council, and heads of not-for-profits and community associations. More than seventeen hundred leaders were interviewed in order to map their social networks and their reputational position with others. The leaders each named five other people to whom they were connected, to determine the most central hubs of the leadership network. The results indicated that the influence of these six primary categories of leaders was directly related to the degree to which they are connected to one another.

And the more reciprocal their relationship, the more effective it was in crossing weak links. For example, a minister might ask a businessman to introduce her to the head of a college so she could convey interest on behalf of a not-for-profit that wished to forge ties to the college.

Sampson's study indicated that the density of leaders' ties and their reputations were directly tied to social efficacy and well-being in their neighborhoods. Neighborhoods with locally powerful but egotistical leaders who did not connect well with others suffered.

Social Networks and the Destiny of Cities

The ways that city leaders respond to global megatrends and the outcomes of their actions are deeply conditioned by the quality of their social networks. In 2004, Sean Safford, a researcher at MIT's Industrial Performance Center, wrote his PhD thesis on the role of social networks in the decline of manufacturing in the American rust belt. His thesis, "Why the Garden Club Couldn't Save Youngstown: Civic Infrastructure and Mobilization in Economic Crisis," mapped out the social networks of Youngstown, Ohio, and Allentown, Pennsylvania, and looked at the role they played in determining the divergent fates of the two cities.

Only 335 miles apart, both cities were founded in the 1800s, and prospered as they became transportation hubs. Both also became steel manufacturing centers, financed by Andrew Carnegie and his circle. (Another very strong social network!) More than a century later, in 1950, Allentown and Youngstown were still very similar. Allentown's population was 208,728, Youngstown's was 218,816. The economies of both cities remained grounded in manufacturing, especially the steel industry, although by the mid-1950s signs of the steel industry's impending decline were already in the air. Each city's leading bankers and industrialists asked local civic associations to hire consultants to study the situation and recommend a course of action. In both cases consultants recommended that the cities diversify their industrial base. Over time manufacturing continued to decline, and each city commissioned more studies. In 1977 a strike dealt the steel industry a terrible blow, and by 1983 the steel plants in both cities had shut their doors.

The fates of two similar cities facing the same global megatrends turned out to be very different. In the 1950s Allentown took the advice of its consultants; Youngstown did not. As a result, by 2015 the population of Allentown was 80 percent higher than that of Youngstown, and its median income was 30 percent higher. How did this happen? In the 1970s Allentown's leaders set out to diversify the city's industrial sector by attracting electronics and specialty chemicals, connecting those industries with local universities, and expanding the region's transportation networks. Community leaders created a private equity fund to invest in new businesses and developed several new industrial parks to house them. As a result, today Allentown's percentage of its population working in electronics, instrumentation, and specialty chemicals is eight times higher than Youngstown's. Its leaders successfully lobbied for a branch of Penn State University to be located in the city so that it could join the statewide Ben Franklin Partnership to develop research and talent to support emerging new businesses. Today Allentown is the fastest-growing city in Pennsylvania.

Over the same time period, the leaders of Youngstown did very little. It was not until the 2000s that the city began to diversify its economy, enhance its community college and university systems, and begin a comeback after decades of decline. In his thesis Sean Safford proposed that the difference between these two cities lay in the social networks of their leaders. The social and civic networks of Allentown brought together a wide range of actors, many of whom were not economically connected, into a few hubs able to make key strategic decisions for the community. The most important of these hubs were local universities and the Boy Scouts of America. The board of the Boy Scouts was made up of CEOs who typically did not do business with one another, so it became a strong connector for an economically diverse group of people who previously had only weak ties. When Allentown's economic leaders decided to form the Lehigh Valley Partnership to attract and grow new industries, they selected the head of the Boy Scouts, a bright, ambitious, effective young man they all knew, but who was not tied to any one clique or point of view. They all signed on to mentor him, and he turned out to be a great leader.

The civic leadership of Youngstown, on the other hand, was concentrated in a few distinguished families whose perspectives were limited by inward-looking, heavily overlapping social networks. For example, the president of the Union National Bank sat on the board of sixteen local businesses and not-for-profits. The city's key civic hubs were the Garden Club and the Red Cross, which were led by the wives of men who banked together and were members of the same country clubs; these hubs did little to cultivate diverse views or new sources of economic power.

Safford writes, "Rather than being forums of interaction, then, these were simply places where social status was affirmed."[31]

Youngstown was limited by strong bonding capital among its leaders that exposed it to few outside perspectives, and also by its lack of bridging and linking capital.

The worldview of a city's or region's leadership also affects how connected it will be to the global economy, with dramatic results. Like Allentown and Youngstown, in 1950, Birmingham, Alabama, and Atlanta, Georgia, had very similar population sizes and economies. But their fates also turned out to be very different.

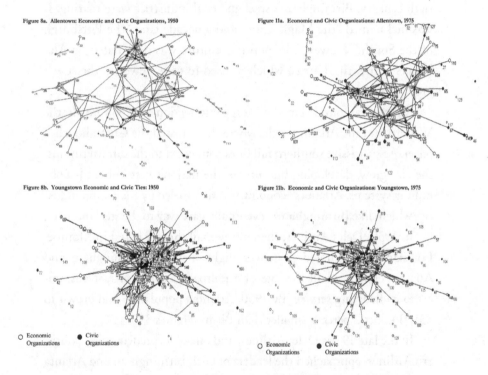

A Comparison of Economic and Civic Organizations in Allentown and Youngstown.

Observe how spread out and lightly connected Allentown's civic and economic ties were versus Youngstown's, in 1950. By 1975, Allentown's diverse networks were strengthening and increasing connections, whereas Youngstown's centralized network was beginning to collapse. *(From Sean Safford,* Why the Garden Club Couldn't Save Youngstown: Civic Infrastructure and Mobilization in Economic Crises *[Cambridge, MA: MIT, 2004], pp. 42, 45)*

Birmingham was incorporated in 1871 by a group of local businessmen who looked at the proposed route maps for the Alabama & Chattanooga and North & South Alabama railroads, and speculated by acquiring the land around the future crossing of the two rail systems. The founders of Birmingham named it after Birmingham, England, in hopes that it, too, would one day become a significant industrial city. The site was blessed with iron, coal, and limestone, the three raw materials used to make steel, and by the turn of the twentieth century, Birmingham's steel and coal industries were roaring. It was nicknamed "the Magic City," and a decade later "the Pittsburgh of the South." However, its political culture was dominated by Alabama's white, rural areas, which refused to cede power to the state's growing cities.

Atlanta was founded in 1847 at the intersection of two railroads, the Western and the Atlantic, right where they crossed the Chattahoochee River. As successive southern rail lines connected to the same terminus, the city grew, developing into one of the nation's first hub-and-spoke railway systems. Atlanta's economy was first fueled by the cotton industry, which, like Birmingham's, eventually gave way to the steel industry.

In 1930, Delta Airlines, then a tiny mail shipper based in Monroe, Louisiana, inaugurated passenger flights between Birmingham and Atlanta, charging half the rate of a railroad ticket to attract customers to its fledgling service. By 1950, Atlanta's population had grown to 331,314, just 2 percent smaller than Birmingham's 336,037.

In the late 1940s Delta Airlines, and one of its predecessors, Southern Airlines, approached the leaders of both Birmingham and Atlanta to see if either city would be willing to invest in its plans to develop the nation's first hub-and-spoke passenger airline network. Delta proposed to connect the South's cities into a regional cluster, and then through its newly built hub to Chicago and New York, and to its first international connection, Mexico City. It was a brilliant concept, connecting the South's structural holes with key national and international centers. Delta proposed the benefits of social network theory before it was articulated!

Atlanta enthusiastically supported the airlines' vision. It issued bonds to expand its airport, and invested heavily in new runways and terminals. Birmingham responded to Delta's request by raising its local aviation fuel tax. It has been said that Birmingham's city leaders, called the "Big Mules," fearing that Chicago's unions would infect its nonunion workers and that Mexicans would flood the city, turned Delta down.

In the 1960s, the civil rights movement swept across the South. On May 14, 1961, Ku Klux Klansmen brutally attacked a group of nonviolent Freedom Riders as they got off the bus in Birmingham's Trailways bus station. The city's police, lead by Chief Bull Connor, stood by. Photographs of the violence shocked the world. In response, Atlanta's mayor, William B. Hartsfield, proclaimed that Atlanta was " too busy to hate."[32]

In 1972, Maynard Jackson was elected Atlanta's mayor, becoming one of the nation's first black big-city mayors. He championed the further transformation of the airport into an international hub. He developed MARTA, one of the nation's first postwar commuter rail systems, to connect the city, the airport, and the region, more tightly tying the fate of the city and its suburbs together, and he resisted cutting up inner-city neighborhoods with highways. In the late 1980s Jackson spearheaded Atlanta's successful effort to host the 1996 Summer Olympics, increasing international prestige. Meanwhile, a local media entrepreneur, Ted Turner, launched the world's first twenty-four-hour global cable news network, CNN. Atlanta was definitely an outward-looking city with diverse leadership networks focused on a common goal.

In the 1960s, as Atlanta moved forward with integration, Birmingham resisted with police dogs, fire hoses, and the arrests that led to Martin Luther King's famous "Letter from a Birmingham Jail." The world was shocked by the horrific bombing of a black church in the city that killed four innocent young girls, solidifying Birmingham's

reputation as a backward-looking, bigoted community. Although today Birmingham is working hard to overcome this legacy, fifty years
later the consequences of these different worldviews generated a tremendous difference between the fates of the two cities.

By 2013 the city of Atlanta's population had grown to 447,841,
anchoring a regional population of 5,529,420, twelve times as large
as the city. During the same time period Birmingham's population
had shrunk to 212,237, and its metropolitan region's population of
1,140,300 was only five times as large as its urban core. Even more
tellingly, in 2011 the Atlanta region had a median income of $51,948
per household, eighth-highest among all cities in the nation, while
Birmingham's median household income was $39,274, with a rank-
ing of 124th. Atlanta's Hartsfield-Jackson airport is the world's bus-
iest, thirty times more active than Birmingham's Shuttleworth Airport. Atlanta has issues to contend with—it continues to grapple with
sprawl and income disparity. Nevertheless, it proved to be much more
of a community of opportunity for its residents than Birmingham.

Once again transportation and social network connectivity played
a large part in the divergent paths taken by two cities. Birmingham's
economic leaders were dominated by a conservative, rural ethos. Atlanta's were more diverse and infused with global aspirations; the social worlds exemplified by Delta Airlines and CNN did not overlap;
instead they reinforced each other and extended the city's reach.

Toward Well-Tempered Communities

We live in a highly connected world in which our relationships, attitudes, and behaviors shape outcomes for ourselves, our neighborhoods, and our cities. The choices we make now contribute to the
metagenome of the city, influencing its level of connectivity and its
future prosperity.

And just as the ecological niche is the basic community unit in a larger ecosystem, the neighborhood is the niche that residents most deeply influence, and are influenced by. The social health of a neighborhood is the key to its function as a community of opportunity, the foundation of a healthy city and extended region. And healthy neighborhoods begin with resilient, adaptable, well-tempered people.

CHAPTER 10

The Cognitive Ecology of Opportunity

COMMUNITIES ARE MADE UP of many elements—streets, schools, stores, offices, parks, and so on—but none is more fundamental than the home. Cities, at their core, are places to live. Housing is the platform from which family success grows. It is typically a family's largest expenditure. Safe, well-located, decent, affordable housing is a fundamental condition for communities of opportunity. Unfortunately, in 2015, 330 million urban families around the globe lived in substandard housing, and by 2025 the McKinsey Global Institute projects that number to grow to 440 million, one third of the world's urban families, almost 1.6 billion people.[1]

In the United States, Harvard University's Joint Center for Housing Studies reports that more than two thirds of America's poor spend more than half of their income on housing.[2] Add the cost of food, transportation, utilities, phone, Internet, clothing, education, and health care, and it's hard to see how they can possibly make it all work. As a result, many lower-income families often double and triple up, living in overcrowded conditions, or are always on the move, finding inexpensive accommodations wherever they can.

Housing comes with a second cost that also disproportionately affects low-wage earners: transportation. In Europe the poor live in isolated suburban housing estates; in the developing world low-wage workers often live in informal slums sprawling from the edges of cities, often spending two to three hours commuting to work; in the United States more than 50 percent of low-income families now live in suburbs, where they spend an additional 20 to 30 percent of their income on auto-based transportation. Adding to this burden, they are likely to live in poorly insulated, energy-inefficient homes with huge utility costs.

Those lower-income families who are able to find a stable place to live survive from paycheck to paycheck. One unexpected medical bill or family emergency can set off a cascade of missed payments and tough choices. In job sectors where many lower-income families work, when a parent misses a day to take a sick child to a clinic, she is likely to be unpaid for that day, demoted, or fired. That often leaves low-income families unable to pay their rent, on the slippery slope to homelessness.

This vulnerability affects a significant number of families. A 2011 study by the National Foundation for Credit Counseling found that 64 percent of Americans have less than $1,000 in savings to deal with an emergency, and 30 percent have no savings whatsoever, other than retirement funds.[3] Savings are a critical element of a family's economic resilience, yet with the combined costs of housing, transportation, utilities, and health care, America's working families simply cannot keep up, much less save. This sense of living on a razor's edge undermines their overall sense of well-being; the stress of just getting by is enormous. Enterprise Community Partners calls this "housing insecurity."

According to Enterprise, in 2015, about 19 million families—one in six households in the United States—were either homeless or paying more than half of their income for housing. The majority of these families rent their homes. America's stock of affordable rental units is older, and in very poor condition. To make matters worse, while demand is going up, the supply of affordable housing is shrinking.

The Joint Center reported that more than 29 percent of the housing stock rented to low-income families in 1999 was abandoned or torn down a decade later.[4] In high-cost cities such as San Francisco, where the median rent in 2015 was $4,225 a month, a family had to earn $169,000 a year,[5] more than twice the city's median household income, to keep its rental costs to 30 percent of its income. Thus, even middle-class families are faced with housing insecurity. The American dream is slipping away.

For low- and moderate-income families, this challenge of finding and keeping a safe, secure, well-located place to live is quite stressful. Less than a quarter are able to find subsidized affordable housing. The rest often live in poorly insulated, poorly maintained toxic homes, subject to eviction if they can't pay the rent. Low-income communities are also rife with other stressors such as crime and neighborhood violence; low-wage, low-opportunity work; racism; lack of access to health care; poor food; and underperforming schools. These endemic stresses never go away. And just as the residents of these neighborhoods have limited financial reserves, they also have few cognitive or emotional reserves to buffer them.

Although these communities are often characterized by their physical and social isolation, they are subject to the same global trends affecting every community on earth—climate change, globalization, growing income inequality, financial volatility, epidemics, and the migration of refugees, among others. These volatile macrotrends add episodic stresses to the endemic ones. When episodic stresses such as Hurricane Katrina, Superstorm Sandy, manufacturing plant closures, or waves of housing foreclosure or job loss strike, endemically stressed communities and their social service systems are overwhelmed, and simply cannot respond.

A Secure Base and Cognitive Ecologies

Advances in cognitive science over the past twenty years have deepened our understanding of how the human brain and mind develop, as well as the critical relationship between cognitive health and the well-being of the individual, the family, and the community. This work points to the importance of a safe, stable home as a secure base upon which psychological well-being is built. In 1988, the British psychologist John Bowlby published *Secure Base*, describing the development of healthy children as requiring "a secure base from which a child or adolescent can make sorties into the outside world and to which he can return knowing that he will be welcomed when he gets there, nourished, physically and emotionally, comforted if distressed, reassured if frightened."[6]

There is a deep interdependence between the cognitive security of individuals, their families and their neighborhoods, and their physical and mental health. The collective cognitive state of a community forms its *cognitive ecology*, its mental landscape of thinking, feeling, and relating. It deeply influences and is influenced by the social networks that it permeates.

The cognitive ecology in which children are raised affects their physical and mental health for the rest of their lives, adding to the metagenome of their community's perceptions, reactions, and behaviors. Endemic stresses such as poverty and housing insecurity corrode a developing child's sense of security. Add to this the episodic stresses that lie beyond the control of any individual or community, and the cognitive security essential to children's healthy growth becomes even more frayed.

A neighborhood's cognitive ecology is particularly affected by trends of increasing violence. For example, during the war in Vietnam, the United States trained millions of young men to use weapons, then shipped them to a foreign land where many were traumatized and introduced to heroin, and then brought them home without an effective plan to heal them or jobs to employ them. Poor neighborhoods that were already destabilized by the flight of jobs, inflation, and rising energy costs were further racked by a surge in violence and drugs as veterans struggled to cope with the aftermath of the traumas they had suffered in Southeast Asia.

In a 1976 study, "Violent Acts and Violent Times: A Comparative Approach to Postwar Homicide Rates," the sociologists Dane Archer and Rosemary Gartner explored the effect of war on the murder rates of fifty countries going back to 1900. They observed that most nations experienced postwar increases in homicide rates, whether the war was fought within their boundaries or not, and regardless of whether they won or not. During the war in Vietnam the murder rate in the United States doubled. In the 1970s the cognitive mechanism of this increase wasn't understood,[7] but now we know much more about the effects of PTSD on war veterans. For example, a 2010 Marine Corps study found that marines who had suffered from PTSD were more than *six times* as likely to engage in antisocial and aggressive behaviors.[8]

There are many other external contributors to a community's cognitive ecology. For example, the persistent racism experienced by young black males who are endlessly stopped and searched reduces their sense of individual and collective efficacy. And many cities are now being flooded with immigrants fleeing the horrors of intergroup violence and displacement in their homelands, or who simply can no longer live in a climate-changed environment, often making journeys of great suffering, bringing with them all the effects of the traumas they experienced. These and many other external factors contribute to the neighborhood effect described by Robert Sampson. Combined with overcrowding, housing instability, and environmental toxins, they can result in very poor places to raise healthy children.

Adverse Childhood Experiences

A few years ago I met with the leader of a not-for-profit community development company who said, "My community suffers from terrible overcrowding. We often have thirteen or more extended family members living in a single home. Inevitably, one evening an uncle comes home drunk and rapes a young niece. Everyone in the home knows it happened, everyone feels complicit, and everyone is damaged by the experience. If we can just move every mother and her children to their own safe, green apartment we can begin to help them move forward with their lives."

The rape of a child is a horrible thing. The medical community labels this an "adverse childhood experience," or ACE. ACEs, significant traumatic experiences that deeply affect a child's development, fall into three categories: abuse, neglect, and household dysfunction. These include emotional abuse, physical abuse, sexual abuse, emotional neglect, physical and emotional neglect, excessive noise at home, sudden eviction, observing one's mother being subjected to domestic violence, property victimization, peer victimization, exposure to community violence, parents always arguing, household substance abuse, household mental illness, parental separation or divorce, and a parent who was sent to prison.[9]

In 1993, Dr. Robert Anda, an epidemiologist at the Centers for Disease Control, and Dr. Vincent Filetti, an internist at Kaiser Permanente in San Diego, began a decade-long study of more than 17,000 people in the Kaiser system in order to better understand the impact of adverse childhood experiences. Approximately 75 percent of the population they studied were white and had a college degree, yet 12.6 percent had an ACE score of four or more—meaning they had suffered through four or more adverse childhood experiences—indicating just how prevalent ACEs are in our society.

ACEs produce a dose/response effect—the greater the exposure to ACEs, the deeper their lifelong effects. Adults who lived through four or more ACEs as children are twice as likely to be smokers, twelve times as likely to attempt suicide, seven times as likely to be alcoholics, and ten times more likely to inject street drugs. Such children are also four times more likely to have intercourse by the age of fifteen, and 40 percent of girls with four or more ACEs become pregnant as teenagers.[10]

There is also a close correlation between a child's ACE score and his or her health. Adults who have experienced four ACEs or more as children are 260 percent more likely to have chronic obstructive pulmonary disease (COPD) than adults with an ACE score of zero; they are 240 percent more likely to have hepatitis, and 250 percent more likely to contract a sexually transmitted disease. Experiencing six ACEs increases one's chances of lung cancer by 300 percent, and reduces life expectancy by thirteen years. There is also a direct relationship between the number of ACEs one has experienced and the risk of being hospitalized for an autoimmune illness such as rheumatic disease.[11] Since Anda and Filetti's initial study there have been dozens of population studies on the effect of ACEs on children, and the results have been confirmed over and over again. These terrible adverse childhood experiences are prevalent all over the world and across income brackets, but they are particularly concentrated in low-income communities.

ACEs and the Brain

When we encounter what we perceive as a threat, the brain sends messages to the hypothalamus, the part of the brain that regulates the body's autonomic and homeostatic systems. The hypothalamus compares the threat with memories in the hippocampus, and if those memories are associated with danger it releases hormones that trigger the pituitary gland to instruct the adrenal glands to release two further hormones: cortisol and adrenaline. This network for responding to potential danger is called the HPA axis (hypothalamus, pituitary, adrenal). Imagine that you're out walking in the woods and you come across a bear. The HPA axis releases adrenaline, which prepares you for fight or flight by speeding up your heart and contracting your pupils to focus your attention. If it looks like you're going to need to run for a long time, your pituitary gland releases cortisol, which increases blood pressure and blood sugar, and turns down your immune response, both of which enhance your long-distance running ability. But after the bear lumbers by, or you've successfully run away from it, your heart calms down and the rest of your body returns to normal.

Under ordinary circumstances the HPA axis relaxes and your system returns to its normal balance. But if the stress is continuous, or if the stresses are traumatic, the HPA pathway is jarred open and remains on, even when it's no longer needed. A child who undergoes several adverse childhood experiences has his or her HPA set permanently in the "on" position. The child also develops a smaller prefrontal cortex, the strategic part of the brain, and less-robust control connections between it and the amygdala, the part of the brain associated with emotions, aggression, and memory. This circuit is a key part of self-regulation, particularly our ability to regulate reactions to perceived threats. An overactive HPA axis generates continuous anger and anxiety.

As a result, children who suffer from continuous toxic stress or frequent ACEs are more likely to be withdrawn, less able to regulate their behavior or pay attention in school, and less likely to participate in activities or to make friends. Until puberty they are stuck in flight mode, and after puberty they shift into fight mode. This neurological condition leads to children dropping out of school, joining gangs, and engaging in crime and other high-risk behaviors. Girls seeking affection without self-control often become pregnant. And then, as resentful, stressed-out mothers, they create an environment that inflicts the same condition on their own children.

The neural damage from ACEs is also inheritable. ACEs are now known to cause methylation variations in genes that contribute to a likelihood of developing psychiatric disorders such as suicide and passing them down from generation to generation. This epigenetic process is undermining the metagenome of communities with higher degrees of trauma, perpetuating poor mental and physical health and difficulties in forming positive social networks.[12]

Overcrowding and Eviction

Not only are ACEs caused by a child's direct traumatic experiences, they can also be caused by the environment in which children live. Chaotic living situations, overcrowding, excessive noise, and transience negatively affect young children. Overcrowding is not a function of family size in itself, or even of family income; rather it is caused by the density, or number of people, in a room. When ten or fifteen people are crowded into a home, the density causes social contagion to soar, and negative behavior such as the drug or alcohol addiction of one affects all. The rate of older males abusing younger females is also substantially higher.

Studies by Gary Evans, a researcher in Cornell University's Departments of Human Development and Design and Environmental Analysis, indicate that overcrowding produces a negative effect on children's interpersonal behaviors, mental health, motivation, cognitive development, and cortisol levels. Parents in crowded homes are less responsive to young children, perhaps due to their own adverse childhood experiences. According to Evans's research, parents who raise children in crowded homes speak less frequently to their children, and use less-complicated words. A study by Betty Hart and Todd Risley of Rice University calculated that after four years children on welfare will have heard 30 million fewer words than children from high-income families. Even worse, the low-income child will have heard 125,000 more discouraging words, whereas the high-income child will have heard 560,000 more words of praise.[13] This, too, has a cognitive effect.

Parents who raise children in overcrowded homes are more likely to engage in punitive parenting, significantly increasing the level of children's distress. As Evans notes, "Elementary school-aged children who live in more crowded homes display higher levels of psychological distress and they also have higher levels of behavior difficulties in school. . . . Chronic overcrowding influences children's motivation to perform tasks. Independent of household income, children aged 6–12 show declines in motivational behavior and also demonstrate a level of learned helplessness—a belief that they have no control over their situation and therefore do not attempt to change it—although they have the power to do so."[14]

Housing evictions are also a driver of ACEs, and the Great Recession made that problem much worse. Between 2010 and 2013 the number of eviction cases in Milwaukee County increased by 43 percent. As Matthew Desmond, a Harvard sociologist who studied evictions in Milwaukee, put it, "You would think that eviction is caused by job loss, but we found that eviction can actually cause you to lose your job."[15] And once evicted, people have higher rates of depression, material hardship, hunger, and inadequate medical care.

Where do families who are evicted end up? In the United States they double up with friends or relatives, camp in their cars, or move to homeless shelters. Globally, families who are displaced by wars, climate change, or intergroup strife end up in refugee camps. All of these housing solutions are overcrowded, chaotic, noisy, and transient. When a child is brought to such a place, rather than receiving the stable base that she or he so desperately needs, the child is further destabilized.

When a significant portion of a community lacks a stable base, ACEs and their attendant behavioral and health issues permeate its social networks, and begin to feed back into the cognitive ecology of the community. The twenty-first-century job markets require people with not only an increasing range of technical skills, but also the cognitive skills of attention, systems thinking, and complex use of language. Children who grow up in overcrowded, chaotic homes, or suffer abuse, are most likely to lack these capacities.

Add Toxicity and Stir

On April 15, 2015, Freddie Gray, a twenty-five-year-old African American man, was arrested by Baltimore police officers, had his hands and legs cuffed, and was thrown into a police van. In the process Gray suffered a spinal cord injury, and died. Six police officers were indicted; none were convicted. The death of yet another young black man in the hands of the police pushed the community over the edge. Small protests grew larger and larger until the night of Gray's funeral, on April 27, when Baltimore erupted into rioting and looting.

Freddie Gray was not destined to become a local hero. He never graduated from high school, and had been arrested more than a dozen times for drug possession. The deck was stacked against Freddie the moment he was born. His mother was a heroin addict. He was raised in an impoverished North Baltimore neighborhood suffused with drugs, violence, and crime. He grew up neglected in a chaotic environment, which as we have seen negatively effects a child's cognitive development. But to make matters worse, when Freddie was a small child, he and his twin sister, Fredericka, were exposed to flaking lead-based paint, tested, and found to have excessive levels of lead in their blood. Both were classified as suffering from ADHD in school, and ultimately dropped out. Freddie turned to drugs, and Fredericka was often violent.

A blood level of more than 5 micrograms of lead per deciliter is likely to severely disturb a child's cognitive development, leading to lack of executive function, lack of emotional self-regulation, and an inability to pay attention. Without these skills, children often fail at school, drop out, and accumulate criminal records. When Freddie was 22 months old, blood tests revealed that he had 37 micrograms of lead per deciliter of blood.

Dan Levy, an assistant professor of pediatrics at Johns Hopkins University who has studied the effects of lead poisoning on youth, said, "Jesus, the fact that Mr. Gray had these high levels of lead in all likelihood affected his ability to think and to self-regulate and profoundly affected his cognitive ability to process information. And the real tragedy of lead is that the damage it does is irreparable."[16] In the fall of 2015, it was revealed that the entire city of Flint, Michigan, was drinking water with five times more lead than the EPA's recommended limit.

Lead is only one of the environmental toxins that negatively affect neural development, degrading the intelligence of children, especially if their mothers were exposed during pregnancy. Philippe Grandjean, a professor of neurology at Harvard Medical School, and Philip Landrigan, dean for global health at Mount Sinai School of Medicine in New York, wrote in the distinguished medical journal *Lancet* that a pandemic of toxins was damaging the brains of unborn children. "Our very great concern is that children worldwide are being exposed to unrecognized toxic chemicals that are silently eroding intelligence, disrupting behaviors, truncating future achievements and damaging societies."[17] Dr. David Bellinger, also at Harvard Medical School, calculated that Americans have lost 41 million IQ points as a result of exposure to lead, mercury, and organophosphate pesticides.[18]

Dr. Fredericka Perrera, the director of the Columbia Center for Children's Environmental Health at the Mailman School of Public Health, notes that exposure to toxic chemicals leads to increased infant mortality, lower birth weight, deficits in lung functioning, childhood asthma, developmental disorders, intellectual disabilities, attention deficit hyperactivity disorder, and an increased risk of childhood cancer. Prenatal or early life exposure to alcohol, nicotine, and cocaine also can have devastating and lifelong effects on the developing architecture of the brain.

Adverse childhood experiences cause what Dr. Jack Shonkoff, director of Harvard's Center on the Developing Child, labeled "toxic stress." There is not a great deal of work on the combined effect of toxic stress and toxic chemicals on cognition, but it cannot be good. If a child's immune response is weakened, a known effect of toxic stress, the child is likely to be more vulnerable to environmental neurotoxins. This toxic soup is pervasive, but usually invisible, often found in the chemicals used in building materials, furniture, insecticides, and other elements of modern daily life. It is critical that future research identify its components and its compounding effects. In addition to lead, mold, pests, pesticides, and excessive dust have been shown to adversely affect children and their families. These may be present in any home, but are typically concentrated in low-income homes and neighborhoods. In these poorly insulated homes, during cold winters, families often use gas-fired ovens, and stoves, for heat, adding to the toxicity of the indoor air.

Contemporary urban life is complex, and getting more so. Cognitive capacity is increasingly required to figure out how to negotiate a city's systems. Emotional and social intelligence are needed to thrive in school, work, and neighborhood life. Children raised in highly stressed, environmentally toxic environments will be far less likely to succeed. And in the competitive twenty-first century, how can a city thrive when a significant portion of its residents can't contribute to its economy and its culture?

The riots in Baltimore revealed how deep the rifts are between prosperous and poor neighborhoods in most American cities. Is the American dream large enough so that every one of our children has the opportunity to live in a safe, affordable home?

It's just not possible to build a well-tempered society on an unstable base. Safe, affordable, toxin-free housing is an essential precon-
dition for a thriving civilization. While this base is essential, it is not
sufficient. We must also repair the cognitive ecology of communities
torn apart by violence, trauma, and adverse childhood experiences,
and grow trust, an essential element for the development of a community's social capital. When children have ACEs they grow wary,
much less trusting. Neighborhoods with high levels of ACEs are less
likely to possess the sense of order and social efficacy necessary for
their residents to thrive.

The Solutions

The corrosive damage wrought by pervasive family or neighborhood
trauma can be overcome, but this requires a systemic approach. There
are four key intervention points: the family, the home, the school, and
the health-care system. When these are integrated, ACEs can be successfully addressed. In the port city of Tacoma, Washington, Michael
Mirra, executive director of the Tacoma Housing Authority (THA),
was struggling to improve the lives of children from homeless and
foster care families when he realized that he couldn't make significant
progress unless local schools were part of the solution.[19]

McCarver Elementary School is located near the Tacoma Housing Authority's main campus. McCarver, the nation's first magnet
school, was originally developed as part of a voluntary desegregation
program, but in recent years its quality had significantly declined.
Overwhelmed with a homeless and low-income population and an
epidemic of ACEs, the school had one of the highest student turnover
rates in the city, with 179 percent of the population changing in a
year. This level of instability undermined the students who were coming and going, and the students who remained and were unable to

form stable relationships. It was also very frustrating for the school's teachers, who left for more stable schools. The combination of high student and teacher turnover made the school itself an ACE generator.

Mirra realized that if he was going to transform the lives of his residents, he had to stabilize their housing tenure and transform their school. He began with fifty homeless or at-risk families with children in McCarver's kindergarten, providing them with rental vouchers that required each family to pay only $25 a month for rent during the first year, with the Tacoma Housing Authority paying the rest. Over the next five years the families would commit to paying an increasing share of their rent, rising to about $770 a month for a two-bedroom apartment. To help families earn enough to come up with rent, the housing authority provided parents with job training, health care, and GED programs, and connected them to more than thirty different supportive services.

At the same time, the housing authority raised philanthropic funds so that the school could increase the quality of its education. As a result of these integrated efforts, in the 2011–12 school year only 4.5 percent of the students on the THA program left McCarver. The number of working parents quadrupled, and the average monthly income of all households in the program doubled. The quality of education at McCarver also significantly improved and is on track for International Baccalaureate certification. Crossing difficult funding barriers, the THA invested some of its own funds in the school's teacher training program. By 2014 annual teacher turnover had declined to only two a year.

Michael Mirra's program is innovative, expensive, and essential. But it is much cheaper than not acting. Homeless individuals can cost cities up to $1 million a year in police, court, jail, hospital, and emergency shelter costs. The city of Denver, Colorado, discovered that providing housing to its homeless population saved an average of $31,545 a year per person, reducing emergency room visits and costs by 34.3 percent, hospital inpatient costs by 66 percent, detox visits by

82 percent, and incarceration days and costs by 76 percent. Even after investing these savings in housing, social services, and medical care, the program saved $4,745 a year per person.[20]

In addition to housing, families, and schools, the health-care system is also an important leverage point, the focus of Dr. Nadine Burke Harris. Dr. Burke Harris grew up in Palo Alto, the daughter of Jamaican immigrants. She earned a master's degree in Public Health from Harvard, and a medical degree from the University of California, Davis, and did her residency at Stanford. She then joined the California Pacific Medical Center, a private health-care network, opening a clinic in the Bayview–Hunters Point neighborhood, one of the poorest in San Francisco, with a 73 percent unemployment rate and 53 percent chronically absent from school. Between 2005 and 2007 there was ten times more violence in this one neighborhood on average than in all the rest of San Francisco.

Dr. Burke Harris was surprised by how many health issues her pediatric patients suffered from, and set out to discover why. After learning about adverse childhood experiences and toxic stress, she concluded that they were the likely cause of the epidemic in Bayview–Hunters Point, and she set out to find a cure. Dr. Burke Harris's project, now called the Center for Youth Wellness, developed a multidisciplinary approach that begins with early screening for ACEs, since prompt interventions can restore healthy cognitive patterns. It takes ninety days for a traumatic event to inflict its damage on the brain, so if effective measures are taken within that time, the harm may be reversed.

The Center for Youth Wellness works with both affected children and their parents, as their issues are interdependent. Its doctors and social workers begin with an assessment carried out in the clinic, the home, and the school to determine the child's exposure to adversity and the extent of its impact on the child's well-being. Then the health system, the home, and the school all join forces to become part of the cure. The center begins by educating the family on the causes and symptoms of chronic stress, and provides its members with strategies for reducing that stress.

Children and their families are also provided psychotherapy by UCSF's Child Trauma Research Program and the Early Life Stress and Pediatric Anxiety Program at the Lucile Packard Children's Hospital. In addition, the Center for Youth Wellness trains patients in mindfulness and coping skills, which help them and their families build their cognitive resilience to manage future stressful events. And San Francisco's public housing program, Hope SF, has initiated a program that integrates trauma awareness into all of its housing work. This begins by recognizing the effects of trauma on both its residents and its staff, and then figuring out how to integrate solutions at every level of the system.

Vicarious Trauma

In 2003, my wife, Diana Rose, founding president of the Garrison Institute, and the noted meditation teacher Sharon Salzberg began a program to address the toxic stress suffered by workers in New York City's shelters for victims of domestic violence. They founded the institute's Contemplative Based Resilience (CBR) program, to understand and help relieve the toxic stress experienced by social service workers. They often work in an invisible, pervasive cognitive ecology of toxic stress that deeply permeates not only families, but also the caregivers who are trying to support them.

The effects of trauma can pass from traumatized people to their caregivers in the form of vicarious, or secondary, trauma. This little-known phenomenon is one of the major causes of the burnout, stress, depression, and even suicide that affect social services and medical workers who deal with traumatized populations. If we are going to successfully address the epidemic of ACEs and toxic stress, we're going to have to protect the helping professionals who come in contact with the victims. CBR training uses a four-pronged approach to healing vicarious trauma: yoga because trauma is embodied, meditation to detoxify the mind, psychosocial work to help explain how vicarious trauma is impacting workers, and community building to help traumatized workers rebuild their social networks and return from isolation. The Garrison team has gone on to apply its work effectively to refugee and humanitarian aid workers around the world. Caring for caregivers, it turns out, is an essential leverage point in creating healthy communities.

The cognitive ecology of communities is the soil of civilization, essential to its well-being. Just as the stresses of climate change, disease, and biodiversity loss reduce the adaptive capacities of biological communities, the stresses of low-income life and the prevalence of PTSD and ACEs are reducing the adaptive capacity of our cognitive ecologies. These conditions are then exacerbated by housing instability, transmitted through social contagion, and amplified by neighborhood effects and environmental toxins. It is a recipe for damaged people and failing neighborhoods.

Healthy neighborhoods require a sense of collective efficacy and strong social networks. Toxic environmental and cognitive stresses undermine the capacity of individuals to trust one another and to develop social cohesion. Housing instability makes it harder for families to connect with their neighbors, undermining the reliability and consistency needed to build strong social networks. And these cognitive deficits make it harder for affected residents to envision a future and work together to plan it. Thus these stresses form a negative feedback loop within the neighborhood, increasing the likelihood of persistent endemic poverty.

Four Strategies to Combat Toxic Stress

Although work on toxic stress is in its early stages, four strategies to relieve it have emerged. The first approach, a stable base, takes us back to housing, a place that is physically, psychologically, and environmentally safe. It is becoming increasingly clear that such housing is essential to the well-being of chronically stressed families, as well as the social and health-care workers who serve them. Enterprise Community Partners identifies four key ways to improve poor and working families' housing. The first is to increase the opportunity for these families to move to better neighborhoods by expanding the Section 8 voucher and other federal programs. The second is to dramatically increase investments to improve low-income neighborhoods so that every child can grow up in a community of opportunity. The third is to raise the minimum wage, increase access to higher education, and make other investments to raise the wage-earning capacity of low-income families. And the fourth is most surprising—to redirect the housing subsidies received by wealthier families to fund these programs. Home owners receive over $100 billion a year in housing subsidies through two tax deductions, the mortgage-interest deduction and the property-tax deduction. Families earning over $200,000 a year receive 37 percent of these subsidies, while families earning less than $50,000 a year receive only 4 percent. If just 25 percent of this subsidy were redirected to lower-income families, it could provide Section 8 housing vouchers to every U.S. family earning less than 150 percent of the poverty level and to all families who currently pay more than 50 percent of their income on rent.[21] If half of the home mortgage subsidies were redirected toward the working poor, we could also develop hundreds of thousands of new affordable housing units each year.

The second strategy is exercise. Bruce McKewen, head of the Margaret Milliken Hatch Laboratory of Neuroendocrinology at Rockefeller University, has demonstrated that among its many benefits exercise stimulates healthy neurogenesis, or brain regeneration. We have already seen that people who live within a ten-minute walk from parks and open space are more likely to exercise. The location, form, and connectivity of neighborhoods also matter. A study published in the *American*

Journal of Preventive Health found that children who live in walkable, smart-growth neighborhoods get significantly more exercise than those who live in environments designed for driving.[22]

The walkability of communities varies significantly. In cities it is affected by residential density, intersection density, land-use mix, subway stop density, and the ratio of retail building area to retail land area. In suburban areas these factors are exacerbated when a neighborhood lacks sidewalks and safe street crossings. People living in walkable neighborhoods engage in 100 minutes a week of physical activity more on average than those people living in neighborhoods with low levels of walkability. This amount of exercise is significant enough to have a considerable impact on health issues such as obesity.[23]

The third strategy for reducing stress is developing mental quiet and space. Dr. Richard Davidson, founder of the Center for the Study of Healthy Minds at the University of Wisconsin's Waisman Center, has extensively studied the effects of mindfulness training on stress, and has documented its positive neurological and immunological benefits.[24] His lab has published research showing that contemplative practices such as meditation can increase children's self-regulation, attention, and pro-social behaviors such as compassion and empathy.[25] Stress-reduction practices can also stimulate the regrowth of healthy brain structures in as little as eight weeks. Meditation nurtures the mind's reflective capacity, which is essential for us to gain perspective on the conditions stressing our lives, our communities, and the world, and to respond not reactively but systemically, a skill increasingly required by the twenty-first-century job market.

The fourth key to fighting toxic stress is the benefit of being part of a community with supportive, healthy human connections. Eric Klinenberg's study of the response of Chicago neighborhoods to the stress of heat waves indicates the importance of social networks in individual and collective resilience. Our brains are not only wired for flight and fight. They are also wired for what psychologists call "tend and friend," a strategy that women, in particular, turn to. The choice between fight and flight or tend and friend is influenced by Sampson's neighborhood effect. Neighborhoods that have a high degree of perceived order, and a sense of collective efficacy, are more likely to respond altruistically in times of volatility and stress.

Cognitive and Environmental Traumas Are Expensive

The Centers for Disease Control and Prevention, in a study based on 2008 data, estimated the total lifetime financial costs associated with just one year of confirmed cases of child physical abuse, sexual abuse, psychological abuse, and neglect as ranging from $124 billion to as high as $585 billion.[26] The costs were arrived at by adding short-term health-care costs, long-term medical costs, child welfare costs, special education costs, criminal justice costs, and productivity losses. Multiply this by a decade of new cases and the costs will overwhelm our city, state, and federal budgets—and this does not even take into account the cognitive effects of toxic stress that pass to caregivers. If we invest in preventing and healing these issues now, the long-term benefit to individuals and society will be enormous.

The costs of environmental toxins are equally devastating. A study by Leonardo Trasande, associate professor in pediatrics, environmental medicine, and health policy at NYU, found that the 2008 costs of environmentally mediated diseases in U.S. children, including lead poisoning, prenatal methylmercury exposure, childhood cancer, asthma, intellectual disability, autism, and attention deficit hyperactivity disorder, were $76.6 billion.[27]

These costs help us think about community development in an entirely different way. Investing in safe, green, well-located housing, excellent schools, and proactive health-care systems saves societies money over the long run. Yet the investment in any one of these—

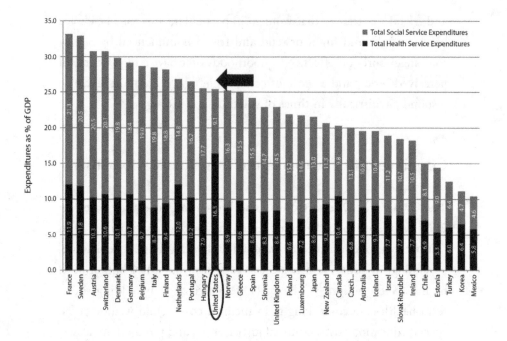

The United States spends far more than other OECD nations on health care, and far less on social services. The result is lower health and well-being outcomes. *(From E. H. Bradley and L. A. Taylor,* The American Health Care Paradox: Why Spending More Is Getting Us Less, *1st ed. [New York: Public Affairs, 2013])*

housing, education, health—alone is not sufficient. We need to invest in all to sever the roots of ACEs, toxic stress, and vicarious trauma, to preempt unsustainable human, social, and economic costs later on. And these need to be accompanied by rigorous regulations to remove environmental toxins from our buildings, food, soils, water, and air.

The funds for these social services are already available, hidden in our government's expenditures. The average OECD nation spends four times as much as the United States does on social services, education, and housing, and, as a result, spends only half as much as the United States on health care.

These nonmedical services are significant determinants of health—stable, affordable housing, early childhood and family services, excellent education and psycho-social care make a great deal of difference to the health of a nation. Shifting expenses from health care to social services not only improves health but also enhances the conditions of opportunity.

Transforming Trauma into Resilience

We are just beginning to understand the interconnection between the well-being of children and that of their families, their housing, their neighborhoods, and the cities in which they live, but we do know that they are all interconnected. Every step we take to relieve the toxic causes and conditions of economic, psychological, and spiritual poverty for even one child provides relief from those conditions for all of us.

We conclude this chapter with the Latin roots of the community of opportunity, the gift of being together and safely returning home from our various ventures to a harbor of peace. We are living in a stressful time. Toxic stress and trauma are socially contagious, and they cause people to hunker down and isolate. They fray social networks and limit the growth of social capital. And although this chapter has focused on low-income communities, where they are often most concentrated, the issues described affect every community.

But just as we have significantly advanced our knowledge of the causes of trauma and stress that so negatively affect communities, we have also learned a great deal about how to foster their well-being. We can apply these strategies to the task of restoring the ecological, social, and cognitive health of our communities, and weave the solutions together to compose a well-tempered city that enhances its cognitive ecology and landscape of opportunity.

CHAPTER 11

Prosperity, Equality, and Happiness

IN 1930, JOHN MAYNARD KEYNES, one of the greatest economists of the twentieth century, wrote an extraordinary article, "Economic Possibilities for Our Grandchildren," in which he ruminated on what the nature of the economy and the quality of people's lives would be one hundred years in the future. The year 2030 is not so far away anymore, so we can begin to see some of its outlines. In light of what has already occurred, some of what Keynes predicted appears remarkably prescient, but he also failed to see much of what came to pass as the twentieth century unfolded.

Keynes was born in 1883 in Cambridge, England. He grew up steeped in an environment of academic rigor, moral philosophy, and social activism. His father taught economics at Cambridge University at a time when economics was considered part of a larger system of morality going back to the earliest thinkers and writers, including Greece's Aristotle, India's Chanakya, and China's Qin Shi Huang. Keynes's mother, Florence, was a social activist. After his graduation from Cambridge in 1904 with a degree in mathematics, Keynes's path took him through the civil service and academia. By the time he wrote "Economic Possibilities for Our Grandchildren" he had been thinking about the social implications of macroeconomic systems for some time. The article, written at the beginning of the Great Depression, begins:

"We are suffering just now from a bad attack of economic pessimism. It is common to hear people say that the epoch of enormous economic progress which characterized the nineteenth century is over; that the rapid improvement in the standard of life is now going to slow down—at any rate in Great Britain; that a decline in prosperity is more likely than an improvement in the decade which lies ahead of us."[1]

Keynes intuited a connection between the degree of optimism or pessimism in a society, which he called "Animal Spirits," and the society's performance in improving the well-being of its members. We now know that a society must believe in its collective efficacy to truly prosper, and as citizens we must believe that the system in which we live gives us at least a glimmer of hope that we can improve our lives going forward.

Keynes saw a positive relationship between growth, prosperity, and happiness. He predicted compounding economic growth over the ensuing century, and assumed that once there were enough resources to take care of everyone on earth, wealth would be more equally distributed. He wrote, "All kinds of social customs and economic practices affecting the distribution of wealth and of economic rewards and penalties, which we now maintain at all costs, however distasteful and unjust they may be in themselves, because they are tremendously useful in promoting the accumulation of capital, we shall then be free, at last, to discard." Ultimately Keynes envisioned a world in which people would essentially be free from economic necessity, their material desires satisfied so they could enjoy leisure and the pursuit of culture while working fifteen hours a week. In such a world, income and wealth would be fairly equally distributed, because, with widespread prosperity, individuals would not need to defend their economic advantages.

The world has become vastly more prosperous than it was in the 1930s, but we still have not shifted our social customs and economic practices away from the accumulation of capital, so the distribution of income has not been equalized. In 2015 the richest 1 percent of the world's population controlled more wealth than the remaining 99 percent. Eighty-five billionaires owned as much wealth as everyone in the lower half of the world's population. The World Economic Forum ranked income inequality as the number one trend facing the world in 2015,[2] and it looks as if the problem is only getting worse.

Prosperity in a Resource-Constrained Future

In Keynes's day the quality of an Oxford don's life was considered to be pretty terrific. Yet in the 1930s the world's most distinguished English-speaking professors lacked material benefits that many lower-middle-class families today consider the norm: central heating, air-conditioning, electric washing machines and dryers, televisions, home computers, smartphones, multiple cars, overnight package delivery, and a wide array of technologies like the Internet, WiFi, CT scanners, and laparoscopic surgery.

Keynes thought that higher Gross Domestic Product, or GDP, which measures the economic output of a city or nation, would inevitably lead to greater happiness and less work. Alas, he was wrong. From 1970 to 2015 the size of the average home in the United States doubled, as did its number of cars, and its number of televisions has tripled, all this while the number of occupants per home halved! However, despite all these outward signs of prosperity, Americans are working longer, harder, and with less job security. Nor are the wealthy exempt from professional stresses and strains: for the first time in history, high-income earners now work more hours per week than working-class people. Soaring production and consumption have not turned out to be the pathway to happiness.

At the beginning of economic history, our global economy was directly linked to the fruits of the earth. Civilization was powered by what we grew, the animals we fed, and a bit of water and wind.

Estimates of global GDP show a bump upward during the Greek, Roman, and Byzantine empires, but surprisingly modest growth until 1780. During this early period there were vast differences in wealth between landowners and the serfs who worked their land, with only a small middle class between. Interestingly, from the end of the Roman Empire until 1820, India and China produced more than 50 percent of the global GDP.[3]

So what happened in 1780? Everything changed, thanks to James Watt's dramatic improvement of the steam engine in 1777. Until then, the world's economies were primarily powered by the current energy of what was harvested. Watt's steam engines were powered by coal, concentrated energy that was grown millions of years ago. Coal was followed by more efficient oil, and the invention of oil-based engines and generators. The expanded EROI of these new forms of energy unleashed the industrial revolution, and along with it, the urbanization of the world.

In the nearly two hundred years between 1780 and 1970 the ratio between gross domestic product, or GDP, and the number of tons of extracted natural resources remained fairly constant: roughly two billion tons of resources were consumed for every trillion dollars of GDP. In 1900, for example, global GDP was about $3 trillion and some 6 trillion tons of primary materials were mined or harvested. By 1970 global GPD had grown to $12 trillion and about 25 trillion tons of materials were being extracted. During these two centuries most of the world's developed nations grew large, fairly comfortable middle classes.

In 1970 the world went off the gold standard and money became less directly linked to production. All of a sudden it became easier to make money from money than it did from manufacturing goods. Agent-based modeling simulations show that under such circumstances those people with more money at the start of a generation will gain a disproportionately larger share of wealth by the end of that generation, which is exactly what happened. One outcome of the new economic system was increased economic inequality. So while Keynes envisioned economic growth producing a more equal distribution of wealth and well-being, in most societies its actual distribution has become increasingly unequal. He foresaw neither the rise of a middle class in the developing world nor the decline of the developed world's middle class. And we are now discovering that the distribution of well-being also does not track with the distribution of the world's wealth.

Well-Being and Wealth

In 2013, UNICEF released a report comparing the well-being of children in twenty-nine of the world's most advanced nations. The report compiled data on health, safety, education, behavioral factors, living environments, material well-being, and subjective "life satisfaction" surveys from children themselves. The United States landed near the bottom on almost all measures, ranking twenty-sixth out of twenty-nine countries; only Lithuania, Latvia, and Romania performed worse.[4] Somehow there is a huge disconnect between this country's prosperity and the well-being of its families. According to the traditional economic view, growth and productivity as measured by GDP are key markers of the success of a society. The UNICEF well-being report underscores just how incomplete is this conventional view. Cities and countries with rising incomes have been confronted by the paradox of unhappy growth, in which increased GDP per capita has not led to increased well-being.

Our early cities appear to have been fairly egalitarian. Engong Ismael, a Balinese anthropologist, describes this as a horizontal caste system with clearly defined roles—each respected for its contribution to the health of the community. But as urban cultures developed they became more hierarchical. Most of the grand monuments of the past were built by slaves or indentured labor. As a city grew more prosperous, if the gap between the richest and poorest was perceived as too great, the social cohesion of the city suffered. As we read in the cases of the Mayan and Russian empires, when stressful environmental conditions were accompanied by a low collective sense of we-ness, social unrest followed, and even collapse.

People move to cities because they seek opportunity, hoping to improve their lives, not to stay mired in a lifetime of poverty. Poverty is extraordinarily debilitating, and its persistence limits the ability of a city to thrive. One goal of any well-tempered city must be to provide opportunity for all of its residents to reduce their suffering and improve their well-being. Material prosperity doesn't necessarily lead to happiness, but grinding poverty certainly makes people more likely to be unhappy, unless they believe that there is a pathway to a better life. As we've seen, some aspects of poverty also have a contagious negative effect on the life of a city, including toxic stress, PTSD, inadequate or insecure housing, joblessness, and low-quality education that doesn't give people a chance to successfully compete in the twenty-first century. Increasing a low-income household's income is an essential step to improve factors that contribute to well-being, such as housing, health, and education.

Urbanization is deeply linked to economic development. For much of the twentieth century cities were correlated with wealth. Those nations with the highest per capita income were the most urbanized.[5] But for a growing number of cities in the developing world, urbanization does not necessarily rise in parallel with economic growth, nor with increased individual wealth. The forces of civil war, tribal and religious violence, rural poverty, and climate change are driving most of the 200,000 people a day, across the globe, who now move to cities. And if the city they reach does not have the economic, technical, political, and social structures needed to create communities of opportunity for these migrants and refugees, that city will grow in numbers, but not in prosperity or well-being.

Following World War II the World Bank focused a great deal of effort on the economic development of cities in order to overcome the negative effects of poverty. In many cases its efforts produced positive economic results, yet many of the people living in cities today are no happier. The complexities and uncertainty of the modern world are stressful and difficult to navigate. Even the wealthy have not been made much happier by economic development. It turns out that although money is essential to thrive, there are many other important elements of happiness, too. But until recently we've known more about how to develop prosperous cities than we have about developing happy ones.

In 1974 the USC professor Richard Easterlin published a ground-breaking paper, "The Economics of Happiness."[6] Easterlin's paper, which analyzed the comparative happiness of nations, indicated that rising incomes increase the happiness of individuals in lower-income countries, but that as the prosperity of nations rises it hits a point beyond which additional income doesn't make people any happier. This phenomenon has come to be known as the Easterlin paradox. There's no doubt that many direct causes of suffering among poor people are alleviated by an increase in their income, yet it's also clear that income is not the only driver of happiness.

In a 2009 study of 450,000 Americans, the economists Angus Deaton and Daniel Kahneman discovered that for Americans happiness seemed to level off at a household income level of $75,000. Earnings beyond that, even far beyond that, didn't seem to make people much happier. Interestingly, the $75,000 limit had nothing to do with the cost of living; people were just as happy earning $75,000 in expensive cities like New York as they were in much lower-cost cities. One reason for this may be that although the cost of housing is higher in larger cities, the cost of transportation and food is lower, and there is a much larger selection of goods and services. In fact, as the size of a city doubles, the number of things to buy increases by 20 percent, and their cost declines by 4.2 percent.[7]

But there is a deeper reason. Happiness is tied to what Deaton calls emotionally enriching social experiences. Dr. Kahneman says, "The very best thing that can happen to people is to spend time with other people they like. That is when they are happiest."[8] The way we spend our time is also a critical component of our sense of well-being. In another study Kahneman and his colleagues tracked how people experience their day by asking them to record events in fifteen-minute intervals and evaluate them. Walking, making love, exercise, playing, and reading ranked as their most pleasurable activities. Their least happy activities? Work, commuting, child care, and personal computer time. How many people really enjoy a night of plowing through endless e-mails?[9]

This survey should not mislead us about the value of work. Work can be deeply gratifying and meaningful, and it can also provide rich social relations. Employment is a key element of well-being. People who are unemployed or underemployed are statistically more likely to die younger and be in worse health. People who lose their job in middle age and have difficulty finding a new one are more likely to become depressed, and have a two to three times higher risk of heart attack and stroke over the next ten years.[10] So one of the key challenges of cities in the twenty-first century is to develop economies that generate stimulating, productive work for all of their residents.

In the past we often held the same job for life, whether as a shepherd, a member of a medieval guild, or an employee of a large corporation. Today the average millennial will have had eleven jobs by the time he or she reaches the age of forty. This underscores the need to acquire many different skills beyond technical ability. Satisfying work often requires not only a high level of education, but the emotional and social intelligence required to work successfully in teams. This wider range of qualifications will be essential in a world where computer coding may become the entry-level position that a factory job once was. As agriculture becomes more and more industrialized, rural people are flocking to cities seeking work. Yet with robots increasingly taking line positions in our factories, there are likely to be fewer jobs for the uneducated in the future.

So what *is* the future of work in our cities? Keynes predicted that automation would lead to more leisure, but achieving that requires a wider distribution of economic benefits than our economy is designed for. Instead of Keynes's vision, we are faced with fewer opportunities not only for the uneducated, but also for those who are educated but poorly adapted to the rapidly changing conditions of work. Unemployed and underemployed people tend not to be happy, so this is an issue we need to approach with a thoughtful plan, or it will tear the guts out of our social contract.

In 2005, when Gallup began polling selected residents of almost every country in the world to gauge their state of well-being, respondents were asked about their employment status, trust in government, confidence in the quality of public education, food security, and a variety of other questions. They were also asked to describe their lives as thriving, struggling, or suffering. It turned out that the answer to that question is a key indicator of the social stability of a society.

In the period from 2005 to 2010 the GDP of Tunisia rose by an impressive 26.1 percent[11] and in Egypt it rose by a remarkable 53.4 percent.[12] But Gallup polls showed something else as well. In 2005, 25 percent of Tunisians said they were thriving, but by 2010, despite the big jump in GDP, the proportion of Tunisians who said that they were thriving had declined to 14 percent. The numbers were even worse for Egypt. In 2005, 26 percent of Egyptians described themselves as thriving, but by 2010 that percentage had dropped by more than half, to 12 percent.[13] A key reason for the declines was that growth was accompanied by an enormous amount of corruption, so its benefits were not fairly distributed. For example, a recent study showed that in Tunisia 22 percent of all corporate profits during that period went to companies owned by relatives of the country's president. So perhaps we should not have been so surprised when mass protests took place in these countries in the fall and winter of 2011–2012.

Sidi Bouzid is a central Tunisian city of just 39,000 people some 160 miles south of Tunis, the capital of this small North African nation. The World Economic Forum ranks Tunisia as Africa's most economically competitive nation, ahead of Europe's Portugal and Greece. Tunisia's economy is based on its role as a bridge between the European Union and the Arab states of North Africa. Unfortunately, little of the Mediterranean trade that benefits the country's port cities reaches the inland residents of Sidi Bouzid. This geographic disadvantage has led to a 41 percent unemployment rate in the city, and the highest poverty rate in the country—almost double the national average. To make matters worse, Sidi Bouzid is plagued by corruption that saps its hardworking small-business owners and entrepreneurs.

Sidi Bouzid was an unlikely candidate for global attention, but on December 17, 2010, an event took place there that shook the world: Mohamed Bouazizi set himself on fire.

Twenty-six years old, Mohamed had been working hard selling vegetables in the local market to support his mother, uncle, and siblings, and to pay for the university tuition of one of his sisters. Each day Mohamed would pull his cart through the city's streets to the market and back, laden with wares. His dream was to save enough money to buy a small pickup truck that would allow him to expand into food distribution, the next step up the income ladder.

On December 17, Mohamed borrowed $200 from a moneylender and purchased a cartload of fruits and vegetables. A policewoman, seeking a bribe, confiscated his unlicensed cart, scales, and wares, and fined him ten dinars. As Rania Abouzeid later reported in *Time*, "It wasn't the first time it had happened, but it would be the last. Not satisfied with accepting the 10-dinar fine that Bouazizi tried to pay ($7, the equivalent of a good day's earnings), the policewoman allegedly slapped the scrawny young man, spat in his face, and insulted his dead father.

Humiliated and dejected, Bouazizi went to the provincial headquarters, hoping to complain to local municipality officials, but they refused to see him. At 11:30 a.m., less than an hour after the confrontation with the policewoman and without telling his family, Bouazizi returned to the elegant double-story white building with arched azure shutters, poured fuel over himself and set himself on fire."[14]

Mohamed Bouazizi's act set the country ablaze with demonstrations by young people, frustrated at the oppression of the police, their own lack of opportunity to advance, corruption, and the widening gap between rich and poor. Twenty-eight days later, in January 2011, Tunisia's president, Zine El Abidine Ben Ali, resigned. A few weeks later the flame lit in Tunisia had spread to the most populous country in the Arab world: Egypt.

On January 25, 2011, a small crowd gathered outside the Hayiss Sweet Shop in Boulaq, one of the informal settlements that had grown on the periphery of Cairo in the 1970s. Egyptians called these communities *ashwaiyyat*, or haphazard places. The first squatters to move to Boulaq came to work at a nearby Coca-Cola bottling plant, a cigarette factory, and the Upper Egypt railroad. By the 1990s the slum had developed into a dense, thriving community with five-story brick buildings, shops, and small factories.[15] Like the banlieues of Paris and the favelas of Rio de Janeiro, Boulaq is not far from wealthier neighborhoods, but is cut off from the rest of the city, in this case by three railway lines, the al-Zumor canal, and a high fence. Only two pedestrian bridges and bus stops connect the community to the rest of the city. The only government presence comes in the form of the occasional visit by police who harass Boulaq's residents.

During the later 1990s and early 2000s Egypt was overwhelmed by the same megatrends that affected much of the rest of the world— explosive population growth, rapid urbanization, and, in the Middle East, increased violence. For decades the government had lived off income from oil and gas, fees from the Suez Canal, and foreign aid from the Soviet Union and the United States, which were competing for the nation's loyalty. With the fall of the Soviet Union and the decline of oil prices, President Hosni Mubarak no longer had sufficient income for his people. Instead of formalizing and growing the economy or further taxing his wealthy friends, Mubarak cut funding and services to places like Boulaq. As a consequence, no public secondary school was built in Boulaq, nor a single public health center, despite the neighborhood's population of 500,000 (larger than Miami, Florida). The Muslim Brotherhood and its network of Islamic charities filled the gap by providing education and health clinics, as well as by helping residents build an informal network of sewer lines.

On January 25, ironically a national holiday established to honor the police, the small group of protesters gathered at the Hayiss Sweet Shop began to march across Boulaq's pedestrian bridges to Cairo's Tahrir Square. The first group of protesters to arrive, they resisted police until others joined them. By sunset 50,000 protesters held Tahrir Square. By the end of the week, the square was filled with millions. Eighteen days later, President Mubarak resigned.

Uprisings followed in Libya, Bahrain, Syria, and Yemen, but social ferment was not limited to North Africa and the Middle East. In the summer of 2011 riots broke out in London. Interestingly, they didn't take place in the poorest areas of the city. They erupted on the edges, between lower-middle-income and middle-income neighborhoods, where the invisible fault lines of British society create barriers to upward mobility. These were followed by demonstrations in Tel Aviv and Jerusalem, where protesters rallied against the lack of affordable housing, jobs, and opportunity, as well as pervasive corruption. On September 17, 2011, the Occupy Wall Street movement took the issue of inequality to the heart of America's financial district, posing a fundamental question: Is the vast gap in income between the top 1 percent of America's income earners and the rest fair? Protesters didn't propose a solution, yet the Occupy movement spread to more than one hundred other cities around the United States.

Protests over inequality continued throughout the world. In 2013 growing concern in China about pollution and toxic neighborhoods boiled over into huge street demonstrations in Beijing, Kunming, Ningbo, Dalian, Qidong (just north of Shanghai), and Guangzhou. At the same time the bus fare protests flared in São Paulo, led by working people who felt that Brazil's massive investment in facilities for the coming Olympics and soccer World Cup had raised their taxes and their bus fares without delivering any benefit to them. In September 2014, 100,000 protesters shut down central Hong Kong over their right to democracy. And in Ferguson, Missouri, the shooting of Michael Brown, a black youth, by Darren Wilson, a white police officer, touched off tense demonstrations that spread around the nation.

Each of these protests started in a city. And each grew not from the city's poorest, but from those who felt that they were unjustly deprived of opportunity by corruption, racial discrimination, or other structural barriers in their political systems and economies. The military historian Elihu Rose (my uncle) noted that almost all revolutions begin with a valid issue that goes unheard. Those protests rise to the level of violence only after other avenues of redress have been tried and the system has failed to respond. Each of these waves of protest took its government by surprise. How could any government or major global institution not have a clue that a revolution was coming? Because they were looking at the wrong data. In the Middle East GDP was rising, and governments believed that increased productivity provided a sufficient pathway to happiness. They were wrong.

The Paradox of Unhappy Growth

Throughout most of human history, governments did not measure their GDP. The idea was developed by the economist Stanley Kuznets, who introduced it in a 1934 report to the U.S. Congress regarding the economy and the Depression. The first to caution that GDP does not measure happiness was Kuznets himself, who included in his report a prescient warning about the risks of single indicators, and the need to better understand income distribution.

"Economic welfare cannot be adequately measured unless the personal distribution of income is known. And no income measurement undertakes to estimate the reverse side of income, that is, the intensity and unpleasantness of effort going into the earning of income. The welfare of a nation can, therefore, scarcely be inferred from a measurement of national income as defined above."[16]

Kuznets made a remarkable observation—that not just the amount of income but the way it was distributed was critical to the happiness of a nation. It was an observation that remained buried under the averaging concept of GDP for seventy-five years, but after the 2008 global financial crisis many woke up to the reality that growth at any cost was not serving to make the world's people much happier.

The Brookings Institute scholars Carol Graham and Eduardo Lora have been studying the relationship between growth and happiness around the world for over a decade. Not only do their findings support the notion that national prosperity and happiness are not directly linked, but high levels of growth seem to make people *less happy*, not more. As Graham put it, "Rapid economic growth typically brings greater instability and inequality with it, and that makes people unhappy."[17]

Graham's most recent work correlates current happiness with the belief in the opportunity to improve our future or the future for our children.[18] People who feel the future can be better are not only happier, but much more willing to work hard and invest to educate themselves and their children. Those who believe that their opportunities are limited are separated from the rest of the world by physical, social, educational, and racial barriers and are less willing to invest in the future. Even if they do aspire to a better future, their additional burden of toxic stress, ACEs, and poisons in the environment makes it extremely difficult to achieve. Remember the lead paint that Freddie Gray grew up with in Baltimore? If things had been different, Freddie and his sister Fredericka might have become scientists, social workers, or community leaders, and the city would have been better off for it.

In 1911, George W. F. McMechen, a Yale-educated lawyer, moved to Baltimore's prosperous Mount Royal neighborhood. McMechen represented the aspirations of the Mount Royal community in every way, including education, occupation, dignity, and leadership, except for one: his skin was black. In response to his move, McMechen's neighbors drafted legislation that imposed apartheid on the city. Cynically designed to pass muster with the equal-protection clause of the Fourteenth Amendment to the Constitution, it stated that Negroes could not move to a block that was more than half white, and whites could not move to a block that was more than half Negro. Called the "Baltimore Idea," the legislation spread throughout cities in or near the South, and was soon adopted by Birmingham, St. Louis, Winston-Salem, Roanoke, Louisville, and many others. These cities are still struggling with the legacy of that decision.

Since the nation's founding, home ownership in the United States has been a way for families to generate wealth and pass it on to future generations. This pathway was cut off for African Americans by "Baltimore ideas" that became policy thanks to the FHA's mortgage regulations of the 1930s. Deprived of an important opportunity to generate wealth, African Americans saw the gap between themselves and white families widen, so that by 1992, when Freddie Gray was born, generations of his ancestors knew their opportunities were limited. With little belief in a better future, they disconnected from education and work. When police harass young African Americans, call them by racial epithets, and arrest them for petty crimes and push them into the criminal justice system, they cement the death of their aspirations. Alas, the broken windows policy, which does reduce disorder, if misdirected can have the countervailing effect of also reducing social efficacy.

Although the deck has been historically stacked against African Americans, they are not alone in their pessimism, at least in the United States. In this country 62 percent of all people, regardless of race or ethnicity, think their children will be worse off than they are. Graham's work shows that the least optimistic cohort of the nation's population, poorly educated, lower-income whites, have declining life expectancies, while poor blacks and Hispanics are more optimistic about their futures, and their life spans are rising.[19] By contrast, people who live in Latin America are much more optimistic about the future; only 8 percent of Chileans think their children will be worse off. Even in Brazil, which has been struggling with a stalled economy, 72 percent of people think their future will be better.[20]

Cities are cauldrons of opportunity, but their overall happiness is dependent on the degree to which that opportunity is open to all their inhabitants. People can intuitively tell when access to opportunity is unfairly distributed. But it also can be measured.

Measuring Income Inequality: The Gini Index

The global standard for measuring income inequality is the Gini index, developed by the Italian statistician Corrado Gini in 1912. A Gini index coefficient of 0 indicates a society of absolute equality, in which every member of the society has exactly the same income. At the opposite end of the spectrum, a Gini coefficient of 1 (or 100 percent) represents a society of maximal inequality, in which one person has all of the income and the rest of the population has none. The United Nations warns that a Gini coefficient above 0.40 increases a society's risk of social unrest.[21]

Ironically, Corrado Gini had no interest in tackling the problem of inequity; he was a fascist and an early advocate of eugenics, the sterilization of any group that would ostensibly dilute a nation's racial purity. Gini postulated that if the ratio of low-income people to high-income people became too extreme, the higher birthrate among low-income families would dilute the genetic virtues of the high-income families, drive the country into decline, and make it vulnerable to conquest. His solution to eliminating poverty was to eliminate the poor!

Today the world's most income-equal cities are found in northern Europe. Copenhagen has a Gini index coefficient of 0.27, and Hamburg and Stockholm have a coefficient of 0.34. Barcelona's Gini coefficient rose from 0.28 in 2006 to 0.33 in 2012, due to reallocation of income from the global financial crisis. But Europe's cities were not always the world's leaders in equality.

The French Revolution of 1789 may have been led by intellectuals, but it was mostly waged by starving farmers who had come to Paris and settled in the slums of Faubourg Saint-Antoine, seeking work in its tanneries and workshops. The district happened to be adjacent to the Bastille prison. Like today's urban immigrants saving to send money home to their families in the countryside, they lived in overcrowded slums, with fifteen or more people sleeping in a room. The cost of bread consumed 60 percent of their wages, and although it seems that Marie Antoinette may never have said, when told of their lack of bread, "So let them eat cake," the phrase stuck as a potent symbol of income inequality. When the call came for revolution, they were highly motivated to storm the Bastille.

In 1875, Berlin became the most densely settled city in Europe. Its new residents were crammed into *Mietskaseren*, human warehouses, built in huge blocks, five stories tall, with little light, air, or sanitation. In 1930, Werner Hegemann's exposé *Das Steinerne Berlin* (Stony Berlin) called Berlin "the largest tenement city in the world." Even in

1962, only 19 percent of the Mietskaseren apartments had a toilet. These tenements were centers of discontent.

But Europe emerged from the collapse of its empires, brutal industrialization, the horror of fascism and Nazism, and its two world wars with a new social contract. Today its cities are the most equal on earth because Europe's leaders and people have intentionally made them so.

In general, the larger a city or metropolitan region, the more likely it is to be unequal. London, the largest city in the UK, has a disproportionate share of both the nation's wealthiest people and its poorest, as do Rio de Janeiro, Bogotá, and Bangkok.[22] The least equal cities are found in the developing world. Officially the worst are Johannesburg and Cape Town, both in South Africa, with Gini coefficents of 0.75, the legacy of a half-century of state-sponsored apartheid. I suspect that some cities in the world are even less equal, but that between corruption and poor management their economic data is not reported as accurately as in South Africa.

Addis Ababa, the capital city of Ethiopia, comes in slightly above bottom-ranked South African cities with a Gini index coefficient of 0.61, followed by Bogotá, Colombia, at 0.59. Brazil's Rio de Janeiro, with its famous slums, has a Gini score of 0.53, and its sister city, São Paulo, weighs in at 0.50. For a decade China claimed that Beijing was one of the most equal cities in the world with a Gini index of 0.22, but after a change in leadership in 2012, China acknowledged that the numbers were inaccurate; the nation's Gini index was changed to 0.61, but through a process that was still not transparent.[23] All these cities with high scores have seething undercurrents of social unrest.

The United States has an overall Gini coefficient of 0.39, just barely below the warning level, and many of its individual cities don't fare so well. New York City and the Miami/Fort Lauderdale region have Gini indexes of 0.50, the same as São Paulo's. New Orleans comes close with a Gini index of 0.49, and San Francisco, Los Angeles, and Houston are only slightly more equal, with indexes of 0.48. The ten U.S. metropolitan areas that come nearest to Europe's level of equality are all smaller cities, none of which has a population of more than a million people. These include Lancaster, Pennsylvania; Salem, Oregon; and Colorado Springs, Colorado. Ogden, Utah, has the lowest Gini index coefficient of any U.S. city, at 0.386, although, for perspective, this is 40 percent higher than Helsinki's 0.26. It seems that if you want to live in a city but want to enjoy the happiness that comes from income equality, you would do better in a moderate-size one!

The ancient Greek philosopher Plato observed, "If a state is to avoid . . . civil disintegration . . . extreme poverty and wealth must not be allowed to rise in any section of the citizen-body because both lead to disasters."[24]

As we have seen with the collapse of the Mayan cities, the fall of Moscow after the starvation of 1603, the French revolution and the Jasmine revolutions, inequality undermines the social fabric that keeps communities together—especially in times of stress. Consider the Argentine paradox. In 1913 Argentina was a rapidly growing country, the tenth most prosperous in the world, and its capital city, Buenos Aires, was regarded as one of the world's most beautiful. It was celebrated for being home to one of the world's finest opera houses, wide boulevards, South America's tallest buildings, and the continent's first subway system, yet *villas miserias*, or shantytowns, surrounded its industrial zones. When the global depression reached Argentina in 1930 the nation's vast chasm between rich and poor— its income inequality—became its undoing. In response to a restless population, a fascist military coup supported by the wealthy overturned seven decades of democracy. Meanwhile, the gap between the opulence of the city's downtown and the squalid living conditions of its disgruntled laborers erupted into a mass mobilization on October 17, 1945. Since then the nation has staggered through cycles of default and economic restructuring. Today, its economy lies in the hands of hedge fund opportunists, who bought Argentina's bonds cheaply.

Infrastructure

Mexico City lies at the heart of the tenth-largest metropolitan region in the world, home to more than 21 million people. It is a thriving metropolis, the sixteenth most prosperous in the world,[25] but its prosperity is not evenly distributed. Many of the city's most affluent families live and work in the secure central city, or in northwestern neighborhoods with fine restaurants and trendy shops, a comfortable drive away from their daily activities. Only 30 percent of Mexico City's residents have cars; except for those living in the finest neighborhoods, its streets are choked with traffic and pollution. The 70 percent who live toward the city's sprawling edges spend an average of three hours a day on their commute to work, carried by the informal *collectivo* system of small independent vans and buses.

Like many of the world's largest cities, Mexico City and its region are rapidly growing, but because this growth has been unplanned, the city has failed to balance the location of jobs and housing in an equitable way. One of the solutions for large, sprawling megacities like Mexico City is to develop multiple downtowns and connect them with a high-capacity mass-transit system. Singapore's 2014 master plan divides the city-state into six regions, each with a dense downtown core as well as health and education facilities, open spaces, civic services, and a superb mass-transit system connecting them.

Infrastructure is the armature upon which civilization advance; it provides the necessary conditions for healthy density—the connections between workers and workplaces, between companies and markets; it also provides the framework for the flow of information, the substrate upon which communities grow their health and well-being.

Cities cannot have a vibrant economic future with congested roads, overloaded airports, a brittle electric grid, slow Internet connections, aging water and wastewater treatment systems, outdated schools, and a lack of ubiquitous information and of smart municipal management systems. Almost every one of these systems needs to be redesigned, or at a minimum updated, in order to dynamically respond to the challenges of climate change, population growth, resource constraints, cybersecurity, and other results of global megatrends.

One of the first ways to improve opportunity for all communities is to provide them with effective mass transit. The design and construction of new infrastructure and the repair and upgrade of existing infrastructure also create new jobs. China has vaulted itself forward economically with twenty-five years of significant infrastructure investments. By contrast, the United States has been underinvesting in its infrastructure for decades. When I last flew to Hong Kong, I departed from Detroit. What a contrast the two cities pose!

Once Again, Neighborhoods Matter

Income inequality in cities always has a spatial dimension, reflected in their more and less prosperous neighborhoods. In 2010 not a single resident of London's three most affluent districts filed for unemployment benefits, while in its poorest neighborhoods 28.9 percent of the population received them.[26] Average life spans decline by a year for every two stops east one goes on the London Underground. The range of life expectancies from the best neighborhoods to the worst varies by twenty years.[27]

In China a residence permit, or *houku*, is needed to live and work in a city. More than 800 million Chinese have only a rural residence permit and are therefore denied the economic opportunities of city life, although an estimated 150 million have illegally migrated to cities anyway. Technically nonresidents, they have no access to public health, education, and social welfare systems, or to the city's housing system. As a result they crowd into dormitories and basements, and sublet apartments. Since their children cannot attend school, parents must leave their children behind in small, isolated villages. Their *houku*-less parents work long hours to earn enough money to send home to grandparents raising their children. A recent *Economist* report estimates that in 2010, the lives of 106 million children were profoundly disrupted, most of them "left behind children" as the Chinese call them. Tong Xiao, director of the China Institute of Children and Adolescents, notes that the emotional and social damage "on left behind children is huge."[28] The full economic consequences of urban workers' salaries subsidizing their parents and children in a declining rural system, because they are not supported by educational, health, and social services in the emerging urban one, have not been addressed. This is not just an issue for China, as almost every nation faces it. The cross-subsidy between urban and rural families has long been a driver of migration, but in the twenty-first century, is this the best way to achieve it?

As we saw from the work of Robert Sampson, the neighborhood effect is extremely potent. Raj Chetty and Nathaniel Hendren, researchers at Harvard University, looked at data from millions of families to study the effects of moving a poor family to a different neighborhood. Their information came from "Moving to Opportunity," a twenty-year-old federal housing program that provided low-income families with a housing voucher to pay the difference between the rent they could afford and market rent in the neighborhood where they wished to move. More than 5 million families received these vouchers, and each family was then encouraged to relocate. Some moved to middle-income neighborhoods, while others remained in low-income communities. Chetty and Hendren discovered that the odds of a poor child escaping poverty as an adult were deeply dependent on the choice the parents made as to where to raise their family, and the age of the child when they made the decision. For example, a poor child born in Baltimore who stayed there earned 25 percent less money as an adult than a poor child born in Baltimore who subsequently moved to a more mixed-income community.

Those cities most conducive to upward mobility share several traits: elementary schools with higher test scores, a higher share of two-parent families, greater levels of involvement in civic and religious groups, and more residential integration of affluent, middle-class, and poor families. And the younger children were when they moved, the better they did economically as adults, the less likely they were to become single parents, and the more likely they were to go to college. These characteristics begin to point to where cities can make investments to create communities of opportunity.

Interestingly, communities that provided more opportunity for poor children also helped wealthier children do better. For example, if a child whose parents were in the bottom 25 percent of income earners in Manhattan moved to Bergen County, New Jersey, just on the other side of the George Washington Bridge from New York City, by the time that child reached the age of twenty-six, she was likely to earn 14 percent more than the national average earned by children of poor families. Yet for children whose families were upper middle class, earning in the 75th percentile, those who lived in Bergen County also had a better future, earning 7 percent more than the average child in their income cohort. Even children who grew up in the top 1 percent of all income-earning families in the nation did better by the age of twenty-six if they lived in mixed-income Bergen County. So place matters.[29]

There Are Many Kinds of Inequality

Income disparity and lack of access to infrastructure are not the only forms of pervasive inequality that affect the well-being of city residents. Health care and education are also unequally distributed. Health outcomes are linked to the effectiveness of the larger nation's health-care systems. Tokyo is considered by many to be the healthiest city in the world, yet its cost per person is only half that of the United States. What makes this achievement even more impressive is the fact that Tokyo's population includes lots of older people. How is this possible? There are many reasons, including Japan's deep commitment to the health of its people; a superb mass-transit system that keeps air pollution, greenhouse gases, and commute times low; strong social networks; and a healthy diet with lots of fresh fish, vegetables, and rice. The city is also perfused with temples, and taking time to reflect, to meditate, is encouraged.

Despite spending twice per person what Japan spends on health care, the United States is ranked thirty-third on the *Economist*'s 2014 "Health Care Outcomes and Cost Report," the same list that placed Japan at the top.[30] The United States is underperforming compared with its peer nations in life expectancy, infant mortality, low birth weight, injuries, homicides, adolescent pregnancy, sexually transmitted diseases, HIV/AIDS, drug-related deaths, obesity, diabetes, heart disease, chronic lung disease, and disability rates.[31] And whereas health outcomes throughout Japan and the other OECD nations are fairly consistent, in the United States they vary widely, indicating the absence of a system that integrates housing, health care, social services, and healthy food systems, and makes them available to everyone.

Creating a healthy city is a collective activity. It is difficult for even the wealthiest citizens to remain healthy if the rest of a city is doing poorly. For a city to be healthy it must provide communal infrastructure for water, wastewater, and sanitation; mass-transit systems; and parks and open spaces for all its citizens. It must establish policies to develop a wide range of housing that is affordable and meets the full diversity of its residents' needs. It must require all citizens to be immunized against early childhood diseases, and undertake concerted efforts to prevent the spread of HIV/AIDS, tuberculosis, Zika, methicillin-resistant *Staphylococcus aureus*, and other rapidly spreading drug-resistant superbugs, as the poor health of a few can threaten the health of all.

Education Equality

In 2011, the Moroccan economists Benaabdelaali Wail, Hanchane Said, and Kamal Abdelhak examined data from 146 nations in order to track levels of educational inequality from 1950 to 2010 and compare it with Gini indexes for those same countries. They concluded that there was a strong correlation between equality in education and equality of income. They noted, "The distribution of education is a key element of human capital, growth and welfare."[32]

Educational equality has two primary components: access and quality. To maximize access, residents' circumstances—where they live, their gender, their socioeconomic status, their disabilities—shouldn't limit their opportunity for academic success. Quality is achieved by the standard of excellence set by a city's schools, and the degree to which excellence is available to everyone. It's no wonder that cities like Singapore, Seoul, and Helsinki, which rank among the world's best for accessible high-quality education, also rank so high in every other category of well-being.

In 1763, King Frederick the Great of Prussia developed the modern world's first great public education system. It mandated that all municipalities must provide and fund education for all boys and girls between the ages of five and fourteen. It required teaching reading, writing, music, religion, and ethics—skills considered essential for citizens to build a modern society. The system quickly adopted an excellent teacher training and testing system, a national curriculum, and mandatory kindergarten. The second public school system was developed in Denmark in 1814. Called "Schools for Life," it combined academics and life skills such as introspection, cooperation, and joy, which provide both the technical skills to succeed and the reflective skills necessary to thrive. As the nineteenth century unfolded, both Prussia and Denmark lost much of their territory—the shrinking of a nation often triggers cultural decline—but the excellence and values of their public schools provided these countries with the cognitive and social capacity to successfully adapt. Today, Denmark is one of the happiest nations on earth, and Germany the most prosperous. Each has a strong social support system, and very green policies. Their universal curriculum has created communities with the shared values, ethics, and knowledge that underlie the ability to adapt and succeed.

In the late 1800s the United States adopted a public education system designed to enhance democracy, with a focus on reading, writing, mathematics, civics, and history. Its early-twentieth-century curriculum was designed to train workers for the industrial economy. However, as the kinds of jobs have rapidly changed, the education system has not kept up. There is a disconnect in the United States between what is being taught and the education needed to thrive in a VUCA world. A Center for Urban Future report on CUNY, New York City's public university, notes that few of the university's 480,000 full- and part-time students are being educated to meet the needs of New York City's largest employers. In a world where robots are taking over menial industrial tasks, the emerging jobs of the twenty-first century require training in systems thinking, collaboration, critical analysis, and rapid adaptation, which are not skills possessed by many of America's tenured faculty, who were trained in the twentieth century.

Geoff Scott, emeritus professor at the University of Western Sydney, polled employers from Australia's top professions to determine what capabilities they most wanted from graduating students. From those answers Scott and his colleague Michael Fullen developed a list of competencies needed to succeed in an increasingly volatile and complex world. Interestingly, employers were not looking for job-specific expertise; they were focusing on the "attitude of mind, set of values, and the personal, interpersonal, and cognitive capabilities identified repeatedly in studies of successful early career graduates and those leaders who have helped create more harmonious, productive and sustainable workplaces and societies."[33] These include character, citizenship, collaboration, communication, creativity, and critical thinking, qualities that make employees capable of thinking like global citizens, with a deep understanding of diverse values and with genuine interest in engaging with others to solve complex problems that impact human and environmental sustainability.

These attributes, which we used to call the soft social and cognitive skills, have become the hard skills cities need from their citizens and leaders if they are to thrive. These are the skills that children with ACEs and toxic exposures struggle to attain. These are the qualities that robots and computers will be unable to provide. And these are the attributes needed in a well-tempered city.

We're All in This Together

In 1972, Louisville, Kentucky, and Detroit, Michigan, received similar court orders to desegregate their schools. Both cities were mandated to create regional plans tying together city schools with those in the suburbs, busing students from their neighborhoods to other schools to ensure an integrated mix. Both populations were 80 percent white and 20 percent black, but each city took a very different approach to the court mandate. Louisville embraced it; Detroit subverted it.

Both plans got off to a poor start. In Detroit the Ku Klux Klan blew up ten school buses in the suburban town of Pontiac. The judge who had ordered the busing of Detroit's students received several death threats, suffered two heart attacks, and died before his case was heard by the Supreme Court. Louisville had a long history of racial segregation; having eagerly adopted the Baltimore idea, it entered the 1970s with highly segregated housing. The court decision that required Louisville's school district to be integrated with surrounding Jefferson County was also met with protests, but they were nonviolent. But leading members of Louisville's elite families, including key Binghams, who owned the local newspaper, and the Browns, who owned the city' most visible employer, the Brown Forman Company, defended integration. Five years later the judge who had imposed the order of segregation was celebrated at a banquet in his honor. The difference in educational outcomes was also significant. In 2011, 62 percent of Louisville's fourth-grade students scored at or above basic levels for math, twice as high as the percentage of Detroit students.

Detroit's approach ended up increasing the city's segregation. In 2006, the public school population was 91 percent black and only 3 percent white, whereas public schools in the wealthy town of Grosse Pointe, which borders Detroit, were 89 percent white and only 8 percent black.

Detroit was not alone. For most American cities, the school desegregation orders of the early 1970s led to white flight to the suburbs. The resulting decline in population, concentration of poverty, and loss of tax base proved to be disastrous. Regions are anchored by their core cities. As the work of Dean Rusk has indicated, the health of the city is key to the health of its suburbs. We are all in it together.

Louisville was one of the few brave cities in the United States to recognize that, even more remarkably because it is a southern city. By integrating its urban and suburban schools, it removed the fear-based motivation to abandon the city. The city called on its residents to be citizens of the region. The strategy worked so well that, in 2003, the city and Jefferson County merged their governments into a new polity they named Louisville Metro, which shares not only students, but also tax revenues, infrastructure responsibilities, and economic development opportunities. This shared sense of destiny has become a key element in the Metro's appeal.

Louisville Metro is home to a great deal of economic diversity, ranging from census tracts in which more than 50 percent of the residents live below the poverty level to some with fewer than 10 percent. But because the schools are all operated as one system, there is no correlation between neighborhood and school quality. In fact, some of Jefferson County's best schools are in its poorest neighborhoods, attracting white families.

Once Louisville's schools were integrated, it was much easier to integrate its neighborhoods, using programs such as the voucher-based Moving to Opportunity, which produced such excellent results when families with young children moved to better neighborhoods. Between 1990 and 2010, neighborhood segregation declined by 20 percent.

The result in Louisville is a workforce better prepared for the twenty-first century. As the Chamber of Commerce states in support of Louisville's busing plan, Louisville is "a city unlike other places, where you could hire people from any school and they would actually be educated, and they would know how to work with others."[34] Louisville intuited what data now clearly shows: the more unequal a region, the worse everyone does, even the wealthy.

In studies of weak market cities and regions in the United States, the social scientists Manuel Pastor and Chris Brenner note that regions with the largest income disparity between central cities and suburbs in 1980 had the lowest level of job growth in the following decade. Pastor and Brenner concluded, "The research presented here suggests that equity is not a luxury but perhaps a necessity. As much as income inequality, poverty concentration, and racial segregation are outcomes of a declining city and regional economy, they are also themselves triggers of decline. Competitiveness strategies for weak-market cities should focus on the basics—infrastructure, good government, and a positive business climate—but it is good to keep the equity piece front and center as well."[35]

Happiness

If wealth and income were the main determinants of happiness, Kuwait City would be the happiest city in the world. Alas, it is not. As the Easterlin paradox predicted, income is not the only contributor to happiness, and as the economist Jeffrey Sachs observed, "We need societies that work, not just economies that work."[36]

The first government to take a wider view of happiness was the Kingdom of Bhutan. In 1972, Jigme Singye Wangchuck, Bhutan's sixteen-year-old Druk Gyalpo, or Dragon King, proposed that the role of government was to increase not the nation's gross national product, but its gross national happiness. The concept continued to be developed by global think tanks and was even adopted in a few cities and provinces, but mostly it was disregarded by other nations until the global financial crisis of 2008. As the tide of financial growth rapidly receded, it revealed deeply unsettled communities. All of a sudden, the idea that the happiness of a society and its people mattered struck a chord.

In 2009 Gallup Healthways began extensive polling in the United States and around the world to report on the degree to which communities were thriving, struggling, or surviving. In 2011 the United Nations issued its World Happiness Report and began convening biannual conferences on happiness, along with report updates. At the same time, the Organization for Economic Cooperation and Development (OECD), an NGO comprising of the world's thirty-four most prosperous nations, proposed its Better Life Index. France, seeking to put its own stamp on well-being, hired the noted economists Joseph Stiglitz, Amartya Sen, and Jean-Paul Fitoussi to develop a well-being index, too. The Stiglitz report noted a disconnect between the quality of a country's health and its GDP. For example, since 1960 life expectancy in France has grown relative to the United States, while its GDP relative to the United States has been declining.[37]

Each of these indexes has a slightly different approach, but they share some common characteristics. Each recognizes the importance of family income, health, education, good governance, vibrant social networks, and a healthy environment to well-being. Bhutan adds to this list psychological well-being, community vitality, cultural diversity and resilience, and time use. The OECD adds work-life balance (another take on time use), safety, and civic engagement. The UN World Happiness report contributes a focus on trust, generosity, and the freedom to make life choices. This list will continue to grow and become more refined as the science of happiness becomes more sophisticated, integrating neuroscience, behavioral economics, sociology, public health, and urban informatics to define and measure healthy communities.

The Prosperity/Well-Being/Equality Matrix

And so it seems that the world's best cities balance prosperity, equality, and happiness to create well-being. But how can we tell if a city is doing a good job of balancing these three attributes of a thriving population? While there are ample data on income, income distribution, and household wealth, and a growing body of information on well-being, few approaches combine these metrics to provide an integrated assessment of a city's performance.

My colleague Will Goodman and I set out to solve this. We began by examining prosperity and well-being indicators from the 100 largest U.S. metro areas, and then synthesized data. To this we added the Gini index for each city, to develop a prosperity, well-being, and equality matrix.[38] The top ten American metropolitan areas for prosperity, well-being, and equality are:

1.　San Jose–Sunnyvale–Santa Clara, CA
2.　Washington–Arlington–Alexandria, DC-VA-MD-WV
3.　Des Moines–West Des Moines, IA
4.　Lancaster, PA
5.　Honolulu, HI
6.　Madison, WI
7.　Salt Lake City, UT
8.　Minneapolis–St. Paul–Bloomington, MN-WI
9.　Ogden–Clearfield, UT
10.　Seattle–Tacoma–Bellevue, WA[39]

Note that these are all medium-sized communities, although Lancaster is fairly small. They have excellent colleges, universities, and health-care systems, and stable, growing economies. Around the world, large cities are often the most prosperous, midsize cities the happiest. (For a full list, see note 39 on page 419.)

The Civic Realm

The most enduring cities envision, grow, and maintain an extraordinary civic realm. We are inspired by public libraries that contain lifetimes of knowledge; museums that recall the past and connect it to the future; performing arts centers that allow us to pause and immerse ourselves deeply in the language of music, dance, and theater; parks that weave together humankind and nature; and sports stadiums that excite us. Taken together, with investments in transportation, housing, health, and education, these institutions of excellence and the infrastructure of opportunity make good cities great ones.

Jaime Lerner, the visionary mayor of Curitiba, Brazil, described the transformation of the city as being accomplished with "urban acupuncture" on its leverage points. Curitiba, the capital of the state of Paraná, has a population of about 1.5 million. In his first term, while the rest of the world was tearing apart its cities to accommodate more cars, Lerner began closing major roads to traffic, and started developing a pedestrian-oriented city. He created an integrated mass transit network with one price per ride, no matter how long, to reduce the cost of transportation for those living at the city's edge.

Lerner then updated Curitiba's zoning code to tie together development and the transit system, requiring higher density close to transit lines and lower density farther away. Lacking the finances to build an extensive subway system, Curitiba created the world's first bus rapid transit system in 1974.[40] To improve education the city developed "Lighthouses of Knowledge," public centers with libraries, Internet access, and cultural programming. These were located next to transit centers to make them easy to get to. By the 1980s job training and social services were also tied into transit locations. From 1970 to 2010, Curitiba's population more than quadrupled, but its green space outstripped that rate, growing from one square meter per person to fifty-two square meters. And the city's park system has been very effective at flood prevention during heavy rains.

Curitiba's "garbage that is not garbage" program collects and recycles more than 70 percent of its waste, and puts funds from selling recyclables into social services. Recyclers are paid for garbage with transit tokens, saving the city cash while expanding their job and educational access. An open university funded by the recycling program provides inexpensive job training. Retired city buses are used as mobile classrooms and service offices. Curitiba's economic development program also widely distributes opportunity. Like most developing-world cities, Curitiba is surrounded by poorly serviced slums, and it's aiming business incubation efforts at growing small businesses in these communities. Entrepreneurial sheds located in low-income communities are supported by the Crafts Lycée, which provides finance and business education.

As a result of these efforts, Curitiba is not the richest city in the world, but it is a contender for the happiest. Ninety-nine percent of its residents reported being happy in 2009, and in 2010 it was awarded the Globe Sustainable City Award. Mayor Lerner says, "I believe that some medicinal 'magic' can and should be applied to cities, as many are sick and some nearly terminal. As with the medicine needed in the interaction between doctor and patient, in urban planning it is also necessary to make the city react; to poke an area in such a way that it is able to help heal, improve, and create positive chain reactions. It is indispensable in revitalizing interventions to make the organism work in a different way."[41] Curitiba's magic came from the belief that "we" must thrive if "me" is to thrive. Jaime Lerner understood the fundamental truth that happiness and well-being are a collective experience. And they make for a better city.

Toward the Purpose of Cities

Our current economic system is based on flawed premises: that markets are efficient, and that efficiency, in itself, will produce the best society. Efficiency is an important function in complicated, linear systems, but it is less so in complex systems. Alas, in the latter half of the twentieth century, economists made efficiency itself our most important value, lauding creative destruction and the rule of the market. The efficient market exacerbates inequality. It knows what Oscar Wilde called the price of everything and the value of nothing. Wynton Marsalis said, "The reason things fall apart is that people create things to celebrate themselves rather than embrace the whole."

But human societies and our cities are complex systems, not complicated ones. And complex systems have both a function and a purpose. The purpose of our cities and societies is well-being, not efficiency.

Complicated systems can be maximized. Complex systems thrive when they are optimized. A city is optimized when all of its components are thriving—the ecology in which it is nested, the metabolism that sustains it, the region that contains it, and its people and businesses. To achieve this, city leaders need to focus on optimizing the whole, not the parts.

Thriving in the twenty-first century requires a cultural shift from an individual-maximizing worldview to an ecological one, recognizing that our well-being derives from the health of the system, not the node. This new cognition is enhanced as a city defines its purpose as the well-being of its wholeness. Then the system will naturally want to equalize its landscape of opportunity and the distribution of health and well-being. Seeking wholeness, the city begins to become more naturally adaptive to the VUCA world.

Funding the Well-Tempered City

Many nations have the financial capacity to make their cities more well tempered. With the federal thirty-year bond interest rate at 2.62 percent in the spring of 2016, the United States could divide its budget into a capital and an operating budget, and borrow, not to cover its deficit, but to invest in new schools; roads and mass transit; smart, renewable energy systems; circular water and wastewater systems; smart city operating systems; affordable housing; community health centers; parks and open spaces; and the other components of communities of opportunity. It would create millions of local jobs and the armature for future well-being while reducing its environmental footprint. And if the nation invested its domestic operating budget in evidence-based solutions to the issues of health, education, and trauma, it could better prepare its people to thrive in the twenty-first century. Its criteria for investment should be determined by the goals of regional well-being indexes, as those are more likely to reflect the needs of communities, and less likely to be distorted by the industry lobbies that pervade Washington.

Investments in infrastructure, human development, and the restoration of nature will make nations much more resilient to the coming megatrends of the VUCA age. Their cities will be refuges of prosperity, equality, and well-being. The only thing missing is the will to make it so. And that requires compassion.

PART FIVE

Compassion

The fifth aspect of the well-tempered city is great compassion, the desire to relieve the suffering of all beings. Compassion harmonizes humans and nature in a framework that gives meaning to human activities. At the physical level this harmony increases the resilience of cities by integrating urban technology and nature. At the operational level it increases the resilience of cities by enhancing their adaptive capacity, so that they can evolve in dynamic balance with megatrends, focused on their core objective: the well-being of both human and natural systems. At the social level, a compassionate temperament provides common values and meaning, key elements of altruism and cultural resilience. And at the spiritual level it enhances a city's sense of common purpose, giving rise to an integrated view of wholeness that generates resilience, healing, and the deepest well-being. Compassion provides the will to imagine and create a better future for all.

We live in a competitive, aggressive world. Every successful city must have protective systems to secure itself from threats. Political and economic power are preconditions for a thriving city. And since cities do not exist in a vacuum, they must be part of strong countries that provide them with, among other things, defense, the rule of law, patent protection, transparent corruption-free governance, and the preservation of individual and collective rights. But while protection is necessary, it is not sufficient. Cities must also grow their capacity for compassion. Interweaving protection and compassion, cities can replace the concept of "stronger" with "better able to adapt."

Altruism as a Protective Factor

When exposed to the same disease, why do some get sick while others do not? People have a range of protective factors. When individuals, families, and communities are exposed to stressors or risks, protective factors are conditions or attributes that enhance the likelihood of positive outcomes and reduce vulnerability.

Protective factors can be found in our DNA. Some people, for example, are born less susceptible to alcoholism than others. Protective factors can be enhanced by inoculations, such as vaccines for measles and mumps. Positive cognitive ecologies are protective, providing a stable and resilient base that helps children deal with stress. And altruism, the selfless concern for the well-being of others, is a protective factor. Individuals who are altruistic are happier, more flexible, and less likely to become sick. Altruistic neighborhoods have stronger social networks and are more resilient in the face of stress. Cities infused with altruism are more trusting, inclusive, and tolerant; have stronger, more diverse volunteer networks; are better able to plan for their future; and can take the necessary steps to carry out those plans effectively. Altruism infuses individuals with a sense of purpose that is greater than themselves. When collective altruism gathers a population around a common purpose, it moves the city toward harmony.

A Vision of Purpose

Jane Chermayeff spent much of her life advising children's museums and planning science playgrounds. She often said that if you want to make a great city, design it to work for children. On the surface this may sound overly simplistic, but what if a city were to follow through on this idea with every project, department, and plan?

For example, a city that really worked for children would be one in which its children would live in safety. That would require safe streets, with protected areas for children to walk and bike to school and around their neighborhoods. It would mean that no child would live in fear of being shot by a stray bullet. Its children would be free from the threat of drugs. And imagine a city in which cognitive opportunity flourished, in which there was no domestic violence, abuse, neglect, or other adverse childhood experience. To achieve that, the city would need ample affordable housing, health care, and social services, and it would need to root out the epigenetic effects of endemic poverty.

In order for every child to have an equal opportunity to thrive, a city would need an exemplary education system, with modern, green, light-filled schools within walking distance of home, every school providing a superb education, no matter the income level of its neighborhood residents. Its teachers would receive respectable wages and lifelong training, and they too would live in safe, comfortable homes with sufficient child care and support for their families.

In order for children to thrive, their families must thrive. Such a city would need to be a cauldron of opportunity for all—the immigrant, the inventor, the coder, and the cardiologist—so that each could reach his or her fullest potential. A city can accomplish these goals only if it is fiscally sound, so it would need an equitable tax system sufficient to meet its needs. As we begin to follow the threads in the fabric of a city dedicated to the well-being of children, it becomes clear that to succeed, the city must dedicate itself to the well-being of all.

And what if we added the health of nature to the city's purpose—inspiring it to restore the wetlands at its water's edges, and weave nature into its streets? Networks of parks, trees, green roofs, and community gardens would enhance its biodiversity, feeding indigenous birds and other pollinators. Rivers would be restored, and swaths of forests and fields in the region would be protected.

It turns out that a city can pick any overarching set of compassionate goals for humans and for nature, and achieve a better outcome by realizing them. As long as those goals have deeply altruistic intentions and the city commits to have those intentions profoundly influence every decision, every project, every action that it makes, then these goals become the flocking rules that guide the city's continuous evolution toward harmony—human and natural. Altruism will be its greatest protective factor. And compassion will be its source.

CHAPTER 12

Entwinement

The Fitness of the City

Kenneth Burke, one of the most important American literary theorists of the twentieth century, wrote that "people may be unfitted by being fit in an unfit fitness."[1]

The current state of many of our cities is an unfit fitness. They may be sufficiently adapted for short-term growth, but they lack the adaptive capacity to thrive in the high-stress environment of the future. They are fitted to unfitness. And that is because they do not understand their true purpose.

Recall that Donella Meadows wrote that "the least obvious part of a system, its function or purpose, is often the most crucial determinant of a system's behavior."[2]

From the rise of Uruk, the world's first known city, the purpose of cities has been to provide for the protection and prosperity of their residents, to oversee the fair distribution of resources and opportunities, and to maintain harmony between human and natural systems. In this time of increasing volatility, complexity, and ambiguity, the well-tempered city possesses systems to help it evolve toward a more even temperament, one that balances prosperity and well-being with efficiency and equity in ways that continually restore its social and natural capital. And having a greater purpose will help it set the course to achieving these goals.

The first aspect of being well tempered, coherence, grows from a pervasive vision; community health indicators that reflect the vision; and a dynamic planning, governance, and feedback system to keep the city moving toward its vision. The second, circularity, requires an adaptive, multiscaled, interconnected infrastructure. The third facet of the well-tempered city, resilience, emerges from the integration of technical and natural urban ecologies. The fourth aspect of temperament, community, requires the stable base of a healthy cognitive ecology, accompanied by fairly distributed opportunity. And the last aspect, compassion, requires a pervasive sense of altruistic purpose. Taken together, these qualities create a city that keeps adapting in a VUCA time by integrating across the scales of the individual to the larger region, while increasingly advancing toward its altruistic purpose. Its people fit into a fitted fitness. It is pervaded by wholeness.

Wolf Singer, director of the Max Planck Institute for Brain Research in Frankfurt, observed that the healthy brain coordinates its different functions not by central control, but by what he calls "binding by synchrony," in which the various systems of the mind share a common wavelength, and send coordinating messages on its pulses, forever talking and listening to one another. Goodness, beauty, truth, dignity, and compassion all share the cognitive signature of neurological coherence, bound by synchrony. When the mind is pervaded by these qualities we feel deeper, more alive, and more whole.[3]

Healthy cities are also bound by a synchrony in which individuals, organizations, neighborhood groups, companies, and city agencies continually perceive their larger environment and independently adapt to it, making adjustments, improving their performance in a distributed but coherent way. And when they are bound by the synchrony of goodness, beauty, truth, dignity, and compassion, they too become whole.

Composing Fitness

Johann Sebastian Bach wrote the second book of *The Well-Tempered Clavier* in 1742, when Europe was undergoing an enormous cultural transition from the Reformation to the Age of Enlightenment. The Enlightenment unleashed scientific rationalism, releasing Europe from centuries of religious dogma. This new thinking gave rise to the American and French revolutions, and to the Industrial Revolution. The sacred and the secular began to diverge. Philosophy and science shifted attention from the cosmos to the individual, from the holy to the human, from the complex to the complicated. But Bach never wavered, and his greatest works resonate with us to this day because they integrate harmonic genius with a deep spiritual aspiration, qualities that were separated in the Enlightenment.

In 1747, three years before he passed away, J. S. Bach was invited by his son Carl Philipp Emanuel Bach to visit the court of King Frederick the Great, where the younger Bach held the position of chief keyboard player. Frederick the Great was powerful, sadistic, difficult to characterize: a series of opposites. He was both liberalizer and despot. He ruthlessly conquered Poland, yet he also created the world's first public education system. He loved nature, but he drained swamps to create new farmland, decimating the area's biodiversity. He believed in the power of science, and disdained the idea of universal morals. He loved his era's new modern music, commissioned to entertain and delight the senses, and he had no interest in Bach's belief that the universe was a sacred and integrated whole suffused with love.

So King Frederick set out to embarrass J. S. Bach, known by then as "Old Bach." Prior to the great composer's arrival at his palace, the king, an amateur flautist, composed (almost certainly with the help of Bach's son) a twenty-one-note theme called the Royal Theme, carefully devised so as to be impossible to harmonize under the strict rules of composition of the time. The moment J. S. Bach arrived from his grueling multiday coach journey, without even a chance to rest or bathe, Frederick took him on a tour of his collection of fifteen claviers, a transitional instrument between the harpsichord and the piano. And then, in front of an audience of educated musicians, the king challenged Old Bach to create a three-part fugue, harmonizing the Royal Theme in three interwoven harmonic threads, and to do it on the spot.

Old Bach sat down at one of the claviers and improvised a magnificent piece of flowing music, incorporating the Royal Theme twelve times in seventeen minutes. Unable to harmonize the theme directly, he created three variations that harmonized with one another, and wove them into an extraordinary tapestry of music. The music soared, each note moving independently yet in perfect relationship to the others. The audience was astounded. Bach had created wholeness from unfitness.

Chagrined, King Frederick recomposed himself and demanded that Bach create a six-part harmony, something that had never been done before. Old Bach said that this would take a bit more time. A few weeks after his return home he delivered a composition integrating six fugues on the Royal Theme, titled "A Musical Offering." It was Bach's answer to the question as to whether harmony had limits—an extraordinary testament to the capacity of humans to create magnificent harmony beyond the dualism of sacred and profane.[4]

The scientific rationalism that Frederick the Great so admired unleashed remarkable technologies. Over the next centuries they gave rise to an extraordinary increase in the prosperity of humankind and enormous environmental destruction. They have been used to save lives and to destroy them.

Technology has produced cities that would have been unimaginable in Bach's time, advancing in waves from the tower of Jericho to the megacities of today. But the essence of humans and nature has not changed. We still feel a great sense of peace and joy when our minds are bounded by the synchrony of music, beauty, truth, dignity, love, and compassion. Our cities today contain many of the technical achievements that Frederick the Great would have been so pleased by, but little of the harmony that Bach and the original makers of cities sought.

The purpose of our cities must be to integrate the science sought by the Enlightenment with the harmony of Bach, to compose the conditions of fitness of their people, their neighborhoods, and nature.

The Great Lisbon Earthquake

Eight years after Bach's encounter with Frederick the Great, another event shook the ground of religion in Europe, hastening the Enlightenment and giving rise to the era's first urban reconstruction. On All Saints' Day, November 1, 1755, a great earthquake struck Lisbon, followed forty minutes later by a powerful tsunami, which itself was followed by five days of raging fire. Eighty-five percent of the city's buildings, including nearly every church, collapsed, burned, or were destroyed by flooding. Lisbon's extraordinary art collections, its libraries, and the records of its extensive colonies all vanished. The royal Ribeira Palace sitting astride the Tagus River collapsed in the earthquake, and then was inundated by the tsunami's massive waves, its 70,000-volume royal library destroyed. Paintings by Titian, Rubens, and Correggio were never seen again. Lisbon's new opera house burned to the ground. It is estimated that 25,000 people, one tenth of the city's population, perished. The only neighborhood fully spared was the red-light district.

The Great Lisbon Earthquake shook the faith of the faithful. How could a tragedy of such proportions take place on such a holy day? How could churches, houses of God, be destroyed and their occupants crushed while the city's whorehouses were spared?

What role did God really have in the affairs of humans and the ways of nature? Was this an expression of His anger over the Inquisition or a sign of His absence?

Intellectuals all over Europe seized on the event to advance the philosophy of the Enlightenment, and the sciences of natural phenomena. Immanuel Kant wrote three texts on the subject, and proposed what would become the science of seismology. Jean-Jacques Rousseau concluded that cities were too densely populated, and proposed that people live a more pastoral life. The earthquake provoked Voltaire to write his satire *Candide*, which mocked the Church and the idea that the world was directed by a benevolent deity. The much-used metaphor of "solid philosophical grounds" was replaced with the concept that certainties were in fact shaky. The Enlightenment replaced absolutes with relativism.

A month after the disaster, King Joseph I, who was spared from the collapse of his palace because his daughter had insisted that the family leave the city for the countryside after sunrise Mass, met with the chief engineer of the realm, Manuel da Maia. Da Maia presented the king with five plans to reconstruct the city, ranging from using the rubble to rebuild it as it was to razing the remains and rebuilding the city in a different location, "laying out streets without restraint."[5] The king chose to build it anew, in the place where it had long been.

The reconstructed Lisbon became the first modern city of Europe, laid out with large squares, wide avenues, and buildings engineered to be earthquake resistant. Da Maia's plan mandated that each block in a neighborhood be built to a universal design, permitting building components such as windows and doors to be mass-produced. This promoted a new egalitarianism—no longer could the wealthy distinguish themselves with individualized, ornate palaces. Lisbon's reconstruction gave birth to the field of modern urban planning, integrating both resistance and resilience to future disasters.

The earthquake also gave rise to a seismic shift in ways to deal with large populations under stress. The government's first response was to call in the army and set up gallows for looters, but Portugal's secretary of state, Sebastião Carvalho, recognized the need to unify Lisbon's residents rather than repress them. He surveyed them to get their perspective on the earthquake, and in the process figured out that it had moved eastward in waves, laying the foundation of seismic science. He expelled the powerful and fundamentalist Jesuits, who blamed the earthquake on the sinfulness of Lisbon's people and claimed that there was no use in rebuilding such a wicked city.

Carvalho seized the opportunity created by the disruption to rip apart the institutional barriers of the old hierarchies and open the gates of human potential. He disempowered the Church and the powerful families who had filled the court with intrigue, continually jockeying for advantage. He mandated the construction of eight hundred national primary and secondary schools. He added mathematics, natural sciences, and the Enlightenment's philosophers to the University of Coimbra's curriculum, and built it a botanic garden and astronomical observatory. His goal was to create *novos homens*, new men, free from fundamentalist prejudice, educated in the latest scientific, philosophical, and social theories. The central power of the king was strengthened, but he broadened the base of his support to an empowered class of entrepreneurs. The reimagination of Lisbon, with symmetrical streets radiating from squares, standardized building blocks, and an overall sense of harmony became a model for the great Haussmann plan of Paris and much that was to follow.

The Power of Trust

To address the coming megatrends of the twenty-first century, cities need all of the solutions described in this book—smart, dynamic regional plans, circular water and sewer systems, renewable-energy-powered microgrids, regional food systems, multimodal transportation systems, integrated natural and technical systems, biodiversity, green buildings, and collaborative consumption. They need affordable housing and health, education, and job-training systems. To inform and inspire their citizens, they need museums, libraries, performing arts centers, clusters of arts and creativity. To operate well, they need inclusive, transparent, efficient, corruption-free governments that tune their progress with clearly defined well-being outcomes, and exchange lessons and best practices with other cities. They need to govern sufficiently to protect humans and nature, but with a light-enough hand so that innovation and entrepreneurship thrive. And they need a pervasive culture of compassion, grounded in neighborhoods, nurtured in houses of worship, places of reflection and retreat, enhanced by the collective efficacy of for-profit and not-for-profit social entrepreneurs, funded by social impact bonds that capture the future value of a healthy society and provide the current funds to make it so, and inspired by selfless leadership. This is the *meh* of the twenty-first century. And it can grow only in the soil of trust.

When Hurricanes Katrina and Rita struck New Orleans, looting and violence increased. When the planes of 9/11 destroyed the World Trade Center, New York City's residents responded with an incredible outpouring of compassion, connection, and courage. Rebecca Solnit, the author of *A Paradise Built in Hell*, describes how people often come together to care for each other in the wake of disaster. After the San Francisco earthquake and subsequent fire of 1906, people spontaneously set up food kitchens to feed the homeless, and hospital tents to care for them. She celebrates this mutual aid: "Every participant is both a giver and a recipient in acts of care that bind them together . . . it is reciprocity, a network of people cooperating to meet each other's needs and wants."[6]

This innate human capacity for mutual aid was described by the Russian economist, geologist, and revolutionary Peter Kropotkin in

his 1902 book *Mutual Aid: A Factor in Evolution*. And he was right—
science is now clear: when there is evolutionary stress, there is a small
chance that selfish individuals will do better by being selfish, but there
is a much larger chance that if altruistic individuals cooperate, they
will collectively outperform those just out for themselves. The fitness
gain of altruism exceeds that of selfishness.

The collective tendency to be altruistic in a crisis arises only in a
society with a high degree of trust. And too many neighborhoods in
our cities have lost that capacity. When a city is infused with ignorance,
intolerance, fundamentalism, selfishness, and arrogance, it becomes
unfit. The unfitness solidifies into the walls of racism that disconnect
people from opportunity; fundamentalism that represses the freedom
of expression of all of a community's people; selfishness that distorts
the distribution of opportunity; fear that corrodes its cognitive ecology;
and ignorance that undermines the emergence of wisdom.

These conditions create an unfit fitness—such a city can never
adapt to the shaky ground of twenty-first-century megatrends.

The ground of fitness begins with a sense of collective efficacy and
neighborhood order. A city's residents must trust that, individually
and collectively, they can make a difference, and they must palpably
perceive the results of their collective efficacy as order.

To build trust, a city must ensure that its landscape of potentiality
is not divided by mountains of unfairness. If opportunity is perceived
to be fairly distributed, then people will grow toward opportunity the
way trees grow toward light.

In cities across the world, protest movements arise from decades
of thwarted opportunity. In the United States, the Black Lives Matter
movement is a legacy of the "Baltimore idea" and its stepchild, the
FHA's restrictive covenants preventing black families from building
home equity for generations. As we've seen in Louisville, such barriers
can be overcome. The future of a nation's children does not have to be
determined by the zip code in which they are raised. We know how to

dissolve the structural barriers to opportunity of housing, education, health, and transportation—and as we do, cities build tremendous trust among their people. That trust is the soil from which adaptive capacity grows.

Collective Impact

The second factor needed to generate altruistic fitness is collective efficacy.

The French aristocrat and political thinker Alexis de Tocqueville came to America in 1831 with the charge to study its prisons. In fact, his real goal was larger, to observe American society firsthand. His classic book, *Democracy in America*, written in 1835, celebrated the contribution of the young nation's informal, nongovernmental social institutions to the county's resilience. He described how effective they were in generating the social cohesion and connectedness needed to maintain a pluralistic society.

America's nongovernmental organizations, or NGOs, continue to enhance collective efficacy in our cities. Cities should encourage the flowering of these traditional and new community-based organizations. The 150-year-old YWCA, now carrying out its mission to eliminate racism and empower women, provides housing and health services to low-income women. Settlement houses such as New York's University Settlement and the Educational Alliance, and community development corporations such as Philadelphia's Asociación Puertorriqueños en Marcha (APM), with deep roots in their neighborhoods, also provide job training, social services, and a collective voice for the communities that they serve. Community service networks like the Federation of Jewish Philanthropies and Catholic Charities share best practices with other agencies. Regional affordable-housing alliances like the Cleveland Housing Network, along with national partners like Enterprise Community Partners, bring resources to fund the revitalization of lower-income neighborhoods. And the national Trust for Public Land supports local community gardens to bring fresh food and nature back into neighborhoods.

Many of these programs, however, are working independently of one another. How can a city integrate them to create communities of opportunity? One way is through a process called "collective impact," a framework for tackling deeply entrenched social problems that was first described in the *Stanford Social Innovation Review* by John Kania and Mark Kramer.[7] The approach has its roots in the work of Strive, a nonprofit devoted to education and job training, based in Cincinnati, Ohio. Strive achieved excellent outcomes despite local budget cuts and a national recession that hit Ohio particularly hard. How did Strive succeed when so many other not-for-profits working on the same issue were losing ground?

Strive brought together a core group of community leaders—funders, educators, elected officials, university presidents, and corporation executives—all of whom agreed to a common set of goals. These objectives, derived from extensive research, focused on key leverage points in educational development of children, such as preschool attendance, fourth-grade reading and math scores, and high school graduation rates. Rather than focus on one favored educational curriculum or program, the Strive partners collectively committed to an entire ecology of programs with one overriding goal: educational excellence. That goal was then divided into fifteen student success networks, each focused on a different part of the educational environment, such as after-school tutoring. Funding decisions were based on independent assessments of effectiveness, the more successful ones receiving more funding. The system was designed with a feedback loop to help it evolve toward excellence.

Kania and Kramer went on to study a wide range of successful urban initiatives, and from their common elements derived the five conditions of collective impact: a common agenda; shared measurement; integrated actions through mutually reinforcing activities; continuous communication; and investment in infrastructure to achieve the goals (which they call the backbone of support). The collective impact model's scope should be enlarged to integrate multiple sectors into a whole community health model, using community health indicators as a guide.

But transformation cannot just be brought to communities, it must also grow *from* communities, harnessing the power of mutual aid. Perhaps the best advocate of mutual aid was Mahatma Gandhi, whose ideas sparked collective efficacy around the world. A superb example is the Sarvodaya Shramadana movement, founded by A. T. Ariyanate in Sri Lanka. Initially, Ariyanate set out to put Gandhi's principles of self-reliance to work by engaging students and teachers to build a rural school. To get materials to the site they had to build a bridge across a river, to get materials to the bridge they had to improve the road leading to it. By the time they were finished, they had not only built a school but significantly improved the connectivity of their village. And they did it themselves, without waiting for the sluggish national government. Empowered by their success, they began to tackle other village issues, and to spread the ideas of self-reliance across the country.

Sarvodaya means "awakening all" in Sanskrit, and *Shramadana* means "to donate effort." By 2015, Sarvodaya Shramadana served more than 15,000 villages with schools, credit unions, orphanages, the nation's largest microcredit network, and 4,335 preschools. It provides communities with clean water systems, sanitation, alternative energy, and other infrastructure improvements. And almost all of this work is performed by donated, community-based labor. Sarvodaya trains thousands of young women and men with methods that motivate and organize people in their own villages to meet their infrastructure, social service, educational, spiritual, and cultural needs. It's an extraordinary model of collective efficacy, sparking engagement, building trust, providing real results, and connecting across scales.

Paul Hawken described the emergence of hundreds of thousands of locally based environmental and social organizations around the world as the "blessed unrest." In a book with the same title, he observed that these organizations are beginning to have a collective impact, serving as a vast immune system, working to heal people and the earth. These movements have arisen spontaneously, have no central leader, and are dealing with big problems whose time for solutions is running out. They are a super-wicked answer to the twenty-first century's super-wicked problems.

Taken together, a community vision, scenario planning, strong and compassionate leadership, dynamic feedback systems, infrastructure investment, the tools of governing, collective impact, and self-reliance help create well-tempered cities.

But to truly succeed, cities need to integrate two worldviews. The first is a systems view, an understanding that nature is deeply interdependent. The second is the evolutionary fitness of altruism. Cities can heal their whole only if they heal all of their parts. This understanding of the interdependence of all living systems, human and natural, is inherent in all religions and science; it is the basis of morality and spirituality; it opens the pathway through the megatrends.

Entangled Altruism Is Entwinement

Quantum physics began with the study of the particle, but quickly observed that particles were interrelated. Quantum theory posits that particles are entangled, or interconnected, across space—change the status of one, and its sibling, even if on the other side of the universe, will respond instantaneously, beyond the speed of light. Albert Einstein called it "spooky action at a distance." The Nobel Prize–

winning Austrian physicist Erwin Schrödinger called this "quantum entanglement."

Entanglement is a necessary condition of life. Isolated subatomic particles, atoms, and molecules are lifeless on their own. Life does not exist as an independent property; it emerges from the relationships between energy, information, and matter. And entropy, the wearing down of systems, the dispersal of heat and information, is also not a condition of individual particles; it too is a quality of an interdependent system.

Cities are magnificently entangled. Every tree, person, building, neighborhood, and business is entwined with every other. And just as living biocomplex systems draw from the same pool of DNA, cities share a metagenome that ties their elements together. Too often our economy, cognitive biases, and social structures amplify disparate expressions of pieces of the code, creating disorder. This may create small zones of fitness, but pushes the larger ecology toward unfitness. For example, our economic system, ignoring what it calls "externalities" of government tax breaks and subsidies, pollution and natural resource depletion, encourages companies to undertake activities that fit for them, but create a larger unfit fitness for the well-being of their communities and for life on earth. Racial segregation may create a community that thinks it fits together, but in fact its "people may be unfitted by being fit in an unfit fitness."

But we have also evolved with an innate metacode that can bind us together with synchrony: altruism. When altruism flows through every bit of a city's interdependent social and cognitive ecologies, and is embedded in the morality of its systems, it can generate synchrony. When altruism profoundly influences every decision, every project, every action that a city makes, then the city will become an extraordinary city. It will become well tempered.

Dr. Martin Luther King, Jr., wrote, "Power properly understood is . . . the strength required to bring about social political, and economic change. . . . One of the great problems of history is that the concepts of love and power have usually been contrasted as opposites—polar opposites—so that love is identified with the resignation of power and power with the denial of love. Now we've got to get this thing right. . . . Power without love is reckless and abusive, and love without power is sentimental and anaemic. Power at its best is love implementing the demands of justice, and justice at its best is power correcting everything that stands against love."[8]

The Well-Tempered City Infuses Its Power with Love

The Greeks described three kinds of love: eros, philia, and agape. Eros is passionate, sexual love that fills us with the urge to merge. Philia is a deep, pervasive attraction, the propensity of things, a quality of the natural world, like gravity. This is the philia of E. O. Wilson's biophilia hypothesis, the human love of nature and life itself, "the urge to affiliate with other forms of life"[9] that we explored in the chapter on green urbanism. Philia physically and spiritually weaves us into the fabric of the world. It entangles us. The third kind of love, agape, is a universal love. The theology professor Thomas Jay Oord describes agape as "an intentional response to promote well-being when confronted by that which generates ill-being. In short, agape repays evil with good."[10] Agape is the impulse to create a society grounded in well-being for all.

When these three kinds of love are woven into the fabric of a city, they create an energized and altruistic culture. They add intention to nature's entanglement. I call this altruistically directed interdependence "entwinement."

Entwinement lies at the core of the world's major religious traditions. In Buddhism the combination of pervasive altruism and the recognition of interdependence is called *bodhicitta*. In Islam the mix of interdependence and altruism is called *ta'awun*, and *ithar* is the peak of altruism. In Judaism, *tikun olam* is the recognition that we have a responsibility to repair any tears in the fabric of the world with acts of goodness, or *mitzvoth*. The Hindu leader Mahatma Gandhi taught *satyagraha*, the power of nonviolent action toward truth and social justice, and Pope Francis's Encyclical Letter "Laudato Si" calls for an *integral ecology* to create a *universal communion* that "excludes nothing and no one."

Composing Wholeness

Bach's music was composed of many notes, but the notes alone lack meaning, grandeur, energy, a sense of purpose. *The Well-Tempered Clavier*'s beauty emerges from patterns of notes that weave across scales, where a pattern of notes may be expanded into a theme across many bars, contributing to a larger multiphrase wave, each phrase composed in counterpoint to another. The note, or particle, through the power of relationship, becomes a wave.

The universe is enlivened not by its notes, or particles, but by their ever-unfolding, complex, adapting patterns. Think of a whirlpool, in which no drop of water ever stays fixed in place, and yet the overall pattern can be very stable. Music, art, film, writing, performance, religious services, prayer, and meditation can all evoke these larger patterns, and help us to align with wholeness, so that our swirling lives may fit into a larger system, helping us understand a bit of the universe and our place in it. And the design of our cities could do the same.

In the aftermath of the astounding suffering caused by Rwanda's uncivil war, aid workers noted that the most traumatized people in refugee camps displayed remarkably different capacities to recover from the unspeakable events they had endured. Those who had a deeply held cosmology that they believed could explain the events they experienced were much more likely to rebound than those who didn't. It was as if the traumas were sharp shards embedded in their minds, and their cosmology helped them assemble the shards into a smooth whole, like pieces of a jigsaw puzzle. Having a cosmology is a protective factor.

Bach wrote music to make such a wholeness. Christopher Alexander, the architectural theorist, wrote, "Making wholeness heals the maker. . . . A Humane Architecture does not only have the power to heal us. The very act of making it is itself a healing act for all of us."[11] And so, making a well-tempered city that reflects a larger harmony increases not only its resilience, but also our own.

Recall the first settlements, with their systems for sharing the responsibility for building irrigation ditches, maintaining them, and equitably distributing their water. These systems succeeded because they were rooted in altruism, in fairness, and with them came the pleasure of being part of a well-tempered society. These qualities are wired into our very neurology; they are the ground of our well-being.

As our cities become more ethnically diverse, we cannot rely on one overarching religion, or creed, or race, or power to give us a common language of entwinement. But we can call upon something deeper: our overarching sense of purpose. When the purpose of our cities is to compose wholeness, aligning humans and nature, with compassion permeating its entire entwined system, then its ways will be ways of love, and all its paths will be paths of peace.

AUTHOR'S NOTE AND ACKNOWLEDGMENTS

THE IDEAS IN this book have been enriched by many people, who have expanded my thinking and exposed me to a wide range of solutions. I am profoundly grateful for all that they think and do, and regret that so many are left unnamed.

The principles of compassion in action in this book were taught to me by my parents, Frederick P. Rose and Sandra Priest Rose. My father was a builder who loved the acts of creating. When I was a boy, he began to build affordable housing in the Bronx while at the same time building market-rate apartments and office buildings in Manhattan. I would join him on visits to the construction sites, savoring the smell of concrete, mud, and diesel fumes, and the coordinated cacophony of the work, but was most moved by the faces of the families in the affordable-housing rental offices, who were eager for a newly built apartment. My father taught me how to build, and inspired me to get things done.

My mother, Sandra P. Rose, is deeply committed to human equality. In the early 1960s she worked to bring voting rights to African Americans who had not been treated equally as citizens. About the same time, she developed a theory of change that has permeated her life: that our communities have a responsibility to teach every child to read equally well. She understood that, even with the vote, a child who could not read well would not have an equal opportunity to thrive. My mother identified teachers as the leverage point, and has spent her life working to improve the way that those in inner-city public schools teach reading. From her work, it became clear to me that if we were to truly rebuild our cities, we had to do so in a way that equalized the landscape of opportunity for all.

I grew up in a home filled with music. I first encountered Johann

Sebastian Bach in a boxed set of 78-rpm records my parents owned of the great humanitarian Albert Schweitzer playing Bach's organ music. That led me eventually to *The Well-Tempered Clavier*. There are many extraordinary recordings of *The Well-Tempered Clavier*, but I wrote much of this book listening to Gerlinde Otto's sublime performance of Book II.

In 1974, as I began to ponder how I would integrate my own sense of social and environmental mission with real estate development, one person towered above all others as a role model: Jim Rouse. Rouse was an extraordinary developer who had the vision, the guts, and the organizational skills to create a new city, Columbia, Maryland, founded on principles of environmental responsibility, social justice, and racial equality. Rouse conceived of Columbia as a place that was, as he said, "a city for growing people." He was a man of tremendous integrity and compassion.

In 1979, Jim and his wife, Patty, formed the not-for-profit Enterprise Foundation (now Enterprise Community Partners) and the for-profit Enterprise Social Investment Corp (now Enterprise Investment) to bring leadership, financing, and technical assistance to the emerging field of low-income community redevelopment. Jim and his colleague Bart Harvey, who succeeded him as Enterprise's chair, have been extraordinary mentors, compassionate and transformational system changers. I joined the Enterprise family as a board member, customer, and co-conspirator, and I have learned an enormous amount from my fellow board members, the organization's leaders, and its staff. Other not-for-profit organizations that have contributed to the development of the thoughts in this book are the American Museum of Natural History, the Center for Neighborhood Technology, the Center For Youth Wellness, the Congress of New Urbanism, the Educational Alliance, the Garrison Institute, the Greyston Foundation, The JPB Foundation, the Max Planck Institute for Human, Cognitive and Brain Sciences, the Mind and Life Institute, the Mindsight Institute, the Natural Resource Defense Council, Projects for Public

Spaces, the Regional Plan Association, the Santa Fe Institute, the Social Venture Network, the Trust for Public Land, the Urban Land Institute, the U.S. Green Business Council, and the Yale School of Forestry and the Environment.

In 1989, I formed the Jonathan Rose Companies with the aid of my assistant, Vivian Weixeldorfer. She has been an extraordinary support ever since, tirelessly managing the many activities related to my work, life, and writing. Our company has grown, realizing many of the ideas I have written about. This work is currently being carried out with the leadership of Mike Arman, Mike Daly, Christopher Edwards, Angela Howard, Chuck Perry, Theresa Romero, Kristin Neal Ryan, Nathan Taft, and Caroline Vary. I am so grateful for their commitment to making these ideas real.

As I sought to bring the many threads of social, environmental, entrepreneurial, and spiritual wisdom together, to find wholeness in what seems like a chaotic world, I found my greatest teacher, Nawang Gelek Rimpoche. His lessons on interdependence, impermanence, and equanimity have permeated every aspect of my thinking, for which I am deeply grateful. I have also learned an enormous amount from Rabbi Zalman Schachter-Shalomi and Father Thomas Keating. The depth, generosity, and love of these three men come from boundless wisdom and compassion.

In 1996, I began writing articles on the emerging concepts of new urbanism, green building, and smart growth. Thanks to Chuck Savitt and Heather Boyer of Island Press, who encouraged me to turn these into a book; and to Kathleen McCormack, Michael Leccese, and David Goldberg, who helped me think through an ancient version of the smart-growth elements of this book. As my ideas began to mature, Rosanne Gold introduced me to my editor, Karen Rinaldi. From the very outset Karen expressed enormous faith in my potential, and when I delivered a sprawling first draft, she said to me, "Take the time to write your best book, not your fastest book." I am so grateful to Karen for her wisdom and her support. Jonathan Cobb provided very helpful guidance to the first draft, then Peter Guzzardi picked up the baton—his passionate and detailed editing significantly focused and improved the text. Hannah Robinson shepherded the book through its birth, Adalis Martinez provided its wonderful cover design, William Ruoto designed the book's interior, Victoria Comella brought it to the world with astute and energetic PR along with Scott Manning and Abigail Wellhouse, Penny Makras marketed it with passion, along with many others on the Harper Wave and HarperCollins teams who have worked to make this book possible. Also thanks to my attorney and friend, Eric Rayman, and Nick Correale for help with the images.

As I was refining the book, I was invited to give lectures which helped work out the development of key ideas. Two of the most helpful were Harvard's Joint Center for Housing Studies' Dunlop Lecture, at the invitation of Eric Belsky, and a TEDX talk at the Met Museum, at the invitation of Limor Tomer and with terrific editing by Julie Burstein, and piano by Tanya Bannister.

As the years of writing unfolded, many friends and colleagues encouraged and supported me: particularly Philip Glass, who kindly read the music sections of the book; Paul Hawken, who was boundlessly generous with his time and thoughts, reading many drafts and rewrites, providing insightful comments, and encouraging me to cut what needed to be cut; Peter Calthorpe, Douglas Kelbaugh, Dan Goleman, Dan Siegel, and Andrew Zolli, who generously gave me feedback on my ideas as they unfolded; Dr. Rita Colwell, who introduced me to the concept of biocomplexity; and Dr. Bruce McEwan, who provided guidance on the pathways forward from trauma.

But the most important have been my family—Diana, Ariel, Adam, Rachel, and Ian—who have tolerated endless discussions of these ideas at meals and contributed references and many refinements. My life has been enriched by their love and support.

PREFACE: THE WELL-TEMPERED CITY

1. Robert Venturi, *Complexity and Contradiction in Architecture* (New York: Museum of Modern Art, 1966), p. 16.

2. Jane Jacobs, *The Death and Life of Great American Cities* (New York: Vintage Books, 1961), p. 222.

INTRODUCTION: THE ANSWER IS URBAN

1. http://www.geoba.se/population. php?pc=world&page=1&type=028&st =rank&asde=&year=1952.

2. https://www.un.org/development/desa/en/news/population/world -urbanization-prospects.html.

3. Le Corbusier, *The Modular, A Harmonious Measure to the Human Scale*, vol. 1, p. 71; reprint 2004.

4. http://www.yale.edu/nhohp/modelcity/before.html.

5. W. J. Rittel and Melvin Webber, "Dilemmas in a General Theory of Planning," *Policy Sciences* 4 (1973): 155–69, http://www.uctc.net/mwebber /Rittel+Webber+Dilemmas+General_Theory_of_Planning.pdf.

6. http://www.acq.osd.mil/ie/download/CCARprint_wForeword_c.pdf Climate Change Adaptation Roadmap.

7. http://www.nytimes.com/2015/03/03/science/earth/study-links-syria -conflict-to-drought-caused-by-climate-change.html?_r=0.

8. https://www.upworthy.com/trying-to-follow-what-is-going-on-in-syria-and -why-this-comic-will-get-you-there-in-5-minutes?g=3&c=ufb2.

9. http://www.donellameadows.org/wp-content/userfiles/Leverage_Points.pdf.

10. George Monbiot, RSA Journal *Nature's Way*, Issue 1, 2015, pp. 30–31.

11. Stephanie Bakker and Yvonne Brandwink, "Medellín's 'Metropolitan Greenbelt' Adds Public Space While Healing Old Wounds," *Citiscope*, April 15, 2016.

12. Donella H. Meadows and Diana Wright, *Thinking in Systems: A Primer* (White River Junction, VT: Chelsea Green Publishing, 2008).

CHAPTER 1: THE METROPOLITAN TIDE

1. http://artsandsciences.colorado.edu/magazine/2011/04/evolving-super -brain-tied-to-bipelalism-tool-making/.

2. Edward O. Wilson, *The Social Conquest of the Earth* (New York: Liveright, 2012), p. 17.

3. Naomi Eisenberger, "Why Rejection Hurts: What Social Neuroscience Has Revealed about the Brain's Response to Social Rejection," http://sanlab .psych.ucla.edu/papers_files/39-Decety-39.pdf.

4. Ian Tattersall, "If I Had a Hammer," *Scientific American* 311, no. 3 (2014).

5. One of the key elements of culture is its embedded worldview. Worldviews frame the way that we think. In fact, the story of the expulsion from the Garden of Eden is a story of a change in worldview.

6. Dennis Normil, "Experiments Probe Language's Origins and Development," *Science* 336, no. 6080 (April 27, 2012): pp. 408–11; DOI: 10.1126 /science.336.6080.408.

7. http://www.newyorker.com/magazine/2015/12/21/the-siege-of-miami.

8. http://en.wikipedia.org/wiki/History_of_agriculture.

9. http://www.newyorker.com/magazine/2011/12/19/the-sanctuary.

10. K. Schmidt, "'Zuerst kam der Tempel, dann die Stadt,' Vorläufiger Bericht zu den Grabungen am Göbekli Tepe und am Gürcütepe 1995–1999." *Istanbuler Mitteilungen* 50 (2000): 5–41.

11. The Birth of the Moralizing Gods Science, http://www.sciencemag.org /content/349/6251/918.full?sid=5cc48fb0-a88f-4b50-aebb-00f4641c67dd; http://news.uchicago.edu/article/2010/04/06/archaeological-project-seeks -clues-about-dawn-urban-civilization-middle-east.

12. Luc-Normand Tellier, *Urban World History: An Economic and Geographical Perspective* (Québec: Presses de l'Université du Québec, 2009); online.

13. This was known by climatologists as the 8.2K Event because it took place 8,200 years ago.

14. "Uncovering Civilization's Roots," *Science* 335 (February 17, 2012): 791; http://andrewlawler.com/website/wp-content/uploads/Science-2012-Lawler -Uncovering_Civilizations_Roots-790-31.pdf.

15. Ibid.

16. Ibid.

17. Gwendolyn Leick, *Mesopotamia: The Invention of the City* (New York: Penguin, 2001), p. 3.

18. William Stiebing, *Ancient Near Eastern History and Culture* (New York: Routledge, 2008).

19. The Guiding Principles of Chengzhou: The urban plan of Chengzhou is a map of the Holy Field, the nine-in-one square. The four squares of even numbers at the corners are imbued with the energy of *yin*; the five axial squares of odd integers are imbued with the energy of *yang*. This balance between yin and yang generated the harmonious flow of *qi*.

     Each side of Chengzhou was 9 *li* (~3 km) long. The edges of the city were defined by walls 20 meters wide and 15 meters high. These were penetrated by three gates on each side, the gates equidistant from one another and from the corners. The interior of the city was subdivided into square zones, with streets following the cardinal axis, running from gate to gate. This gave rise to three north–south and three east–west main roads. Running parallel to these major avenues were six minor avenues. These were all sized to be nine times the width of a carriage.

     Each of the city's nine main squares had a function. The palace sat in the center square, 5, the ancestral temple in the square to its left in square 7. The Sheji altars for the god of land and the god of grains occupied square 3. The market, which was considered to be less important, was located in the square to the north. The hall for public audiences was in square 1.

     The palace square was enclosed by a second set of walls and gates, forming an inner city, such as Beijing's Forbidden City.

     Regional capitals, and their subsidiary primary and secondary towns, also followed similarly prescribed dimensions. Because the form of cities was believed to be essential for the flow of *qi* from heaven to emperor to the society, their form remained constant until the modern era, although their architecture and gardens evolved over time.

20. http://www.smithsonianmag.com/history-archaeology/El-Mirador-the-Lost-City-of-the-Maya.html#ixzz2ZfcGXkot.

21. David Webster, *The Fall of the Ancient Maya: Solving the Mystery of the Maya Collapse* (New York: Thames & Hudson, 2002), p. 317.

22. Kevin Kelly, *What Technology Wants* (New York: Viking, 2011).

CHAPTER 2: PLANNING FOR GROWTH

1. http://eawc.evansville.edu/anthology/hammurabi.htm.

2. http://www.fordham.edu/halsall/ancient/hamcode.asp; http://www.uh.edu/engines/epi2542.htm.

3. http://www-personal.umich.edu/~nisbett/images/cultureThought.pdf.

4. R. H. C. Davis, *A History of Medieval Europe: From Constantine to Saint Louis*, 3rd ed. (New York: Pearson Education, 2006).

5. http://www.muslimheritage.com/uploads/Islamic%20City.pdf.

6. http://icasjakarta.wordpress.com/2011/01/20/the-virtuous-city-and-the
-possiblity-of-its-emergence-from-the-democratic-city-in-al-farabis-political
-philosophy/.

7. From Paul Romer in *Atlantic* magazine, written by Sebastian Mallaby,
July 8, 2010. http://m.theatlantic.com/magazine/archive/2010/07/the
-politically-incorrect-guide-to-ending-poverty/8134/.

8. http://legacy.fordham.edu/halsall/mod/1542newlawsindies.asp

9. Daniel J. Elazar, *The American Partnership: Intergovernmental Co-operation in the
Nineteenth-Century United States* (Chicago: University of Chicago Press, 1962).

10. *The Plan of Chicago* (New York: Princeton Architectural Press, 1993 reprint).

11. http://www.planning.org/growingsmart/pdf/LULZDFeb96.pdf;
https://ceq.doe.gov/laws_and_executive_orders/the_nepa_statute.html.

12. http://lawdigitalcommons.bc.edu/cgi/viewcontent.cgi?article=1963
&context=ealr.

13. John McClaughry, "The Land Use Planning Act—An Idea We Can Do
Without," Boston College *Environmental Affairs Law Review* 3 (1974), issue
4, article 2.

CHAPTER 3: SPRAWL AND ITS DISCONTENTS

1. Kenneth Jackson, *Crabgrass Frontier: The Suburbanization of the United
States* (New York: Oxford University Press, 1987).

2. "The Great Horse-Manure Crisis of 1894," *Freeman*, Ideas on Liberty.

3. http://www.livingplaces.com/Streetcar_Suburbs.html.

4. David Kushner, *Levittown: Two Families, One Tycoon, and the Fight for Civil
Rights in America's Legendary Suburb* (New York: Walker, 2009), p. 7.

5. W. W. Jennings, "The Value of Home Owning as Exemplified in American
History," *Social Science*, January 1938, p. 3, cited in John P. Dean,
Homeownership, p. 4.

6. Federal Housing Administration, *Underwriting Manual: Underwriting and
Valuation Procedure under Title II of the National Housing Act with Revisions
to February, 1938* (Washington, DC), Part II, Section 9, Rating of Location.

7. Kushner, *Levittown*, p. 30.

8. Harry S Truman, president's news conference, July 1, 1948; http://www
.presidency.ucsb.edu/ws/index.php?pid=12951.

9. http://www.policy-perspectives.org/article/viewFile/13352/8802.

10. Will Fischer and Chye-Ching Huang, *Mortgage Interest Deduction Is Ripe for
Reform*, Center on Budget and Policy Priorities, June 25, 2013.

11. Sam Roberts, "Infamous Drop Dead Was Never Said by Ford," *New York Times*, December 28, 2006; http://www.nytimes.com/2006/12/28/nyregion/28veto.html?_r=0.

12. Richard Nixon, State of the Union Address, January 22, 1970.

13. http://www.uli.org/research/centers-initiatives/center-for-capital-markets/emerging-trends-in-real-estate/americas/.

14. http://news.forexlive.com/!/the-massive-us-bubble-that-no-one-talks-about-20121205; http://blog.commercialsource.com/retail-closings-new-numbers-are-on-the-way/.

15. http://www.brookings.edu/research/papers/2010/01/20-poverty-kneebone.

16. https://cepa.stanford.edu/sites/default/files/RussellSageIncomeSegregation report.pdf.

17. http://www.csmonitor.com/World/Europe/2012/0501/In-France-s-suburban-ghettos-a-struggle-to-be-heard-amid-election-noise-video; http://en.wikipedia.org/wiki/Social_situation_in_the_French_suburbs.

18. http://www.csmonitor.com/World/Europe/2012/0501/In-France-s-suburban-ghettos-a-struggle-to-be-heard-amid-election-noise-video.

19. Ibid.

20. http://www.athomenetwork.com/Property_in_Vienna/Expat_life_in_Vienna/Districts_of_Vienna.html.

21. http://www.nytimes.com/2002/10/04/us/2-farm-acres-lost-per-minute-study-says.html.

22. https://www.motherjones.com/files/li_xiubin.pdf.

23. http://io9.com/in-california-rich-people-use-the-most-water-1655202898.

24. http://people.oregonstate.edu/~muirp/landlim.htm; http://www.citylab.com/work/2012/10/uneven-geography-economic-growth/3067/.

25. http://scienceblogs.com/cortex/2010/03/30/commuting/.

26. https://ideas.repec.org/p/zur/iewwpx/151.html.

27. https://worldstreets.wordpress.com/2011/06/23/newman-and-kenworth-on-peak-car-use/.

28. 2015 Urban Mobility Scorecard, http://d2dtl5nnlpfr0r.cloudfront.net/tti.tamu.edu/documents/mobility-scorecard-2015.pdf.

29. http://www.brookings.edu/blogs/future-development/posts/2016/02/10-digital-cars-productivity-fengler?utm_campaign=Brookings+Brief&utm_source=hs_email&utm_medium=email&utm_content=26280457&_hsenc=p2ANqtz--94peln9ll-DLQyM4sYN0HX0-ncQ26aIuiwUsrPVo

GnavPBBZtNF-oRxqW3vf8RFziZIr3LMpa8e9-_KQMBAqjbWMdBw& _hsmi=26280457.

30. http://www.ssti.us/2014/02/vmt-drops-ninth-year-dots-taking-notice/.

31. http://uli.org/wp-content/uploads/ULI-Documents/ET_US2012.pdf.

32. http://www.treehugger.com/cars/in-copenhagen-bicycles-overtake-cars .html.

33. Ibid.

34. http://www.jchs.harvard.edu/sites/jchs.harvard.edu/files/son2008.pdf.

35. Chris Benner and Manuel Pastor, *Just Growth: Inclusion and Prosperity in America's Metropolitan Regions* (New York: Routledge, 2012).

CHAPTER 4: THE DYNAMICALLY BALANCING CITY

1. http://envisionutah.org/eu_about_eumission.html.

2. Ibid.

3. Ibid.

4. Talk at the Garrison Institute, June 11, 2013.

5. Peter Calthorpe comments on text to author, December 2013.

6. http://www.anielski.com/publications/gpi-alberta-reports/.

7. http://www.slate.com/articles/technology/future_tense/2013/03/big _data_excerpt_how_mike_flowers_revolutionized_new_york_s_building _inspections.single.html.

8. http://www.thomaswhite.com/global-perspectives/south-korea-provides -boost-to-green-projects/.

9. http://www.igb.illinois.edu/research-areas/biocomplexity/research.

10. http://www.brookings.edu/research/papers/2016/02/17-why-copenhagen -works-katz-noring?hs_u=jonathanfprose@gmail.com&utm_campaign =Brookings+Brief&utm_source=hs_email&utm_medium=email&utm _content=26459561&_hsenc=p2ANqtz-_xy1AxOwMnwgvdYwg3wghqfm 8ROOqgZhUNtvn7_.

CHAPTER 5: THE METABOLISM OF CITIES

1. http://en.wikipedia.org/wiki/Sparrows_Point,_Maryland.

2. Marc V. Levine, "A Third-World City in the First World: Social Exclusion, Race Inequality, and Sustainable Development in Baltimore," in *The Social Sustainability of Cities: Diversity and the Management of Change*, edited by Mario Polese and Richard Stern (Toronto: Toronto University Press, 2000).

3. Abel Wolman, "The Metabolism of Cities," *Scientific American* 213, no. 3

(September 1965): 178–90; and see http://www.irows.ucr.edu/cd
/courses/10/wolman.pdf.

4. http://www.economist.com/news/christmas-specials/21636507-chinas
    -insatiable-appetite-pork-symbol-countrys-rise-it-also.

5. http://www.ft.com/intl/cms/s/0/8b24d40a-c064-11e1-982d-00144feabdc0
    .html#axzz3P5iyrFue.

6. http://www.researchgate.net/publication/266210000_Building_Spatial
    _Data_Infrastructures_for_Spatial_Planning_in_African_Cities_the
    _Lagos_Experience.

7. http://www.bloombergview.com/articles/2014-08-22/detroit-and-big-data
    -take-on-blight.

8. Ibid.

9. http://articles.baltimoresun.com/2010-06-30/news/bs-ed-citistat-20100630
    _1_citistat-innovators-city-trash-and-recycling.

10. http://www.resilience.org/stories/2005-04-01/why-our-food-so-dependent
    -oil#.

11. Karin Andersson, Thomas Ohlsson, and Pär Olsson, "Screening Life Cycle
    Assessment (LCA) of Tomato Ketchup: A Case Study," VALIDHTML SIK,
    the Swedish Institute for Food and Biotechnology, Göteborg.

12. http://www.fao.org/docrep/014/mb060e/mb060e00.pdf.

13. https://www.nrdc.org/food/files/wasted-food-ip.pdf.

14. http://www.newyorker.com/reporting/2012/08/13/120813fa_fact
    _gawande?currentPage=all.

15. http://www.ruaf.org/urban-agriculture-what-and-why.

16. http://www.worldwatch.org/node/6064.

17. http://www.cbsnews.com/news/do-you-know-where-your-food-comes
    -from/.

18. http://www.usatoday.com/money/industries/retail/story/2012-01-21/food
    -label-surprises/52680546/1.

19. http://www.theatlantic.com/health/archive/2012/01/the-connection
    -between-good-nutrition-and-good-cognition/251227/.

20. "The Cognition Nutrition: Food for Thought—Eat Your Way to a
    Better Brain," *Economist*, July 17, 2008; http://www.economist.com
    /node/11745528.

21. http://www.cityfarmer.info/2012/06/03/detroit-were-no-1-in-community
    -gardening/.

22. http://dailyreckoning.com/urban-farming-in-detroit-and-big-cities-back-to
    -small-towns-and-agriculture/.

23. http://www.grownyc.org/about.

24. http://www.usatoday.com/money/industries/energy/2011-05-01-cnbc-us
-squanders-energy-in-food-chain_n.htm.

25. http://www.veolia-environmentalservices.com/veolia/ressources/files
/1/927,753,Abstract_2009_GB-1.pdf.

26. http://waste-management-world.com/a/global-municipal-solid-waste-to
-double-by.

27. http://www.epa.gov/smm/advancing-sustainable-materials-management
-facts-and-figures; http://detroit1701.org/Detroit%20Incinerator.html.

28. E-mail from Dr. Allen Hershkowitz, August 21, 2012.

29. Sven Eberlein, "Where No City Has Gone Before: San Fransisco Will Be the
World's First Zero Waste Town by 2020," Alternet.

30. https://recyclingchronicles.wordpress.com/2012/07/19/conditioned-to
-waste-hardwired-to-habit-2/.

31. http://www.seattle.gov/council/bagshaw/attachments/compost%20
requirement%20QA.pdf.

32. Nickolas J. Themelis, "Waste Management World: Global Bright Lights,"
www.waste-management-world/a/global-bright-lights.

33. http://www.greatrecovery.org.uk, http://www.theguardian.com/sustainable
-business/design-recovery-creating-products-waste.

34. *Solid Waste Management in the World's Cities: Water and Sanitation in
the World's Cities* (2010), p. 43, http://www.waste.nl/sites/waste.nl/files
/product/files/swm_in_world_cities_2010.pdf.

35. http://phys.org/news/2014-02-lagos-bike-recycling-loyalty-scheme.html.

36. Ibid.

37. Towards_the_circular_economy, Ellen McCarthy Foundation, 2012.

38. Ibid.

39. "Building an Ecological Civilization in China—Towards a Practice Based
Learning Approach," http://www.davidpublisher.org/Public/uploads
/Contribute/5658259511d47.pdf.

40. https://www.yumpu.com/en/document/view/19151521/guo-qimin-circular
-economy-development-in-china-europe-china-/63.

41. http://europa.eu/rapid/press-release_MEMO-12-989_en.htm.

42. http://www.circle-economy.com/news/how-amsterdam-goes-circular/.

CHAPTER 6: WATER IS A TERRIBLE THING TO WASTE

1. Simon Romero, "Taps Run Dry in Brazil's Largest City," *New York Times*,
February 17, 2015, p. A4.

2. http://learning.blogs.nytimes.com/2008/04/16/life-in-the-time-of -cholera/?_r=0.

3. Doug Saunders, *Arrival City: The Final Migration and Our Next World* (New York: Vintage, 2011), p. 136.

4. http://mygeologypage.ucdavis.edu/cowen/~gel115/115CH16fertilizer.html.

5. http://www.ph.ucla.edu/epi/snow/indexcase.html.

6. http://www.ph.ucla.edu/epi/snow/snowgreatestdoc.html.

7. http://bluelivingideas.com/2010/04/12/birth-control-pill-threatens-fish -reproduction/.

8. http://sewerhistory.org/articles/whregion/urban_wwm_mgmt/urban _wwm_mgmt.pdf.

9. http://web.extension.illinois.edu/ethanol/wateruse.cfm.

10. http://www.nytimes.com/2002/11/03/us/parched-santa-fe-makes-rare -demand-on-builders.html?pagewanted=all&src=pm.

11. http://www.cityofnorthlasvegas.com/departments/utilities/TopicWater Conservation.shtm.

12. http://www.nyc.gov/html/dep/html/drinking_water/droughthist.shtml.

13. Ibid.

14. "Urban World: Cities and the Rise of the Consuming Class," McKinsey Global Institute, 2012, p. 8.

15. http://www.impatientoptimists.org/Posts/2012/08/Inventing-a-Toilet-for -the-21st-Century.

16. http://www.lselectric.com/wordpress/the-top-10-biggest-wastewater -treatment-plants/.

17. http://www.sciencemag.org/content/337/6095/674.full?sid=fd5c8045-4dee -43e5-a620-ca6faba728dc.

18. Magdalena Mis, "Sludge Can Help China Curb Emissions and Power Cities, Think Tank Says," Reuters, April 8, 2016.

19. http://www.wateronline.com/doc/shortcut-nitrogen-removal-the-next-big -thing-in-wastewater-0001.

20. Petrus L. Du Pisani, "Water Efficiency I: Cities Surviving in an Arid Land— Direct Reclamation of Potable Water at Windhoek's Goreangab Reclamation Plant," *AridLands Newsletter* no. 56 (November–December 2004).

21. http://greencape.co.za/assets/Sector-files/water/IWA-Water-Reuse -Conference-Windhoek-2013.pdf.

22. http://www.sciencemag.org/content/337/6095/679.full?sid=349ace41 -4490-4f6c-b5bf-4e68a7eb054fan.

23. Ibid.

24. http://www.pub.gov.sg/water/Pages/default.aspx.
25. http://www.infrastructurereportcard.org.

PART THREE: RESILIENCE

1. C. S. Holling, "Resilience and Stability of Ecological Systems," *Annual Review of Ecology and Systematics* 4 (1973): 1–23.
2. http://www.newyorker.com/magazine/2015/12/21/the-siege-of-miami.

CHAPTER 7: NATURAL INFRASTRUCTURE

1. Edward O. Wilson, *Biophilia* (Cambridge, MA: Harvard University Press, 1984).
2. https://mdc.mo.gov/sites/default/files/resources/2012/10/ulrich.pdf.
3. http://www.healinglandscapes.org.
4. Richard Louv, *Last Child in the Woods: Saving Our Children from Nature-Deficit Disorder* (Chapel Hill, NC: Algonquin Books, 2005).
5. http://www.jad-journal.com/article/S0165-0327(12)00200-5/abstract.
6. http://ahta.org.
7. Irving Finkel, "The Hanging Gardens of Babylon," in *The Seven Wonders of the Ancient World*, edited by Peter Clayton and Martin Price (New York: Routledge, 1988), pp. 45–46.
8. C. J. Hughes, "In the Bronx, Little Houses That Evoke Puerto Rico," *New York Times*, February 22, 2009.
9. http://www.communitygarden.org/learn/faq.
10. Peter Harnik and Ben Weller, "Measuring the Economic Value of a City Park System," additional assistance by Linda S. Keenan. Published by the Trust for Public Land, 2009.
11. "Active Living by Design," New Public Health Paradigm: Promoting Health Through Community Design, 2002.
12. http://www.hsph.harvard.edu/obesity-prevention-source/obesity-consequences/economic/.
13. Sarah Goodyear, "What's Making China Fat," *Atlantic Cities*, June 22, 2012.
14. Sarah Laskow, "How Trees Can Make City People Happier (and Vice Versa)," Next City, February 3, 2015.
15. http://www.coolcommunities.org/urban_shade_trees.htm.
16. Sandi Doughton, "Toxic Road Runoff Kills Adult Coho Salmon in Hours, Study Finds," *Seattle Times*, October 8, 2015.
17. http://www.governing.com/topics/energy-env/proposed-storm water-plan-philadelphia-emphasizes-green-infrastructure.html.

18. John Vidal, "How a River Helped Seoul Reclaim Its Heart and Soul," *Mail and Guardian* (online), January 5, 2007.

19. Ibid.

20. Ibid.

21. http://www.terrapass.com/society/seouls-river/.

22. Ibid.

23. Curitiba Convention on Biodiversity and Cities, March 28, 2007.

24. Singapore Index on City Biodiversity, https://www.cbd.int/doc/meetings /city/subws-2014-01/other/subws-2014-01-singapore-index-manual-en.pdf.

25. http://www.moe.gov.sg/media/news/2012/11/singapore-ranked-fifth-in -glob.php; http://www.timeshighereducation.co.uk/world-university- rankings/2013-14/world-ranking.

26. http://www.nytimes.com/2011/07/29/business/global/an-urban-jungle-for -the-21st-century.html?_r=0.

27. https://www.cbd.int/authorities/doc/CBS-declaration/Aichi-Nagoya -Declaration-CBS-en.pdf.

28. "The Economics of Ecosystems and Biodiversity for Water and Wetlands," TEEB report, October 2012.

29. http://www.pwconserve.org/issues/watersheds/newyorkcity/index.html.

30. https://www.billionoysterproject.org/about/.

31. http://www.rebuildbydesign.org .

CHAPTER 8: GREEN BUILDINGS, GREEN URBANISM

1. E. F. Schumacher, *Small Is Beautiful* (New York: HarperPerennial, 2010); http://www.centerforneweconomics.org/content/small-beautiful-quotes.

2. http://www.eia.gov/tools/faqs/faq.cfm?id=86&t=1/.

3. Richard W. Caperton, Adam James, and Matt Kasper, "Federal Weatherization Program a Winner on All Counts," Center for American Progress, September 28, 2012.

4. http://thinkprogress.org/climate/2011/09/19/321954/home-weatherization -grows-1000-under-stimulus-funding/.

5. http://fortune.com/2015/01/16/solar-jobs-report-2014/.

6. http://citizensclimatelobby.org/laser-talks/jobs-fossil-fuels-vs-renewables/.

7. http://www3.weforum.org/docs/WEF_GreenInvestment_Report_2013.pdf.

8. http://www.usgbc.org/articles/green-building-facts.

9. The design team included, from Richard Dattner, Bill Stein, Steven Frankel, Adam Watson, Venesa Alicea; from Grimshaw, Vincent Chang, Nikolas Dando-Haenisch, Robert Garneau, Virginia Little, and Eric Johnson.

10. http://www.buildinggreen.com/auth/pdf/EBN_15-5.pdf.

11. http://www.gallup.com/poll/158417/poverty-comes-depression-illness.aspx.

12. http://living-future.org/living-building-challenge-21-standard.

13. http://energy.gov/sites/prod/files/2013/08/f2/Grid%20Resiliency%20 Report_FINAL.pdf.

14. Robert Galvin and Kurt Yeager with Jay Stuller, *Perfect Power: How the Micogrid Revolution Will Release Cleaner, Greener, and More Abundant Energy* (New York: McGraw-Hill, 2009), p. 4.

15. "Efficiency in Electrical Generation—Eurelectric Preservation of Resources," Working Group's "Upstream" subgroup in collaboration with VBG 2003.

16. http://www.eia.gov/cfapps/ipdbproject/iedindex3.cfm?tid=90&pid=44 &aid=8.

CHAPTER 9: CREATING COMMUNITIES OF OPPORTUNITY

1. "Building Communities of Opportunity: Supporting Integrated Planning and Development through Federal Policy." This framing paper was prepared by PolicyLink to inform the September 18, 2009, White House Office of Urban Affairs Tour to Denver, Colorado.

2. *Community Development 2020: Creating Opportunity for All.* A Working Paper. Enterprise Community Partners, 2012. http://www.washington post.com/local/seven-of-nations-10-most-affluent-counties-are-in -washington-region/2012/09/19/f580bf30-028b-11e2-8102-ebee9c 66e190_story.html.

3. Eric Klinenberg, "Dead Heat: Why Don't Americans Sweat over Heat-Wave Deaths?" *Slate.com*, July 30, 2002.

4. "Adaptation: How Can Cities Be Climate Proofed?" *New Yorker*, January 7, 2013; http://archives.newyorker.com/?i=2013-01-07#folio=032.

5. Eric Klinenberg, *Heat Wave: A Social Autopsy of Disaster in Chicago* (Chicago: Chicago University Press, 2002).

6. "Adaptation: How Can Cities Be Climate Proofed?"

7. http://en.wikipedia.org/wiki/2003_European_heat_wave.

8. http://www.communicationcache.com/uploads/1/0/8/8/10887248/note _on_the_drawing_power_of_crowds_of_different_size.pdf.

9. D. W. Haslam and W. P. James, "Obesity," *Lancet* 366 (9492): 1197–209; doi:10.1016/S0140-6736(05)67483-1. PMID 16198769.

10. http://www.huffingtonpost.com/2012/04/30/obesity-costs-dollars -cents_n_1463763.html.

11. http://ucsdnews.ucsd.edu/archive/newsrel/soc/07-07ObesityIK-.asp.

12.   Nicholas A. Christakis and James H. Fowler, *Connected: The Surprising Power of Our Social Networks and How They Shape Our Lives* (New York: Little, Brown, 2009), p. 131.

13.   Mark Granovetter, "The Strength of Weak Ties," *American Journal of Sociology* 78, no. 6 (May 1973): 1360–80; https://sociology.stanford.edu /sites/default/files/publications/the_strength_of_weak_ties_and_exch _w-gans.pdf.

14.   Ibid.

15.   Ibid.

16.   http://www.wttw.com/main.taf?p=1,7,1,1,41.

17.   Francis Fukuyama, *Trust: The Social Virtues and the Creation of Prosperity* (New York: Free Press, 1995).

18.   Eric Beinhocker, *The Origin of Wealth: Evolution, Complexity, and the Radical Remaking of Economics* (Boston: Harvard Business School, 2006), p. 307.

19.   John Gottman, *Trust Matters*, http://edge.org/response-detail/26601.

20.   E. Fischbacher and U. Fischbacher, "Altruists with Green Beards," *Analyse & Kritik* 2 (2005).

21.   http://www.uvm.edu/~dguber/POLS293/articles/putnam1.pdf.

22.   Peter Hedström, "Actions and Networks—Sociology That Really Matters . . . to Me," *Sociologica* 1 (2007).

23.   Robert J. Sampson, *Great American City: Chicago and the Enduring Neighborhood Effect* (Chicago: University of Chicago Press, 2012); http:// www.positivedeviance.org/about_pd/Monique%20VIET%20NAM%20 CHAPTER%20Oct%2017.pdf.

24.   Ibid.

25.   Terrance Hill, Catherine Ross, and Ronald Angel, "Neighborhood Disorder, Psychological Distress and Health," *Journal of Health and Social Behavior* 46 (2005), pp.170–86.

26.   https://www.ptsdforum.org/c/gallery/-pdf/1-48.pdf.

27.   "Perceived Neighborhood Disorder, Community Cohesion, and PTSD Symptoms among Low Income African Americans in Urban Health Setting," *American Journal of Orthopsychiatry* 81, no. 1 (2011): 31–33.

28.   http://infed.org/mobi/robert-putnam-social-capital-and-civic-community/.

29.   David D. Halpern, *The Hidden Wealth of Nations* (Cambridge: Polity Press, 2010).

30.   Michael Woolcock, "The Place of Social Capital in Understanding

Social and Economic Outcomes," http://www.oecd.org/innovation
/research/1824913.pdf.

31. Sean Safford, *Why the Garden Club Couldn't Save Youngstown: Civic Infrastructure and Mobilization in Economic Crisis,* MIT Industrial Performance Center Working Series, 2004.

32. http://blogs.birminghamview.com/blog/2011/05/16/the-picture-that -changed-birmingham/.

CHAPTER 10: THE COGNITIVE ECOLOGY OF OPPORTUNITY

1. Jonathan Woetzel, Sangeeth Ram, Jan Mischke, Nicklas Garemo, and Shirish Sankhe, *A Blueprint for Addressing the Global Affordable Housing Challenge,* McKinsey Global Institute (MGI) report, October 2014.

2. http://www.jchs.harvard.edu/sites/jchs.harvard.edu/files/sonhr14-color-ch1 .pdf.

3. http://www.nfcc.org/newsroom/newsreleases/floi_july2011results_final.cfm.

4. http://www.jchs.harvard.edu/sites/jchs.harvard.edu/files/americas rentalhousing-2011-bw.pdf.

5. http://sf.curbed.com/archives/2015/05/22/san_franciscos_median_rent _climbs_to_a_whopping_4225.php.

6. John Bowlby, *Secure Base: Parent-Child Attachment and Healthy Human Development* (New York: Basic Books, 1988), 11.

7. Dane Archer and Rosemary Gartner, "Violent Acts and Violent Times: A Comparative Approach to Postwar Homicide Rates," *American Sociology Review* 4 (1976): 937–63.

8. Stephanie Booth-Kewley, "Factors Associated with Anti Social Behavior in Combat Veterans," *Aggressive Behavior* 36 (2010): 330–37; http://www.dtic .mil/dtic/tr/fulltext/u2/a573599.pdf.

9. David Finkelhor, Anne Shattuck, Heather Turner, and Sherry Hamby, "Improving the Adverse Childhood Study Scale," *JAMA Pediatrics* 167, no. 1 (November 26, 2012): 70–75; published online.

10. http://acestudy.org/yahoo_site_admin/assets/docs/ARV1N1.127150541 .pdf.

11. Nadine Burke Harris, "Powerpoint: Toxic Stress—Changing the Paradigm of Clinical Practice," Center for Youth Wellness, May 13, 2014, presented at the Pickower Center, MIT.

12. http://www.pbs.org/wgbh/nova/next/body/epigenetics-abuse/.

13. http://centerforeducation.rice.edu/slc/LS/30MillionWordGap.html.

14. http://www.human.cornell.edu/hd/outreach-extension/upload/evans.pdf.

15. "Evictions Soar in a Hot Market, Renters Suffer," *New York Times*, September 3, 2014.

16. http://www.washingtonpost.com/local/freddie-grays-life-a-study-in-the-sad-effects-of-lead-paint-on-poor-blacks/2015/04/29/0be898e6-eea8-11e4-8abc-d6aa3bad79dd_story.html.

17. http://www.theatlantic.com/health/archive/2014/03/the-toxins-that-threaten-our-brains/284466/.

18. Ibid.

19. Patrick Reed and Maya Brennan, "How Housing Matters: Using Housing to Stabilize Families and Strengthen Classrooms," a profile of the McCarver Elementary School Special Housing Program in Tacoma, Washington, October 2014.

20. http://denversroadhome.org/files/FinalDHFCCostStudy_1.pdf.

21. "An Investment in Opportunity—A Bold New Vision for Housing Policy in the U.S.," Enterprise Community Partners, February 2016, https://s3.amazonaws.com/KSPProd/ERC_Upload/0100943.pdf.

22. http://usa.streetsblog.org/2013/09/11/study-kids-who-live-in-walkable-neighborhoods-get-more-exercise/.

23. http://www.nyc.gov/html/doh/downloads/pdf/epi/databrief42.pdf.

24. http://www.investigatinghealthyminds.org/ScientificPublications/2013/.RosenkranzComparisonBrain,Behavior,AndImmunity.pdf.

25. http://www.investigatinghealthyminds.org/ScientificPublications/2012/DavidsonContemplativeChildDevelopmentPerspectives.pdf.

26. http://www.cdc.gov/violenceprevention/childmaltreatment/economiccost.html.

27. http://wagner.nyu.edu/trasande.

CHAPTER 11: PROSPERITY, EQUALITY, AND HAPPINESS

1. http://www.gutenberg.ca/ebooks/keynes-essaysinpersuasion/keynes-essaysinpersuasion-00-h.html.

2. http://www.pewresearch.org/fact-tank/2015/01/21/inequality-is-at-top-of-the-agenda-as-global-elites-gather-in-davos/.

3. http://www.ritholtz.com/blog/2010/08/history-of-world-gdp/.

4. http://www.unicef-irc.org/publications/pdf/rc11_eng.pdf.

5. David Satterthwaite, "The Scale of Urban Change Worldwide 1950–2000 and Its Underpinnings," International Institute for Environment and Development, 2005.

6. http://www-bcf.usc.edu/~easterl/papers/Happiness.pdf.

7. http://www.citylab.com/work/2015/06/why-groceries-cost-less-in-big
cities/394904/?utm_source=nl_daily_link3_060515.

8. http://gmj.gallup.com/content/150671/happiness-is-love-and-75k.aspx.

9. http://www.sciencemag.org/content/306/5702/1776.full.

10. http://www.ncbi.nlm.nih.gov/pmc/articles/PMC1351254/.

11. http://www.gfmag.com/gdp-data-country-reports/158-tunisia-gdp-country
-report.html#axzz2YBUSAgM0.

12. http://www.gfmag.com/gdp-data-country-reports/280-egypt-gdp-country
-report.html#axzz2YBUSAgM0.

13. http://www.gallup.com/poll/145883/Egyptians-Tunisians-Wellbeing
-Plummets-Despite-GDP-Gains.aspx.

14. http://www.time.com/time/magazine/article/0,9171,2044723,00.html.

15. Doug Saunders, *Arrival City: How the Largest Migration in History Is
Reshaping Our World* (New York: Vintage, 2012), pp. 328–32.

16. Simon Kuznets, "National Income, 1929–1932," 73rd US Congress, 2d
session, Senate document no. 124, 1934, pp. 5–7.

17. http://www.brookings.edu/research/articles/2010/01/03-happiness-graham.

18. Carol Graham, *The Pursuit of Happiness in the U.S.: Inequality in Agency,
Optimism, and Life Chances* (Washington, DC: Brookings Institution Press,
2011).

19. http://www.brookings.edu/blogs/social-mobility-memos/posts/2016/02/10
-rich-have-better-stress-than-poor-graham.

20. http://www.pewglobal.org/2014/10/09/emerging-and-developing
-economies-much-more-optimistic-than-rich-countries-about-the-future/.

21. http://www.un.org/News/briefings/docs/2005/kotharibrf050511.doc.htm.

22. Danielle Kurtleblen, "Large Cities Have Greater Income Inequality," *U.S.
News and World Report*, April 29, 2011.

23. http://www.theguardian.com/world/2014/jul/28/china-more-unequal
-richer.

24. UN-Habitat, *State of the World's Cities 2008–2009: Harmonious Cities*,
(Nairobi: UN-Habitat, 2008).

25. http://www.citylab.com/work/2011/09/25-most-economically-powerful
-cities-world/109/#slide17.

26. http://blog.euromonitor.com /2013/03/the-worlds-largest-cities-are-the
-most-unequal.html.

27. "Life Expectancy by Tube Station," *Telegraph*, http://www.telegraph.co.uk
/news/health/news/9413096/Life-expectancy-by-tube-station-new
-interactive-map-shows-inequality-in-the-capital.html.

28. http://www.economist.com/news/briefing/21674712-children-bear
-disproportionate-share-hidden-cost-chinas-growth-little-match-children.

29. http://www.nytimes.com/interactive/2015/05/03/upshot/the-best-and
-worst-places-to-grow-up-how-your-area-compares.html?abt=0002&abg=1.

30. http://www.eiu.com/Handlers/WhitepaperHandler.ashx?fi=Healthcare
-outcomes-index-2014.pdf&mode=wp&campaignid=Healthoutcome2014.

31. Elizabeth H. Bradley and Lauren A. Taylor, *The American Health Care
Paradox: Why Spending More Is Getting Us Less* (New York: PublicAffairs,
2013), pp. 181–86.

32. Benaabdelaali Wail, Hanchane Said, and Kamal Abdelhak, "Educational
Inequality in the World, 1950–2010: Estimates from a New Dataset," in
*Inequality, Mobility and Segregation: Essays in Honor of Jacques Silber, Edition:
Research on Economic Inequality*, vol. 20, ed. John A. Bishop, Rafael Salas
(Bingley, UK: Emerald Group Publishing, 2012), pp. 337–66.

33. "Assuring the Quality of Achievement Standards in H.E.: Educating
Capable Graduates Not Just for Today but for Tomorrow," Emeritus
Professor Geoff Scott, University of Western Sydney, November 14, 2014.

34. Alana Semuels, "The City That Believed in Desegregation," Atlantic City
Blog, March 27, 2015.

35. Manuel Pastor and Chris Brenner, "Weak Market Cities and Regional
Equity," in *Re-Tooling for Growth: Building a 21st Century Economy in
America's Older Industrial Areas* (New York: American Assembly, 2008),
p. 113.

36. World Happiness Report launch, Columbia University, April 24, 2015.

37. Report by the Commission on the Measurement of Economic Performance
and Social Progress. Professor Joseph E. Stiglitz, Chair, Columbia University,
Professor Amartya Sen, Chair Advisor, Harvard University, Professor Jean
Paul Fitoussi, Coordinator of the Commission, IEP, 2011, p. 45.

38. To measure metropolitan area prosperity, we used U.S. Department of
Commerce Bureau of Economic Analysis 2011 data on real GDP per
capita. To measure metro area well-being, we used the Gallup-Healthways
2011 polling data for its U.S. Well-Being Index. The Gallup-Healthways
methodology includes survey data in six key "domains": Life Evaluation,
Emotional Health, Physical Health, Healthy Behavior, Work Environment,
and Basic Access. Gallup-Healthways combines results in each of these areas
to reach a total Well-Being Index score for each metro area.

39. To see the full list of the prosperity/well-being/equality matrix, go to http://
www.rosecompanies.com/Prosperity_wellbeing_Zscore.pdf.

40. Bus Rapid Transit, or BRT, treats buses like trains. They move on a dedicated pathway, they stop at stations, and they quickly load and unload their passengers through wide side doors. However, because the pathway is simply a lane of roadway set aside for their use, BRT is much cheaper to build and operate than train lines, and much more flexible.

41. Jaime Lerner, *Urban Acupuncture* (Washington, DC: Island Press, 2014).

CHAPTER 12: ENTWINEMENT

1. Kenneth Burke, *Permanence and Change* (Berkeley and Los Angeles: University of California Press, 1935; 3rd ed., 1984), p. 10; https://books .google.com/books?id=E4_BU8v2TPUC&pg=PA10&lpg=PA10&dq= "people+may+be+unfitted+by+being+fit+in+an+unfit+fitness&source=b l&ots=cow7nmf4ie&sig=fJJxTxML25m41GQ_kWlgHSR-__0&hl=en &sa=X&ved=0CD4Q6AEwCWoVChMIpc_e9d6ZxwIVzDw-Ch1s0A -z#v=onepage&q="people%20may%20be%20unfitted%20by%20 being%20fit%20in%20an%20unfit%20fitness&f=false.

2. Donella H. Meadows, *Thinking in Systems: A Primer*, edited by Diana Wright, Sustainability Institute (White River Junction, VT: Chelsea Green Publishing, 2008), p. 17.

3. Jean Pierre P. Changeaux, Antonio Damasio, and Wolf Singer, eds., *The Neurobiology of Human Values* (Berlin and Heidelberg: Springer-Verlag, 2005).

4. The story of King Frederick, Bach, and the "Musical Offering" is described in: James R. Gaines, *Evening in the Palace of Reason: Bach Meets Frederick the Great in the Age of Enlightenment* (New York: HarperPerennial, 2006).

5. Nicholas Shrady, *The Last Day: Wrath, Ruin, and Reason in the Great Lisbon Earthquake of 1755* (New York: Penguin, 2008), pp. 152–55.

6. Rebecca Solnit, *A Paradise Built in Hell* (New York: Penguin, 2009), p. 86.

7. http://www.ssireview.org/articles/entry/collective_impact.

8. Martin Luther King Jr., "Where Do We Go from Here?" Annual Report Delivered at the 11th Convention of the Southern Christian Leadership Conference, August 16, Atlanta, GA.

9. Edward O. Wilson, *Biophilia* (Cambridge, MA: Harvard University Press, 1984), p. 85.

10. Thomas Jay Oord, "The Love Racket: Defining Love and *Agape* for the Love-and-Science Research Program," *Zygon* 40, no. 4 (December 2005).

11. Christopher Alexander, *The Nature of Order*, 4 vols. (Berkeley, CA: Center for Environmental Structure, 2002), Vol. 4, pp. 262–70.

SELECTED BIBLIOGRAPHY

Akerlof, George A., and Robert J. Shiller. *Animal Spirits: How Human Psychology Drives the Economy, and Why It Matters for Global Capitalism*. Princeton, NJ: Princeton University Press, 2009.

Alexander, Christopher. *The Nature of Order: An Essay on the Art of Building and the Nature of the Universe*. Vol. 1, *The Phenomenon of Life*. Berkeley, CA: Center for Environmental Structure, 2002.

———. *The Nature of Order: An Essay on the Art of Building and the Nature of the Universe*. Vol. 2, *The Process of Creating Life*. Berkeley, CA: Center for Environmental Structure, 2002.

———. *The Nature of Order: An Essay on the Art of Building and the Nature of the Universe*. Vol. 3, *A Vision of a Living World*. Berkeley, CA: Center for Environmental Structure, 2002.

———. *The Nature of Order: An Essay on the Art of Building and the Nature of the Universe*. Vol. 4, *The Luminous Ground*. Berkeley, CA: Center for Environmental Structure, 2002.

———. *The Timeless Way of Building*. New York: Oxford University Press, 1979.

Alexander, Christopher, Sara Ishikawa, Murray Silverstein, Max Jacobson, Ingrid Fiksdahl-King, and Shlomo Angel. *A Pattern Language: Towns, Buildings, Construction*. New York: Oxford University Press, 1977.

Amiet, Pierre. *Art of the Ancient Near East*. Ed. Naomi Noble Richard. New York: Harry N. Abrams, 1980.

Anderson, Ray C. *Mid-Course Correction: Toward a Sustainable Enterprise: The Interface Model*. White River Junction, VT: Chelsea Green Publishing, 1998.

Architecture for Humanity and Kate Stohr. *Design Like You Give a Damn: Architectural Responses to Humanitarian Crises*. New York: Metropolis Press, 2006.

Arendt, Randall, Elizabeth A. Brabec, Harry L. Dodson, Christine Reid, and Robert D. Yaro. *Rural by Design: Maintaining Small Town Character*. Chicago: Planners, American Planning Association, 1994.

Ariely, Dan. *Predictably Irrational: The Hidden Forces That Shape Our Decisions*. New York: Harper, 2009.

Arthur, W. Brian. *The Nature of Technology: What It Is and How It Evolves*. New York: Free Press, 2009.

Aruz, Joan, and Ronald Wallenfels. *Art of the First Cities: The Third Millennium B.C. from the Mediterranean to the Indus*. New York: Metropolitan Museum of Art, 2003.

Babbitt, Bruce E. *Cities in the Wilderness: A New Vision of Land Use in America*. Washington, DC: Island/Shearwater, 2005.

Ball, Philip. *The Self-Made Tapestry: Pattern Formation in Nature*. Oxford, UK: Oxford University Press, 1999.

Barabási, Albert-László. *Linked: How Everything Is Connected to Everything Else and What It Means for Business, Science, and Everyday Life*. New York: Plume Books, 2003.

Barber, Benjamin. *Consumed*. W. W. Norton, 2007.

Barber, Dan. *The Third Plate: Field Notes on the Future of Food*. New York: Penguin, 2014.

———. *If Mayors Ruled the World*. New Haven, CT: Yale University Press, 2013.

Barnett, Jonathan. *The Fractured Metropolis: Improving the New City, Restoring the Old City, Reshaping the Region*. New York: HarperCollins, 1995.

Bateson, Gregory. *Steps to an Ecology of Mind*. Chicago: University of Chicago Press, 1972.

Batty, Michael, and Paul Longley. *Fractal Cities: A Geometry of Form and Function*. London: Academy Editions, 1994.

Batuman, Elif. "The Sanctuary: The World's Oldest Temple and the Dawn of Civilization." *New Yorker*, December 19 and 26, 2011.

Beard, Mary. *The Fires of Vesuvius: Pompeii Lost and Found*. Cambridge, MA: Belknap Press of Harvard University Press, 2008.

Beatley, Timothy. *Green Urbanism: Learning from European Cities*. Washington, DC: Island, 2000.

Beatley, Timothy, and E. O. Wilson. *Biophilic Cities: Integrating Nature into Urban Design and Planning*. Washington, DC: Island Press, 2011.

Beinhocker, Eric D. *The Origin of Wealth: Evolution, Complexity, and the Radical Remaking of Economics*. Boston: Harvard Business School, 2006.

Bell, Bryan. *Good Deeds, Good Design: Community Service through Architecture*. New York: Princeton Architectural Press, 2004.

Bell, Bryan, and Katie Wakeford. *Expanding Architecture: Design as Activism*. New York: Metropolis Press, 2008.

Benfield, F. Kaid. *People Habitat: 25 Ways to Think about Greener, Healthier Cities*. Washington, DC: Island Press, 2014.

Benner, Chris, and Manuel Pastor. *Just Growth: Inclusion and Prosperity in America's Metropolitan Regions.* London: Routledge, 2012.

Benyus, Janine M. *Biomimicry: Innovation Inspired by Nature.* New York: Quill, 1997.

Berube, Alan. *State of Metropolitan America: On the Front Lines of Demographic Transformation.* Washington, DC: Brookings Institution Metropolitan Policy Program, 2010.

Bipartisan Policy Center. *Housing America's Future: New Directions for National Policy Executive Summary.* Washington, DC: Bipartisan Policy Center, February 2013.

Bleibtreu, John N. *The Parable of the Beast.* Toronto: Macmillan, 1968.

Blum, Harold F. *Time's Arrow and Evolution.* 3rd ed. Princeton, NJ: Princeton University Press, 1968.

Bohr, Niels. *Essays 1958–1962 on Atomic Physics and Human Knowledge.* New York: Vintage Books, 1963.

Botsman, Rachel, and Roo Rogers. *What's Mine Is Yours: The Rise of Collaborative Consumption.* New York: Harper Business, 2010.

Botton, Alain de. *The Architecture of Happiness.* New York: Pantheon Books, 2006.

Brand, Stewart. *The Clock of the Long Now: Time and Responsibility.* New York: Basic Books, 1999.

———. *How Buildings Learn: What Happens after They're Built.* New York: Penguin, 1994.

———. *The Millennium Whole Earth Catalog: Access to Tools and Ideas for the Twenty-first Century.* San Francisco: Harper San Francisco, 1994.

———. *Whole Earth Discipline: An Ecopragmatist Manifesto.* New York: Viking, 2009.

———. *Whole Earth Ecology: The Best of Environmental Tools and Ideas.* Ed. J. Baldwin. New York: Harmony Books, 1990.

Briggs, Xavier De Souza, Susan J. Popkin, and John M. Goering. *Moving to Opportunity: The Story of an American Experiment to Fight Ghetto Poverty.* New York: Oxford University Press, 2010.

Brockman, John. *The New Humanists: Science at the Edge.* New York: Barnes & Noble, 2003.

———. *This Explains Everything: Deep, Beautiful, and Elegant Theories of How the World Works.* New York: HarperPerennial, 2013.

Bronowski, J. *The Ascent of Man.* Boston: Little, Brown, 1973.

Broome, Steve, Alasdair Jones, and Jonathan Rowson. "How Social Networks Power and Sustain Big Society." *Connected Communities,* September 2010.

Broome, Steve, Gaia Marcus, and Thomas Neumark. "Power Lines." *Connected Communities,* May 2011.

Burdett, Ricky, and Deyan Sudjic. *The Endless City: The Urban Age Project*. London: Phaidon, 2007.

Burney, David, Thomas Farley, Janette Sadik-Khan, and Amanda Burden. *Active Design Guidelines: Promoting Physical Activity and Health in Design*. New York: New York City Department of Design and Construction, 2010.

Burrows, Edwin G., and Mike Wallace. *Gotham: A History of New York City to 1898*. New York: Oxford University Press, 1999.

Calthorpe, Peter. *The Next American Metropolis: Ecology, Community, and the American Dream*. New York: Princeton Architectural Press, 1993.

———. *Urbanism in the Age of Climate Change*, Washington, DC: Island Press, 2010.

Calthorpe, Peter, and William Fulton. *The Regional City: Planning for the End of Sprawl*. Washington, DC: Island Press, 2001.

Campbell, Frances, Gabriella Conti, James J. Heckman, Seong Hyeok Moon, Rodrigo Pinto, Elizabeth Pungello, and Yi Pan. "Early Childhood Investments Substantially Boost Adult Health." *Science*, March 28, 2014.

Campbell, Tim. *Beyond Smart Cities: How Cities Network, Learn and Innovate*. New York: Earthscan, 2012.

Capra, Fritjof. *The Web of Life: A New Scientific Understanding of Living Systems*. New York: Anchor Books, 1996.

Carey, Kathleen, Gayle Berens, and Thomas Eitler. "After Sandy: Advancing Strategies for Long-Term Resilience and Adaptability." *Urban Land Institute* (2013): 2–56.

Caro, Robert A. *The Power Broker: Robert Moses and the Fall of New York*. New York: Vintage Books, 1975.

Carter, Brian, ed. *Building Culture*. Buffalo: Buffalo Books, 2006.

Castells, Manuel. *The Rise of the Network Society*. Malden, MA: Wiley-Blackwell, 1996.

Chaliand, Gerard, and Jean-Pierre Rageau. *The Penguin Atlas of Diasporas*. New York: Penguin, 1995.

Chang, Amos I. T. *The Existence of Intangible Content in Architectonic Form Based upon the Practicality of Laotzu's Philosophy*. Princeton, NJ: Princeton University Press, 1956.

Changeux, Jean-Pierre, A. R. Damasio, W. Singer, and Y. Christen. *Neurobiology of Human Values*. Berlin: Springer-Verlag, 2005.

Chermayeff, Serge, and Christopher Alexander. *Community and Privacy: Toward a New Architecture of Humanism*. Garden City, NY: Doubleday, 1963.

Chivian, Eric, and Aaron Bernstein. *Sustaining Life: How Human Health Depends on Biodiversity*. Oxford, UK: Oxford University Press, 2008.

Christakis, Nicholas A., and James H. Fowler. *Connected: The Surprising Power of Our Social Networks and How They Shape Our Lives.* New York: Little, Brown, 2009.

Christiansen, Jen. "The Decline of Cheap Energy." *Scientific American,* April 2013.

Cisneros, Henry. *Interwoven Destinies: Cities and the Nation.* New York: W. W. Norton, 1993.

Cisneros, Henry, and Lora Engdahl. *From Despair to Hope: HOPE VI and the New Promise of Public Housing in America's Cities.* Washington, DC: Brookings Institution, 2009.

The City in 2050: Creating Blueprints for Change. Washington, DC: Urban Land Institute, 2008.

Ciulla, Joanne B. *The Working Life: The Promise and Betrayal of Modern Work.* New York: Crown Business, 2000.

Clapp, James A. *The City: A Dictionary of Quotable Thoughts on Cities and Urban Life.* New Brunswick, NJ: Center for Urban Policy Research, 1984.

Clarke, Rory, Sandra Wilson, Brian Keeley, Patrick Love, and Ricardo Tejada, eds. *OECD Yearbook 2014: Resilient Economies, Inclusive Societies.* N.p.: OECD, 2015.

Climatewire. "How the Dutch Make 'Room for the River' by Redesigning Cities." *Scientific American,* January 20, 2012.

Costanza, Robert, et al. "Quality of Life: An Approach Integrating Opportunities, Human Needs and Subjective Well Being." *Ecological Economics* 61 (2007).

Costanza, Robert, A. J. McMichael, and D. J. Rapport. "Assessing Ecosystem Health." *Tree* 13, no. 10 (October 1988).

Cowan, James. *A Mapmaker's Dream: The Meditations of Fra Mauro, Cartographer to the Court of Venice.* Boston: Shambhala, 1996.

Cuddihy, John, Joshua Engel-Yan, and Christopher Kennedy. "The Changing Metabolism of Cities." *MIT Press Journals* 11, no. 2 (2007).

Cytron, Naomi, David Erickson, and Ian Galloway. "Routinizing the Extraordinary, Mapping the Future: Synthesizing Themes and Ideas for Next Steps." *Investing in What Works for America Communities.*

Darwin, Charles. *The Origin of the Species and the Voyage of the Beagle.* New York: Everyman's Library, 2003.

Davis, Wade. *The Wayfinders.* Toronto: House of Anansi Press, 2009.

Day, Christopher. *Places of the Soul: Architecture and Environmental Design as a Healing Art.* Oxford, UK: Architectural, 1990.

Deboos, Salome, Jonathan Demenge, and Radhika Gupta. "Ladakh: Contemporary Publics and Politics." *Himalaya* 32 (August 2013).

Decade of Design: Health and Urbanism. Washington, DC: American Institute of Architects, n.d.

Diamond, Jared. *Guns, Germs and Steel: The Fates of Human Societies.* New York: W. W. Norton, 1997.

Doherty, Patrick C., Col. Mark "Puck" Mykleby, and Tom Rautenberg. "A Grand Strategy for Sustainability: America's Strategic Imperative and Greatest Opportunity." New America Foundation.

Dreyfuss, Henry. *Designing for People.* New York: Simon & Schuster, 1955.

Duany, Andres, and Elizabeth Plater-Zyberk. *Towns and Town-Making Principles.* New York: Rizzoli, 1991.

Duany, Andres, Elizabeth Plater-Zyberk, and Jeff Speck. *Suburban Nation: The Rise of Sprawl and the Decline of the American Dream.* New York: North Point, 2000.

Ebert, James D. *Interacting Systems in Development.* New York: Holt, Rinehart and Winston, 1965.

Economist. Hot Spots 2025: Benchmarking the Future Competitiveness of Cities. London: Economist Intelligence Unit, n.d.

———. "Lost Property." February 25, 2012.

Eddington, A. S. *The Nature of the Physical World.* New York: Macmillan, 1927.

Ehrenhalt, Alan. *The Great Inversion and the Future of the American City.* New York: Alfred A. Knopf, 2012.

Eitler, Thomas W., Edward McMahon, and Theodore Thoerig. *Ten Principles for Building Healthy Places.* Washington, DC: Urban Land Institute, 2013.

Enterprise Community Partners. "Community Development 2020—Creating Opportunity for All." 2012.

Epstein, Paul R., and Dan Ferber. *Changing Planet, Changing Health: How the Climate Crisis Threatens Our Health and What We Can Do about It.* Berkeley: University of California Press, 2011.

Ewing, Reid H., Keith Bartholomew, Steve Winkelman, Jerry Walters, and Don Chen. *Growing Cooler: The Evidence on Urban Development and Climate Change.* Washington, DC: Urban Land Institute, 2008.

Feddes, Fred. *A Millennium of Amsterdam: Spatial History of a Marvellous City.* Bussum: Thoth, 2012.

Ferguson, Niall. "Complexity and Collapse." *Foreign Affairs* (March-April 2010).

Florida, Richard L. *The Rise of the Creative Class.* New York: Basic Books, 2012.

Foreign Affairs: The Rise of Big Data. 3rd ed. Vol. 92. New York: Council on Foreign Relations, 2013.

Forrester, Jay W. *Urban Dynamics.* Cambridge, MA: MIT Press, 1969.

Foundations for Centering Prayer and the Christian Contemplative Life. New York: Continuum International Publishing Group, 2002.

Frank, Joanna, Rachel MacCleery, Suzanne Nienaber, Sara Hammerschmidt, and

Abigail Claflin. *Building Healthy Places Toolkit: Strategies for Enhancing Health in the Built Environment*. Washington, DC: Urban Land Institute, 2015.

Freudenburg, William R., Robert Gramling, Shirley Bradway Laska, and Kai Erikson. *Catastrophe in the Making: The Engineering of Katrina and the Disasters of Tomorrow*. Washington, DC: Island Press/Shearwater, 2009.

Friedman, Thomas L. *Hot, Flat, and Crowded: Why We Need a Green Revolution—and How It Can Renew America*. New York: Farrar, Straus and Giroux, 2008.

Fuller, R. Buckminster. *Operating Manual for Spaceship Earth*. Carbondale, IL: Touchstone Books, 1969.

Gabel, Medard. *Energy, Earth, and Everyone: A Global Energy Strategy for Spaceship Earth*. New Haven, CT: Earth Metabolic Design, 1975.

Gaines, James R. *Evening in the Palace of Reason: Bach Meets Frederick the Great in the Age of Enlightenment*. New York: HarperCollins, 2005; HarperPerennial, 2006.

Galilei, Galileo. *Dialogue Concerning the Two Chief World Systems*. Trans. Stillman Drake. Berkeley: University of California Press, 1967.

Galvin, Robert W., Kurt E. Yeager, and Jay Stuller. *Perfect Power: How the Microgrid Revolution Will Unleash Cleaner, Greener, and More Abundant Energy*. New York: McGraw-Hill Books, 2009.

Gamow, George. *One Two Three . . . Infinity: Facts and Speculations of Science*. New York: Bantam, 1958.

Gang, Jeanne. *Reverse Effect: Renewing Chicago's Waterways*. N.p.: Studio Gang Architects, 2011.

Gans, Herbert J. *The Levittowners: Ways of Life and Politics in a New Suburban Community*. New York: Columbia University Press, 1967.

Gansky, Lisa. *The Mesh: Why the Future of Business Is Sharing*. New York: Portfolio/Penguin, 2010.

Garreau, Joel. *Edge City: Life on the New Frontier*. New York: Doubleday, 1988.

Gehl, Jan. *Cities for People*. Washington, DC: Island Press, 2010.

Georgescu-Roegen, Nicholas. *The Entropy Law and the Economic Process*. Boston: Harvard University Press, 1971.

Gibbon, Edward. *The Decline and Fall of the Roman Empire*. New York: Penguin, 1952.

Gilchrist, Alison, and David Morris. "Communities Connected: Inclusion, Participation and Common Purpose." *Connected Communities*, 2011.

Glaeser, Edward. *Triumph of the City: How Our Greatest Invention Makes Us Richer, Smarter, Greener, Healthier, and Happier*. New York: Penguin, 2011.

Glass, Philip. *Words without Music*. New York: Liveright, 2015.

Gleick, James. *Chaos: Making a New Science*. New York: Viking, 1987.

Goetzmann, William N., and K. Geert Rouwenhorst. *The Origins of Value: The Financial Innovations That Created Modern Capital Markets.* Oxford, UK: Oxford University Press, 2005.

Goleman, Daniel. *Emotional Intelligence.* New York: Bantam, 1994.

Goleman, Daniel, Lisa Bennett, and Zenobia Barlow. *Ecoliterate: How Educators Are Cultivating Emotional, Social, and Ecological Intelligence.* San Francisco: Jossey-Bass, 2012.

Goleman, Daniel, and Christoph Lueneburger. "The Change Leadership Sustainability Demands." *MIT Sloan Management Review,* Summer 2010.

Gollings, John. *City of Victory: Vijayanagara, the Medieval Hindu Capital of Southern India.* New York: Aperture, 1991.

Gorbachev, Mikhail Sergeevich. *The Search for a New Beginning: Developing a New Civilization.* San Francisco: Harper San Francisco, 1995.

Gore, Al. *Earth in the Balance: Ecology and the Human Spirit.* Boston: Houghton Mifflin, 1992.

Gould, Stephen Jay. *Time's Arrow, Time's Cycle: Myth and Metaphor in the Discovery of Geological Time.* Cambridge, MA: Harvard University Press, 1987.

Gratz, Roberta Brandes. *The Battle for Gotham: New York in the Shadow of Robert Moses and Jane Jacobs.* New York: Nation, 2010.

Greene, Brian. *The Elegant Universe: Superstrings, Hidden Dimensions, and the Quest for the Ultimate Theory.* New York: Vintage Books, 1999.

Grillo, Paul Jacques. *Form, Function and Design.* New York: Dover, 1960.

Grist, Matt. *Changing the Subject: How New Ways of Thinking about Human Behaviour Might Change Politics, Policy and Practice.* London: RSA, n.d.

———. *Steer: Mastering Our Behaviour through Instinct, Environment and Reason.* London: RSA, 2010.

Groslier, Bernard, and Jacques Arthaud. *Angkor: Art and Civilization.* London: Readers Union, 1968.

Guneralp, Burak, and Karen C. Seto. "Environmental Impacts of Urban Growth from an Integrated Dynamic Perspective: A Case Study of Shenzhen, South China." www.elsevier.com/locate/gloenvcha. October 22, 2007.

Habraken, N. J. *The Structure of the Ordinary: Form and Control in the Built Environment.* Cambridge, MA: MIT Press, 1998.

Hall, Jon, and Christina Hackmann. *Issues for a Global Human Development Agenda.* New York: UNDP, 2013.

Hammer, Stephen A., Shagun Mehrotra, Cynthia Rosenzweig, and William D. Solecki, eds. *Climate Change and Cities.* Cambridge, UK: Cambridge University Press 2011.

Harnik, Peter, and Ben Welle. "From Fitness Zones to the Medical Mile: How Urban Park Systems Can Best Promote Health and Wellness." Trust for Public Land, 2011. www.tpl.org.

———. "Smart Collaboration—How Urban Parks Can Support Affordable Housing." Trust for Public Land, 2009. www.tpl.org.

Hawken, Paul. *Blessed Unrest.* New York: Viking, 2007.

———. *The Ecology of Commerce: A Declaration of Sustainability.* New York: Harper Business, 1993.

Hawken, Paul, Amory B. Lovins, and L. Hunter Lovins. *Natural Capitalism: Creating the Next Industrial Revolution.* Boston: Little, Brown, 1999.

Hayden, Dolores. *Building Suburbia: Green Fields and Urban Growth, 1820–2000.* New York: Pantheon Books, 2003.

Heath, Chip, and Dan Heath. *Switch: How to Change Things When Change Is Hard.* New York: Broadway Books, 2010.

Helliwell, John F., Richard Layard, and Jeffrey Sachs, eds. *World Happiness Report, 2013 Edition.* New York: Earth Institute, Columbia University, 2012.

———. *World Happiness Report, 2015 Edition.* New York: Earth Institute, Columbia University, 2016.

Hersey, George L. *The Monumental Impulse: Architecture's Biological Roots.* Cambridge, MA: MIT Press, 1999.

Hershkowitz, Allen, and Maya Ying Lin. *Bronx Ecology: Blueprint for a New Environmentalism.* Washington, DC: Island Press, 2002.

Herzog, Ze'ev. *Archaeology of the City: Urban Planning in Ancient Israel and Its Social Implications.* Tel Aviv: Emery and Claire Yass Archaeology, 1997.

Heschong, Lisa. *Thermal Delight in Architecture.* Cambridge, MA: MIT Press, 1979.

Hiss, Tony. *The Experience of Place: A Completely New Way of Looking at and Dealing with Our Radically Changing Cities and Countryside.* New York: Alfred A. Knopf, 1990.

———. *In Motion: The Experience of Travel.* New York: Alfred A. Knopf, 2010.

Hitchcock, Henry-Russell. *In the Nature of Materials, 1887–1941: The Buildings of Frank Lloyd Wright.* New York: Da Capo, 1942.

Holling, C. S. "Understanding the Complexity of Economic, Ecological, and Social Systems." *Ecosystems* 4 (2001): 390–405.

Hollis, Leo. *Cities Are Good for You: The Genius of the Metropolis.* New York: Bloomsbury Press, 2013.

Homer-Dixon, Thomas F. *The Upside of Down: Catastrophe, Creativity, and the Renewal of Civilization.* Washington, DC: Island Press, 2006.

Horan, Thomas A. *Digital Places: Building Our City of Bits*. Washington, DC: Urban Land Institute, 2000.

Housing America's Future: New Directions for National Policy. Washington, DC: Bipartisan Policy Center, 2013.

Howard, Albert. *An Agricultural Testament*. London: Oxford University Press, 1943.

Howard, Ebenezer, and Frederic J. Osborn. *Garden Cities of To-morrow*. Cambridge, MA: MIT Press, 1965.

Howell, Lee. *Global Risks 2013*. 8th ed. Geneva: World Economic Forum, 2013.

Hutchinson, G. Evelyn. *The Clear Mirror*. New Haven, CT: Leete's Island Books, 1978.

Interim Report. "The Economics of Ecosystems and Biodiversity." Welling, Germany: Welzel+Hardt, 2008.

Isacoff, Stuart. *Temperament: How Music Became a Battleground for the Great Minds of Western Civilization*. New York: Vintage Books, 2003.

Jackson, Kenneth T. *Crabgrass Frontier: The Suburbanization of the United States*. New York: Oxford University Press, 1985.

Jackson, Tim. *Prosperity without Growth: Economics for a Finite Planet*. London: Earthscan, 2009.

Jacobs, Jane. *Cities and the Wealth of Nations: Principles of Economic Life*. New York: Vintage Books, 1985.

———. *The Death and Life of Great American Cities*. New York: Vintage Books, 1961.

———. *The Economy of Cities*. New York: Vintage Books, 1969.

———. *Systems of Survival: A Dialogue on the Moral Foundations of Commerce and Politics*. New York: Vintage Books, 1994.

Jencks, Charles. *The Architecture of the Jumping Universe: A Polemic—How Complexity Science Is Changing Architecture and Culture*. London: Academy Editions, 1995.

Johnson, Jean Elliott, and Donald James Johnson. *The Human Drama: World History From the Beginning to 500 C.E.* Princeton, NJ: Markus Wiener, 2000.

Johnson, Steven. *Emergence: The Connected Lives of Ants, Brains, Cities, and Software*. New York: Scribner, 2001.

Johnston, Sadhu Aufochs, Steven S. Nicholas, and Julia Parzen. *The Guide to Greening Cities*. Washington, DC: Island Press, 2013.

Jullien, François. *The Propensity of Things: Toward a History of Efficacy in China*. New York: Zone, 1995.

Kahn, Matthew E. *Green Cities: Urban Growth and the Environment*. Washington, DC: Brookings Institute, 2006.

Kahneman, Daniel. *Thinking, Fast and Slow*. New York: Farrar, Straus and Giroux, 2013.

Kandel, Eric R. *In Search of Memory: The Emergence of a New Science of Mind*. New York: W. W. Norton, 2006.

Katz, Bruce, and Jennifer Bradley. *The Metropolitan Revolution: How Cities and Metros Are Fixing Our Broken Politics and Fragile Economy*. Washington, DC: Brookings Institution, 2013.

Kauffman, Stuart A. *At Home in the Universe: The Search for Laws of Self-Organization and Complexity*. New York: Oxford University Press, 1995.

———. *The Origins of Order: Self-Organization and Selection in Evolution*. New York: Oxford University Press, 1993.

Kayden, Jerold S. *Privately Owned Public Space*. New York: John Wiley & Sons, 2000.

Kelbaugh, Doug. *The Pedestrian Pocket Book: A New Suburban Design Strategy*. New York: Princeton Architectural Press in Association with the University of Washington, 1989.

Kellert, Stephen R. *Building for Life: Designing and Understanding the Human-Nature Connection*. Washington, DC: Island Press, 2005.

———. *Kinship to Mastery: Biophilia in Human Evolution and Development*. Washington, DC: Island Press, 1997.

Kellert, Stephen R., and Timothy J. Farnham, eds. *The Good in Nature and Humanity: Connecting Science, Religion, and Spirituality with the Natural World*. Washington, DC: Island Press, 2002.

Kellert, Stephen R., and James Gustave Speth, eds. *The Coming Transformation: Values to Sustain Human and Natural Communities*. New Haven, CT: Yale School of Forestry and Environmental Studies, 2009.

Kellert, Stephen R., and Edward O. Wilson, eds. *The Biophilia Hypothesis*. Washington, DC: Island Press, 1993.

Kelly, Barbara M. *Expanding the American Dream: Building and Rebuilding Levittown*. Albany: State University of New York Press, 1993.

Kelly, Hugh F. *Emerging Trends in Real Estate: United States and Canada 2016*. Washington, DC: Urban Land Institute, 2015.

Kelly, Kevin. *What Technology Wants*. New York: Viking, 2010.

Kemmis, Daniel. *The Good City and the Good Life*. Boston: Houghton Mifflin, 1995.

Kennedy, Christopher M. *The Evolution of Great World Cities: Urban Wealth and Economic Growth*. Toronto: University of Toronto Press, 2011.

Kennedy, Lieutenant General Claudia J. (Ret.), and Malcolm McConnell. *Generally Speaking*. New York: Warner Books 2001.

Khan, Khalid, and Pam Factor-Litvak. "Manganese Exposure from Drinking Water and Children's Classroom Behavior in Bangladesh." *Environmental Health Perspectives* 119, no. 10 (October 2011).

King, David, Daniel Schrag, Zhou Dadi, Qi Ye, and Arunabha Ghosh. *Climate Change: A Risk Assessment*. Boston: Harvard University Press, n.d.

Klinenberg, Eric. *Going Solo: The Extraordinary Rise and Surprising Appeal of Living Alone*. New York: Penguin, 2012.

Koebner, Linda. *Scientists on Biodiversity*. New York: American Museum of Natural History, 1998.

Koeppel, Gerard. *City on a Grid: How New York Became New York*. Philadelphia: Da Capo Press, 2015.

Koren, Leonard. *Wabi-Sabi for Artists, Designers, Poets and Philosophers*. Berkeley, CA: Stone Bridge, 1994.

Kramrisch, Stella. *The Hindu Temple*. 2 vols. Delhi: Motilal Banarsidass, 1976.

Krier, Lèìon, Dhiru A. Thadani, and Peter J. Hetzel. *The Architecture of Community*. Washington, DC: Island Press, 2009.

Krueger, Alan B. *The Rise and Consequences of Inequality in the United States*. Washington, DC: Council of Economic Advisers, 2012.

Kunstler, James Howard. *The City in Mind: Meditations on the Urban Condition*. New York: Free Press, 2001.

———. *Home from Nowhere: Remaking Our Everyday World for the Twenty-First Century*. New York: Simon & Schuster, 1996.

Kushner, David. *Levittown: Two Families, One Tycoon, and the Fight for Civil Rights in America's Legendary Suburb*. New York: Walker, 2009.

Lakoff, George. *Don't Think of an Elephant! Know Your Values and Frame the Debate: The Essential Guide for Progressives*. White River Junction, VT: Chelsea Green Publishing, 2004.

Landa, Manuel de. *A Thousand Years of Nonlinear History*. New York: Swerve, 2000.

Lansing, John Stephen. *Perfect Order: Recognizing Complexity in Bali*. Princeton, NJ: Princeton University Press, 2006.

Lauwerier, Hans. *Fractals: Endlessly Repeated Geometrical Figures*. Princeton, NJ: Princeton University Press, 1991.

Leakey, Richard, and Roger Lewin. *The Sixth Extinction: Patterns of Life and the Future of Humankind*. New York: Anchor Books, 1995.

Ledbetter, David. *Bach's Well-Tempered Clavier: The 48 Preludes and Fugues*. New Haven, CT: Yale University Press, 2002.

Lehrer, Jonah. *How We Decide*. Boston: Houghton Mifflin Harcourt, 2009.

———. *Proust Was a Neuroscientist*. Boston: Houghton Mifflin, 2007.

Leick, Gwendolyn. *Mesopotamia: The Invention of the City*. London: Penguin, 2001.

Leiserowitz, Anthony A., and Lisa O. Fernandez. *Toward a New Consciousness: Values to Sustain Human and Natural Communities: A Synthesis of Insights and Recommendations from the 2007 Yale FE&S Conference*. New Haven, CT: Yale Printing and Publishing Services, 2007.

Leopold, Aldo, and Robert Finch. *A Sand County Almanac: And Sketches Here and There*. Oxford, UK: Oxford University Press, 1949.

Longo, Gianni. *A Guide to Great American Public Places: A Journey of Discovery, Learning and Delight in the Public Realm*. New York: Urban Initiatives, 1996.

Louv, Richard. *Last Child in the Woods: Saving Our Children from Nature-Deficit Disorder*. Chapel Hill, NC: Algonquin Books of Chapel Hill, 2005.

———. *The Nature Principle: Human Restoration and the End of Nature-Deficit Disorder*. Chapel Hill, NC: Algonquin Books of Chapel Hill, 2011.

Lovins, Amory B. *Soft Energy Paths: Toward a Durable Peace*. San Francisco: Friends of the Earth International, 1977.

Lovins, Amory B., and Rocky Mountain Institute. *Reinventing Fire: Bold Business Solutions for the New Energy Era*. White River Junction, VT: Chelsea Green Publishing, 2011.

Mahler, Jonathan. *The Bronx Is Burning: 1977, Baseball, Politics, and the Battle for the Soul of a City*. New York: Farrar, Straus and Giroux, 2005.

Mak, Geert, and Russell Shorto. *1609: The Forgotten History of Hudson, Amsterdam, and New York*. Amsterdam: Henry Hudson 400, 2009.

Mandelbrot, Benoit B. *The Fractal Geometry of Nature*. New York: W. H. Freeman, 1982.

Marglin, Stephen A. *The Dismal Science: How Thinking Like an Economist Undermines Community*. Cambridge, MA: Harvard University Press, 2008.

Mayne, Thom. *Combinatory Urbanism: A Realignment of Complex Behavior and Collective Form*. Culver City, CA: Stray Dog Cafe, 2011.

Mazur, Laurie. *State of the World 2013: Is Sustainability Still Possible*. Washington, DC: Worldwatch Institute 2013. See esp. chapter 32, "Cultivating Resilience in a Dangerous World."

McCormick, Kathleen, Rachel MacCleery, and Sara Hammerschmidt. *Intersections: Health and the Built Environment*. Washington, DC: Urban Land Institute, 2013.

McDonough, William, and Michael Braungart. *Cradle to Cradle: Remaking the Way We Make Things*. New York: North Point, 2002.

McGilchrist, Iain. *The Master and His Emissary: The Divided Brain and the Making of the Western World*. New Haven, CT: Yale University Press, 2009.

McHarg, Ian L. *Design with Nature*. Garden City, NY: American Museum of Natural History, 1969.

McIlwain, John K. *Housing in America: The Baby Boomers Turn 65*. Washington, DC: Urban Land Institute, 2012.

———. *Housing in America: The Next Decade*. Washington, DC: Urban Land Institute, 2010.

Meadows, Donella H., and Diana Wright. *Thinking in Systems: A Primer*. White River Junction, VT: Chelsea Green Publishing, 2008.

Mehta, Suketu. *Maximum City: Bombay Lost and Found*. New York: Vintage Books, 2004.

Melaver, Martin. *Living above the Store: Building a Business That Creates Value, Inspires Change, and Restores Land and Community*. White River Junction, VT: Chelsea Green Publishing, 2009.

Miller, Tom. *China's Urban Billion: The Story behind the Biggest Migration in Human History*. London: Zed, 2012.

Mitchell, Melanie. *Complexity: A Guided Tour*. Oxford, UK: Oxford University Press, 2009.

Modelski, George. *World Cities: 3000 to 2000*. Washington, DC: Faros 2000, 2003.

Moe, Richard, and Carter Wilkie. *Changing Places: Rebuilding Community in the Age of Sprawl*. New York: Henry Holt, 1997.

Moeller, Hans-Georg. *Luhmann Explained: From Souls to Systems*. Chicago: Open Court, 2006.

Montgomery, Charles. *Happy City: Transforming Our Lives through Urban Design*. New York: Farrar, Straus and Giroux, 2013.

Moore, Charles Willard, William J. Mitchell, and William Turnbull. *The Poetics of Gardens*. Cambridge, MA: MIT Press, 1988.

Moretti, Enrico. *The New Geography of Jobs*. Boston: Houghton Mifflin Harcourt, 2013.

Morris, A. E. J. *History of Urban Form: Before the Industrial Revolutions*. Harlow, Essex, UK: Longman Scientific and Technical, 1979.

Morse, Edward S. *Japanese Homes and Their Surroundings*. New York: Dover Publications, 1961.

Mulgan, Geoff. *Connexity: How to Live in a Connected World*. Boston: Harvard Business School, 1997.

Mumford, Lewis. *The City in History: Its Origins, Its Transformations, and Its Prospects*. New York: Harcourt, Brace & World, 1961.

———. *The Myth of the Machine: The Pentagon of Power*. New York: Harcourt, Brace, Jovanovich, 1970.

Nabokov, Peter, and Robert Easton. *Native American Architecture*. Oxford, UK: Oxford University Press, 1989.

Narby, Jeremy. *The Cosmic Serpent: DNA and the Origins of Knowledge*. New York: Jeremy P. Tarcher, 1998.

Neal, Peter, ed. *Urban Villages and the Making of Communities*. London: Spon, 2003.

Neal, Zachary P. *The Connected City: How Networks Are Shaping the Modern Metropolis*. New York: Routledge, 2013.

Newman, Peter, and Isabella Jennings. *Cities as Sustainable Ecosystems: Principles and Practices*. Washington, DC: Island Press, 2008.

New York City Department of City Planning. *Zoning Handbook*, 2011 ed. New York: Department of City Planning, 2012.

New York City Department of Transportation. *Sustainable Streets 2009: Progress Report*. New York: New York City Department of Transportation, 2009.

Nijhout, H. F., Lynn Nadel, and Daniel L. Stein, eds. *Pattern Formation in the Physical and Biological Sciences*. Reading, MA: Addison-Wesley, 1997.

Nolan, John R. *The National Land Use Policy Act*. New York: Pace Law Publications, 1996.

Norberg-Hodge, Helena. *Ancient Futures*. N.p.: Sierra Club Books, 1991.

Novacek, Michael J. *The Biodiversity Crisis: Losing What Counts*. New York: The New Press, 2001.

OECD. *How's Life? Measuring Well-Being*. Paris: OECD Publishing, 2015.

———. *Ranking of the World's Cities Most Exposed to Coastal Flooding Today and in the Future. Executive Summary*. Paris: OECD Publishing, 2007.

Ormerod, Paul. *N Squared: Public Policy and the Power of Networks*. RSA, Essay 3, August 2010.

Orr, David W. *Design on the Edge: The Making of a High-Performance Building*. Cambridge, MA: MIT Press, 2006.

———. *Down to the Wire: Confronting Climate Collapse*. Oxford, UK: Oxford University Press, 2009.

Ostrom, Elinor. *Governing the Commons: The Evolution of Institutions for Collective Action*. New York: Cambridge University Press, 1990.

Pagels, Heinz R. *The Cosmic Code: Quantum Physics as the Language of Nature*. New York: Penguin, 1982.

———. *The Dreams of Reason: The Computer and the Rise of the Sciences of Complexity*. New York: Simon & Schuster, 1988.

———. *Perfect Symmetry: The Search for the Beginning of Time.* New York: Simon & Schuster, 1985.

Palmer, Martin, and Victoria Finlay. *Faith in Conservation: New Approaches to Religions and the Environment.* Washington, DC: World Bank, 2003.

Pecchi, Lorenzo, and Gustavo Piga. *Revisitng Keynes: Economic Possibilities for Our Grandchildren.* Cambridge, MA: MIT Press, 2008.

Peirce, Neal R., Curtis W. Johnson, and John Stuart Hall. *Citistates: How Urban America Can Prosper in a Competitive World.* Washington, DC: Seven Locks, 1993.

Pelikan, Jaroslav. *Bach Among the Theologians.* New York: Penguin Books, 2008. First published in 1986 by Wipf and Stock.

Pennick, Nigel. *Sacred Geometry: Symbolism and Purpose in Religious Structures.* New York: Harper & Row, 1980.

Peterson, Jon A. *The Birth of City Planning in the United States, 1840–1917.* Baltimore: Johns Hopkins University Press, 2003.

Piketty, Thomas. *Capital in the Twenty-First Century.* Cambridge, MA: Belknap Press of Harvard University Press, 2014.

Pittas, Michael J. *Vision/Reality: Strategies for Community Change.* Washington, DC: United States Department of Housing and Urban Development, Office of Planning and Development, 1994.

Pollan, Michael. *The Botany of Desire: A Plant's Eye View of the World.* New York: Random House, 2001.

Reed, Henry Hope. *The Golden City.* Garden City, NY: Doubleday, 1959.

Revkin, Andrew. *The North Pole Was Here: Puzzles and Perils at the Top of the World.* Boston: Kingfisher, 2006.

Ricard, Matthieu. *Happiness.* New York: Little, Brown, 2003.

Ricklefs, Robert E. *Ecology.* Newton, MA: Chiron, 1973.

Ridley, Matt. *Genome: The Autobiography of a Species in 23 Chapters.* New York: Perennial, 1999.

Riesman, David. *The Lonely Crowd: A Study of the Changing American Character.* Cambridge, MA: Yale University Press, 1961.

Rimpoche, Nawang Gehlek. *Good Life, Good Death.* New York: Riverhead Books, 2001.

Rocca, Alessandro. *Natural Architecture.* New York: Princeton Architectural Press, 2007.

Rodin, Judith. *The Resilience Dividend: Being Strong in a World Where Things Go Wrong.* New York: PublicAffairs, 2014.

Rosan, Richard M. *The Community Builders Handbook.* Washington, DC: Urban Land Institute, 1947.

Rose, Dan. *Energy Transition and the Local Community: A Theory of Society Applied to Hazleton, Pennsylvania.* Philadelphia: University of Pennsylvania Press, 1981.

Rose, Daniel. *Making a Living, Making a Life.* Essex, NY: Half Moon Press. 2014.

Rose, Jonathan F. P. *Manhattan Plaza: Building a Community.* Philadelphia: University of Pennsylvania Press, 1979.

Rosenthal, Caitlin. *Big Data in the Age of the Telegraph.* N.p.: Leading Edge, 2013.

Rosenzweig, Cynthia, and William D. Solecki. *Climate Change and a Global City: The Potential Consequences of Climatic Variability and Change; Metro East Coast.* New York: Columbia Earth Institute, 2001.

Rosenzweig, Cynthia, William D. Solecki, Stephen A. Hammer, and Shagun Mehrotra. *Climate Change and Cities: First Assessment Report of the Urban Climate Change Research Network.* Cambridge, UK: Cambridge University Press, 2011.

Roveda, Vittorio. *Khmer Mythology: Secrets of Angkor Wat.* Bangkok: River Books Press, AC, 1997.

Rowson, Jonathan. *Transforming Behavior Change: Beyond Nudge and Neuromania. RSA Projects* (n.d.), 2–32. Web.

Rowson, Jonathan, and Iain McGilchrist. *Divided Brain, Divided World.* London: RSA, 2013.

Rudofsky, Bernard. *Architecture without Architects: A Short Introduction to Non-Pedigreed Architecture.* New York: Museum of Modern Art; distributed by Doubleday, Garden City, NY, 1964.

Rybczynski, Witold. *Home: A Short History of an Idea.* New York: Penguin, 1987.

Rykwert, Joseph. *The Idea of a Town: The Anthropology of Urban Form in Rome, Italy, and the Ancient World.* Princeton, NJ: Princeton University Press, 1976.

———. *The Seduction of Place: The City in the Twenty-First Century.* New York: Pantheon Books, 2000.

Saarinen, Eliel. *The City: Its Growth, Its Decay, Its Future.* New York: Reinhold, 1943.

Sachs, Jeffrey D. *Common Wealth: Economics for a Crowded Planet.* New York: Penguin, 2009.

Sampson, Robert J. *Great American City: Chicago and the Enduring Neighborhood Effect.* Chicago: University of Chicago Press, 2012.

Sanderson, Eric W. *Mannahatta: A Natural History of New York City.* New York: Harry N. Abrams, 2009.

———. *Terra Nova: The New World after Oil, Cars and the Suburbs.* New York: Harry N. Abrams, 2013.

Saunders, Doug. *Arrival City: How the Largest Migration in History Is Reshaping Our World.* New York: Vintage Books, 2012.

Saviano, Roberto. *Gomorrah: A Personal Journey into the Violent International Empire of Naples's Organized Crime System.* New York: Picador, 2006.

Scarpaci, Joseph L., Roberto Segre, and Mario Coyula. *Havana: The Faces of the Antillean Metropolis.* Chapel Hill: University of North Carolina Press, 2002.

Schachter-Shalomi, Rabbi Zalman. *Paradigm Shift.* Northvale, NJ: Jason Aronson, 1993.

Schama, Simon. *Landscape and Memory.* New York: Alfred A. Knopf, 1995.

Schell, Jonathan. *The Fate of the Earth.* New York: Avon, 1982.

Schinz, Alfred. *The Magic Square: Cities in Ancient China.* Stuttgart: Axel Menges, 1996.

Schoenauer, Norbert. *6,000 Years of Housing.* New York: W. W. Norton, 1981.

Schorske, Carl E. *Fin-de-siècle Vienna: Politics and Culture.* New York: Alfred A. Knopf, 1979.

Schrödinger, Erwin. *What Is Life? The Physical Aspect of the Living Cell; and Mind and Matter.* Cambridge, UK: Cambridge University Press, 1944.

Senge, Peter, et al. *The Dance of Change: The Challenges of Sustaining Momentum in Learning Organizations.* New York: Doubleday, 1999.

Sennett, Richard. *The Conscience of the Eye: The Design and Social Life of Cities.* New York: Alfred A. Knopf, 1990.

Sheftell, Jason. "Best Places to Live in NY." *Daily News,* September 9, 2011.

Shipman, Wanda. *Animal Architects: How Animals Weave, Tunnel, and Build Their Remarkable Homes.* Mechanicsburg, PA: Stackpole, 1994.

Shorto, Russell. *The Island at the Center of the World: The Epic Story of Dutch Manhattan and the Forgotten Colony That Shaped America.* New York: Vintage Books, 2004.

Shrady, Nicholas. *The Last Day: Wrath, Ruin, and Reason in the Great Lisbon Earthquake of 1755.* New York: Penguin, 2008.

Singer, Tania. "Concentrating on Kindness." *Science* 341 (September 20, 2013).

Smith, Bruce D. *The Emergence of Agriculture.* New York: Scientific American Library, 1995.

Solnit, Rebecca. *A Paradise Built in Hell: The Extraordinary Communities That Arise in Disaster.* New York: Penguin, 2009.

Solomon, Daniel. *Global City Blues.* Washington, DC: Island Press, 2003.

Speth, James Gustave. *The Bridge at the Edge of the World.* New Haven, CT: Yale University Press, 2008.

———. *Red Sky at Morning: America and the Crisis of the Global Environment.* New Haven, CT: Yale University Press, 2004.

Standage, Tom. *The Victorian Internet: The Remarkable Story of the Telegraph and the Nineteenth Century's On-Line Pioneers.* New York: Walker, 1998.

Steadman, Philip. *Energy, Environment and Building.* Cambridge, UK: Cambridge University Press, 1975.

Steinhardt, Nancy Shatzman. *Chinese Imperial City Planning.* Honolulu: University of Hawaii Press, 1999.

Steven Winter Associates. *There Are Holes in Our Walls.* New York: U.S. Green Building Council, New York Chapter, 2011.

Stiglitz, Joseph E. *The Price of Inequality: How Today's Divided Society Endangers Our Future.* New York: W. W. Norton, 2012.

Stiglitz, Joseph E., Amartya Sen, and Jean-Paul Fitoussi. *Mismeasuring Our Lives: Why GDP Doesn't Add Up.* New York: The New Press, 2010.

Stohr, Kate, and Cameron Sinclair. *Design Like You Give a Damn: Building Change from the Ground Up.* New York: Harry N. Abrams, 2012.

Stoner, Tom, and Carolyn Rapp. *Open Spaces Sacred Places.* Annapolis, MD: TKF Foundation, 2008.

Stuart, David E., and Susan B. Moczygemba-McKinsey. *Anasazi America.* Albuquerque: University of New Mexico Press, 2000.

Surowiecki, James. *The Wisdom of Crowds.* New York: Doubleday, 2004.

Sustainable Communities: The Westerbeke Charrette. Sausalito, CA: Van der Ryn, Calthorpe & Partners, 1981.

Swimme, Brian, and Mary Evelyn Tucker. *Journey of the Universe.* New Haven, CT: Yale University Press, 2011.

Tainter, Joseph A. *The Collapse of Complex Societies.* Cambridge, UK: University Printing House, 1988.

Taleb, Nassim Nicholas. *Antifragile: Things That Gain from Disorder.* New York: Random House, 2012.

Talen, Emily, and Andres Duany. *City Rules: How Regulations Affect Urban Form.* Washington, DC: Island Press, 2012.

Tavernise, Sabrina. "For Americans Under 50, Stark Finding on Health." *New York Times,* January 9, 2013.

———. "Project to Improve Poor Children's Intellect Led to Better Health, Data Show." *New York Times,* March 28, 2014.

Teilhard de Chardin, Pierre. *The Phenomenon of Man.* Trans. by Julian Huxley. New York: Harper Torch Books, 1959.

Tellier, Luc-Normand. *Urban World History: An Economic and Geographical Perspective.* Québec, Canada: Presses de l'Université du Québec, 2009.

Thaler, Richard H., and Cass R. Sunstein. *Nudge: Improving Decisions about Health, Wealth, and Happiness.* New York: Penguin, 2008.

Thomas, Lewis. *The Medusa and the Snail: More Notes of a Biology Watcher.* New York: Viking, 1979.

Thompson, D'Arcy. *On Growth and Form.* Cambridge, UK: Cambridge University Press, 1961.

Tough, Paul. "The Poverty Clinic—Can a Stressful Childhood Make You a Sick Adult?" *New Yorker,* March 21, 2011.

Tufte, Edward R. *Visual Explanations: Images and Quantities, Evidence and Narrative.* Cheshire, CT: Graphics Press, 1997.

UN-Habitat. *State of the World's Cities 2012/2013: Prosperity of Cities.* N.p.: United Nations Human Settlements Programme, 2012.

United States of America. Office of Management and Budget. *Fiscal Year 2016: Budget of the U.S. Government.* Washington, DC: U.S. Government Printing Office, 2015.

Urban Land Institute. *America's Housing Policy—The Missing Piece: Affordable Workforce Rentals.* Washington, DC: Urban Land Institute, 2011.

———. *Beltway Burden—The Combined Cost of Housing and Transportation in the Greater Washington, DC, Metropolitan Area.* Washington, DC: Urban Land Institute–Terwilliger Center for Workforce Housing, 2009.

———. *Building Healthy Places Toolkit: Strategies for Enhancing Health in the Built Environment.* Washington, DC: Urban Land Institute, 2015.

———. *Infrastructure 2011: A Strategic Priority.* Washington, DC: Urban Land Institute, 2011.

———. *What's Next? Getting Ahead of Change.* Washington, DC: Urban Land Institute, 2012.

———. *What's Next? Real Estate in the New Economy.* Washington, DC: Urban Land Institute, 2011.

Van der Ryn, Sim, and Peter Calthorpe. *Sustainable Communities: A New Design Synthesis for Cities, Suburbs, and Towns.* San Francisco: Sierra Club, 1986.

Van der Ryn, Sim, and Stuart Cowan. *Ecological Design.* Washington, DC: Island Press, 1996.

Venkatesh, Sudhir Alladi. *American Project: The Rise and Fall of a Modern Ghetto.* Cambridge, MA: Harvard University Press, 2000.

Vergara, Camilo J. *The New American Ghetto.* New Brunswick, NJ: Rutgers University Press, 1995.

Von Frisch, Karl. *Animal Architecture.* New York: Harcourt Brace Jovanovich, 1974.

Wallace, Rodrick, and Kristin McCarthy. "The Unstable Public-Health Ecology of the New York Metropolitan Region: Implications for Accelerated National Spread of Emerging Infection." *Environment and Planning A* 39, no. 5 (2007): 1181–92.

Warren, Andrew, Anita Kramer, Steven Blank, and Michael Shari. *Emerging Trends in Real Estate.* Washington, DC: Urban Land Institute, 2014.

Watkins, Michael D., ed. *A Guidebook to Old and New Urbanism in the Baltimore/Washington Region.* Washington, DC: Congress for the New Urbanism, 2003.

Weinstein, Emily, Jessica Wolin, and Sharon Rose. *Trauma Informed Community Building: A Model for Strengthening Community in Trauma Affected Neighborhoods.* N.p.: Health Equity Institute, 2014.

White, Norval. *The Architecture Book: A Companion to the Art and the Science of Architecture.* New York: Alfred A. Knopf, 1976.

Whithorn, Nicholas, trans. *Sicily: Art, History, Myths, Archaeology, Nature, Beaches, Food.* English ed. Messina, Italy: Edizioni Affinita Elettive, n.d.

Whyte, William H. *City: Rediscovering the Center.* New York: Doubleday, 1988.

———. *The Social Life of Small Urban Spaces.* Washington, DC: Conservation Foundation, 1980.

Wilkinson, Richard G., Kate Pickett, and Robert B. Reich. *The Spirit Level: Why Greater Equality Makes Societies Stronger.* New York: Bloomsbury, 2010.

William, Laura. *An Annual Look at the Housing Affordability Challenges of America's Working Households.* Housing Landscape, 2012.

Wilson, David Sloan. *The Neighborhood Project.* New York: Little, Brown, 2011.

Wilson, Edward O. *Consilience: The Unity of Knowledge.* New York: Alfred A. Knopf, 1998.

———. *The Meaning of Human Existence.* New York: Liveright, 2014.

———. *The Social Conquest of Earth.* New York: Liveright, 2012.

Wolman, Abel. "The Metabolism of Cities." *Scientific American* 213, no. 3 (September 1965): 179–80.

Wong, Eva. *Feng-shui: The Ancient Wisdom of Harmonious Living for Modern Times.* Boston: Shambhala, 1996.

Wood, Frances. *The Silk Road: Two Thousand Years in the Heart of Asia.* Berkeley: University of California Press, 2002.

World Economic Forum. *Global Agenda: Well-Being and Global Success.* World Economic Forum, 2012.

———. *Insight Report: Global Risks 2012, Seventh Edition.* World Economic Forum, 2012.

Wright, Robert. *NonZero: The Logic of Human Destiny*. New York: Pantheon Books, 2000.

Wright, Ronald. *A Short History of Progress*. Cambridge, UK: Da Capo, 2004.

Yearsley, David. *Bach and the Meanings of Counterpoint*. Cambridge, UK: Cambridge University Press, 2002.

Yoshida, Nobuyuki. *Singapore: Capital City for Vertical Green (Xinjiapo: Chui Zhi Lu Hua Zhi Du)*. Singapore: A+U Publishing, 2012.

Zolli, Andrew, and Ann Marie Healy. *Resilience: Why Things Bounce Back*. New York: Free Press, 2012.

Page numbers in *italics* refer to illustrations.

JONATHAN F. P. ROSE has focused his business, public policy, and not-for-profit work on creating more environmentally, socially, and economically resilient and equitable cities. In 1989, Mr. Rose founded Jonathan Rose Companies LLC, a multidisciplinary real estate development, planning, and investment firm to develop communities of opportunity. The firm touches many aspects of community and environmental health, working with cities and not-for-profits to build green, affordable, and mixed-income housing, as well as cultural, health, and educational facilities.

Jonathan and his wife, Diana Calthorpe Rose, are the cofounders of the Garrison Institute, which develops rigorous ways to apply contemplative practices to key social, education, and environmental issues; growing new fields of practice; and helping build a more resilient, compassionate society.

Jonathan graduated from Yale University in 1974 with a B.A. in psychology and philosophy, and received a master's degree in regional planning from the University of Pennsylvania in 1980.

Mr. Rose is also the founder of Gramavision Records and a musician.